A HISTORY OF THE
THAMES VALLEY
TRACTION COMPANY
1946 ~ 1960

Written and published by Paul Lacey

With Best Wishes
Paul

The Thames Valley Bus Station off Bridge Avenue in Maidenhead offered a convenient interchange for bus and coach passengers. Indeed, when this photo was taken from the rooftop of the Rialto Cinema in the Spring of 1952, the Coach Station was taking shape between York Road and the embankment of the London – Bristol railway line. Demonstrating how necessary this would be are the four ECW 'Queen Mary'-bodied Bristol LL-type coaches in white and on the Bristol Greyhound service between their home town and Victoria Coach Station. The numerous bus routes have allocated platforms, which do not require potentially dangerous reversing, together with shelters and good signage. In the middle of the island site is the new cafeteria and toilet block, offering all-day facilities to the travelling public. Beyond the buses is the bungalow 'Yorkstream', used as a staff canteen and a base for the resident gardener, whilst to its left is the site of the Enquiry Office, which has yet to be constructed. The site fulfilled a long-held ambition of the Company to provide an off-road bus station, and was part of the daily life of Maidenhead for decades before being needlessly sacrificed for a re-development to provide some office blocks.

A HISTORY OF THE THAMES VALLEY TRACTION CO. LTD., 1946 ~ 1960

Written, designed, typeset and published by
Paul Lacey, 17 Sparrow Close
Woosehill, Wokingham
Berkshire, RG41 3HT

ISBN 978-0-9510739-9-5

Printed by the MPG Books Group in the UK

Sunningdale was a point served right through from British days, originally being the terminus of the route from Maidenhead. In due course it was served by buses from Reading and Ascot, being part of the Reading – Ascot – Windsor through service. In later years the journeys between Ascot and Sunningdale, then by way of two different routes, became a shuttle service, allowing the journey time between Reading and Windsor to be reduced. However, the link remained important, particularly for commuters by train or those travelling to London or Reading for shopping. Ascot Garage covered the duties which, by 1951, fell to its remaining Strachan utility-bodied Bristol K6A's, and Car 426 (CRX 196) is seen at Sunningdale Station in company with an Aldershot & District Dennis 'Lancet' saloon bound for Woking. The scene also recalls the estate agents office, the original 1939 Southern Electric sign and the prominent advert for the Carlton Hotel, though nothing from this view now survives.

The classic lines of the Windover coachwork on 1947 Bristol L6B Car 460 (DMO 664) seen prior to delivery.

CONTENTS

Subject	Page	Subject	Page
Chapter 1946	5	Chapter 1959	165
Chapter 1947	15	Chapter 1960	177
Chapter 1948	23	*The Guest Pages*	194
Chapter 1949	31	Operators Acquired 1946 – 1960	197
Chapter 1950	43	*Appendix 1* Fleet List	198
Chapter 1951	63	*Appendix 2* Service Vehicles	210
Chapter 1952	77	*Appendix 3* Livery Notes	212
Chapter 1953	95	*Appendix 4* Newbury & District M.S. Ltd.	215
Chapter 1954	109	*Appendix 5* South Midland M.S. Ltd.	217
Chapter 1955	121	*Appendix 6* Scheduled Allocations to Garages	219
Chapter 1956	131	*Appendix 7* Scheduled Workings 1958	220
Topless on the 'Valley 1957-1959	139	*Appendix 8* Official Fleet Allocation 1952	221
Chapter 1957	141	*Appendix 9* Official Fleet Allocation 1958	222
Chapter 1958	149	*Appendix 10* Official Fleet Allocations 1960	223
A Route Map appears on the outer back cover		Index to Other Operators	224

Standard Body Codes - Throughout this work the standard codes are used to describe the configuration of bodywork, e.g. B32F is a single-deck bus seating 32 with a front entrance. See Appendix 1 Fleet List on page 198 for full listing of codes.

OTHER TRANSPORT TITLES FROM PAUL LACEY

A History of the Thames Valley Traction Co. Ltd., 1920 –1930   £15.00

The detailed history of this vibrant period, including the 207 other operators sharing the roads with TV, published in 1995, 144 pages A4, perfect bound, 144 half-tones, route map, full fleet list, line drawings.

Thackray's Way – A Family in Road Transport   £10.00

An in-depth study of this enterprising family, written with assistance from their descendants, published in 2001, 136 pages A5, perfect bound, 62 half-tones, plans of premises, route maps, full fleet list.

A History of the Thames Valley Traction Co. Ltd., 1931 – 1945   £25.00

Continuing the story of development through the expansion of the 1930's, railway shareholdings, and then through the difficult years of the wartime era, published in 2003, 208 pages A4 with laminated covers, 300 half-tone illustrations, maps and plans, full fleet lists and specialised appendices.

50 Years of South Midland, 1921 – 1970   £11.00

A comprehensive study of Oxford's premier coach operator and express service pioneer, written by David Flitton. Published in 2004, 192 A5 pages and laminated covers, 142 half-tone illustrations, full fleet list, details of premises and period adverts.

All titles in print are available direct from the author, post free, or through good book suppliers.

For further details see the website at http://uk.geocities.com/paul_lacey_transport_books

ACKNOWLEDGEMENTS

This work is dedicated to all those who were involved in the daily operation of *Thames Valley* and its competitors, many of whom I have had the interesting task of interviewing over some 40 years of research. I also wish to say a big Thank You to everyone who has helped me in any way, no matter how small, to piece together this interesting history. So many people have been consulted over all those years, it is difficult to try to list them all, so suffice it to say that you know who you are. My thanks also go to the photographers, whose names are often unrecorded, who had the fore-thought to record the daily activities of the erstwhile 'Thames Valley Traction Company Limited' and its fleet.

This impressive line up of 8 Bristol coaches and a Bedford OB was taken in London Street on 3rd December 1951 on the occasion of the Reading Pensioner's Association Outing organised by the Women's Voluntary Service. Note that hats are still much in evidence, whilst the drivers are neatly turned out in their white summer issue jackets with red collars with Thames Valley embroidered thereon.

1946

To describe the *Thames Valley* fleet as war-worn by the start of 1946 would indeed be something of an understatement. The operational area had seen a very large increase in population and war-related industries and well as being home to numerous establishments of the military. Evacuated schoolchildren had further increased the local population, and all sections of the above required transport at some time or another.

Unfortunately the Company had favoured single-deck vehicles rather than double-deckers for the bulk of its intake between 1935-9, which had made the task of moving the masses even more problematical. Indeed, it was out of sheer necessity that the working lives of the 1928-31 Leyland 'Titan' TD1's were extended well beyond their originally intended span. Making do and mending was the national order of the day, and TV had done just that, rebuilding ageing bodywork and fitting new engines throughout the wartime era, resulting in a fleet with nigh on 57 varieties!

Car 412 (HF 6041) aptly demonstrates the numerous changes wrought on the old 'Titan' TD1s, with a new upper deck front, modified destination boxes and cab line by ECW, but by then bearing an older style radiator.

So, 1946 opened with a fleet made up of 210 vehicles:

Double-deckers (total 102 buses)
Leyland 'Titan' TD1 (total 45, Leyland or Short body)
Cars 164-175, 179-187, 190, 199-208, 219-224, 232-237 and 412 (originally Wallasey CT)
Leyland 'Titan' TD2 (total 2, Mumford bodies)
Cars 435/6 (ex Plymouth CT, both being rebuilt)
Leyland 'Titan' TD4 (total 8, Brush bodies)
Cars 272-277and 335-336
Leyland 'Titan' TD5 (total 5, Brush or ECW bodies)
Cars 339-341 and 369-370
Bristol K5G (total 25, ECW or Duple bodies)
Cars 391-410 and 413-417
Bristol K6A, (total 9, Strachan bodies)
426-434
Guy 'Arab' Mk1 5LW (total 8, Duple, Strachan or Brush bodies)
Cars 418-425

Single-deckers (97 buses and 11 coaches)
Leyland 'Lion' LT1 (total 10, Brush bodies)
Cars 2, 4, 6, 8, 10, 12, 20, 22, 38 and 42
Leyland 'Lion'LT2 (total 5, Brush bodies)
Cars 14, 46, 50, 52, 54
Leyland 'Tiger' TS3 (total 3, Brush or Leyland body)
Cars 230 and 258-259 (originally Premier Line)
Leyland 'Tiger' TS4 (total 10, Brush bodies)
Cars 245-250, 252, 253, 255 and 256
Leyland 'Tiger' TS7 (total 37, Brush or ECW bodies)
Cars 18, 24, 26, 28, 30, 32, 34, 36, 40, 44, 48, 265-277, 295-299, 302-308, 327-330, 332-334
Leyland 'Tiger' TS7 (total 1, Duple body)
Car 262 (coach back from WD, still in store)
Leyland 'Tiger' TS8 (total 27,Brush or ECW bodies)
Cars 342-348, 359-368 and 371-380
Leyland 'Tiger' TS8 (total 10, Harrington bodies)
Cars 381-390 (coaches with TD1 petrol engines)
Leyland 'Cub' KPZ2 (total 2, Brush bodies)
Cars 337-338
Leyland 'Cub' KP3 (total 1, Brush body)
Car 411 (ex Crosville MS)
Bedford OWB (total 2, Duple bodies)
Cars 437-438

At that point in time there were still a number of vehicles taken by the military authorities and not yet returned, comprising:
Tilling-Stevens B9A (total 9, Brush bus bodies)
Cars 145, 147, 148, 151, 154, 155, 157, 158 and 161
Leyland 'Tiger' TS4 (total 6, Brush coach bodies)
Cars 239-241, 244*, 251 and 254
Leyland 'Tiger' TS7 (total 2, Duple coach bodies)
Cars 263 and 264*
*Only the two cars marked * were eventually returned*

The above fleet was largely based on the main garages in Reading, Maidenhead and High Wycombe, as well as the smaller garage in Ascot, though *Thames Valley* still relied to some extent on its Dormy Sheds, where it kept vehicles to reduce dead mileage and provide better links at the ends of the day. At January 1946 the allocations of the smaller locations were as follows:

The wartime Guys were a useful addition to deal with the large increase in the local population, though their wooden seats were unpopular. For those reasons they were largely concentrated on the High Wycombe local services, with Car 422 (CJB 141), a Brush-bodied example clearing damp shoppers from the High Street market.

Ascot Garage (for routes 2, 2b and 2c)
'Lion' LT1 14, 'Titan' TD1 181 and K6A's 426-434
Crowthorne Dormy Shed (for routes 3 and 3a)
'Tiger' TS7' 32 and 'Tiger' TS8's 344, 371 and 372
Fingest Dormy Shed (for routes 36 and 37)
'Tiger' TS7's, usually 295 and 296
Newbury (parked at Railway Station for route 10)
2 Bristol K5G's changed in rotation
Princes Risborough Dormy Shed (for route 30)
2 double-deck Leylands changed in rotation
Stokenchurch Dormy Shed (for routes 39/40/41)
Bristol K5G's 413 and 414
Tadley Dormy Shed (for routes 9 and 9a)
'Tiger' TS7 271 and 'Titan' TD5 369

It should be noted that the single-decker at Ascot was provided to cover worker's relief runs on route 2 from Bracknell (High Street) through to the Miles Aviation Factory at Woodley Airfield, after which the crew had a break at Frank's Café at Loddon Bridge, then doing a relief 3 to Wokingham and from there dead to Ascot. Similar return journeys were made during the home-going period, as aircraft production was still very busy at that site.

Under the circumstances it was perhaps ironic that *Reading Corporation Transport* actually approached TV to see if it had any surplus buses for sale. At the time there were only a few old Tilling-Stevens buses awaiting immediate disposal, but these were evidently rejected! Indeed, had TV been in a position to release any of the old 'Titans', the situation might have been a different matter, as RCT already had examples of that type. In fact the only new stock for TV since the last of the drawn out deliveries of utility Bristol K6A's during November 1945, was a pair of 26-seat

Bedford OWB buses with Duple bodies, Cars 437/8 (CRX 546/7), licensed from 1st January for use on the weight-restricted route between Maidenhead and Marlow.

It is worth noting that two former TV buses survived the war in the yard of the well-known scrap dealer Harold Goodey of Twyford, as former Cars 18 (RX 188), a Thornycroft A2 Long 20-seater, and 101 (MO 6845), a 32-seater Tilling-Stevens B9A had both been disposed of before the war. However, time did catch up with most of the surviving Tilling-Stevens B9A's during January, with Car 150 (MO 9322) being collected on the first day of that month, whilst Cars 144, 153 and 156 (MO 9316, 9325 and 9328) departed on the 26th, mostly for showmen.

Another positive step to peacetime normality came on 7th January, with the re-opening to the public of the Colonnade for parking and petrol. Attendants were on duty from 7am to 11pm for the supply of petrol, oil and other sundries, whilst cars could also be cleaned or polished. The facility was obviously popular with those attending the nearby Granby Cinema, whilst its former owners *Thackray's Way* had indeed promoted it as a sort of park-and-ride for those not wishing to drive right into the centre of Reading, there be frequent buses and trams from very close by.

The pair of former *Plymouth Corporation* Leyland 'Titan' TD2's had been entrusted to Vincents for their refurbishment, but no doubt TV had anticipated using them somewhat sooner. Car 435 (DR 9636) returned on 4th January, but had been at the Station Hill works since 18th April the previous year – whilst Car 436 was still not ready for release! The bodies on these buses were unlike anything else in the TV fleet and were built by Mumfords of Plymouth, featuring a very deep waist rail and bands between decks.

The second of the Plymouth TD2's to enter service was Car 436 (DR 9846), seen by the canteen in the Southern Railway yard parking area.

January also saw the return of a quartet of Leyland 'Tigers' from refurbishment at Eastern Coach Works, with TS7 Cars 34 (ABL 753) and 329 (ABL 759) on 18th, followed by TS7 Car 24 (JB 8348) and TS8 Car 348 (AJB 820) on the last day of the month.

At times, through either shortage of rolling stock or a need to work cars back to home depots, this was a period when a number of unusual workings could be noted. Also the older stock sometimes reappeared on former 'mainline' duties, whilst 'odd' cars could turn up almost anywhere.

On 28th January Route 11 (Reading – Bucklebury) was converted to double-deck operation, with 'Titan' TD4 Car 335 (ABL 765) as the first to cover it.

The regulations on standing passengers were altered from Monday 4th February, with 10 standing permitted on saloons with standard seating or 20 when perimeter seating was in place. TV's cars with perimeter seating were fairly soon returned to the conventional layout once peace returned, as they passed through the works or went away for refurbishment.

History was made when the final Tilling-Stevens bus was sold on 4th February, the B9A type being the first full-size saloons bought new by TV in 1926. Car 152 (MO 9324) went for its new role as a showman's bus and, as with other similar examples, it actually received a repaint by TV in all-over green as part of the deal. However, that was not to be the end of the story, as happily 'MO' has survived into preservation through *Thames Valley* enthusiast and pioneer bus preservationist Michael Plunkett and can now be seen both at Amberley and various events.

Unfortunately February also saw 'Tiger' TS3 saloon 230 (RX 6250) involved in an accident where an elderly pedestrian was knocked down outside the Weldale Street entrance, which led to a request to the Reading Borough Engineer to improve the lighting.

On a happier note, the other ex-*Plymouth CT* 'Titan' TD2 Car 436 (DR 9846) finally escaped from the Vincent works, having been there since the previous July! As with 435 before it, a Leyland oil engine had been fitted during the process of getting these vehicles into serviceable condition.

Of course it was not only vehicles that had suffered from a lack of maintenance during the hostilities, as the driver of a double-decker on Route 4a found out on the road between Barkham and Arborfield during February. As he pulled over to allow another vehicle to pass, the road collapsed into the adjacent ditch.

Thoughts also turned to the reintroduction of coaching work, so one of the Harrington-bodied 'Tiger' TS8's was experimentally painted as green with a cream flash on one side, whilst on the other side the colours were reversed for inspection by the management.

The Company also had a visit from the Bristol K5G with prototype lowbridge bodywork. Delivered as *Eastern National* No. 3885 (JVW 430), it was operated on Route 2 (Windsor – Ascot – Bracknell – Wokingham – Reading) out of Ascot depot for a week from Saturday 16th March. Indeed, experimental buses were usually run on this route, which was 21 miles long, but also had drivers and Garage Foreman Tucker who Basil Sutton knew would take care of their buses and pass on their valued comments.

The prototype K5G loaned from the Eastern National fleet. Note that the high pre-war style radiator had still been retained, whilst the sliding cab door was not a usual feature for ECW bodies.

Also at Ascot, the regular Leyland 'Lion' LT2 saloon Car 14 (RX 6249) went away for overhaul and a much-needed repaint from Friday 22nd March, so its place was taken by LT1 Car 20 (RX 5577) instead.

From Monday 25th March a number of new model Setright Ticket Machines were issued experimentally to selected conductors for evaluation. With the war over, attention was also turned to the improvement of facilities for passengers and staff alike. During March discussions started on providing new passenger shelters on Station Hill, Reading, whist a refreshment hut was authorised for erection in the *Southern Railway* yard, for crew use on Sundays when the other local facilities were not available. At High Wycombe, attention once again turned to consolidating the land held in the Frogmoor area. Discussions took place over acquiring the Old Cattle Market area, whilst other land adjacent to the Old Technical College was also taken in. In order to offset these purchases and also to provide further garage accommodation in that town, it was decided to sell off the former *Chiltern Bus Co.* garage in Lane End. The premises were sold to local garage owner (and one-time charabanc operator) R. Smith. Meanwhile, in Maidenhead the Company had already planned an off-road bus station in Bridge Avenue, where it also acquired an existing bungalow, known as 'Yorkstream' after the nearby brook, which would be converted for staff facilities.

Once Car 14 (RX 6249) was released from the works, it saw use on 11th-12th April by Reading depot on some of the varied saloon routes from that town, then returning to its regular duties at Ascot, resplendent in its new paintwork.

Bedford OWB Car 438 (CRX 547) at Maidenhead.

From 14th April the mileage restriction on private hire work was lifted, resulting in a new programme of excursions also being put in place. The Company was also hoping to improve the frequency of stage carriage services as soon as the vehicle situation eased. Indeed, there were plans for delivery of 22 double-deckers to replace the 12 1928 and 10 1929 'Titan' TD1's, with 20 single-deckers to replace the Tilling-Stevens buses recently disposed of, together with 10 1930 'Lion' LT1's and the pair of 1931 'Tiger' TS3's. It was hoped to receive these during 1946 (16 double-deckers and 5 single-deckers) and 1947 (6 double-deckers, 15 single-deckers and also 6 coaches). These plans were, however, subject to quite a bit of slippage

due to shortages of materials and skilled labour that extended through to the early 1950's.

Refurbishment of vehicles continued, with Leyland 'Tiger' TS7 Car 306 (JB 8345) returning from ECW on 9th May. The new post-war interior standard for Tilling Group buses was a dark red, which soon became applied to various vehicles as they were dealt with either by TV or outside firms, with that colour going on in place of the pre-war blue or even polished woodwork in some cases! Red roofs soon replaced the pre-war standard of white, whilst white bands gave way to a creamier shade. Further amendments to regulations on the number of standing passengers from 27th May returned to the pre-war level of 5, though one source of extra passengers was lost from early May, with the departure of the Polish troops from their resettlement camps in the Nettlebed area.

Over at Newbury, the TV crews were transferred from their wartime base at the firewatchers hut at Newbury Station, where they had taken refuge when the dormy shed was requisitioned by the Ministry of Supply, to the recently extended *Newbury & District* garage. The N&D garage was very close to the TV shed, and with *Red & White* cash had been considerably extended They also benefited from the new bus wash there when the transfer took place on Saturday 18th May.

During May the first pair of post-war buses arrived and were pressed straight into service as Cars 439/440 (CRX 548/9), being followed by Cars 441/4 (CRX 550/1) the following month. All were Bristol K6A's with ECW L27/28R bodies. On delivery all lacked rear fleet numbers, but they were soon added. All four were initially allocated to Reading and used mainly on Route 1 (Reading - Maidenhead) and Route 9 (Reading – Mortimer), though 440 was soon sent to Newbury to cover Route 10 (Reading - Newbury). However, hopes for further deliveries before the busy Summer period were soon dashed due to delays.

K6A Car 441 (CRX 550) with newly-painted adverts is seen on route 10 at the Station Hill bus stands.

Seen in their latter days and after body rebuilds are former private hire Leyland 'Tiger' TS4 Car 252 (RX 9706) and Leyland 'Lion' LT1 Car 10 (RX 5575), both in reserve at the Colonnade yard.

Car	Reg. No.	Radiator Notes	Engine Notes
244	RX 9541	Standard TS4 by 1.5.48, later had TS1/TS2 type	Leyland oil engine by 1.5.48
245	RX 9699	TS1/TS2 type by 9.45, standard TS4 from 1.46	Leyland oil engine from 1.46
246	RX 9700	TS1/TS2 type by 9.45, standard TS4 from 12.45	Leyland oil engine fitted 12.45
247	RX 9701	Standard TS4, then black-painted long CovRad from 1.46	Leyland oil engine fitted 1.46
248	RX 9702	Always carried standard TS4 unit	Leyland oil engine fitted 10.45
249	RX 9703	Standard TS4 to 7.45, then long CovRad from 7.45	Leyland oil engine fitted 12.45
250	RX 9704	Standard TS4 to 11.45, then TS1/TS2 type from 11.45	Leyland oil engine fitted 10.45
252	RX 9706	From WD 3.42 with long CovRad, later TS1/TS2 type	Leyland oil engine fitted 10.45
253	RX 9707	Returned from WD 3.43 with long CovRad, which it retained	Leyland oil engine fitted 1.46
255	RX 9709	Long CovRad fitted at rebuild 10.45, TS4 unit to 258 (a TS3)	Leyland oil engine fitted 11.45
256	RX 9710	Standard TS4 to 9.45, TS1/TS2 type 9.45, long CovRad 10.45	Leyland oil engine fitted 10.45

As can be seen from the above table, the surviving Leyland 'Tiger' TS4's received a variety of radiator types in the early post-war period which, combined with body refurbishments made each virtually unique in appearance. It had originally been planned for those with coach bodies to be rebuilt as service saloons just as the war started, but when that did eventually occur it was out of sheer necessity. Neither did they sound the same once the oil engines were fitted. The shortage of coaches was also vexatious, meaning that bookings for private hire could only been taken for days when excursions were not planned, though progress was soon made on repainting the 1939 TS8's with Harrington bodies, Cars 381-390 (BMO 980-9) from their wartime grey into the green and cream livery. Attention also turned to the future of the 1935 Duple-bodied 'Tiger' TS7 Car 262 (JB 5841), though the body was in very poor shape and there was no immediate prospect for returning it to service.

However, with the lowering of fuel restrictions and the return of called-up employees to their old tasks, it became possible to improve service levels in the area covered by Reading depot and its associated dormy sheds with effect from Saturday 18th May. In almost all cases the services returned to their pre-war levels, but the opportunity was taken to make some operational changes. Route 8 (Reading – Binfield Heath – Henley) went over to double-deck operation, but without journeys beyond Henley. A temporary Route 28a (Reading – Twyford – Henley – Fingest) was put on to incorporate the section between Henley and Fingest, also dispensing with the wartime Route 8a workings. The timetables did, however, note that this arrangement was only a stopgap until it became possible to improve Route 37 which served the area from the High Wycombe end. Indeed, it was still not practical to raise service levels in the High Wycombe and Maidenhead areas, though that was mainly due to loss of labour to industries in Wycombe and Slough. The other winners were the residents along the former *Blue Star* 6B route, which had been cut back to a Saturdays-only double journey each way as far as Stratfieldsaye. The route was now extended onto Bramley Station and given five return journeys on Mondays to Saturdays.

9

With improved services and the departure of many who had swelled the local population, travel returned to being more pleasant again. Not everyone did return though, as many bombed-out Londoners had no homes to go back to, whilst many Poles settled in the area as they felt, effectively, they had no country to return to. A few of each category inevitably made their way to the *Thames Valley* ranks, which helped to ease the labour shortage. A further stage in the return to normality came with the reintroduction of the Summer Sunday express route from High Wycombe to Southsea from 2nd June, though 'Tiger' TS7 or TS8 saloons were used at times due to the lack of coaches.

A further issue of new Setright Ticket Machines took place on 6th June to selected conductors. The staff refreshment hut at the *Southern Railway* Reading yard had come into use by June, but their were soon representations that it was also required after 6pm in the evenings due to lack of other local facilities.

As will be recalled, the Dormy Sheds at Yateley and Stoke Row had ceased to be operational, but both had been retained and used to store vehicles at times. The Stoke Row shed was sold in August but Yateley was still retained.

The Harrington-bodied 'Tiger' TS8's returned to coach duties, and Car 381 (BMO 980) was posed in the gateway of Reading Blue Coat School at Sonning. The TV monogram was retained on the front dome, as were those on the body sides.

Bristol K6A Car 440 (CRX 549) seen at Reading Stations Square bound for Windsor on busy route 2. Note the 'Titan' TD1 acting as relief, and also that the starting handle has been left in situ. Painted adverts were often still applied, with those for Maidenhead's Nicholson's Brewery, Simond's Brewery of Reading and Huntley & Palmer's Biscuits being widespread.

July saw a return to Royal Ascot Races, though in deference to the widespread shortages still in place nationally, the meeting took place on 19th to 20th only. TV buses were widely employed again to link the course with Windsor Central Station, plus enhanced coverage on Route 2 (Reading – Ascot – Windsor), the Company making use of the Grange Car Park as a terminus for Ascot traffic. Arrangements were also made for further meetings on 27th and 28th September and 11th and 12th October, with same off-road area close to the TV garage being used.

The Summer was a busy one for coach work, but with no immediate prospects of new vehicles, it was also a frustrating time. Indeed, it was during that period that other operators managed to raise their profile, none more so than *Smith's Luxury Coaches* of Reading. Due to Alf Smith's foresight in acquiring secondhand vehicles in quantity, he was in a good position to greatly increase his range of excursions, in particular the regular coastal express runs. Although TV still retained a good level of coach work, it never did quite regain its pre-war position in the Reading area.

Meanwhile, over at High Wycombe, further parcels of land in the vicinity of Frogmoor were added, though some were initially leased out pending completion of plans for an off-road bus station once materials and labour permitted. As those who were alive at that time will recall, the end of the war brought no immediate relief from shortages of all kinds. Also in Wycombe, TV set about acquiring the garage in Desborough Road formerly used by *T&B Haulage* but recently occupied by the Ministry of Supply. Maidenhead also saw improvements to garage facilities, with two additional inspection pits.

Desborough Road Garage was a very useful addition that eased the burden on the Wycombe Marsh site, operating effectively as a running-shed for the latter, which also saved quite a lot of dead mileage in and out of the town.

The land adjacent to Frogmoor had been surfaced, so it became possible to end the long-standing practice where buses turned at Bellfields, this taking effect from Tuesday 27th August and resulting in the saving of a 1000 miles per week. A small canteen was also provided, which was an improvement on the private facility previously frequented by crews. One of the old warehouses was also converted to take 4 buses and equipped with an inspection pit and a fuel oil tank and pump, plus new sliding doors. Buses on Routes 20 (Windsor), 25 (Flackwell Heath), 27 (Great Missenden), 28 (Reading), 31 (Lacey Green) and 34 (Speen) all laid over there, though passengers were still picked up at the Forgmoor bus stands.

Exactly how long the on-site garaging continued for is unclear, though buses were also parked overnight in other local yards etc. in the period leading to the occupation of Desborough Road. Wycombe Marsh was completely full, with 8 buses having to be left out at night, so the purchase of Desborough Road was timely, the garage having space for at least 30 buses.

The TV workshops managed to find room for 'Tiger' TS7 Car 328 (ABL 758), which received a thorough body overhaul before reappearing resplendent on 30th August. Indeed, repainting of the fleet continued at a good rate throughout 1946.

Also on the vehicle front, the four Leyland 'Beaver' Petrol Tank Wagons 5, 7, 9 and 11 (ABL 769-772) had been kept very busy as fuel rationing eased, with a pair being kept at the GWR Goods Yard in Coley and the others based in East Ham, the latter pair taking supplies from Silvertown in the London Docks. They had of course been operated under 'Pool' arrangements throughout the war years.

Duple 'camel-back' coach 262 (JB 5841) on a Leyland 'Tiger' TS7 chassis and new in 1935, had returned after military service and was in a very poor state. It was sent to Cawoods on 14th August for a complete refurbishment, but no doubt the driver had to check it over for any bits likely to fall off before the long journey to Doncaster!

Unfortunately little progress had been made with the plans for new passenger shelters on Station Hill when the Standing Joint Committee considered the topic in September, even though the *Great Western Railway* owned the land and was TV's major shareholder. The maintenance facilities at Reading depot did, however, improve from that month with the addition of two further inspection pits.

The general introduction of the Autumn timetable from 14th September also heralded the long-awaited service improvements for the Maidenhead and High Wycombe areas. The Desborough Road garage opened for business that day, though it had still to be completely cleared of Ministry of Supply items, the initial allocation being 16 buses. As a result of the new schedules for that area, the temporary Route 28a (Reading – Twyford – Henley – Fingest) arrangement ceased, with journeys on Route 37 (High Wycombe – Fingest) once again extended through to Henley, the operation being covered by Fingest Dormy Shed with its pair of 'Tiger' TS7's. Provisions were also made on Route 28 (Reading – Twyford – Henley – Marlow – High Wycombe) for additional short-workings to cater for the military based at 'Danesfield', just east of Medmenham on the Buckinghamshire bank of the River Thames. These journeys soon proved popular and provided a valuable link for social activities and useful additional income for the route.

11

Another route affected by the September changes was the 21 (Maidenhead – Waltham St. Lawrence), which saw some journeys covering the old *Beta Bus Service* section through Binfield – Warren House Crossroads – Wokingham once again, which also meant 'Tiger' TS4's making rare appearances in Wokingham after some years of absence. Also in the Wokingham area, Route 3a was amended to run as Reading – Wokingham – Barkham – Finchampstead only, the projected journeys to Crowthorne Station being taken off. By coincidence this operation also brought one of the TS4's to the area occasionally, though an early TS7 model was a more likely performer.

This rear view of Car 436 (DR 9846) highlights the unusual proportions of the Mumford bodywork, none of which were improved during the time at Vincents.

On the other hand, some routes were extended, with Route 19 (Maidenhead Station – Courthouse Road) projected onto Pinkneys Green, which gave a useful link for commuters. In the Wycombe area Route 31 (High Wycombe – Naphill – Walters Ash) was extended onto Lacey Green, whilst Route 36 (High Wycombe – Sands – Lane End) once again reached Cadmore End on most journeys. Both Routes 36 and 37 received additional early-morning journeys from 5th October, whilst Routes 3 (Reading – Crowthorne – Camberley), 10 (Reading – Thatcham – Newbury) and 19 all received additional work-related journeys from various dates in November as both the vehicle and staffing situations eased a little. However, much to the regret of TV's management, re-introduction of the London express routes still had to be deferred.

In fact only a trio of Bristol K6A's were received in September, becoming Cars 443-5 (DBL 151-3), all 3 being put into use at Reading on Route 1 along the Bath Road to Maidenhead and Route 9 to Mortimer. TV had hoped for more of the batch in time for the Autumn service improvements, but production was still affected by widespread shortages, for although Britain had won the War, it was a long way from full recovery.

Operationally the Company had continued to be administered under 2 areas, with Area 1 based on Reading, and Area 2 on High Wycombe, this situation originating from the huge expansion of TV interests in the latter area throughout the mid-1930's. Area 1 was under the daily control of Traffic Superintendent J. A. Dear, aided by Chief Inspector H. Guley, together with Local Inspectors T. H. Reed (Maidenhead), Frank Williams (Ascot) and C. W. Ankerson (Reading). Area 2 was in the hands of former *Marlow & District* manager Ernest Jeffries, aided by Chief Inspector S. Hammond and Local Inspector W. E. Hobbs.

October saw the arrival of a further pair of Bristol K6A's with standard ECW L27/28R bodies as Cars 446/7 (DBL 154/5), both of which were allocated to High Wycombe. Most of these double-deckers were to see long years of service, and fortunately Car 446 has survived in the care of local enthusiast Ward Jones.

Having previously dealt with replacing the engines in the 'Tiger' TS4's, the Works now turned its attention to the 1930 'Lion' LT2 types, with Car 50 (RX 6246) receiving a Gardner 4LW oil engine during its full overhaul during October/November 1946. Cars 46 and 54 (RX 6245 and 6248) were similarly dealt with during November, then finally Car 52 (RX 6247) in March 1947. A further 4LW unit was also obtained for 'Tiger' TS3 Car 230 (RX 6250), but work was not put in hand just yet.

Car 417 (CJB 136) was the only K5G with Duple body, and is seen after a post-war repaint working in the High Wycombe area.

Business at the Colonnade was further boosted by a contract to base 7 tipper lorries on behalf of the Reading Demolition Company there from 12th October, the arrangement being for about 7 months and involving the provision of all fuel and oil, as well as the parking fees. On the debit side, the contract to serve the Ministry of Supply depot near Prestwood came to an end on 31st October, though the general increase in Private Hire helped to offset the loss of wartime contracts.

There was further involvement between the M-o-S and TV throughout October and November 1946, with the Company representing the Tilling Group at the extensive disposal sales held at Mount Farm, near Dorchester in Oxfordshire. The main purpose of the visit by Engineer Basil Sutton and his loyal sidekick Elmet Abberfield was to identify lorries suitable for use as recovery tractors by associated companies. 90 Ford V8 gun tractors were inspected for this purpose and 38 were purchased. Sutton earmarked 2 for TV's use, together with a very impressive 6-wheel Dodge, of which we will hear more during 1947. Another of the latter type was also secured for *Hants & Dorset*, whilst the Fords were worked on to produce as many complete examples as practical. 2 went to *Aldershot & District*, whilst 1 each went to *Eastern National, United Counties, Hants & Dorset, Crosville* and *West Yorkshire*, plus 1 to the *Great Western Railway*, and 5 to *United Automobile Services*, with deliveries taking place through November and December.

Based on a Canadian Ford gun tractor was Service Vehicle No.19, which sometimes ran on trade plates 533 MO.

The Service Vehicle fleet received other attention in the shape of a Vauxhall 10hp car (DJB 865) for use by Inspectors, which arrived in October, plus Bedford 10/12cwt depot van No.15 (DJB 914) in November, both of these being sent to High Wycombe. Only one new bus arrived during November, Car 448 (DBL 156) being a further ECW-bodied Bristol K6A, which was allocated to Reading and initially used on Route 4 (Reading – Yateley – Camberley).

During November Traffic Manager Dally and Area 2 Superintendent Jeffries met with representatives of the *Great Western Railway* to discuss improving connections between bus services and trains on the lines from High Wycombe to Oxford, Watlington and Stokenchurch, someone also being present to represent *City of Oxford*. Railway co-operation of another kind was forthcoming that same month, with TV crews at Maidenhead Station being allowed to use the buffet at staff rates.

Ascot's wartime Bristol K6A's were still the backbone of Route 2 until gradually ousted by newer buses. Car 434 (CRX 545) was the last of the batch with Strachan utility bodies and was at Reading Stations Square. The angular features of the utility body are evident, as is the lack of opening windows. In later years these buses were extensively used on contracts.

Staff shortages still presented a problem, and there were 4 vacancies for drivers and 12 for conductors at Reading, 2 drivers and 11 conductors at Maidenhead and for 5 drivers and 14 conductors at Wycombe. The lack of conductors at the latter location resulted in many of the wartime 'clippies' staying on, whilst it was that location which also suffered from a shortage of engineering staff with so much competition around.

Movements of ex-WD vehicles assisted TV once again during the latter months of 1946, when the Colonnade became a staging post for Jeeps in transit.

The Company's own ex-WD vehicles were converted to their new role as Recovery Vehicles, the Fords as Nos.17 (DJB 943) and 19 (trade plate 533 MO or 111 RD), both initially being based at Reading. One saw use on 2nd December, after a Bristol double-decker was ditched in floods between Cookham and Hedsor Turn. The Dodge came into use in January 1947 as No.21 (trade plate 112 RD), being based at Reading.

During December two buses were sent to Cookham-based builders and decorators G&R Harding in order to increase the rate of repaints. 'Tiger' TS8 Car 361 (ARX 983) was with them from 8th – 14th, and 'Titan' TD1 Car 204 (RX 5566) from 14th – 21st. However, the standard of workmanship was not up to Sutton's requirements, so no more were sent at that time.

Another hard-working batch in the early post-war period were the 1939 Bristol K5G's with Eastern Coach Works bodies. Car 402 (BRX 918) was still operating over the lengthy Route 4 between Reading and Camberley when caught by the camera at the latter terminus in Park Street. Behind it is a rebuilt 'Tiger' TS4 covering the equally long Route 3 between those two towns, the latter running by way of Crowthorne and Wokingham.

TS7 coach 262 (JB 5841) was away at Cawoods, but the subject of how it should be painted was discussed during December. As it was now an odd-man-out in the fleet, it was decided it would be painted in service red and cream, as it was envisaged that one of its duties would be as a relief coach for the London Route A. An inspector from Cawoods had also looked at the Harrington-bodied TS8's 381-390 (BMO 980-9), and a programme was agreed to overhaul their bodies over the Winter months. At that stage no one could have realised for how many more years that batch of coaches would in fact last!

Also in the interests of passenger comfort, utility K6A Cars 426/7 (CRX 196/7) had their wooden slatted seats upholstered during late 1946, the remainder of that batch having been built to relaxed standards as new. Deliveries of ECW-bodied K6A's continued with Cars 449-452 (DBL 157-160) during December, with 449 going to Newbury for Route 10, 450/1 onto Route 1 from Maidenhead and 452 based at Reading.

Discussions took place in November and December regarding the proposal for a local service between Windsor and new housing in Dedworth by *Moore's*. There was a suggestion of a joint route, particularly as the independent wanted to use the *Southern Railway* yard at the Windsor & Eton Riverside Station. However, such co-operation was not forthcoming and *Moore's* service terminated on Castle Hill instead, whilst TV still operated the short-workings originating at the takeover of Jimmy Harris's *Pixey Bus Service*.

The levels of service had been returned to largely pre-war standards, and in some cases there had even been improvements. The workshops had been very busy indeed, with 80% of the fleet receiving a full repaint, as well as recovering from the general maintenance deficit of the war years. New engines in older chassis would see them through for a few more years until new buses could be obtained in sufficient quantities to finally retire cars originally earmarked for 1939/40 disposal.

However the necessity to continue operating older types over still high mileages did have an adverse effect on all the improvements that years of refining technical details had tried to achieve on fuel costs.

During 1946 the fleet had run a total of 8,539,999 miles and carried 38,634,447 passengers. Revenue from advertising had been much improved, being up by 400% since 1943, though this was partly due to old contracts having ended, plus advertisers feeling a new sense of optimism. Adverts for new houses were noticeable amongst those carried on the rear panels of vehicles, there being a further boost in the 'ribbon development' already found along the bus routes. On the other side of the coin, adverts for private cars now became more commonplace, a sign of the future and to the mixed fortunes for bus operators over the next two decades, as we will witness in due course. The first full year of Peace had been a very busy one for the Company, though progress had been thwarted by the general shortage of materials and manpower.

1947

We British are often accused of having an obsession about the weather, but as anyone who lived through 1947 will testify, that was a year with great cause to do so! Before we return to the chronological sequence of events, a review of the weather and its effects on bus operations in the *Thames Valley* is appropriate.

Exceptionally heavy snowfalls covered the area, with the High Wycombe being particularly badly affected. This led to operational difficulties, with roads un-passable, hills un-climbable and numerous buses with burst radiators, including all of the Guy 'Arabs' based in that town. Many services only operated for part of the day, with the local managers being given discretion to deal as they felt best. The service levels were also determined by the ability of crews to reach their bases from home. Radiator 'muffs' were soon fitted to reduce the incidence of bursts, but added to that was the problem of broken leaf springs where chassis were twisted over packed snow. If that was not bad enough, frequent power cuts also affected work at the Company's garages.

So throughout the months of January and February the Company's operating area resembled the Arctic, and it continued into early March. Indeed, transport observer Mac Head recalls how he got a new bike for Christmas, but it was late March before he got to take it out!

Maidenhead was severely affected by the floods, and 1930 Leyland 'Lion' LT1 Car 12 (RX 5576) waits on at the edge of the waters on the Berkshire side. Note the rebuilt bodywork with longer flared-out side panels and larger destination aperture.

A number of buses were kept on the Buckinghamshire side for the service to Slough, whilst the large Dodge service lorry No.21 (112 RD) was used to service them and is seen outside the famous 'Skindles' club.

As the snow began to melt, all the local ditches and water courses soon flooded. Once the waters reached the rivers the situation became serious, and at times life-threatening. Although local flooding was an annual Spring event, the 1947 floods were far deeper than anything experienced that century, whilst in most years the towns were largely unaffected. At Windsor the Thames even reached the Maidenhead Road and flooded the quadrangle of the Boys School, and that other school establishment over in Eton also suffered.

Leyland 'Tiger' TS8 Car 344 (AJB 816) looks more like a boat as it passes under Caversham Road railway bridge.

In Reading the floods extended beyond the bridge of the main London to Bristol railway line on the Caversham Road, but fortunately the TV garage was on a rise and was not affected.

At Maidenhead it had long been the practice to operate through to High Wycombe despite riverside floods along by Boulters Lock and over Widbrook Common in the hands of picked drivers, but this time the waters were too deep, so a service was provided via Pinkneys Green instead. Also the TV service lorries Nos. 19 (111 RD) and 21 (112 RD) provided a passenger ferry service over Maidenhead Bridge to link with the service to Slough, also working with the Fire Service, Army and WVS on general relief duties.

Dodge No. 21 ferrying through the Bridge Street flood, and Ford lorry No. 19 follows along behind it.

The bus terminus in Bridge Avenue was duly flooded and buses had to stop at other points in the town. At one point the flood waters actually reached the rear of the *Thames Valley* garage. Indeed, the officers and crews were only too aware of the scale of the floods throughout the area, and they soon set up a Flood Distress Fund. The contributions to that fund, together with the sterling effort put into maintaining services resulted in letters of gratitude from the Mayors of the towns worst affected.

Bridge Avenue and the rear of Maidenhead garage.

At times when Caversham Road was impassable, buses ran via Vastern Road instead whilst, as noted above, buses including 'Tiger' TS8 Car 373 (BBL 559) and 'Titan' TD1 Car 185 (RX 4347) maintained the eastern section of the route to Slough from the Buckinghamshire bank of Maidenhead Bridge.

Takings at the Colonnade were badly affected as motorists laid up their cars during the bad weather, whilst a further consequence was the slower delivery of new vehicles, the latter resulting in no buses being disposed of during 1947.

A further pair of Ford Gun Tractors were obtained in early January on behalf of the *Bristol Omnibus Co. Ltd.,* whilst on the 9th 'Tiger' TS7 coach 262 (JB 5841) returned from Doncaster after an extensive refurbishment at Cawoods.

During the early months of 1947 several items of road and rail co-operation were discussed, one being the possibility of a rail halt at Loddon Bridge, though TV was adamant that the bus services could cope. On the other hand, TV urged the *Great Western Railway* to abandon the Marlow – Bourne End section in favour of an improved bus service, however neither of these amounted to anything.

January saw the delivery of a further Bristol K-type with Eastern Coach Works L27/28R body, but this was fitted with a 6-cylinder Bristol engine, becoming Car 453 (DBL 161), and which was initially used from Reading on Route 10 (Reading – Newbury). The first of the post-war saloons began to arrive that month as Cars 455-8 (DBL 163-6). These were all Bristol L6A's with ECW B35R bodies and were in fact earmarked for the resumption of London Route A, though in the meantime Cars 455/6 went to Maidenhead for Route 24 (Maidenhead – Cookham) and Cars 457/8 were sent to High Wycombe for Route 38 (High Wycombe – Booker). The other new buses in course of preparation were held up by weather disruption until April, as Bristol K6B/ECW L27/28R Car 454 (DBL 162), which went to Reading and entered service on Route 10, whilst the outstanding saloon was Bristol L6A/ECW B35R Car 459 (DBL 167), which followed in May and was also sent to work for Reading.

It was against the above situation that the decision was taken in early February to touch-up and reinstate the dozen open-staircase 1928 'Titan' TD1's for yet another reprieve. All of those cars had spent the Winter in store at Newbury, Stokenchurch and Yateley. At the same time it was also decided to sell off the land behind the Newbury garage, as TV's hold in the town had never come up to expectations. It also soon became apparent that new coaches would not be received in time for the start of the season, so work on the Harrington-bodied 'Tiger' TS8 Cars 381-390

16

(BMO 980-9) was authorised. It was also decided that the roof quarter-lights would be removed during overhaul, and in early February Drivers Dixon and Mullett (the latter a former *Thackray's Way* man) took the first pair through the Winter landscape to Cawoods. These first two certainly came up to Basil Sutton's exacting requirements, so the programme got underway to do the rest, full details being as follows:

Car No.	Reg. No.	Date Out	Date Back
381	BMO 980	31.3.47	5.5.47
382	BMO 981	13.10.47	24.11.47
383	BMO 982	early 2.47	25.2.47
384	BMO 983	17.3.47	24.4.47
385	BMO 984	24.2.47	1.4.47
386	BMO 985	7.11.47	22.12.47
387	BMO 986	7.11.47	6.12.47
388	BMO 987	23.4.47	31.5.47
389	BMO 988	early 2.47	19.3.47
390	BMO 989	5.5.47	6.6.47

No one could have envisaged then quite how long the Harrington-bodied TS8's would remain in service. Car 385 is seen in the later red and cream livery at Goodwood Races. Note the TV monograms above the dome and on the vehicle sides retained from new.

The Company had previously had a Dormy Shed over at Stoke Row, which had ceased to be operational in 1940, and was sold in May 1946. Michael Plunkett lived locally to it, and used Route 7 on schooldays, noting on 23rd March 1947 that it had burnt down!

With the continuing need to keep the older types in service, it once again became necessary to seek help from outside. Basil Sutton and Works Foreman Foulke paid a visit to the Tooting works of Express Motor Bodies on 5th March to investigate if they could undertake body overhauls. That firm specialised in bodies for delivery vehicles, in particular for the news trade and, as they met the criteria, Leyland 'Cub' Car 338 (ABL 768) was sent to them on 17th March. It did not return until 3rd June, though to be fair to Express,

the wooden framework was found to be more gone once the panels had been removed! Identical Car 337 (ABL 767) was also sent there on 14th March, coming back with 338.

The Bristol K's became widespread on the main trunk routes, and Car 445 (DBL 153) is seen on the Reading – Camberley Route 4 at the latter terminus in original form with painted 'Corona' adverts.

Despite some dissatisfaction with the full repaints undertaken by Hardings of Cookham, the touch-ups on 2 of the 1928 TD1's were entrusted to them, with Cars 171/2 (RX 1760/1) going their singly between 12th March and 11th April, whilst others were dealt with in the Company's own works.

On Saturday 19th April Pony Racing at Hawthorn Hill re-commenced so, by agreement with the railway partners, the *Valley* provided bus links from stations at Maidenhead and Bracknell, the site being between Jealotts Hill and Holyport. In pre-war days a further service had been provided from High Wycombe, with pickups in Loudwater, Wooburn Green, Bourne End and Marlow. Some 30 meetings were held annually, so it was a worthwhile venture, though competition from Maidenhead came from *Alpha Coaches*.

During April Sutton, Balls, Jeffries and Dally went to Vincent's Reading coachworks, just opposite Station Hill, to see a new coach body being built for Timpsons on an AEC 'Regal' chassis. The Company would have liked to have placed a larger order, but Vincents agreed to do just 2 bodies at that time, the remainder of the order going to Windovers at Hendon.

Over at Newbury the *Newbury & District* garage was becoming crowded, so TV was asked to park their 2 Bristol K-type double-deckers on the forecourt overnight with effect from Saturday 26th March.

The Spring saw some of the Austin Staff Cars getting a well-earned overhaul, although they too went away for the work to Sands Garage of Burnham. The service fleet was enhanced in May with the arrival of a Vauxhall 10hp car (DRX 476), which was allocated to Reading for Engineering use. Basil Sutton visited Samuelson's Garage, across the road from Victoria Coach Station, during early May to view where the pair of double-deckers would be shedded overnight for Route B. As parts of the garage were of low height, it was agreed to issue a warning through the Staff Bulletin and to mark the low girders with warnings. Whilst in the area, it was also agreed to site an aluminium hut at the Coach Station for the use of the Inspector 'Jock' McCrindle.

Bristol K6A Car 452 (DBL 160) was one of the buses selected for the re-commencement of Route B, though curiously it is seen at the Kings Cross Coach Station with 'Private' and Route B on the blinds!

The re-introduction of the two London routes was eagerly anticipated, and finally became a reality from Saturday 17th May. A number of recently delivered buses were re-allocated to cover those routes, with Bristol L6Λ Cars 457-9 (DBL 165-7) going on the Λ (Reading – Wokingham – Bracknell – Ascot – Staines – Victoria), whilst Bristol K-type Cars 448/50-4 (DBL 156/8-62) were for the B (Reading – Twyford – Maidenhead – Slough – Victoria). It should be noted that the saloons had high-backed seats in an otherwise standard saloon body, whereas the double-deckers were just standard bus seats. 'Tiger' TS7 coach 262 (JB 5841) was officially earmarked for relief duties on the A, though at busy times virtually anything might turn up, including the Harrington-bodied TS8's.

The two London routes still differed very much in their character, with the A being bookable in advance and serving a far more rural route in those days, whilst the B was more an inter-urban bus route. The A was slightly longer at 41 miles, with a journey time of 2 hours, whilst the 40-mile B took 2 hours and 10 minutes due to having more stopping places.

During May Michael Plunkett observed that 'Titan' TD1 Cars 166/7/9/72/3/5 were in Reading depot after their touch-up work and ready for service, these being very much his favourites in the fleet. His other fancy

at that time were the little Guy buses still with *Reading Corporation,* and to that end he suggested that one should be preserved. However, the idea of bus preservation was at that time virtually unheard of, so such efforts went in vain.

The idea of a Bus Station at Camberley was raised at fairly regular intervals, but in the Spring of 1947 land at Knoll Road was offered for that purpose by Frimley & Camberley UDC. However, the Council then changed its intention and designated that land as a car park, offering an alternative at Obelisk Road when a joint meeting took place with representatives of TV, the *Southern Railway* and *Aldershot & District* on 23rd May, though again nothing resulted on the issue.

However, work at Maidenhead on 'Yorkstream' was completed by May, and the planning permission for the Bus Station had been obtained. The old bungalow had been rebuilt for staff use and featured a canteen and toilets, whilst at the same time Ascot garage had been provided with a new canteen.

As previously noted, a number of vehicles had been requisitioned by the Military at the outbreak of war, and again after the losses of hardware at Dunkirk. Although some had been returned to operators, the actual level of compensation had still not been resolved. During the various attempts to settle the matter on an ad hoc basis, disputes over the value of vehicles had arisen, so a General Claims Tribunal was set up. In respect of the Tilling Group companies, it had been decided that *Thames Valley* would represent all of the operators involved, lists of all vehicles and the written-down values being prepared. As the sitting commenced on 3rd June Basil Sutton, representing TV, had to forego his planned holiday, the hearing in the Royal Courts lasting until 19th June.

The Royal Ascot Race Week had long been a busy time on the Thames Valley calendar, and 1947 saw the event back to its full pre-war glory. Utility-bodied Bristol K6A Car 431 (CRX 542) heads the queue of buses returning the crowds to Windsor after the races.

Also helping out at Ascot is 1939 Bristol K5G Car 406 (BRX 922), about to depart for Reading.

Royal Ascot Races returned to a full programme from Tuesday 17th to Saturday 20th June, with The Grange car park once again being used as a Bus Station, with the usual effort to provide as many vehicles as possible, all routine maintenance being suspended for that week. As the very popular Aldershot Tattoo ran on much the same dates, vehicles often had to cover both the daytime racing and the evening excursions, so long hours were worked. As some compensation though, off-duty crews were permitted to enjoy those events, as in those days the wearing of uniform was respected and free entry often granted.

'Cubs' 337/8 (ABL 767/8) returned to their Marlow route duties after being received from Tooting on 3rd June, followed by TS8 coach 390 (BMO 989) from Cawoods on the 6th, and TD1 Car 168 (RX 1757) back from a touch-up at Hardings on the 11th. However, a mishap occurred when the driver of TS7 coach 262 (JB 5841) ran into the back of newly-refurbished TS8 390 as they were being transferred from Wycombe to Reading, so Bob Hepburn had to organise urgent attention to both on Sunday 15th June!

Parcels traffic was a significant source of income, and the conductor of K6A Car 449 (DBL 157) loads up.

'Beaver' Tanker required specialist welding to its tank so Driver Warman took it to a firm in Slough on 19th June to be done whilst he was taking his holiday. TS7-type saloon 305 (JB 8344) was the next vehicle to go to Express at Tooting on the last day of that month. Former 'London' TS4 coach 244 (RX 9541) had been recovered from the Military in poor shape and stored pending decisions on its future, re-appearing in Reading depot on 26th October 1946 in khaki paint. It was sent away in November to Cawoods, with a brief to rebuild it as a service saloon. New seats were ordered from G. D. Peters of Slough, and those were dispatched direct to Doncaster in the hope that the bus

The toll over Cookham Bridge was finally removed in the Summer of 1947, as up until then the Company had to pay for each of its vehicles crossing it. Bristol K5G Car 404 (BRX 920) makes the free crossing with the old toll house to the left behind it.

would return in time for the August Bank Holiday traffic. Indeed, it was collected by Driver Dixon on 24th July, but on inspection it was found that the new wheel arches were too wide and required alteration.

In the meantime on the staff front, with effect from 5th July, Conductor Arthur 'Nobby' Clarke was made up to Inspector at Ascot, fitting recognition for a man who was one of the original Ascot outstation crew at the barn at Englemere Farm!

Also from 9th July public parking at the Colonnade came to an end, as pressure of space at Lower Thorn Street was becoming a problem. The Tilling Contracts vans provided for the GEC contract were transferred to the Colonnade, as were some vans and cars, along with breakdown vehicles, coaches and relief vehicles. Despite the competition over Hawthorn Hill traffic, TV disposed of a 'Tiger' TS4 petrol engine to *Alpha Coaches* on 15th July and, as one of their coaches was also noted sporting a TV radiator – the timing perhaps suggests that the units may have come from Car 244?

Despite the delivery of newer buses the Leyland 'Titan' TD1 was still numerically significant in the fleet in 1947. Most were still engaged on full-day turns, such as Car 223 (RX 6243) waiting time at Reading Stations, and sporting one of the series of adverts for Milwards Shoes. This vehicle still retains much of the original appearance of the type, other than having had the rear staircase enclosed.

Although the 1928 TD1's had been prepared for further use, the work was only fairly superficial, but it still came as a shock when Stop Notices were placed on Cars 166/8/70 (RX 1755/7/9) on 23rd July! The trio were taken into Reading Works to investigate the extent of rotting body pillars and what could be done.

The return of 'Tiger' TS7 Car 305 (JB 8344) was not recorded, but by 22nd August the former *Crosville MS* 'Leyland 'Cub' 411 (FM 7455) was at Express in its place, and it too was discovered to have rotting pillars.

During August it had to be recognised that one of the serious impediments to recruitment of crews for work at Maidenhead was the shortage of cheap lodgings in that town. As the Company was already the landlord of a number of properties in the garage area, priority was to be given to potential employees. Although that eased the situation a little, other industries were by then offering a 5-day week, so some vacancies both on the crew front and in the workshops still remained.

The Standing Joint Committee had fostered closer links with the *Red & White Group* during the Summer of 1947. The intention was to work more closely with its local subsidiaries *Newbury & District* and *Venture*, but little came of it other than displaying timetables for connecting services. However, TV plans to make fuller use of Station Hill in Reading received a knock-back in September, when the Corporation announced that it intended using the stands for its trolleybuses! Also on the subject of Bus Stations, land at Frogmoor in High Wycombe was chosen as the site for an new Bus Station and Garage complex, though only the former was actually progressed in due course. The main operational difficulty in High Wycombe was the out-of-town siting of the Marsh garage, which led to a lot of dead mileage, plus generous time allowances for crews to reach Frogmoor, something the Union would not forego even once there was a garage in the town!

As the Summer months of 1947 passed by, so did the hope of further new deliveries of vehicles, particularly the much needed coaches from Windover and Vincents. From 30th September the Winter timetable brought a few significant changes to routes, with the journeys between Ascot and Sunningdale re-organised as two routes: Route 2a (Ascot – Sunninghill – Sunningdale Station) and Route 2c (Ascot – South Ascot – Sunninghill – Sunningdale Station). Route 18 gained journeys via Pinkneys Green, shown as Route 18a, whilst Route 19 reverted as a consequence to serve Maidenhead Station – Seeley's Stores once again.

'Titan' TD1 Car 175 (RX 1764) was the next to receive a Stop Notice on 3rd September, and as a result of which Basil Sutton accepted a suggestion from his opposite number at *Hants & Dorset* to seek quotes from Portsmouth Aviation, a company that had undertaken refurbishment work on its behalf. A visit was arranged to inspect one of the 1928 'Titans', but the turnaround would be too long and the price high.

On 22nd September a new Bedford 10/12cwt van was collected from Thomes Tilling Ltd., becoming No. 23 (EBL 533) for use as the Depot Van at Maidenhead.

The first of the new 32-seater Bristol L6B coaches were also received in September as Cars 460/2 (DMO 664/6), followed by Cars 463/5 (DMO 667/9) during October, these being the Windover-bodied examples, those at Vincents being far from completion! 460/2/3 were all allocated to Wycombe and 465 to Maidenhead, wearing a livery of cream with green wings, mudguards and radiator grilles.

Windover-bodied coach 460 (DMO 664) seen as new, a truly stylish vehicle. Note the use on the side of TV monograms again, though the fleetname was painted in the nearside destination aperture, whilst below is shown the interior looking forward. The heater of the Clayton-Dewandre system is on the front bulkhead.

An additional excursion introduced that Autumn was to the Public Viewing Gallery at Heathrow Airport, and passengers were also advised that the London Routes A and B could provide links there too.

The deliberations of the General Claims Tribunal came to an end on 19th September, and it was generally regarded that TV had put up a very good case on behalf of the Tilling Group. The officers were given a hearty vote of thanks for their dogged work, whilst Sutton was compensated for having to cancel his holiday. As regards the outcome for *Thames Valley,* it received £11,152 for the 23 vehicles taken.

Whilst 'Cub' 411 (FM 7455) was away at Express work was put in hand at Maidenhead re-trimming the seats removed from it, the vehicle being transferred from Tooting to the Leyland works at Kingston for the fitting of a replacement engine on 12th November.

During October and November more of the 'Tiger' TS8 coaches were dealt with by Cawoods, the programme having been interrupted by the delayed delivery of new coaches in time for the Summer.

The use of the Colonnade as a Paint Shop and a supplementary works commenced on Monday 27th October. Mr. H.H.N. Huggings was the Chargehand Painter and reported to the Works Superintendent, whilst movements of vehicles between the sites came under the control of the Reading Garage Foreman. The overall control of the Colonnade site was given to Mr. Abberfield, with assistance from Garage Wardens R. Soley and W. Barker.

From 11th October buses had started to appear with their registration numbers painted on the front dash, the work often being done whenever laidover for long enough, 'Lion' LT2 Car 14 (RX 6249) and 'Titan' TD1 Car 234 (RX 8167) being the first two treated. The rest of the fleet had been done by 27th November when all cars were fitted with radiator muffs for the Winter.

Further contractors were sought for refurbishment work, so the horsebox constructors Lambourn Garages, based in the West Berkshire horse-training centre, was sent 1935 'Tiger' TS7 Car 298 (JB 7498) in early November. Although it was still there in December, Mr. Foulke reported that the work was to a high standard.

Although it was obvious that the older 'Titans' would require further intention if they were to be retained, fate intervened in the case of Car 199 (RX 5561), when Driver Ewer ran up the bank on Witheridge Hill whist working the last journey out to Peppard on the 7 Route on 9th November. The bus completely blocked the road, landing on its nearside. It was righted the following morning by the joint effort of the Ford and Dodge Wagons, and as he was local to the scene, the repair job was given to D.J. Hawkins of Stoke Row. The same firm was also entrusted with remedial work on TD1 Car 172 (RX 1761), though little progress had been made with either project when Sutton called by on 13th November, the timber on order having not yet apparently arrived.

The scene that greeted the recovery crew after Car 199 (RX 5561) was overturned on Witheridge Hill. One of the Ford lorries is seen in the background and a start has been made assembling the framework for winching the bus to the more conventional position.

The repaints undertaken at the Colonnade resulted in a further 3 cars per week being dealt with, with one car being dispatched to Reading, High Wycombe and Maidenhead each Saturday morning. The Company also dealt with an internal refurbishment on 1928 TD1 Car 166 (RX 1755) during November in the Reading Works, also trying a new maroon interior paint scheme. This appears to have been done to evaluate the prospects of preparing the batch for further use at minimal cost.

The utility-bodied Bristol K6A's, Cars 426-34 (CRX 196-8, 540-5) were also worked on, with improved interiors and seating. Consideration was also given to the re-bodying of the 1935-8 Leyland 'Titan' TD4 and TD5's, or even perhaps the newer 'Tiger' TS7's and TS8 saloons, as had been done in other Tilling Group fleets, where sometimes even older vehicles had been selected to receive new ECW bodies.

1939 Bristol K5G Car 392 (BRX 908) is seen working Route 10 to Newbury in St. Mary's Butts, Reading. The 'Regent Ice Cream Parlour' had previously been the Thames Valley office in the town centre, remaining there still as a pizza restaurant.

Only one new bus was delivered during November, in the shape of Car 466 (DMO 670), another standard ECW L27/28R body on a Bristol K-type chassis, but the engine choice again reverted to the 6-cylinder AEC unit. That was followed during December by identical Car 467 (DMO 671), both of which were allocated to Reading.

During November the Board approved the ordering of 15 single-deck and 15 double-deck bodies from ECW for the re-bodying programme, but no vehicles were put forward after all.

1928 'Titan' TD1 Car 165 (RX 1754) looks quite sound in this view waiting in the sunshine at Reading Stations, but the real problems lay under the surface, in particular the wooden body framing, which was actually constructed as separate lower and upper decks. Newer batches had been rebuilt during the war years and generally received full-height framing as a result.

The prospects for completion of the pair of Bristol L6B coaches entrusted to Vincents was still poor, as work was slow, and the one thing that Basil Sutton certainly wouldn't get for Christmas 1947 was Cars 461 and 464! In retrospect, it also seems strange that the pair did not have had consecutive fleet numbers?

In the meantime over at Maidenhead, permission had been obtained to start development of the off-road Bus Station on land in Bridge Avenue. Drainage and surface works got underway, though there were still shortages of steel to contend with, so the proposed new cafeteria would have to be added at a later date. The plans for the semi-circular bus station were indeed quite comprehensive and would overcome the often crowded situation by the Rialto Cinema, made even worse when express coaches called in there too.

1948

The Nationalisation of road public transport, road haulage and the railways was seen as essential by the post-war Labour Government, though at the time it was by no means fully achieved. In the case of the Tilling Group, and therefore *Thames Valley,* the high financial involvement of the railway companies made this inevitable. And so, from 1st January 1948, the shares of the Tilling Group passed to the new British Transport Commission (Road Transport Executive), though this had little immediate effect for the travelling public in the area.

As noted a little earlier, Leyland 'Tiger' TS4 Car 244 (RX 9541) had been reconstructed as a service saloon and is seen lurking in the entrance from Reading depot into Lower Thorn Street. The destination box has been enlarged and the registration moved to the front dash, both of which altered its general look.

Lambourn Garages completed the work on 'Tiger' TS7 Car 298 (JB 7498) on 7th January and, as the work was very good, TS8 Car 368 (ARX 990) was sent there on 2nd February. 'Cub' 411 (FM 7455) came back from Leyland's Kingston works on 19th January, similar bus 337 (ABL 767) going in its place to receive an overhauled engine. The latter returned on 20th April, its place then being taken by the third example Car 338 (ABL 768). Ultimately the shortage of new coaches had led to a series of decisions that effectively extended the working lives of this trio of small buses, as we shall see in due course.

A vacancy arose for a Petrol Tanker Driver during January, and the new East Ham-based driver A.W.C. Smith collected Petrol Tank Wagon No.7 (ABL 770) from Reading Works to take up his duties that month. At that time Wagon Nos.5 (ABL 769) and 7 were at East Ham and Nos.9 and 11 (ABL 771/2) were kept at the Coley Goods Yard in Reading. The tanker contract had long been an unusual facet of TV operations, and its survival into the Nationalised era is remarkable.

Route 5 between Reading and Oxford was one of the services to benefit from the new Bristol L6A's fitted with high-backed seating, and Car 476 (DMO 680) is seen at Gloucester Green Bus Station in Oxford.

Further discussions took place over the future of bus stands in the Reading Stations area, with Reading Corporation still earmarking the Station Hill stands for trolleybuses, mainly for the ease of positioning the wiring for such vehicles to turn and the use of a loop to allow through-working trolleys to pass by. The alternative site considered for the *'Valley'* buses was the area of land beyond the current bus parking area between the *Southern Region* and *Western Region* Stations. There was certainly plenty of potential space there and the scheme, which would see buses enter by way of Stations Square and exit via Vastern Road, gained the approval of the Chief Constable of the Reading Borough Police.

Car 484 (DMO 688) is seen at Reading Stations on Route 3 after having spent a spell on the A Route. The odd saloon to the left is Kemp's Motor Service former Green Line T-type coach re-registered as BRD 922.

During January supplies of Bristol L6A single-deckers came through, with Cars 472-7 (DMO 676-81), fitted with ECW DP31R with semi-luxury seating. The rest of the batch were spread out in delivery, with Cars 478-484 (DMO 682-8) arriving in March, followed by Car 485 (DMO 689) in April and finally by Car 486 (DMO 690) in May. Ultimately their intended duties were to cover the longer routes such as the 3 (Reading – Crowthorne - Camberley), 5 (Reading – Oxford) and 28 (Reading – Henley – High Wycombe), but in the short-term some were required to cover London Route A until coaches on order could be delivered. So Reading initially received 476/7/84-6, whilst 481-3 went to Maidenhead and 472-5/8-80 to Wycombe.

Seen at High Wycombe Station on Route 36 to Lane End is Bristol L6A Car 478 (DMO 682).

Double-deck deliveries also continued, with Cars 468/9 (DMO 672/3) arriving in March and Cars 470/1 (DMO 674/5) in April, being a quartet of Bristol K6B chassis with ECW L27/28R bodies, and all were for use at Reading. However, there were a number of technical problems besetting these batches, with wheel wobble noticeable on cars used at higher speed on the London routes, resulting in a number of visits from the Bristol Commercial technical men.

Bristol K6B Car 470 (DMO 674) halts by the Red Cow at the junction of Southampton Street and Crown Street working Route 4a to Wokingham via Shinfield and the Arborfield Garrison.

As noted earlier, a Gardner 4LW engine oil engine had been ordered for 'Tiger' TS3 Car 230 (RX 6250), and the fitting of that was completed on 14th February. On the same day Reading Works released 'Titan' TD1 Car 170 (RX 1759) after a thorough overhaul. Similar

buses 172 (RX 1761) and 199 (RX 5561) were still in the hands of Hawkins of Stoke Row, and during that month they were joined by 'Tiger' TS8 coach 389 (BMO 988), which had suffered rear end damage. The firm had actually built up some expertise in allied trades during the War, making aircraft sub-assemblies for Woodley Airfield factories. On 15th February Cawoods were sent their first double-deck project, in the shape of Bristol K5G Car 391 (BRX 656), now in need of a thorough body overhaul.

The first of the pair of Bristol L6B 32-seater coaches from Vincents was collected on 18th February, but it had to be returned to have a modified driver's seat, as their were instant complaints regarding the lack of forward vision. Car 461 (DMO 665) was modified and followed by identical coach 464 (DMO 668) soon after – though both were back at Vincents again during April, when seasonal showers showed that the sliding roofs were by no means water-tight! Both were based at Reading initially, and wore a livery of cream relieved with green side-flash, wings and mudguards and radiator grille.

One of the pair of Vincent-bodied Bristol coaches as new, the body being pure pre-war in style, especially the anachronistic stepped waistrail!

Reading through the Engineer's Reports of the period, there seems at last the sense that the Reading Works, aided by the Colonnade Paintshop and some outside firms, was at last turning the tide on the deficit of vehicle maintenance caused by the War years. Sutton also instructed his assistants to seek out Leyland spare parts through dealers and other operators, which was a further acceptance that older types would not be cleared for the foreseeable future.

A plan of the expanding use of the site off Frogmoor in High Wycombe drawn up in March 1948 shows that Nos.37/37a facing the Frogmoor terminus were let out as shops below, but upstairs were used for the Traffic Office, whilst No.35 was the Booking Office, as inherited from the *Penn Bus Company* in 1935. The Inspectors were accommodated nearby at No.55, and a Staff Canteen was provided to the south side of the vehicular entrance at No.49. Vehicles went both ways between Nos. 49 and 51 at that point, though later a one-way system came in and will be reviewed in due course. The use of this site for a garage facility is not

Bristol L6A Car 475 (DMO 679) climbs up Castle Hill out of Maidenhead on Route 21 to Woodlands Park. Also note the style of the road signage of the period.

thought to have lasted for long, probably ceasing once Desborough Road became fully available. The Company also provided overnight parking for one *Royal Blue* coach for the Portsmouth – High Wycombe – Hitchin route at Frogmoor, though that was re-located to Desborough Road by 1957 (when the next major phase of re-development took place).

Given the ex-Military background of the Engineer, and the close proximity of the Army Apprentices School at Arborfield, it is understandable that TV was an eager participant in the Pre-release Vocational Training Scheme for soldiers. The scheme gave opportunities for courses in the Works in various trades or for training as PSV Drivers. As a number of the candidates duly filled vacancies with the Company, it was certainly a worthwhile involvement.

With the need to bring the 1928 'Titan' TD1's out of store for the Summer timetable, Car 165 (RX 1754) was driven all the way to Doncaster on 4th March for attention at Cawoods! However 'Tiger' TS4 saloon was the subject of yet another setback, being served a Stop Notice when inspected around the same time, yet another car in need of urgent work, though it was seen out again in service on 10th June. Despite this, TV did manage to find the capacity to overhaul engines for the *Brighton, Hove & District* Company during April, with one each of Gardner 5LW and 8.6-litre Leyland oil engines dealt with. By sheer coincidence, the same operator requested TV's assistance in recovering an AEC 'Regent' double-decker from the Mount Farm disposal sales on 5th April, a *BH&D* driver collecting it 3 days later.

A strike at Cawoods during April was another rock in the road to recovery and, so although Bristol K5G Car

391 (BRX 656) was returned on 1st June, 'Titan' TD1 Car 165 was delayed and missed the crucial Ascot Race Week!

Although originally conceived in the latter pre-war years, the off-road Bus Station in Maidenhead finally opened on Monday 26th April. The new arrangement gave much more space for vehicles and passengers alike, whilst also continuing to serve as a significant point for express coach services from various parts of the country. Indeed, the roadway in Bridge Avenue at times looked more like a coach park, with service coaches and numerous reliefs travelling between the town and London, Oxford, Worcester, Bristol and all points West. As materials for construction were still in short supply, the planned waiting room/cafeteria could not be built, so the large wooden passenger shelter by the Rialto Cinema was relocated to the new facility. It was later replaced by a brick-built structure, evidently being donated to the Reading Blue Coat School at Sonning, where it had a new role as a sport's pavilion. When inspected on re-discovery in 2005, the original perimeter bench seats were still in place, as were the leaflet racks in what had been the Inspector's kiosk! It was rescued by preservationist Colin Billington, and so will hopefully rise yet again.

Upper deck interior looking rearward on Car 468.

25

Maidenhead Bus Station in its original form, with the old wooden passenger shelter relocated to a central position. More individual shelters were later provided at the stands. Note the little 'Cub' on the Marlow 18 Route stand at the far end, with the white-painted staff facility at 'Yorkstream' to its right. The photo was taken from the roof of the Rialto Cinema and also shows the additional ribbing used to strengthen the sagging roofs on the utility Guys, one of which stands in the left foreground.

However, the prospects for an improved Bus Station at Reading still came to nothing, despite a number of meetings with the railway representatives and the GM of Reading Corporation Transport Mr. W. J. Evans.

Sutton had his assistant S.V. Read prepare a list of double-deckers that might benefit from re-bodying, this time including the 1939/40 Bristol K5G's, the latter being due for an thorough mechanical overhaul.

'Titan' TD1 Car 172 (RX 1761) returned from Hawkins on 5th May, with Car 199 (RX 5561) coming back on an unrecorded date, though it was noted in use on 28th April. The latter did, however, suffer another setback just before the busy Ascot Week, as the seats were slashed overnight at Reading depot yard – the first record of such vandalism by TV. Also in connection with the Race Week, a Staff Tea Tent was provided at the Grange Car Park, crews prior to that having to walk to the garage in Course Road.

Further Staff Cars were dealt with during May and June, with the overhaul on Austin 8 hp CJB 670 dealt

with over at Sands of Burnham, though others passed through the Reading Works. On 27th May a further pair of AEC 'Regent' double-deckers were collected on behalf of *BH&D* from Mount Farm, whilst during the following month three more engines, one apiece of Gardner, Leyland and AEC were overhauled for that Company.

Those of you have had the benefit of reading Basil Sutton's finely detailed accounts will understand how enthusiastic he was about events, but he felt that one particular item deserved a special mention, so I will quote the man himself – ''On 26th May we had a very interesting visit from Reading schoolboy Michael Plunkett and a friend. Michael, aged 17.5, had left for display on our stand at the recent War Savings Exhibition in Reading a beautifully made model of Leyland 'Titan' Double Deck No.204, which he had constructed and had occupied him for nearly 3 years. He asked that he might be permitted to look at our records. He showed great interest in these and afterwards produced an amazingly complete record of our vehicles, showing vehicles past and present. He had prepared scale drawings of almost every type of vehicle that had ever been included in the fleet''.

By June 1948 the single-deck requirement at Ascot had been changed to Leyland 'Lion' LT1 Car 10 (RX 5575). It was indeed a period of numerous allocation changes, with vehicles still being worked on under the reconstruction programme, new deliveries arriving, another phase of changes as the London routes re-commenced and new coaches arriving. It is therefore useful to review the allocations of 1st June 1948:-

Brush-bodied Leyland 'Tiger' TS8 Car 343 (AJB 815) is seen on Station Hill in the shadow of the far end of the huge Vincents site. It is on Route 5b to Yattendon, whilst Routes 5 to Oxford and 5a to Wantage also ran from this stand.

Vehicle allocations at 1st June 1948

Ascot Garage
Single-deckers: Leyland 'Lion' LT1 Car 10.
Double-deckers: Leyland 'Titan' TD1 Car 181; Bristol K6A Cars 426-34.
Maidenhead Garage
Single-deckers: Leyland 'Lion' LT1 Cars 6, 8, 12; Leyland 'Lion' LT2 Cars 42, 46, 50, 52; Leyland 'Tiger' TS4 Cars 245-50; Leyland 'Tiger' TS7 Cars 36, 295; Leyland 'Tiger' TS8 Cars 345-7, 373-5, 379/80; Leyland 'Cub' KPZ2 Cars 337/8; Leyland 'Cub' KP3 Car 411; Bedford OWB Cars 437/8; Bristol L6A Cars 455/6, 475, 481-3.
Double-deckers: Leyland 'Titan' TD1 Cars 180, 182-6, 205, 206, 208, 235/6; Leyland 'Titan' TD4 Cars 274-7; Bristol K5G Cars 403/4, 408-10, 416; Guy 'Arab' I 5LW Cars 418-20; Bristol K6A Cars 443, 450.
Coaches: Leyland 'Tiger' TS8 Cars 382, 388, Bristol L6B Car 465.

Guy 'Arab' Car 419 (CJB 138) stands in the new Maidenhead Bus Station on a Local Service.

High Wycombe Garage, including Dormy Sheds at Fingest, Princes Risborough and Stokenchurch:
Single-deckers: Leyland 'Tiger' TS7 Cars 24, 26, 28, 40, 44, 48, 266/7, 269/70, 296-9, 303, 306, 327-30, 332-4; Leyland 'Tiger' TS8 Cars 348, 359-68, 376-8; Bristol L6A Cars 472-4, 478-80.
Double-deckers: Leyland 'Titan' TD1 Cars 201, 221, 224, 237; Leyland 'Titan' TD5 Cars 339/40; Bristol 407, 413/4, 417; Guy 'Arab' I 5LW Cars 421-5; Bristol K6A Cars 446/7, 451.
Coaches: Leyland 'Tiger' TS7 Car 262; Leyland 'Tiger' TS8 Cars 383-5, 387, 389; Bristol L6B Cars 460, 462/3.

Bristol K's were the newest buses at High Wycombe, though Car 469 (DMO 673), seen at Crendon Street on the 38 to Booker, arrived there a little later on.

Reading Garage, including Dormy Sheds at Tadley, Newbury, Crowthorne, and Victoria O/S:
Single-deckers: Leyland 'Lion' LT1 Cars 2, 4, 14, 20, 22, 38; 'Lion' LT2 Car 54; Leyland 'Tiger' TS3 Cars 230, 258/9; Leyland 'Tiger' TS7 Cars 18, 30, 32, 34, 265/8/71, 302/4/7/8,: Leyland 'Tiger' TS8 Cars 342-4, 371/2; Bristol L6A Cars 476/84-6.
Double-deckers: Leyland 'Titan' TD1 Cars 164-75, 179, 187, 190, 199, 200, 202-4, 207, 219/20, 222/3, 232-4, 412; Leyland 'Titan' TD2 Cars 435/6; Leyland 'Titan' TD4 Cars 272/3, 335/6; Leyland 'Titan' TD5 Cars 341, 369/70; Bristol K5G Cars 391-402/5/6, 415; Bristol K6A Cars 439-42/4/5/9/50/2, 466/7; Bristol K6B Cars 453/4, 468-71.
Coaches: Leyland 'Tiger' TS8 Cars 381, 386, 390; Bristol L6B Cars 461, 464.

The excursions programme had settled down with the arrival of the new Bristol coaches, so by July they ran to the coastal resorts of Bognor Regis, Hayling Island and Lee-on-Solent, horse-racing at Goodwood and Hawthorn Hill, to Whipsnade Zoo, as well as day tours taking in Savernake Forest & the Hampshire Downs, Hindhead & Waggoners Wells, and Gems of the Surrey Scenery. Evening tours were also available through the Beechwoods to Fairmile & the Berkshire Downs. Prices varied from 2 shillings and 3 pence for an evening tour to 8 shillings and 9 pence for Bognor.

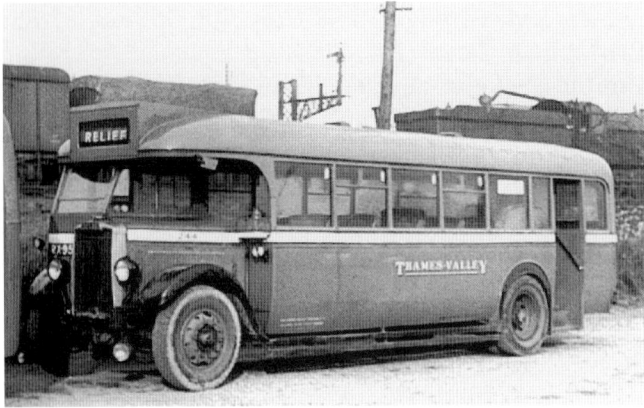

'Tiger' TS4 Car 244 (RX 9541) rebuilt as a bus is seen at the parking area between Reading Stations.

From Saturday 10th July five journeys on Route 3 (Reading – Wokingham – Crowthorne – Camberley) were diverted to take in other local areas not served, going via Little Sandhurst between Camberley and Crowthorne, then after the latter running via Honey Hill and Gardeners Green into Wokingham.

1937 Leyland 'Beaver' TSC8 Petrol Tanker No.7 was repainted into full 'Regent' livery, having run in 'Pool' grey since the War, and re-emerged on 15th July. It was collected by Driver Smith, whilst Driver Burns brought No 5 (ABL 769) in its place. Both men then took it down to Caversham Promenade, where Jimmy Lewington, Reading Stores Superintendent and TV's in-house photographer, recorded the event. After that it was driven to the 'Regent' headquarters in London's Park Lane for inspection by the Directors. This diversion evidently gave a good impression of the TV Paintshop, resulting in a number of such jobs for the fuel company after No.5 emerged on 7th September. 'Regent' Dennis 1200-gallon tanker No.349 was in the shops from 4th October, then an International 1500-gallon tanker No.432 from 19th October, then before December a similar lorry No.432 and a new Bedford, each taking around 2 weeks to do.

'Beaver' No.7 (ABL 770) resplendent in new paint.

Despite plans for the new Bus Station at Reading being stalled, it was agreed that a joint road and rail Enquiry Office would be built adjacent to the north frontage of the *Southern Region* Station, the design work to be undertaken by the Tilling architects.

'Titan' TD1 Car 165 (RX 1754) finally returned from Cawoods on 30th July, though only in undercoat, but the interior was blue with blue refurbished seats. Bristol K5G Car 398 (BRX 914) had been taken to Doncaster in its place, though again Stop Notices placed on cars put the serviceable fleet back yet again! The TD1's affected were Cars 167 and 173 (RX 1756/62), both with bad body movement, as once again the dilemma was how to keep these vehicles going until replacements finally came. It is also noted that radiator swaps around this period saw some of the old hollow-sided type of units appearing on newer batches and vice-versa, and some of these units may have even been secondhand?

Thames Valley was always publicity conscious and went to a lot of trouble to design posters and other display materials. The themes of royalty and the river, the latter often personified by the mute swan, were recurrent, as seen on the hoardings situated outside the Head Office at Lower Thorn Street in Reading.

Vehicle disposals at Mount Farm were still continuing and on 4th August Basil Sutton went there on behalf of *Hants & Dorset* to view a 'Tiger' coach they were in mind of re-purchasing. Imagine his surprise when he found that the sorry-looking vehicle next it was once his pride-and-glory Duple-bodied 'Tiger' TS7 coach 264 (JB 5843). Enquiries were immediately put in hand and the re-purchase sanctioned by the Board, as 264's 'return from the dead' was most unexpected! A further *H&D* 'Tiger' was inspected there on 26th August, but no further TV examples were found, the third of the batch of TS7's, Car 263, never returning.

Once the Summer peak had ended, the opportunity was taken to de-license the older generation of saloons from 31st August, these being Leyland 'Lion' LT1 Cars 2-14 (even numbers only), 20, 22, 38 and 42 (RX 5571-80) and 'Tiger' TS3 Cars 258/9 (GN 5145, 5139). Cars 6, 8, 10, 12, 14 and 42 went to the Colonnade yard, the others being stored at Newbury, Stokenchurch, Fingest and Desborough Road.

The 'Tiger' TS7 was still numerically the backbone of the saloon fleet in early postwar days, and Car 267 (JB 5846) was a 1935 Brush-bodied example. It is seen at High Wycombe Station after a repaint with red roof, though the blind is set to blank for some reason.

The 'Lion' LT1 Car 10 at Ascot had been replaced by 'Tiger' TS4-type 245 (RX 9699) transferred from its former allocation at Maidenhead. However, the extra journeys to Woodley ceased in January 1949, aircraft production now being reduced, so Ascot lost its only saloon for the time being.

The trawl for Leyland spares drew results when Bob Hepburn paid a visit to a clearance sale at the North London operator *Birch Bros.* in September, returning from Kentish Town with 4 Leyland radiators, 2 'Tiger' oil engines and a quantity of other spares. It should be noted that around this period a number of 'wrong' radiators appeared on various buses, mostly between 'Titan' TD4's and 'Tiger' TS7's, whereby some had the other model name at the base of the radiator, whilst some TS7's even got radiators that had once graced the saloons earmarked for the London routes or the TS8 coaches, noticeable for the *Thames Valley* script diagonally across the grille.

Car 32 (ABL 752) was another 'Tiger' TS7, but new in 1937 and carrying an ECW body. It carries one of the former 'coach' radiators, though there is no model name at the base. By the time this view was taken at the entrance to the Southern Yard at Reading Stations, the bus had reverted to its original fleet no. 322, having been in the Ledbury Transport fleet.

Although the old Newbury Dormy Shed had been vacated by the Ministry of Supply earlier in 1948, it was not until 1st September that all the repairs had been completed, allowing the 2 Bristol K-types for Route 10 to return home once again. The shed's other main function during this period was for storing buses and coaches delicensed for the Winter.

Over the Summer months further land off Frogmoor had been drained and surfaced to give more parking space, whilst the general cleanliness of the fleet was enhanced by the purchase of 3 new 'Essex' washing machines, ordered during September and November for use at Reading, Maidenhead and the 'Marsh.

'Titan' TD1 Car 168 (RX 1757) was the next one to be served with a Stop Notice in September, but in view of its impending withdrawal for the Winter, it was sent straight to store to await a decision on any possible future use.

Windover-bodied Bristol L6B coach 487 on Route A.

The new batch of Bristol L6B coaches for London Route A, Cars 487-91 (EJB 209-13) arrived in time for use from 1st September. They had Windover bodies seating 33, having 5 rear seats against the 4 of earlier deliveries, but were finished ii service red with cream waistrail and side fleetnames. Their arrival released Bristol L6A saloons 484-6 (DMO 688-90), which were transferred to Crowthorne to work the 19-mile Route 3 (Reading – Crowthorne – Camberley). That Dormy Shed lost all of its Leyland buses, except TS7 Car 18 (JB 7494), which was retained to cover Route 3a (Reading – Wokingham – Finchampstead).

An order for lightweight buses on Bedford OB chassis had also been placed which, in view of the weak bridge linking Haying Island, and the difficulty in obtaining vehicles to full coach specification, would be equipped with semi-luxury seating. Indeed, the order was increased from 3 to 4, the intention being to transfer the quartet to the equally restricted Route 18 (Maidenhead – Marlow) in due course, which would then allow disposal of the trio of Leyland 'Cub' buses. On the Service Vehicle front, a 3-ton Commer Q4 lorry about 1 year old was obtained during one of the visits to the Mount Farm Sales, becoming No.25 (JGF 406) at the end of September for use at Wycombe Marsh. Also at the end of September the forecourt of Reading Garage leading into Lower Thorn Street was concreted over for a possible extension to the garage. Due to the number of buses parked out night, it was even necessary to leave some at the Cattle Market Car Park in Great Knollys Street, and so it was on the night of 29th September Michael Plunkett had the opportunity to fully explore 'Titan' TD1's 165, 170 and 175 (RX 1754/9/64) and 'Tiger' TS3 Car 230 (RX 6250).

The General Manager, Leonard Balls was able to report in his Autumn Report that repaints were now being undertaken at 15-month intervals. He also drew attention to the fact that the Company would need to plan for the increased rowing activity at Henley-on-Thames in connection with the Olympic Games of 1950.

Bristol K5G Car 398 (BRX 914) returned from Cawoods on 1st October still in undercoat, the driver delivering similar bus 395 (BRX 911) in its place. As before though, there were elements of reversed fortunes, as 'Titan' TD1 Car 164 (RX 1753) was also served a Stop Notice and was hurried into store. Then on 9th October 'Tiger' TS4 Car 252 (RX 9706) was badly damaged in a collision when on Ascot Races duties, ending up in a front garden in Bracknell, and spent some time being repaired as a result.

The Winter timetable came into effect from Saturday 1st October, but it contained few major changes. Some journeys on Route 9a (Reading – Grazeley – Tadley) were diverted to run via Ufton Nervet. To the east Route 22b (Slough – Cippenham – Maidenhead) was brought in to assist in handling local traffic, but the changeover day was somewhat marred by a one-day strike at High Wycombe, where 7,570 scheduled miles were lost over a dispute over new duty rosters, that location having quite a reputation for militancy. From Monday 18th October new Setright Ticket Machines were brought in to replace the Automaticket System at Ascot and Reading Garages.

In a slightly unexpected move, 'Lion' LT1 Cars 6, 8, 10, 12 and 42 (RX 5573-6) and 'Lion' LT2 Car 14 (RX 6249) were brought out of the Colonnade and re-licensed for service at Maidenhead from 30th October, the purpose being to allow other newer buses to be sent for attention or re-allocation. At the same time 'Tiger' TS7 coach 262 (JB 5841) and TS8 coaches 382-5 (BMO 981-4) were stored for the Winter.

During November a new design of Request Stop sign came into use, remaining a familiar sight throughout the remainder of the Company's existence. Cawoods continued their way through the 1939 Bristol K5G's, with 396 (BRX 912) taking the place of 395 on 29th

November. On 3rd December Duple-bodied 'Tiger' TS7 coach 264 (JB 5843) was sent to Lambourn Garages, where it was subsequently decided that the sliding roof was beyond economical repair and would be panelled instead. Bristol L6B coach 463 (DMO 667) suffered a bad smash and had to be sent to Windovers on 6th Decenber, whilst 'Titan' TD1 Car 203 (RX 5565) ran into a hedge out at Kennylands whilst its driver attempted to overtake the service car on Route 7 to Peppard on the 23rd of that same month!

At the close of November TD1 Cars 172/5 (RX 1761/4) were put in store at Newbury, whilst similar buses 165/6/70/1 (RX 1754/5/9/60) went north to Stokenchurch for the Winter. Also withdrawn again then were 'Lion' LT1's 6, 8, 10, 12 and 42, as well as 'Tiger' TS4 Car 244 (RX 9541) and TS7 coach 262 (JB 5841), which had returned to use for a short time, and TS8 coaches 387/9/90 (BMO 986/8/9), some of the saloons went to Crowthorne and Fingest for store, the coaches to Stokenchurch and Desborough Road.

The only new vehicles delivered in the last 2 months of the year were ECW-bodied Bristol K6B's 492 (EJB 214), which arrived in November, followed by Cars 493-6/9 (EJB 215-8/21) in December, all of them being allocated to Reading, which also had allowed the withdrawal of the TD1 Cars mentioned above.

Bristol K6B Car 494 in original condition, but seen on hire to City of Oxford during the Royal Show of July 1950, when it operated under temporary fleet no.1, as displayed in the front nearside bulkhead window at Gloucester Green Bus Station.

Thames Valley agreed to undertake some work on the *Thomas Tilling Ltd.* contract vans for GEC that were kept at the Colonnade during December.

On the services front, a new Route 60 (Maidenhead – Bourne End – Little Marlow – Marlow) commenced on December 18th, which avoided the need to pass over the weight-restricted Marlow Bridge, also adding to the links for pupils of Borlaise School in Marlow.

1949

Due to slippage of chassis completions at the Bristol works, it was necessary to earmark 6 of the L6B's intended for coaching work to receive saloon bodies instead, later examples finally making up the quota of coaches in the following year. In reaction to this, it was decided to repaint the Harrington-bodied 'Tiger' TS8 coaches 381-90 (BMO 980-9) into red and cream for the forthcoming season.

January also saw delivery of a pair of Vauxhall 10hp cars (ERX 580 and 601), the former going for use by the Clerk of Works, and the latter for the Private Hire Manager, both based at Reading. Also on the Service Fleet front, TV sent one of the Reading Recovery Wagons out on 24th January to near Cookham Bridge to rescue a *Regent* Dennis tanker that had left the road en route for High Wycombe.

Further new Setright Ticket Machines were obtained, with Maidenhead changing over on Monday 31st January, followed by High Wycombe on Monday 28th February. On the subject of duty rosters, the system of alternating duties between the Marsh and Desborough Road garages was running into difficulties. Such rotas resulted in a rotation of 2-3 weeks between duties, but many crews were based in the Marsh area due to cheaper accommodation being available, whilst it should be appreciated that the Wycombe area had a lot of very early starts, making travelling to the other garage less than convenient. After discussions with the Union representatives, it was agreed to seek staff preferences for permanent allocations to one or other garage, whilst the Company reiterated its ultimate goal of having a single depot located centrally, with bus station combined if possible.

Further standard ECW-bodied Bristol K-types were added during 1949 and took over most major routes. Car 500 (EJB 222) is seen at Maidenhead bound for the busy Route 22 to Slough along the main Bath Road, complete with painted Hickies Piano advert.

Car 499 (EJB 221) went to Wycombe from new and is seen on Route 38 to Booker at the railway station terminus in High Wycombe before receiving adverts.

Further consideration was also given to a bus station at Reading, with a proposal to construct one in the forecourt of the Reading garage at Lower Thorn Street, or possibly in place of that garage if a site was found to relocate and combine the capacities of both the garage and the Colonnade Works. Although such schemes had worked for other companies, in reality the garage was already very constrained, so the idea was soon dropped.

Vincent-bodied coach 464 (DMO 668) in the red and cream livery applied for the 1949 season.

During January Bristol K6B Cars 497/8, 500-6 (EJB 219/20/2-8), all with ECW L27/28R bodies arrived, with 498 and 500 initially going to Reading, 501/2/4-6 to Wycombe and 503 to Maidenhead (soon to be joined there by 500).

Bristol K5G Car 396 (BRX 912) returned from work at Cawoods on 2nd February, but nothing was sent in its place. Work on Leyland 'Tiger' TS7 coach 264 (JB 5843) over at Lambourn was progressing very well, that concern already having developed a reputation for sound workmanship in the construction of horseboxes. However, the same had not necessarily been true of the Bristol L6B coaches of the 1947/8 deliveries, but the real culprit was the shortage of quality materials. A number of panels had cracked, so it was decided to repaint them all in a red and cream scheme for the new season. Whereas their original schemes had made use of such body features as streamlined wings and side flashes, the repaints imposed an overall red scheme, relieved only by a cream waistrail. This work also resulted in some of the TS8 coaches returning to use earlier than planned.

One of the Bedford OB chassis called into the Reading for inspection en route to the Beadle works in early March creating a favourable impression.

A new motorcycle to replace the Crowthorne Dormy Shed Inspector's 1938 BSA 600cc example (GJO 54) was ordered from Phillips & Bloomfield of South Street, Reading, being collected during March from there by Charlie Hester. He was another example of long service often found on the 'Valley, having served as a driver at Ascot from about 1925, later transferring as a driver at the Crowthorne Shed, and marrying in the village. He duly became the Shed Inspector, though he did return to work from Ascot before leaving around 1958.

Young Susan Hester tries out her father's new BSA in the Spring of 1949. Note the goggles perched on the brim of his official headgear and also his greatcoat.

What was *Thames Valley's* first acquisition of another operator for some time took place on 26th March, when the long-established *Gem Bus Service* of Harry Farmer of Hughenden Valley was purchased. Harry was also the publican of the Harrow Inn in that fairly remote area, soon recognising the need for a bus link to High Wycombe, running his succession of small buses continuously since 1923. One assumes that he

had decided to retire, as there is no record of the Company making any overtures to entice him to sell, though it was happy to take the opportunity of adding his route.

Typifying Farmer's buses was this Dodge (ADF 797) seen in High Wycombe under wartime conditions.

His route had varied slightly over the years, but as taken over it stood as High Wycombe – Lacey Green – Hampden – Princes Risborough. TV extended that onto Longwick and Aylesbury, starting a new route number series at 80. The existing Route 31 between High Wycombe and Lacey Green also had some runs extended to The Whip at Lacey Green as a result. TV paid £1200 for the goodwill, but no vehicles were involved in the takeover.

Although the Maidenhead Bus Station was already in use, there remained a number of works still to be carried out, so the Board gave approval for additional passenger shelters and lavatories for the public, though the grander scheme for the café remained on the drawing board due to lack of steel stocks. Over at Reading No.94 Chatham Road was added to the local properties around the garage site, most being acquired as they became available against the possibility of further garage extensions or to create additional exits.

Bristol K6B Car 498 (EJB 220) took up duties on the London Route B and is seen at Reading Stations.

32

Following the acquisition of Harry Farmer's route, 1938 TS8 'Tiger' Car 361 (ARX 983) is seen on Route 80 at the Aylesbury terminus in Kingsbury Square. Next to it is new Bristol K6B Car 508 (EJB 230) on the main-road High Wycombe – Aylesbury Route 30.

During the early months of 1949 the only petrol-engined cars were based at Maidenhead and were the trio of Leyland 'Cub' buses 337/8 (ABL 767/8) and 411 (FM 7455), and the pair of Bedford OWB's 437/8 (CRX 546/7). However it soon became apparent that it would be necessary to re-license 4 of the 1928 'Titans' and 5 of the 'Tiger' coaches, all of which still had petrol units. 'Tiger' TS7 262 (JB 5841) and TS8's 387-90 (BMO 986-9) came out of hibernation from 12th April, as did Bristol L6B coaches 460-3/5 (DMO 66-7/9) following repaints. The TD1's selected were Cars 165/6/70/1 (RX 1754/5/9/60), all of which were in store at Stokenchurch. However, tyres and other items had actually been removed, as no one had foreseen yet another reprieve for these aged buses! In fact, whilst local enthusiasts rubbed their eyes with disbelief, the decision was taken to put a further trio of TD1's and 6 of the old 'Lions' back on the road as soon as practical!

On a brighter note, Duple-bodied TS7 coach 264 (JB 5843) returned from Lambourn on 13th April, though it had to wait a further week for re-certification – its last one having expired in 1940! However, whereas 262 had retained a petrol engine, 264 was now fitted with a diesel unit, probably out of necessity?

Despite TV's dominance in the area for so many years, there were still others willing to operate local routes, and the Spring of 1949 brought several examples. *Bray Transport* represented the successor to the West Bros. *Blue Bus* of Bray, near Maidenhead,

who had managed to survive competition from both *Thames Valley* and the *Great Western Railway* buses. It reinstated the link between Maidenhead and Bracknell from 4th April 1949, which also linked the Jealotts Hill experimental farm operated by ICI, a link from Maidenhead that had once passed from the GWR to TV. The latter didn't retain the route for long, not even deeming it worthwhile to run through to Bracknell, so various facilities existed over the pre-war years, even including a period when ICI ran a pair of Guy saloons to take its workers to Maidenhead or Bracknell. Although the usefulness of the service was perhaps weakened by the lack of any Sunday journeys, the Easthampstead Rural District Council welcomed the regained link, especially as patients were often referred to the Taplow Hospital, now that its wartime role had evolved into the public domain.

The Council also noted that S. R. Gough of *Gough's Garage,* London Road, Bracknell had applied for a license for a service between Touchen End, just south of Holyport, and Crowthorne, the route effectively duplicating the *Bray Transport* one as far as Bracknell. As it was, only the Bracknell - Crowthorne section was granted by the Traffic Commissioner, but nonetheless *Gough's* had stolen the march on TV, as the latter had not provided a link between those points, despite having a Dormy Shed in Crowthorne since 1926!

Gough's Bus Service commenced on Monday 25th April, offering 3 return journeys a day on Mondays to Fridays and 4 on Saturdays. The route ran by way of Bracknell High Street (Police Station) – Bracknell (Railway Station) – Bagshot Road (Horse & Groom) – Church Hill House – Easthampstead Park Camp – Pinewood Crossroads – Crowthorne (High Street). Due to not having been granted the northern end of the proposed route, *Gough's* duly sought alternative facilities to serve Warfield Park Camp – Goose Corner – Warfield School – Warfield Park Camp (the other entrance) – Bracknell (Hinds Head) – Bracknell (Regal Cinema car park, Station Road), the latter point taking the place of the Police Station, then situated some 50 yards further west at the end of the High Street. The revised service commenced on Monday 28th November, with 4 journeys daily, though those on Saturday were at different times, and no Sunday runs were provided. A second bus were required to cover the expanded route, and *Gough's* were notable in using one of the few other Leylands to be found in the area, as they had a former *Central Scottish Motor Traction* 'Lion' LT5A with Leyland B32R body new in 1934 (VD 3503), which even featured a cut-away rear entrance favoured by Scottish operators!

For those readers less familiar with the area, it is worth noting that a number of displaced civilians had taken residence at the caravan park at Warfield Park, mainly due to the Blitz, whilst the old Easthampstead army camp of Nissen huts had been converted for use as temporary housing, both sites therefore benefiting from having a bus link, something that *Gough's* knew from local contacts, whilst there were also regular visitors to the Pinewood Sanatorium, some of whom would have arrived via Bracknell Station.

Leyland 'Tiger' TS7 coach 264 (JB 5843) after being thoroughly rebuilt by Lambourn Coachworks. Note the Thames Valley script across the radiator mesh.

Although efforts were made to sell off the remaining 'Titan' TD1 buses, several attempts fell through for one reason or another. Mr. & Mrs. Harmon, landlords of the Leathern Bottel pub at Goring, inspected several TD1's stored at Newbury Shed, though they only really wanted a body. It was agreed to sell one for £35 plus £5 delivery charge, so Car 168 (RX 1757) was taken to be de-bodied on site, just the way the bodies from the old Thornycroft buses of the 1920's were disposed of! However, the site chosen was steeper than expected, so on the following day, 6th

Still hard at work was 1929 'Titan' TD1's Car 183 (RX 4345) on the busy Slough – Maidenhead run, albeit with a Gardner 5LW engine and a new front profile courtesy of a rebuild at Eastern Coach Works.

May, one of the Ford Recovery Wagons was taken over to winch the body into position. A number of prominent locals took exception to the siting of this rather large 'shed', taking the matter up with the owners, Brakspear's Brewery of Henley-on-Thames, the outcome being that the publicans had to ask TV to take it back! On 19th May the process of delivery was reversed and the dejected bus was taken to a corner of the Colonnade yard, where it remained, minus radiator, never to see service again.

Other attempts involved approaching prominent local scrap dealers Harold Goodey of Twyford and Mr. J. Dunnaway of Reading, the latter having recently taken vehicles from *Reading Corporation*. However, neither was really interested. One bus was inspected at the old Yateley Dormy Shed, where it had been placed in store, but the private owner from Lower Wokingham Road, Crowthorne was refused planning permission to site it for use as a summerhouse! The Company also wanted to dispose of the remaining trio of Morris-Commercial lorries Nos.2, 3 and 4 (PP 5930 and DP 7413/4), with the same lack of success.

In the meantime, on 20th January, the first pair of the four Bedford OB's with Beadle bodies were received as Cars 512 and 520 (EJB 234 and 242), the latter being the 4th example ordered a little later, hence the gap in the numerical sequence. Although this chassis and body combination also featured in other former Tilling Group fleets, TV was unique in specifying the additional comforts such as semi-luxury seats. These were initially to supplement to coach fleet, partly in order to satisfy the weight restriction on the bridge link to Hayling Island, though they were intended for the Marlow Bridge route in due course. In a number of interviews, the subject of their unladen weight has been raised, as the ''3.0.0.0.'' seemed rather precise –

Bedford OB Car 511 (EJB 233), one of the quartet with Beadle 27-seater bodies, is seen at Maidenhead after transfer to the Marlow Bridge route.

all the interviewees agreeing that the inscription was not necessarily accurate, but rathermore convenient! It might be that a few items were removed to reach the desired figure, though one correspondent claimed they were never actually weighed when new. The other pair was received as Cars 510/1 (EJB 232/3) on 2nd and 3rd June, and all were allocated to operate from the Colonnade. Car 512 was also displayed to the public outside the entrance there, together with boards advertising forthcoming excursions.

For operational reasons, the routine maintenance of the London-based pair of Petrol Tankers was placed under the Maidenhead Garage from January 1949.

Local enthusiasts had noted with some interest that TD1 Car 169 (RX 1758) was being rebuilt at the Colonnade Works, but because the project failed to be completed in time for use during the busy Ascot Race Week, it was decided to use it as the basis for a new Route Servicing Vehicle to replace the old Morris No.3, which had been equipped with high platforms for tree-cutting work. Work was somewhat erratic, being progressed as time permitted, and Bob Crawley noted the following stages: in from store at Newbury on 17th August; being stripped down in Reading Works; transferred over to the Colonnade Works by 25th September; back at Reading Works by 8th October; out of shops re-numbered as No.29 (but still showed 169 over petrol filler cap until at least the end of October); back to Reading 17th-26th October for the fitting of double-doors across the rear end. It was then in a livery of all-over red with gold lettering, and at that time retained a petrol engine. Also throughout the

same period 'Lion' LT2 Car 54 (RX 6248) spent some time in Reading Works receiving straight side panels in place of the flared ones resulting in its wartime rebuild, which was rather unexpected given its age.

The third week of June was another very busy time for the *Thames Valley* fleet, with the popular Royal Counties Show being held at Sonning from 22nd-25th, whilst the High Wycombe Royal Show was on Saturday 25th. The latter event required duplicates run on Route 28 (Reading – Twyford – Henley – Marlow –High Wycombe) throughout the day, but the Sonning event called for even more organisation. Indeed, joint working was *Reading Corporation* was arranged, the only other time the two concerns had joined forces being for the transport of wartime evacuees!

Route Servicing Vehicle No.29 is seen assisting with the clearance of the scrag-end of the Southern yard being the two Reading stations.

Extra buses were run between Reading and Sonning, many of the passengers reaching the former by train, but for those coming from the London direction, TV also provided a shuttle service between Twyford and the showground. Numerous (and varied) vehicles were used , and on one day Bob Crawley noted 'Lion' LT1 Car 2 (RX 5571), 'Titan' TD1 Car 175 (RX 1764), 'Tiger' TS7 coach 264 (JB 5843), Bristol L6B Vincent-bodied coach 461 (DMO 665), Bedford OB Car 512 (EJB 234) and a number of AEC 'Regent' double-deckers from the Corporation fleet. On that day the Twyford shuttle was in the hands of 1928 TD1 Car 166 (RX 1755). Michael Plunkett also recorded travelling back to Reading on RCT's 1948 'Regent' No.80 (CRD 869), which bore a sticker proclaiming it as on hire to TV – however the official records state clearly that it was a joint operation, so the hire stickers may have been to conform to licensing requirements? Additionally, relief journeys were worked on Route 28 between High Wycombe and Sonning, with all-day turns by Harrington-bodied Leyland 'Tiger' TS8 Cars 381-3 (BMO 980-2). During the 4 days of the show 19,846 passengers were conveyed by these services!

Bus washing was part of the daily routine of garage maintenance to the fleet, and 1938 ECW-bodied TS8 Car 372 (BBL 558) in seen receiving attention in the Reading garage.

An interesting contact occurred during June or July, when a Mr. Groombridge approached TV regarding the purchase of one of the 1928 TD1's for use as staff transport. His Company was Associated Deliveries, so named because of its connection with the supply of bodies suitable for the biscuit trade, where products were relatively bulky in comparison to their weight, was based at Theale aerodrome. During the war years work was directed to aircraft production, but the local directory of the period also lists them as 'coach body builders', though the author has never come across any examples of complete bodies built on PSV's by them. Despite TV's desperation to sell the old TD1's, it responded instead by offering to improve timings on the 10 Route to suit the workforce! Indeed, this actually took place, only for Associated Deliveries to purchase Leyland 'Titan' TD1 No.43 (RD 2721) from the Corporation rather than one of the TV examples!

Brush-bodied TS8 Car 347 (AJB 819) at Maidenhead.

However, as we shall see in due course, the contact with Associated Deliveries would prove more useful in the future.

There was a glimmer of hope regarding the disposal of the old TD1's, as during July *Westcliff-on-Sea Motor Services* expressed an interest in taking 6 double-deck buses for contract work, and more of that a little later.

As various of the buses delivered during the war years reached re-certification, a number of problems were highlighted, mainly as a result of the poor quality of materials utilised in their construction. Some gangway widths also did not conform to the regulations, whilst the more widespread problems were weak floors and platform areas, sagging roofs and lots of leaks to cabs, windows and roofs! Each car was assessed and given remedial attention during 1949, though Bristol K6A Cars 426/7 (CRX 196/7) had already been dealt with, and the slightly later examples of that type, Cars 428-34 (CRX 198, CRX 540-5) were generally in better state from the outset, which considering their daily use on the long Route 2 (Reading – Ascot – Windsor) was a compliment to the workforce at Strachans and the high standards generally found at Ascot garage.

During July 1949 former Premier Line 'Tiger' TS3 Car 258 (GN 5145) was given a final role as a static Staff Rest Room at the Southern Railway yard whilst the new Canteen was under construction. Similar Car 259 (GN 5139) returned to relief work for the Summer months, operating from Reading.

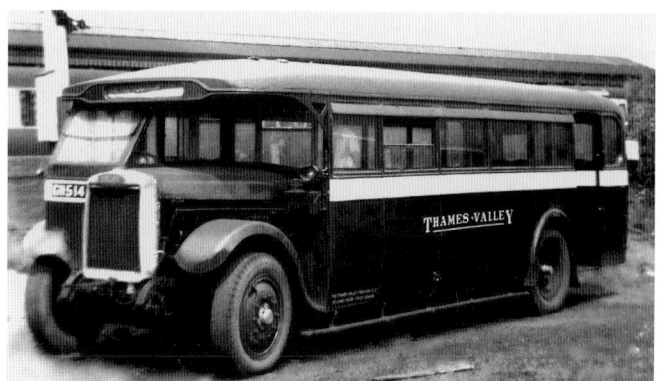

As more Bristol K6B's arrived, so the variety of duties they were found on increased. Car 502 (EJB 224) is seen on one of the extended journeys on Route 21 (Maidenhead – Boyn Hill – Cox Green - White Waltham – Waltham St. Lawrence – Shurlock Row – Binfield – Wokingham) as it passes The Ship pub and turns into Peach Street en route for Wokingham Town Hall.

During July a new Bedford 10/12cwt van arrived in the shape of No.27 (FJB 99), having been supplied by Thomas Tilling Ltd. It was allocated to Reading and allowed the transfer of Austin 7hp van No.6 (RX 3755) to Ascot, where it replaced the BSA 7.7hp motorcycle with massive sidecar (DP 9140) that had served that garage since November 1927!

The Reading-based Inspectors got a new Ford 'Anglia' 8hp car on 15th August (EDP 247), making Austin 10hp car FXD 202 redundant. Another car was also approved to replace the Engineer's 1940 Austin 10hp (PV 6530), which was advertised for sale. It is worth noting that TV had very little luck selling off its surplus Service Vehicles during the Summer of 1949, so it offered them for sale to staff instead. Whilst the Austin car PV 6530 attracted 150 bids, only 1 was made in respect of the 3 1926 Morris lorries (Nos. 2, 3 and 4) and 4 for the 1927 BSA motorcycle combination (DP 9140). The draw for the car was held with Conductress Goddard making the selection, and Conductor Partridge became the proud owner of what must have been one of the best maintained cars in the area! Both the trio of lorries and the motorcycle went to the bids by Maidenhead Cleaner Brandon, but as he left the Company's employ in late September (before the deal was completed), his bid was voided and only the car had actually been disposed of!

On the plus side, further Bristol K6B's with ECW L27/28R bodies were received, with Cars 507-9/13 (EJB 229-31/5) arriving in July, followed by Cars 514-9 (EJB 236-41) during August. These were widely distributed, many staying with those depots for life, with Cars 507-9/13 going to High Wycombe, Cars 514-6 to Maidenhead and Cars 517-9 to Reading. The arrival of more double-deckers led to quite a lot of depot re-allocations during this period, particularly affecting the line-up at the Wycombe garages, as well as reducing the need for relief vehicles in general.

As noted several times previously, the subject of the bus stands on Station Hill, Reading had been discussed, even prompting proposals for a new bus station. However, the finance for the latter was not forthcoming, so a compromise was reached, allowing the stands on the hill to be used by both TV and the *Reading Corporation* services. The revised arrangements came into effect on Sunday 7th August, with Routes 9 (Reading – Mortimer – Tadley), 9a (Reading – Grazeley – Tadley), 10 (Reading – Newbury) and 11 (Reading – Bucklebury) all still stopping on the northern side of the road, though Routes 5 (Reading – Oxford), 5a (Reading – Wantage), 5b (Reading – Yattendon), 7 (Reading – Nettlebed), 8 (Reading – Henley) and 28 (Reading – High Wycombe) were moved to the south side of the hill near the far end of the Vincent premises, whilst a number of changes were made to the roads traversed for buses to reach those positions within the locality.

The popularity of the London Routes A and B in the late Summer of 1949 resulted in the use of various reliefs, with the Harrington-bodied 'Tiger' TS8 coaches being seen more than usual, whilst saloons also helped out on occasions.

Bristol L6A saloon 458 (DBL 166) is seen helping out on the London B Route at Victoria in the Summer of 1949. Also note the appropriate advert on its side for the London services.

It was decided to make greater use of the Colonnade premises in order to relieve pressure on the Reading garage, so all car park permit holders were given notice to quit by 24th September. Work was also put in hand to remove the 'dummy' petrol pumps by the way in to the yard, and also to provide a barrier to the site. From 1st October the Reading-based private hire coaches were re-allocated there, along with some scheduled relief buses. Bob Elder, longtime Fitter at Reading Works, as offered the position of Charge Hand at the Colonnade, but had to decline for personal reasons, so Fitter B.J. Rackley was promoted. In a similar vain, the coaches at Wycombe Marsh were re-allocated to Desborough Road from Friday 23rd September. At the same time it was discussed whether the Stokenchurch Dormy Shed could be disposed of, though in reality that may have just seen it re-acquired by *City of Oxford*, the original owners, who had continued to keep more vehicles in active service than *Thames Valley*!

It was also during the Summer of 1949 that Michael Plunkett wrote his ground-breaking letters appealing that some of the historic buses in the Reading area should be preserved for posterity. Whilst that concept would not be regarded as unusual today, there were very few examples outside of London of buses retained for historic reasons. To *Reading Corporation* Michael wrote regarding the surviving Corporation-bodied Guy B-type buses new in 1926, in particular No.20 (DP 7258), whilst Basil Sutton was urged to save Car 164 (RX 1753) of the 1928 Leyland 'Titan' TD1's. The type had been quite revolutionary when announced, and Sutton had acknowledged the fact that he came away from the 1927 Commercial Motor Show ready to place the first order for *Thames Valley*. He had also often noted in the trade press how reliable the type had been in constant service on high mileage routes. However, the proposals came to nothing and no vehicles were preserved as suggested. However,

the seeds were undoubtably sown for Michael's own entry in the very early ranks of bus preservationists. As a footnote, it is well worth reading that other well-known preservationist Michael Sutcliffe's book 'The Leyland Man' in respect of the fledgling movement.

When one considers the very rural nature of much of the *'Valley's* operating area, accidents of significance were not frequent, much of this being due to the pride and care taken by drivers of buses in those days. The Company promoted this through the Royal Society for the Prevention of Accidents (RoSPA) Safe Driving Awards, with very good results.

Conductress Jenny Swanborough at Wycombe Marsh.

However, August saw two 'Tiger' buses involved in serious accidents. TS7 Car 265 (JB 5844) was in a bad smash on an unspecified date at Ruscombe Turn, near Shurlock Row, when several passengers were injured. The TV driver was not at fault, but the driver of the offending lorry was prosecuted by the police. But a much worse accident occurred on the late afternoon of 31st August, when TS4-type Car 248 (RX 9702) was working Route 21 into Maidenhead past the Beehive in White Waltham when, without warning a Corporal on a bicycle emerged from the entrance of the RAF Camp on the other side of the road. Driver Cummings tried to avoid the cyclist, but he was struck and killed, and the bus went up the opposite embankment and turned onto its nearside. Incredibly, there were no serious injuries to the passengers, and the bus no longer having a petrol engine did not catch fire. The Company Recovery Wagons were dispatched and the bus was righted by 8pm, but it was left until the following day for towing away, whilst the driver was fully exonerated of any blame. Most of the nearside windows were broken, but the bus was back in use at Maidenhead a fortnight later without any signs of the mishap it had experienced on that fateful afternoon.

Offering a rare opportunity to study the underside of a Leyland 'Tiger' TS4, Car 248 (RX 9702) is seen where it came to rest at White Waltham, with Ford V8 Recovery Wagon No.17 (DJB 943) in attendance.

Negotiations with the *Westcliff-on-Sea* Company led to 6 of the 1928 'Titan' TD1's being prepared for use, but only one was actually requested, so on 7th September their driver collected Car 171 (RX 1760). It was for use as construction workman's transport on the oil refinery at Shell Haven in Coryton, Essex. It will also be recalled that the *Westcliff* concern had assisted *Thames Valley* with the loan of double-decker Bristol buses during the war years, though TV was only being paid £1 per day in this case!

Car 171 was of course the Company's own in-house rebuilding project and only one of that batch modernised. With a sloping frontal profile and built-in stairs, it was similar to the ECW rebuilds of the wartime years, though it retained its petrol engine to the end. The other quintet of TD1's earmarked for the above project, Cars 164/7/8/73/4 (RX 1753/6/7/62/3) were advertised for sale. Car 174 was one of a pair then stored in the old Yateley Dormy Shed, whilst 164/8 were known to be at Newbury.

Delicensed for the Winter from 19th September were a number of vehicles, with Reading hosting 'Lion' LT1 Cars 2, 4, 6 and 8 (RX 5571-4), 'Tiger' TS7 Cars 267 and 268 (JB 5846/7), 'Tiger' TS8 coaches 387-9 (BMO 986-8) and Bedford OB's 511/2 (EJB 233/4). At Maidenhead there were Guy 'Arab' double-decker 420 (CJB 139), 'Tiger' TS7 saloon 36 (ABL 754), 'Lion' LT1 Car 42 (RX 5580), 'Lion' LT2 Car 14 (RX 6249) and 'Tiger' TS8 coach 385 (BMO 984). The Wycombe contingent consisted of 'Tiger' TS7 coach 262 (JB 5841), 'Tiger' TS8 coach 383 (BMO 982) and utility-bodied Bristol K5G 417 (CJB 136). The older saloons were then earmarked for disposal.

However, in apparent contrast to the above, some ageing saloons suddenly re-appeared on full-day turns in late September, with LT1 Car 4 (RX 5572) working the Henley 'shorts' on Route 8, LT2 Car 54 (RX 6248) on the 1b to Shurlock Row, LT1 Car 2 (RX 5571) also to be found on the Henley Route 8, with similar Car 6 (RX 5573) covering the 5b to Yattendon. 'Tiger' TS4 Car 256 (RX 7910) also appeared on the 1b, whilst similar bus 244 (RX 9541) provided full-time turns on Route 3 (Reading – Crowthorne – Camberley).

During September the call came through Purley Parsh Council that residents wanted an improved link into Reading, with the suggestion that a railway halt should be built. However, when discussed by the Standing Joint Committee, it was suggested by TV that double-deckers might be introduced, though in the end the high number of large trees that would have required lopping made that unpractical. Over to the east, there had been another request for a service improvement, and in that case the Company could oblige. The last journey on Route 28 from High Wycombe to Marlow was extended onto the RAF base at Danesfield, near Medmenham with the Winter timetable introduced on Saturday 24th September. A report made approximately 3 months later stated that some 825 personnel had made use of the late-night facility, making it a worthwhile amendment.

With the Winter timetable came the opportunity to dispose of some of the older stock, most of which had enjoyed several Summers more than anticipated. The two former *Premier Line* Leyland 'Tiger' TS3 buses, wee ousted, with Car 259 (GN 5139) being sold on 6th October, followed by 258 (GN 5145) the following day, both finding private owners locally. The 5 'Titan' TD1s not taken by *Westcliff*, together with the 3 Morris lorries still not sold, were all taken by a scrap dealer at Darby Green after seeing Car 174 at Yateley.

TD1 Cars 165/6/70/2/5 (RX 1754/5/9/61/4) had remained in use for the Summer of '49, but were now taken to the Colonnade for 'the final gathering' before disposal. They were caught on film one damp morning.

Car 166 was collected by a new owner from Colnbrook, near Slough on 4th October, with 165 going nearby to Chesham on 25th. However, on the 28th Driver Harding took Car 175 on the long trek to its new owner in Airedale, near Castleford in Yorkshire! As had always been a TV tradition, all the sold cars were given a 'touch-up' before disposal.

So, apart from the rebuilt Car 171 away at the Essex seaside, the only 1928 TD1's left were Cars 170/2 (RX 1759/61), both of which went to the well-known showman Traylen at Feltham, Middlesex on 3rd November. An era had truly ended, the batch having served the Company well for 21 years. Some of them did re-appear on their old patch from time to time in the guise of showman's buses, with the roof dropped, but otherwise in the old livery at first. Although I was not alive then, conversations with Michael Plunkett and Bob Crawley, as well as many old employees, including Basil Sutton, indicate that the Colonnade seemed strangely eerie once the TD1's had departed, though former Car 169 survived in its new guise as Route Servicing Vehicle, whilst Car 171 was 'out but not gone'. Hopefully Basil took some consolation in the arrival of his new Morris 'Oxford' car FMO 152 during November.

Bristol L6B Car 521 (FBL 23) at High Wycombe Station on Route 35 up Plomer Hill to Downley.

November also saw the delivery of Bristol L6B buses with Eastern Coach Works B35R bodies which were Cars 522/3 (FBL 24/5), both of which were sent to High Wycombe. On the double-deck front, Bristol K6B/ECW L27/28R Car 524 (FBL 26) also arrived and was allocated to Reading.

With the Winter timetable and the influx of further new buses, a re-distribution of older vehicles took place, and Gardner-engined 'Titan' TD1 Cars 182-6 (RX 4344-8) were finally dislodged from many years at Maidenhead to cover relief duties at Reading, plus High Wycombe 'Tiger' TS7 Cars 266/7/9 (JB 5845/6/8) and 297/8 (JB 7497/8) all travelled south to join the Reading allocation.

The new Bristol saloons also started to appear on the long Route 28 (Reading – Henley – High Wycombe), and Car 522 (FBL 24) is seen on the stand on the south side of Station Hill – note the Corporation trolleybus on the opposite stands.

On the debit side, two more saloons had seen accident damage during October, with the 'Tadley Tiger' TS7 Car 271 (JB 5850) in a fatal collision with a motorcyclist on 24th between Grazeley and Wokefield, whilst a Polish motorcyclist collided with TS8 Car 372 (BBL 558) on the Barkham Road, Wokingham on the 28th.

Also adding pressure to the fleet was the findings of the Certifying Officer on 11th November, which resulted in work being required on the roofs and rear platforms of Wycombe-based Bristol K5G Car 413 (CJB 132) and Guy 'Arab' Cars 423/4 (CMO 653/4), as well as similar Maidenhead-based Guy 'Arab' Car 425 (CMO 655).

On 3rd November outside assistance was once more forthcoming with the dispatch of 'Tiger' TS8 Car 345 (AJB 817) to the Brislington Body Works at Bristol refurbishment, including new seat frames and re-seating from 32 to 35 passengers, TS8 Car 371 (BBL 557) following it to BBW on 19th November.

Another busy trunk route was the 20 (High Wycombe – Cookham – Windsor) and Bristol K6B Car 515 (EJB 237) is seen near Cookham on one of the hourly runs extended to Windsor Hospital.

There was another spate of accidents during November, with London A Route Bristol L6B 488 (EJB 210) involved on the 4th, followed by 'Tiger' TS7 Car 48 (ABL 761) on the 13th, though on the latter occasion a fitter had driven it into the entrance of Desborough Road, then lastly Bristol K5G Car 393 (BRX 909) was hit by a lorry at Reading Stations at an unrecorded date.

The earlier contact with Associated Deliveries led to Mr. Groombridge meeting with Basil Sutton at Newbury Shed in late December, where the Harrington TS8 coaches in store were inspected. It was agreed to give the batch a general refurbishment, including dealing with problems with the sliding roofs, modification of the luggage racks and revamping the rear seats to take 5 passengers to raise the capacity from 32 to 33. This work would be undertaken at the coachbuilder's works on the Huntley & Palmers biscuit factory site off Kings Road, Reading, with the programme also to include Duple-bodied TS7 coach 262, as follows:-

Car No.	Reg. No.	Date Sent	Date Back
262	JB 5841	06.02.50	29.03.50
381	BMO 980	30.01.50	10.03.50
382	BMO 981	06.02.50	Not known
383	BMO 982	21.12.49	02.02.50
384	BMO 983	28.02.50	05.04.50
385	BMO 984	22.12.49	24.02.50
386	BMO 985	27.02.50	03.04.50
387	BMO 986	28.12.49	21.02.50
388	BMO 987	21.12.49	02.02.50
389	BMO 988	13.01.50	03.03.50
390	BMO 989	13.03.50	14.04.50

Deliveries of new buses for December were just two vehicles, as the Bristol Works and Eastern Coach Works were still working hard to meet demand from BTC fleets all over the Country. Bristol K6B with ECW L27/28R body Car 525 (FBL) was joined by L6B Car 534 (FMO 9) with ECW B35R bodywork. Both buses were allocated to Reading, with the saloon going straight onto the 32.7 mile Route 5 (Reading – Wallingford – Oxford), which was a joint operation with *City of Oxford.*

The standard of the fleet had now much improved, so as a result it was decided that the active strength would be reduced to 255 from the New Year, which led in late December to the placing in store of Leyland 'Titan' TD1-types 220 (RX 6111), 224 (RX 6244) and 233 (RX 8166), all with Leyland bodies rebuilt to one extent of another. The first two examples were delivered in 1930, though the latter was new in 1931.

Despite many new deliveries, the Leyland saloons of the mid-'30's were still kept hard at work. Car 308 (JB 8347) was a Brush-bodied example of 1936 on a 'Tiger' TS7 chassis, seen here on Route 1b to Hurst, and still fitted with a sliding 'sunshine' roof'.

On the other hand, the newest double-decker was Car 525 (FBL 27), very much the standard issue for BTC fleets at that time, with Bristol chassis and ECW body. It is seen laid over at the Southern Railway yard.

41

An aerial view of the Reading Garage and Offices in 1949, the front yard featuring half-a-dozen Leyland saloons, some 'Titans' and a new Bristol double-deck bus. This photo can be compared with the plan of the garage development in the 1931 – 1945 volume p100.

It should be noted that Basil Sutton would soon notch up 30 years service with the Company, during which time the operations had expanded considerably. He had a trusted and loyal team in his Works Staff and the Garage Foremen, all largely hand-picked of course, but with only 6 years to his retirement, the management had to consider the future. The outcome of this was the appointment of an Assistant Engineer, which led to Ian Campbell transferring from that same position at *Eastern Counties* from 16th January 1950. Campbell had previously served with *Northern General*, each of those fleets offering him the opportunities to extend his skills. It is not recorded exactly what Basil thought of having such an assistant for the first time in his long career at the 'Valley', though they were to compliment each other well as time went by. Ultimately though, they were skilled engineers, both passionate about achieving the best results and the development of chassis and oils. The *Eastern Counties* fleet also featured lots of old Leyland types rebuilt or re-bodied, together with new Bristols of both pre-war and post-war deliveries.

In terms of the make up of the *Thames Valley* fleet at the close of 1949, the following types were in stock:-

Double-deckers	Total 140
Leyland 'Titan' TD1	34
Leyland 'Titan' TD2	2
Leyland 'Titan' TD4	8
Leyland 'Titan' TD5	5
Guy 'Arab' I 5LW	8
Bristol K5G	25
Bristol K6A	25
Bristol K6B	33
Single-deckers	**Total 124**
Leyland 'Lion' LT1	10
Leyland 'Lion' LT2	5
Leyland 'Tiger' TS3	1
Leyland 'Tiger' TS4	11
Leyland 'Tiger' TS7	37
Leyland 'Tiger' TS8	27
Leyland 'Cub' KPZ2	2
Leyland 'Cub' KP3	1
Bedford OWB	2
Bedford OB	4
Bristol L6A	20
Bristol L6B	4
Coaches	**Total 23**
Leyland 'Tiger' TS7	2
Leyland 'Tiger' TS8	10
Bristol L6B	11

1949 Bristol K6B Car 505 (EJB 227) at Aylesbury.

1950

The passage of *Thames Valley* into State ownership had been a smooth one because the *Tilling Group* had sold out voluntarily. However, not all operators, either individuals or other groups, had adopted the same attitude. One such significant group was *Red & White United Transport Ltd.*, a very successful and efficient group based in Chepstow, Monmouthshire. This group had even continued its expansion during the war years and, with local relevance, had acquired *South Midland* at Oxford, *Newbury & District* based in Newbury, and *Venture* of Basingstoke.

These acquisitions were part of a larger plan to cut a swathe through from South Wales to the South Coast of England, whilst also strengthening express coach links to London and other parts of the country. Indeed, had the proposal to purchase *Hants & Sussex* gone through, that aim would have been finally achieved. In each case *R&W* had improved services, renewed or refurbished ageing fleets and introduced its sound brand of management and high maintenance standards. It also nurtured the natural talent within the workforce, a very key factor in its overall success, and the widespread communications referred to the 'R&W family', and always recognised long service and those deserving promotion through merit.

The group also had interests in Guernsey and abroad, so a decision had to be made regarding the possibility of a compulsion to sell to the State, the result of which was to sell out voluntarily before that situation arose. As a result of the sale, which was effective from 1st January 1950, the issue arose of how the diverse companies would be managed. In respect of the local holdings, it was decided that *Thames Valley* would manage both *Newbury & District* and *South Midland*, those two concerns having already been brought closer together by *R&W*, whilst *Venture* was assigned to Salisbury-based *Wilts & Dorset*.

Rebuilt 'Titan' TD1 Car 200 (RX 5562) on Reliefs, and TS8 Car 371 (BBL 557) on the Moulsford Special.

During the Winter of 1949/50 Bristol K5G Cars 393, 397, 400, 401, 402, 404, 405, 409 had their Eastern Coach Works bodies thoroughly refurbished in the TV workshops. Car 409 (BRX 925) is seen stripped down, and then again on completion of the work.

The acquisition of the Newbury and Oxford-based operations represented a considerable expansion both geographically and in fleet strength. It also increased the Company's involvement in express coach routes, though of course most of those ran through its area. It was around this time that Charlie Chun joined TV from *London Transport* as Assistant Traffic Manager based at Reading. He brought with him a degree of planning hitherto unseen at the 'rural' '*Valley*, and introduced the highly-detailed Scheduled Working Arrangements, which in turn helped to reduce the size of the fleet through more efficient allocations.

A summary of the development of *South Midland* and *Newbury & District* will be found in Appendix 4 and 5, though each has already been the subject of separate volumes. Although the *N&D* volume has long been out of print, that for *South Midland* written by David Flitton remains available (see p4 for details).

Fortunately for *Thames Valley, Red & White* had already invested in an expansion of the Newbury garage, addressed the fleet maintenance issues at both Oxford and Newbury, and developed good working relationships between both concerns and also *Venture*. In each case there were no plans for removing the identity of these concerns, particular as *South Midland* had beat of opposition in Oxford for nearly 30 years!

TV buses had of course reached Newbury for many years on Route 10 from Reading. Although this was generally covered by the latest Bristol K-types, there was a time around 1950 when some of the 'Titans' could be found on that run. Brush-bodied TD4 Car 336 (ABL 766) new in 1937 is seen by the TV shelter at Newbury Wharf.

South Midland had three main facets to its operations. It had developed express coach services almost from its inception in 1922, with private hire being work also very prominent despite strong competition from *City of Oxford Motor Services Ltd.* However, during the war years the fleet had survived mainly on contract work, of which there was no shortage with all the 'shadow factories', Government stores, air fields and other military camps in the area. A number of these sites also formed the basis of large post-war building projects which would require contracts for a number of years more. Good relations other express coach operators also keep the Oxford-based fleet in demand for seasonal relief work, particularly on the *Associated Motorways* network, meaning that drivers and coaches were often away for 2 or 3 days at a time on 'triangular' workings – e.g. relief coach between Cheltenham and London, then relief to Bournemouth for overnight stay, next day relief on Bournemouth to Bristol or Cheltenham, then finally home to base!

SM's own Worcester – Oxford – Henley – London route could be very busy at times, requiring up to 6 coaches on each departure, whilst the seasonal Oxford – Newbury – Southsea route also experienced heavy loadings at times, often using relief coaches starting at Newbury and provided by *N&D*. Worcester and the Southsea route were also linked at peak times.

The Newbury Company was always known locally as 'Newbury District', though some of the old TV crews referred to it disparagingly as 'Newbury & Risk It' due to its rather motley fleet! However, having studied this operator for many years, it must certainly be acknowledged that it was a very important factor in the lifeblood of the area. West Berkshire has very few

towns of any real size, with Newbury at its heart, and Hungerford and Wantage being the only other places of any significance (though the latter is now in Oxfordshire of course). This, however, brought the issue of transport more to the fore for the residents of the numerous scattered villages and hamlets, creating opportunities to visit markets, socialise or to reach links for journeys farther afield. The Country Carriers had established much of this pattern before motorised transport had come along, and the original collection of individual operators had formed the nucleus of the development of *Newbury & District.* On taking over, *Red & White* had recognised the significance of this process, so there had been no rash changes to the local pattern of services. Indeed, due to subtle management and investment in premises and vehicles, the coming under *R&W* was widely accepted as a good thing by the employees and public alike.

Another 1937 'Titan' with Brush body, Car 340 AJB 812) was a TD5-type, seen here laid over at Reading between journeys on Route 4a to Arborfield. Buses such as this enjoyed a longer lifespan due to the adding of the Newbury area operations.

There are numerous examples that could be quoted of the way in which the 'personal touch' of *N&D* had been fundamental in its success. One such example was Ted White, who came into the fold in March 1934, after his father decided to merge his *W. J White & Son* bus and coach operations with *N&D*. As part of the deal Ted was given employment, as was the usual practice with concerns amalgamating with it, and he rose to become Private Hire Manager. This was largely based on his sound local knowledge and links to groups likely to want coaches for outings and other events. He continued in this role through the *R&W* era, coping with the demands of contract operations, then on through the TV era, still based at The Wharf Enquiry Office. He remained there until his retirement many years later – ask any old Newburian, and they'll remember him, the result of his personal and efficient service always delivered with a cheerful smile!

44

Coaching work had always had a high priority at Newbury, usually fitting in nicely with the peaks days of the local markets. Newbury was very busy on Thursdays, so coaches were widely used as reliefs, but as with *South Midland*, the war years had seen the coaches mainly on contract work. As peace returned *Red & White* had wisely started to re-equip the coach fleet at Newbury, and fuller details are given in due course.

TV's Leyland saloons also saw an increase in use around this time, and 1937 'Tiger' TS8 Car 346 (AJB 818) is seen at Slough on Route 22 – little suspecting that it would soon be sent west to join the N&D fleet!

There were still many contracts in operation to Shaw Factory, the Military Depots at Bramley, Milton and Thatcham, as well as various RAF and Army Camps. The development of the Atomic Energy Research Establishment at Harwell, the Atomic Weapon Research Establishment at Aldermaston and the Royal Ordnance Factory at Burghfield all required large numbers of builders to be transported, followed by the staff employed there in due course.

By sheer luck, the highest numbered vehicle in the Newbury fleet was 172, whereas TV's own fleet now started with 179. Similarly, the Oxford-based fleet were numbered between 39 and 70, whereas the lowest number at Newbury was now 94, so there was no needed for any renumbering!

The Newbury area routes were in a series 1 to 29, so these had 100 added to produce a new series, TV's highest route number then being 80. The routes taken over were as follows:

Route 101:	Newbury – East Ilsley – Chilton
Route 101A:	Newbury – Chieveley – Peasemore
Route 102:	West Ilsley – East Ilsley – Reading
Route 103:	Newbury – Greenham – Ecchinswell
Route 104:	Newbury – Headley – Kingsclere
Route 104A:	Newbury – Headley - Ashford Hill
Route 105:	Newbury – Shefford – Wantage
Route 106:	Newbury – Shefford - Lambourn – Upper Lambourn
Route 106A:	Lambourn – Shefford – Hungerford

Route 107:	Newbury – Lambourn Woodlands – Swindon
Route 108:	Newbury – Wickham – Hungerford Newtown or Newbury – Wickham – Lambourn Woodlands – Baydon
Route 109:	Newbury – Thatcham – Cold Ash
Route 110:	Newbury – Thatcham – Thatcham Station
Route 111:	Newbury – Thatcham – Bucklebury
Route 112:	Newbury – Abingdon – Oxford
Route 113:	Newbury – Inkpen – Hungerford
Route 114:	Newbury – Ball Hill – East Woodhay
Route 114A:	Newbury - Ball Hill – West Woodhay
Route 115:	Newbury – Woolton Hill – Highclere
Route 116:	Newbury – Bath Road – Hungerford
Route 119:	Newbury – Hermitage – Yattendon
Route 119A:	Newbury – Hermitage – Aldworth – Ashampstead
Route 120:	Newbury – Hermitage – Frilsham
Route 121:	Shaw – Newbury (The Broadway) – Highclere Station – Whitway
Route 127:	Newbury (The Broadway) – Wash Common
Route 128:	Bartlemy Close – Maple Crescent
Route 129:	The Broadway – Hambridge Road

The Newbury & District fleet had become far more standardised under Red & White direction, but still offered variety. Seen above is utility-bodied Bedford OWB No.96 (CMO 657), whilst AEC 'Regal' No.155 (AGP 841) was a wartime rebuild of a former coach from the London-based Blue Belle express fleet.

Leyland 'Tigers' also featured in the Newbury fleet, though Harrington-bodied TS7 No.167 (BWL 349) had originated with South Midland and had been part of exchanges between the two fleets. The coach also displays the high standard of maintenance at Newbury, where both fleets received major attention.

No.122 (FS 8560) was another rebuilt AEC 'Regal', originally of the 0642 variety but now equipped with a Gardner 5LW oil engine and new to Scottish Motor Traction in 1934. R&W had re-bodied a number of these with Eastern Counties bodies that started life on North Western Tilling-Stevens, so they were quite a mixture! The one is seen shortly after the takeover in 1950 outside the Mill Lane garage.

Of particular note in the list of routes is that between Newbury and Oxford, which came into being through the suggestion by R&W that the Newbury Company should join its service to Rowstock with that to the same place operated by *City of Oxford*. This produced a route of almost 30 miles 'up-and-over' the Berkshire Downs and commenced in July 1945.

As a consequence of the passing of *Venture* to *Wilts & Dorset,* the former's outstation at Whitchurch was closed in favour of keeping a bus at the N&D garage. By January 1951 that was the duty of a Bristol K-type,

which worked Route 135 with a dedicated W&D crew. However, few journeys covered the full route, with many turning at Whitway. At certain times of day it was even possible to change at Whitchurch onto the *King Alfred* Route 11 to reach Winchester.

In respect of premises, N&D benefited from a much enlarged garage with excellent facilities, situated only 100 yards from the TV Dormy Shed. Messrs. Sutton and Campbell soon paid a visit and met with Manager Grimmett and Engineer Taylor, leading to the decision to use the Dormy Shed as a paintshop, with the pair of TV buses shedded there for Route 10 once again returning to the N&D garage. It should also be appreciated that the N&D garage had assumed responsibility for major dockings on the SM fleet, and had even handled some extensive body overhauls on behalf of *Venture*.

Due to the wide geographic area covered by the N&D fleet, together with its origins through the absorption of other operators, a network of outstations had been developed, latterly extended even further to meet the needs of contract routes. At the time of transfer there were vehicles operating out of Chilton Foliat, East Ilsley, Hungerford, Kingsclere, Lambourn and West Ilsley.

Many of the outstations had long-serving crews, and the Lambourn location was renowned for its reliable and friendly staff. Driver Ernie Church and his wife Conductress Kathleen worked together for years, and Bill Allington was also a long-serving Driver. Later, when Arthur Waldron had responsibility for Newbury area operations, he recalled their dedication, though on one occasion he did have to administer a warning, after they were found to have used a bus one Sunday to take a party of friends to a social event!

South Midland also had outstations in Worcester (Newport Road Coach Station) and in London at Samuelson's Garage over the road from Victoria Coach Station. Full details will be found in Appendix 7, Scheduled Vehicle Allocations to Garages etc.

Thames Valley had for some years organised its traffic management into areas, so that inherited from N&D became Area No.3, continuing to run largely under the control of the inherited management and inspectors. Although the Oxford-based operations were retained as a separate identity, reporting was direct to Head Office at Reading. Once matters settled down, certain staff in the Traffic Office dealt almost exclusively with SM matters, particularly the development of tours, for which it was to become quite notable. Indeed, such was the magnitude of the extra work involved in the enlarged concern, that a number of staff received bonuses during the transitional period. TV had of course been quite prominent on coach work, though it was never the force of pre-war days.

By the start of 1950 Ascot's last 'Titan' TD1, Car 181 (RX 4343) had been transferred to Reading for relief duties. Its place was taken by a pair of 1946 Bristol K6A's instead, Cars 440/2 (CRX 549/51), making the allocation there 100% of that chassis type.

In the meantime a new series of practical tests commenced using TV buses using detergent oils, the Company working very closely with the oil refiners and technicians based at Chobham, Surrey at the Fighting Vehicle Development & Research Establishment. A number of buses were selected over a 2-year period, running exclusively on one grade or another, with consumption and performance under constant review. This often involved buses being away at FVDRE, whilst others were monitored in service conditions, and other tests took place on bench-run engines. Comparisons were also made between the AEC, Bristol and Gardner engines fitted to the various Bristol buses selected.

The remaining Leyland 'Titan' TD1's were mainly to be found on regular relief duties, and 1930 Car 206 (RX 5568) is seen by the old canteen on the parking ground off Stations Square in Reading. It had been rebuilt by Willowbrook with a utility-style front end. Many of the wartime rebuilds had route number apertures but few were ever used.

A number of re-allocations had naturally followed the sale of older stock and the arrival of newer types by January 1950. Up at Stokenchurch Dormy Shed new buses were planned but not yet available, so Duple utility-bodied Bristol K5G Car 417 (CJB 136) stood in for the usual performers, Bristol K5G's 413/4 (CJB 132/3) at various times between January and March.

The contribution of the Colonnade Paintshop has already been acknowledged but, by January 1950, it was becoming hard to find buses not requiring more

thorough attention to bodywork, and which therefore were directed to Reading Works. Therefore the Skilled Painters were returned to work from Maidenhead, whilst the Brush Hand was transferred to Reading Works.

Although its days were numbered, the Enquiry & Booking Office at Reading Stations Square was still the focus for such activities. Note the extensive use of adverts for excursions and other events, including the forthcoming Festival of Britain.

Possibly due to a pre-occupation with his enlarged remit, the Engineer had only succeeded in disposing of one old bus during January, with Leyland 'Lion' LT2 Car 14 (RX 6249) departing on 18th of that month. Only two new buses were received that month, with Bristol K6B/ECW L27/28R Car 526 (FBL 28) and Bristol L6B/ECW B35R Car 535 (FMO 10), both allocated to Reading, the latter going initially on the long Reading – Oxford Route 5.

Somewhat heavier inroads were made into the ranks of withdrawn saloons during February, heralding the demise of Leyland 'Lion' LT1 Cars 2, 4, 6, 8, 12, 22 and 42 (RX 5571-4/6/8/80), these being followed by similar Cars 20 and 38 (RX 5577/9) during March, which left only Car 10 (RX 5575) of the batch unsold.

The 1950 Bristol L6B's took over duties on Route 5, and Car 534 (FMO 9) is seen on that service when new and before side adverts had been applied.

As more new saloons arrive they took over a variety of duties, and Car 539 (FMO 14) was sent to Tadley to replace the 'Tadley Tiger' TS7 Car 271 (JB 5850). It is seen on the stand towards the Tudor Road end of Station Hill, under the building of the Star Upholstery Company and the extensive billboard hoardings.

During February the Route Servicing Vehicle No.29 (RX 1758) was kept busy clearing accumulated items from the far end of the *Southern Railway* yard between the Reading Stations, where a soakaway was constructed to cater for the improved canteen in the form of a Nissen Hut available for refreshments all day long. Good use was also made of the rubble piles dumped in the old Toomer's Coal Yard, which made the parking area larger. It is interesting to note that Sutton still refers to this vehicle as '169' in his notes of the time! Also, as the Colonnade was no longer a public area, the signboards were removed and placed at Stations Square, whilst the details of the new Road and Rail enquiry Office to replace the old wooden one were also progressed. Following the clipping of a London Plane tree outside the Royal Berkshire Hospital by Bristol K6B Car 517 (EJB 239) during February whilst working Route B, a warning notice was posted to drivers to avoid the potential hazard.

Also during that month, representatives of Brown Brothers, who had a branch in Caversham Road, came to demonstrate the Weaver 'Steam Jenny' cleaning machine on the chassis of TS7 Car 268 (JB 5847) – an order for one being placed as a result. TS8 Cars 363/6 (ARX 985/8) were taken down to Brislington for a refurbishment at BBW on 23rd February, though on arrival it was noted that little progress had been made with similar Cars 345 (AJB 817) and 371 (BBL 557), as apparently new seat frames were proving difficult to obtain. In the Engineer's report it was also noted that the only petrol-engined vehicles in active use

were those on Route 18 (Maidenhead – Marlow), all others being in store or away (in the case of TD1 Car 171). The latter actually returned from service with *Westcliff-on-Sea* on 27th February and was noted as earmarked for contract use by *Thames Valley*, though notwithstanding that comment it was delicensed the following day, along with 'Titan' TD1's 201 (RX 5563) and 236 (RX 8169), Bristol K5G's 402/7 (BRX 918/23), 'Tiger' TS8 saloon 343 (AJB 815) and TS8 coaches 384/6 (BMO 983/5). On 1st March their places were taken by 'Tiger' TS7 Car 48 (ABL 761), Bristol K5G's 394/9 (BRX 910/5) and 'Tiger' TS8 coaches 387/9 (BMO 986/8)

New vehicles arrived during February, as Bristol K6B/ECW L27/28R Cars 527/8 (FBL 29 and 30), and L6B/ECW B35R Car 536 (FMO 11). The latter plus Car 528 was sent to Wycombe, with the double-decker earmarked in due course for Stokenchurch Shed, whilst Car 527 was allocated to Maidenhead.

ECW-bodied Bristol L6B Car 541 (FMO 16) gleams in the sunshine at Maidenhead Bus Station awaiting its duty on Route 22a to Slough via Clivedon.

Also received were vehicles originally ordered for the Newbury fleet by *Red & White,* all of which were typical of the types then being supplied throughout that group. A pair of lowbridge double-deckers on Guy 'Arab' Mk111 chassis, fitted with Gardner 5LW engines and bearing very stylish Duple bodies with 54 seats and rear platform doors, arrived as Cars 170/1 (FMO 515/6). These had been ordered to improve the standard of the Newbury – Lambourn route, which required passing under the low railway bridge near Boxford.

Above: Guy 'Arab' Car 171 (FMO 516) as new and in the Red & White style livery. These were used on the Newbury – Oxford route initially whilst tree-cutting was completed on the Lambourn route. The bodies were to a high finish both inside and out, several features duly influencing TV's double-deck coaches.
Below: The trio of Lydney-bodied AEC 'Regals' were also very much a R&W product, and Car 161 (FBL 919) is seen outside the Mill Lane garage, these vehicles being used mainly on contract work.

The single-deckers ordered for N&D were three AEC 'Regal' 6821A-types fitted with B35F bodies built by the *Red & White*-associated Lydney Coachworks. The bodies on these had quite stylish bodies, though lacking the design skills of the Duple 'deckers, with some odd window arrangements and quite a high cab window line. Cars 161/2 (FBL 919/20) arrived during February and were joined by 163 (FBL 921) in March.

The other outstanding vehicle was Car 172 (FMO 517), another Guy 'Arab' Mk111, but with a Gardner 6LW engine and fitted with a highbridge version of the Duple body, seating 57 but lacking the rear doors, arrived during April or May. This had originally been the 5th of a batch ordered for the *Venture* fleet but had been re-assigned to Newbury, the rest of which we will hear of again in due course. The diversion had been in exchange for N&D's Car 159 (HAD 745), an AEC 'Regent' which had itself been diverted to the *Cheltenham District* fleet during those busy post-war days, before finally passing to the Newbury fleet. As a matter of standardisation, the exchange of 159 with the awaited 172 took place from 1st January 1950, so the vehicle did not pass into the TV era. A further AEC 'Regent', Car 151 (EJB 521) would also transfer in due course, but more of that also later.

The Lambourn route tree-cutting saw 'Titan' TD1 No.29 busy for some time, and it is worth considering the largely unsung heroes of the Route Servicing Gang. They worked over the whole system in all weathers, lopping trees, erecting bus stop signs, updating timetable cases, repairing and repainting bus shelters, dormy sheds and garages, saving the need for outside contractors and answering directly to Elmet Abberfield.

The crew of Bristol K6B Car 529 (FBL 31) enjoy the sunshine whilst laid over at West Wycombe awaiting departure on Route 42 to Loudwater. The Milward's advert is for K Shoes, one of a series of slogans used on the bus ads for many years for that Reading firm.

March saw the arrival of more new vehicles, the rate of supply being markedly improved on the previous year, with Bristol K6B/ECW L27/28R Car 529 (FBL 31), Bristol L6B/ECW B35R Cars 537-9 (FMO 12-14), and Bristol L6B/Windover C33F coaches 545-9 (FMO 20-4). At this point K6B's 528/9 were sent to Stokenchurch Dormy Shed in place of the 'unfrozen' Bristol K5G's 413/4 (CJB 132/3), whilst the saloons went one each to Wycombe, Maidenhead and Reading respectively. There was great relief that the coaches had come through before the start of the main season, and all were allocated to work from the Colonnade.

Windover-bodied coach 548 (FMO 23) was put on display outside the Colonnade, advertising excursions and for inspection by the public – something of a TV tradition at both Reading and High Wycombe.

March also saw the return from Brislington of 'Tiger' TS8 Car 345 (AJB 817) on 24th, followed by 371 (BBL 557) on 29th, the time away being rather excessive for the amount of work undertaken.

On the services front very little had changed during the year, again largely because of the additional task of absorbing the workload which came with *N&D* and *South Midland*. However, the experimental journeys through Ufton Nervet village had proved worthwhile, so with effect from 11th March all journeys on Route 9a (Reading – Grazeley – Tadley) went that way.

The Windover coaches were attractive vehicles, but this type of design would quite soon appear dated once under-floor engined chassis came along. Car 547 (FMO 22) is seen on a private hire job.

It is worth noting that Staff Bulletins often contained letters from members of the public or Local Councils that were thought worthy of airing to all staff. It seems that late-running of Route 3a led to complaints that passengers were missing train connections, whereas on the other side of the coin, the crew on a Route 27 journey were praised for holding the departure of the last run one evening when they heard that the incoming train had been delayed! Again, both letters illustrate how important the bus operations were to the daily lives of so many people, and in fact complaints were a rarity, which is testament to a well-run company and its dedicated staff.

The Traffic Superintendent at Reading, Mr. J.A. Dear, got a new Morris 'Oxford' car (FRX 9) from March 1950. Not to be outdone, his counterpart over at Wycombe, Mr. E. Jeffries, received a similar vehicle (FRX 647) in June, leading to the September disposal of an number of Staff Cars.

Bristol K6B Car 533 (FMO 8) is seen working as a relief on Route A, although the service was still then not the usual haunt of double-deckers, so it is likely this was during a bank holiday.

In respect of the fleet inherited from *South Midland*, rationalisation by *Red & White* between the Oxford fleet and *Newbury & District* had produced an active fleet consisting entirely of Duple-bodied AEC 'Regal' coaches. These 30 vehicles had been constructed between 1947 and 1950 (including 3 still outstanding at the time of the takeover), though their seating varied between C30F for touring and C35F for general work, and all carried the standard *R&W* inspired livery of red panels, white relief and black mudguards, which was well suited to that style of bodywork.

The *Newbury & District* fleet, encompassing a greater variety of tasks, was rather more varied, with various sizes and types of vehicles. However, *Red & White* had still managed to instill a greater degree of standardisation than hitherto associated with the '57 varieties' found in earlier times at Newbury!

With much of the old stock swept away, the fleet now consisted of a surviving trio of Bedford OWB's, 8 Guy 'Arab' double-deckers, 1 AEC 'Regent' double-deck, and almost all the rest being AEC 'Regals' of various varieties. The exceptions were a pair of Bedford OB coaches, a trio of Leyland 'Tiger' TS7 coaches, plus a curious hybrid in the form of a 1947 Leyland 'Tiger' PS1 which was carrying a 1936 ECOC body! All of these had been transferred from *South Midland* prior to the takeover by TV. Although now officialy in the Newbury fleet, most actually spent much of the time on hire to their former owner.

The 33 'Regals' in stock came in a variety of forms and ages. Those not familiar with the activities of the *Red & White Group* should note that it had long been known for its ability to breathe new life into older types, with early experiments in the fitting of diesel engines and re-bodying programmes, both of which stood it in good stead when wartime conditions made 'make do and mend' a national necessity. Indeed, Reg Hibbert in the Newbury Garage had served at the Chepstow Works, and recalled how it was equipped with all the latest equipment, together with the sheer thoroughness of all the work undertaken both on the mechanical side and in the bodyworks.

In order to find vehicles for rebuilding, scrapyards and dealers yards had been searched, resulting in some interesting end results. As regards the Newbury stable, a large batch of former *Scottish Motor Traction* AEC chassis of the 0642-type had been acquired, and fitted with Gardner 5LW engines, and then united with 1936 Eastern Counties bodies originally from the *North Western Road Car* fleet. In addition 5 other old 0662-type chassis emanating from with *R&W Group* fleets were given new leases of life for use at Newbury, one receiving one of the 1936 ECOC body, whilst the others were rebodied by Burlingham with utility bus bodies. The remainder of the 'Regals' were of new deliveries between 1947 and 1948 (plus the 3 1950 examples received after TV took control), all on 0662 or 'Mark 111' chassis and fitted with bus or coach bodies by Duple, the livery being the same as that applied to the *South Midland* fleet.

Full details of the vehicles acquired from *Newbury & District* and *South Midland* will be found in Appendix One.

In order to help out at Newbury, *Thames Valley* sent a number of buses from its fleet, and Leyland 'Lion' LT2 Car 50 (RX 6246), 'Tiger' TS4 Cars 246 and 255 (RX 9700/9), along with 'Tiger' TS7 coaches 262/4 (JB 5841/3) were all transferred from 1st April. On the same date Bedford OB coaches 164/5 (LJO 756/7) were transferred to TV ownership, though they still spent much of the time working for *South Midland*! On 12th April 1929 Leyland 'Titan' TD1 Cars 179/81 (RX 4341/3) were also sent to Newbury. Also, though not noted in official sources, 'Titan' TD1 Car 184 (RX 4346) and 'Tiger' TS4's 247/52 (RX 9701/6) were at Newbury at various times during the Summer of 1950, perhaps rotating with those officially noted?

'Titan' TD1 Car 181 (RX 4343), still retaining the original piano-fronted front profile, seen at Newbury. Vehicles of this type were of course no strangers to The Wharf, having been the mainstay of Route 10 for many years.

During April a number of N&D vehicles, including the Bedford OWB's were parked up at the newly extended *Southern Railway* yard, where they were stoned by some boys, though the Police caught and prosecuted them.

1930 Brush-bodied Leyland 'Lion' LT2 Car 50 (RX 6246) was transferred to assist at Newbury, and is seen outside the Mill Lane garage. Note the lack of a destination blind roll in the enlarged front box as a result of wartime refurbishment. The radiator badge leaves the maker's name in no doubt though.

As further new saloons arrived they took over a wider variety of duties. The single-deck workings at Reading were fairly diverse and some inter-working had been arranged to even out duty hours. Car 544 (FMO 19) is shown above when working for on the 3a to Finchampstead, whilst below it is seen parked in the Southern Yard between contract runs to AERE at Harwell. More will be heard of this bus and its duties in due course.

At the first meeting of the Standing Joint Committee since the acquisition of the former *Red & White* areas it was agreed to dismantle the previous liaison arrangements with the *Venture* company, and also that Mr. Grimmett, manager of *Newbury & District* would attend. Plans for the new joint road and rail enquiry office were well advanced, but the subject of a more comprehensive bus station remained unresolved. One suggested site discussed during the Spring of 1950 was the large yard used by Vincents, on the south side of Station Hill, and in fact leased from the *GWR*.

By the Spring Leyland 'Titan' TD1 Car 206 (RX 5568) was at the Colonnade looking rather forlorn and without a radiator. However, it was duly fitted with

one of the 1928-style radiators, complete with *Thames Valley* lettering, repainted and returned to service.

Still an important aspect of income in Spring 1950 was the early-morning newspaper distribution by bus on behalf of W. H. Smith & Son. Pre-stamped labels were available for this and the packages were handed directly to the conductors of buses departing from the main termini. There were also arrangements for mail bags to be dropped at many an out-of-the-way post office. The Parcels Service also continued, providing as it did a convenient and relatively cheap means of sending packages to places within the route system. Indeed, a consignee could send a package of 7lbs weight for 6 old pence, or up to 28lbs at just 1 shilling and 3 old pence. At the time there were 175 agents for dispatch and receipt of parcels, and it difficult to identify places not covered in that network, the agents being listed in the timetable books and their premises marked by a red and white enamelled Parcel Agent sign. In the Newbury area there had also been a well-developed parcels service, understandable in view of the origins of many of the links under the old Country Carriers.

Parcels remained an important source of revenue and this photo records the moment when the conductor on the 'Valley's Bristol K-type Car 468 (DMO 672) signs the receipt for packages transferred from the bicycle of the Reading Corporation 'boy' kitted out in uniform and cycle clips. Also note the full-width destination displays in use at the time, and the neat round hole punched in the rear panel by the starting handle of another bus!

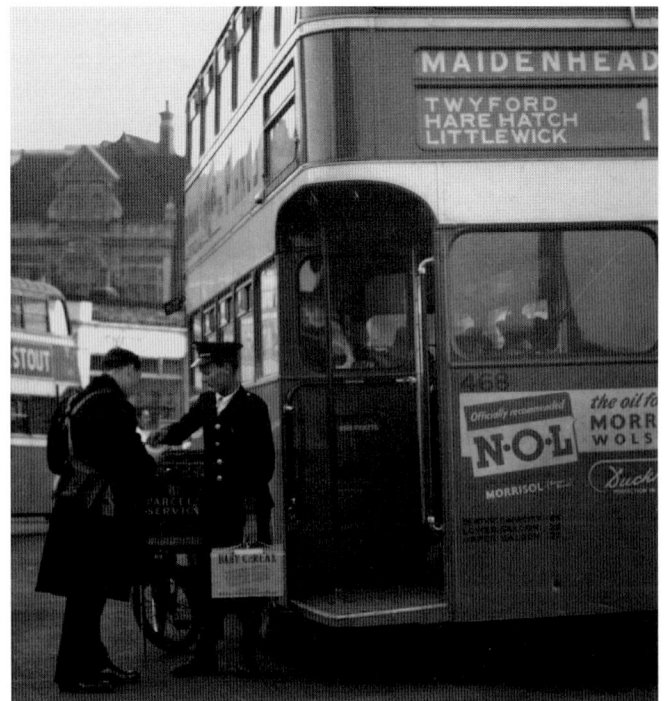

From 22nd April Route 5a (Reading – Wantage) was given an extension that has an interesting story behind it. An early-morning contract with a corresponding afternoon journey called for a Reading-based saloon to run out to the AERE at Harwell, the route travelling via Crays Pond. The run was in the daily care of a regular crew known as 'Bill & Ben', who also had assigned to them a regular bus. Ben Parker was the driver, and he had previously served at the Fingest Dormy Shed, whilst the conductor was Bill Haines (who was also known as 'Granny'). There was a lot of new housing being built as part of the Harwell project, and the local residents soon suggested to the crew that an improved service would be welcomed. The incoming contract journey was extended on Chilton (Horse & Jockey), where the crew took a break before forming the 9.30am service run to Reading, which provided a useful shopping link, and was certainly more useful than running back dead. In the afternoons the bus left Reading at 3.50pm, which positioned it in time for the return contract run. As there was a layover of an over an hour each morning the crew soon took to giving the bus a clean, which meant that the bus was very well kept. From June they were given new Bristol L6B saloon 544 ((FMO 19), which by virture of the relatively low mileage worked, plus the daily polish by the crew, was quite a bargain when sold to *United Welsh* in 1960!

Bristol K6B Car 532 (FMO 7) is seen in the Southern Yard between runs on the London Route A. Note it has another of the Milwards adverts, this example being 'for Physical Culture'.

On Saturdays the link to Chilton was maintained by working out from Reading at 8.10am, plus several extended return journeys for the afternoon and evening, which catered for general passengers and anyone needing transport to AERE on that day. The bus could also often be seen laid over during the day in the Southern Yard, usually with Private on the blinds to ensure it was not taken for other duties. The crew also had a few other duties around the garage at Lower Thorn Street to complete their day, one of which was to replenish the large enamelled teapot for the Traffic Office Staff, which when empty was lowered on a piece of string from the window above!

Turning out from Frogmoor past the distinctive shop front of the Fifty Shilling Tailors, is Bristol L6B Car 543 (FMO 18), en route to Desborough Castle Estate on Route 33.

April brought the delivery of a quartet of Bristol K6B's with Eastern Coach Works L27/28R bodies as Cars 530-3 (FBL 32/3, FMO 7/8), all being allocated to Reading other than 530, which went to Maidenhead. May saw further saloons arrive in the shape of Bristol L6B/ECW B35R Cars 540-3 (FMO 15-8), allocated on a 3-way split between Reading (540), Maidenhead (541) and Wycombe (542/3). A trio of Bedford OB coaches with Duple C29F bodies were delivered ready for licensing for the season, and these were Cars 604-6 (FRX 313-5), with all being allocated Reading initially. The large gap in fleet numbers reflected large orders for 1950-1 delivery.

Bedford OB coach 606 (FRX 315) at the coast.

Bedford coach 606 was displayed outside the entrance to the Colonnade from 8th May, but from 13th May its place was taken by Windover-bodied Bristol L6B coach 548 (FMO 23), which remained there until the 19th. The Spring display of coaches became something of a TV tradition, and also occurred at Stations Square, Wycombe Marsh, Maidenhead and Marlow.

It should of course be recalled that the Colonnade was now the base for the Reading coach fleet, so arrangements were also made for excursions to pick up from that point. A new Enquiry Office was opened at that location in the former café building in the frontage of the Crown Colonnade, all of those properties having come into the *Thames Valley* portfolio with the acquisition of *Thackray's Way*. Bookings could also be taken for coach services throughout the country, as well as the extended tours operated by *South Midland.*

The Colonnade Enquiry Office shortly after it opened, with Festival of Britain excursion posters and others depicting the South Midland extended tours.

As the Newbury Company still existed as a separate entity, arrangements were made for the inter-availability of return tickets between Newbury and Thatcham on Route 10, or between Reading and Upper Basildon with Routes 5, 5a and 5b, conductors being notified of this on 16th May. Elsewhere, over at Victoria Coach Station, the long-held Stand No.2 was vacated by Route A, when it joined Route B on Stand 14 from 25th May. Such items were communicated through the weekly Staff Bulletins, which also at times included rather more unusual items. On 22nd May crews in the High Wycombe area were asked to keep an eye out for an elderly lady who had gone missing for 5 days. Nothing more is heard on that score, but on 5th July an item concerned a black dog well known to crews on the Booker service. The dog from Limmer Lane had the habit of boarding buses, but had always managed to find his way back from wherever he was put off. The third interesting notice, issued on 10th October 1950, was on behalf of Reading Borough Police, who were keen to trace a burglar with 2 suitcases, who it is thought had made his escape from the Cemetery Junction area by bus!

Leyland 'Tiger' TS8 Cars 363/6 (ARX 985/8) finally returned from the BBW works on 25th May, re-seated as B35R, which meant that for the first time for many years no TV vehicles were receiving external work.

Further new coaches were licensed for June, being Bristol L6B's with Windover C33F bodies as 550-2 (FMO 25/6 and FMO 934), the batch being completed the following month with the arrival of Cars 553-5 (FMO 935-7). The only service saloon received in

June was Bristol L6B/ECW B35R Car 544 (FMO 19), which we have already noted above. The coaches were split between Reading (554), Maidenhead (550/1) and Wycombe (552/3/5). Their arrival brought the coach fleet to its highest level for many years. However, the Standing Joint Committee noted with concern the rapid expansion of *Smith's Luxury Coaches* of Reading in the early post-war period. The coastal express network had received particular attention, whilst the large amount of contract work was also sustaining, *Smith's* ploy in refurbishing secondhand stock having put it in a good position to meet these demands at a time when new deliveries were often problematical. However, *Thames Valley* still attracted a goodly share of the private hire work in Reading, whilst the High Wycombe and Marlow areas were still strong for coaching work, and indeed the popular Southsea express route. The latter operated on Summer Sundays, often requiring 4 coaches, one of which was provided by Maidenhead as a relief for local bookings. In fact June 1950 also marked the official end of fuel rationing, so operators of private hire vehicles were no longer obliged to log mileages run or work to the restrictions originally introduced 11 years beforehand!

Over at Crowthorne Dormy Shed, Leyland 'Tiger' TS7 Car 18 (JB 7494) was displaced during June on Route 3a (Reading – Wokingham – Finchampstead) by Bristol L6B Car 540 (FMO 15).

Bristol L6B (FMO 25) rests with the graceful lines of its Windover coachwork in the sunshine on a day trip to Arundel in Sussex.

As already noted, there had been many refugees in the Company's area during the War years, with some hut camps featuring in the post-war effort to resolve the shortage of housing. One such location was east of the village of Wargrave, and the residents of the camp in Victoria Road appealed for a bus service. As a result, some short-workings on Route 1 were diverted at Carlisle Corner on the Bath Road to Wargrave village, turning right at The Greyhound, up Victoria Road, and then back down the Bath Road to reach Twyford, this arrangement commencing on 3rd June.

The Ascot Race Week was a busy affair in June 1950, and TV found itself having to hire vehicles from *City of Oxford, Reading Corporation* and *Brimblecombe Bros.* of Wokingham. In respect of inter-company relations, Messrs. Sutton and Campbell paid a visit to Salisbury during June, to see how *Wilts & Dorset* was coping with work on the *Venture* vehicles. It seems likely that the subject of standardisation of types was raised during this occasion, no doubt leading to some vehicle exchanges in due course. During that month a suggestion was put forward to raise the roof of the Colonnade garage in order that double-deckers might be admitted, but after inspection that was ruled out.

Staff on duty for the Ascot Race Week were provided with sustenance through this tea tent erected at the Grange Car Park. The TV Ascot Garage can be seen behind the tent, and this arrangement saved crews having to go to the canteen there.

As part of planning the specification for the next batch of double-deckers earmarked for London Route B, a representative from ECW came to look at the rear doors of the pair of Duple-bodied lowbridge Guys at Newbury, with results we shall see during 1951.

On 20th June a party of 12 came from the London Transport Executive to view the Reading Works, after which they were taken to lunch at Sonning, followed by a tour back through the Woodcote area, carried by Bedford OB coach 604 (FRX 313).

Bristol K5G Car 413 (CJB 132) at Gloucester Green Bus Station on hire to City of Oxford for the Royal Counties Show in July.

Bob Hepburn in 1918.

However the month of June was marred by the untimely death of Works Manager Bob Hepburn on the 29th. He had served the Company for 35 years, right through from bringing the original secondhand Leylands down from Barnsley in 1915. In those early days he was Fitter, Driver and anything else required as *British* set the foundations for *Thames Valley*. From 1920 he had been Basil Sutton's right-hand man in the Works, so his death ended that long association.

As already noted, the *'Valley* had borrowed *City of Oxford* buses for several Ascot Race Weeks, but the opposite loan was made for 4th-7th July, when the Oxford operator found itself catering for the demands of the Royal Counties Show. Five double-deckers were required, each running with a temporary fleet no. shown on a paper sticker, the vehicles being: 1 (TV Car 494, Bristol K6B), 2 (TV Car 495, Bristol K6B), 3 (TV Car 413, Bristol K5G), 4 (N&D Car 99, Guy 'Arab'), and 5 (N&D Car 160, Guy 'Arab').

In addition to the vehicles already in hand for delivery to the Newbury and Oxford fleets, there were other orders originally placed by *Red & White* that needed either honouring or cancellation. A trio of underfloor-engined coaches had been intended for *South Midland*, two on Guy LUF-type chassis and one on the AEC 'Regal' MkIV model, whilst *Newbury & District* was intended to receive a pair of similar Guys. Once the decision was made to accept these, it was also decided that all would go to the Oxford-based fleet. The story of the Guys was a protracted one, as we shall see over the next couple of years, but it should be noted that at this point the AEC had already been reserved a body to be built by Duple, and TV apparently resigned itself to the inevitability of accepting that. However, there were further twists to this story, which again we will re-visit in due course.

55

South Midland Car 38 (LWL 995), a Leyland 'Tiger' PS1 of 1947 fitted with 1936 ECOC body.

At the same time some serious thought was given to the future of the 'Tiger' PS1 with older ECOC body, new as *South Midland* Car 38, but exchanged with *Newbury &District* as the latter's Car 169 (LWL 995). The original matching of the 1936 body to the 1947 chassis had been a necessity of the time, as bodies were harder to obtain than chassis. Basil Sutton could see that the chassis would in fact make the basis of a nice coach, particularly as the Festival of Britain would make 1951 a very busy year for the coach fleet. As the legal maximum length for PSV's had recently been increased from 27ft 6ins to 30ft, it was also desirable to utilise the full dimensions for the 'new' vehicle, so Sutton paid a visit to the Kingston Works of Leyland Motors to see a demonstration of a kit for extending the wheelbase of post-war 'Tigers' from 17ft 6ins to 18ft 9ins, and thereafter the project got the go ahead, as we shall see a little later on.

The ever-popular selection of Road/Rail/River Trips re-commenced from July, including one that involved a rail journey from Cheltenham, which picked up at stations en route, from Reading by various boat trip options, then bus travel back to Reading. For these journeys a complex 'exchange ticket' was issued in 3 parts, the first part for the initial rail journey, then the second and third could be used for boat or bus trips depending on the order of transport. Fully detailed tour options were produced, some being to certain set times, whereas as others were go-as-you-please. All options were clearly laid, making some memorable tours available.

Unfortunately July also saw the death of another long service employee, and Driver F. C. Butler's funeral was set for 24th July at Earley St. Peter's Church on the eastern edge of Reading. As a large number of colleagues wished to attend, the Company provided a bus as a mark of respect, a volunteer driving it there. Such a situation occurred again in May 1951, following the death of Assistant Foreman J. J. Metcalfe of Reading, which was another mark of the genuinely goodwill that existed between management and staff at that time.

A pair of Leyland rear ends at Maidenhead Garage in 1950, with Brush-bodied 'Tiger' TS7 Car 269 (JB 5848) of 1935 and Brush-bodied 'Tiger' TS8 Car 345 (AJB 817) new in 1937.

As may be recalled, following the takeover of the fleet of *Ledbury Transport* on 1st January 1936, the coaches were gradually replaced by TV vehicles to form a 'paper fleet', continuing the former owner's practice of using only even numbers. This situation was mainly due to *Thames Valley's* fear that application to transfer the lucrative license for Route B might not be granted, but on 26th July 1950 *Ledbury* was finally wound up and the vehicles were to revert to their former fleet numbers (though some were sold still bearing their *Ledbury* fleet numbers, as noted below):

LT No.	TV No.	Reg. No.	Type	Notes
10	213	RX 5575	LT1	Sold as 10 in 8/50
18	294	JB 7494	TS7	Reverted to 294
24	309	JB 8348	TS7	Reverted to 309
26	310	JB 8349	TS7	Sold as 26 in 7/50
28	311	JB 8350	TS7	Reverted to 311
30	321	ABL 751	TS7	Reverted to 321
32	322	ABL 752	TS7	Reverted to 322
34	323	ABL 753	TS7	Reverted to 323
36	324	ABL 754	TS7	Reverted to 324
40	325	ABL 755	TS7	Reverted to 325
44	326	ABL 756	TS7	Reverted to 326
46	225	RX 6245	LT2	Sold as 46 by 9/51
48	331	ABL 761	TS7	Reverted to 331
50	226	RX 6246	LT2	Sold as 50 by 9/51
52	227	RX 6247	LT2	Sold as 52 in 7/50
54	228	RX 6248	LT2	Sold as 54 in 3/51

ECW-bodied 'Tiger' TS7 Car 36 (ABL 754) was still carrying its Ledbury Transport fleet number when seen at Maidenhead Bus Station during Summer 1950.

During July there were quite a few disposals and, despite all the work wrought upon it, the final petrol-engined Leyland 'Titan' TD1 Car 171 (RX 1760) was amongst them, surviving as a caravan behind the New Inn at Heckfield for a few years. TD1 Cars 224 (RX 6244) and 233 (RX 8166) also went, as did Leyland 'Lion' LT2 Cars 14 (RX 249) and 52 (RX 6247), as well as the sole 'Tiger' TS3 new to the Company, Car 230 (RX 6250). The latter went to *Reliance* over at Brightwalton, though sadly as a non-runner, its seats and engine been used whilst the rest faded into the orchard at the rear of their garage. However, 'Tiger' TS7 Car 330 (ABL 760) also went to them at the same time, but did see further service. Quite a number of 'Tigers' were cleared out during July now that new saloons were coming through steadily, these being TS7's 297 (JB 7497) and 26 (JB 8349), and TS8's 359/60/4 (ARX 981/2/6) and 376 (BBL 562). Some of these had been lifelong Wycombe cars and probably hardest worked of all the saloons in the fleet.

Despite inroads into the 1938 Leyland 'Tiger' TS8's, Car 366 (ARX 988) found itself stretching its legs whilst on hire to South Midland at Oxford in 1950.

I have already noted the numerous family connections in the ranks of employees at N&D, and the same was also commonplace on the *'Valley*. One such example was Jack Edwards, who joined the Company at Reading Works in 1950, his father having started his driving career at Maidenhead, seduced by the shiny new Leyland 'Titan' TD1 buses in 1928. Due to their respective occupations they became known as 'bend 'em and mend 'em'!

It would have been difficult to take any photographs in the centre of High Wycombe without a bus in it, and this wet market day view looking across to the old Corn Market shows a Bristol L-type saloon working in from Flackwell Heath on Route 25, whilst Bristol K6B 528 (FBL 30), a Stokenchurch-based bus, heads for Radnage on Route 40. The network of routes in the area ensured good links from the scattered villages.

Bus work was good solid work, hard at times, but something you could count on as long as you did your duty. There were even occasional consolations, such as journeys to special events or private hires, where the crews would benefit from a change of scenery. One such regular run was the 'Moulsford Special' between Reading and the Berkshire Mental Hospital near Cholsey, a service that had started back in August 1917 and ran on Thursdays and Sundays only. Two, sometimes three, saloon buses were required and were crew-worked as passengers were also picked up in St. Mary's Butts, harking back to when the main terminus was situated there. Only return tickets were issued, and checked to ensure none of the unfortunate patients tried to getaway by bus! However, once the buses were parked up in the nearby gravel lane, the crews were free to enjoy a couple hours of layover, some even taking a dip in the River Thames!

At Maidenhead the Bus Station became so crowded with service coaches at times that they spilled out into Bridge Avenue itself, leading to the decision in the Summer of 1950 to take up the option to purchase the plot of land running from York Avenue to the railway embankment of the London to Bristol line, upon which a Coach Station would be constructed. South Midland AEC 'Regals' 57 (NJO 218) and 68 (EJB 649), plus a Thames Valley Windover-bodied Bristol L6B line up with the Rialto Cinema in the background.

Further along the river at Henley, the Council was of the opinion that the bus stops should be relocated over at the railway station. Although that would have been handy for rail passengers, it would not be so useful for shoppers. The citing of traffic congestion just shows how we have allowed our daily lives to be ruled by that one issue for so many years but to so little effect!

As noted previously, the maximum dimension for single-deck PSV's had been increased from 1st June to 30ft, so Bristol Commercial Vehicles developed their L-type to the LL-type, TV's first examples being Cars 556-9 (FMO 938-41) which arrived during August. At the same time double-deck lengths were only increased from 26ft to 27ft, and BCV constructed the KS-type, TV's first example being Car 586 (FMO 968), one of the first pair of that type to leave ECW. As BCV and ECW were both under State control,

existing orders were modified automatically unless the operator specified overwise. Whereas the LL increased capacity from 35 to 39 passengers, the extra length on double-deckers was merely absorbed. Cars 556 and 586 both went to Reading, whereas 557-9 were the first new buses allocated to Newbury.

Bristol LL6B Car 558 (FMO 940) seen on a layover in the Southern Yard between runs on Route 6B between Reading and Bramley Station, at this time allocated to Reading.

As an 8ft maximum width for PSV's soon followed, a number of vehicles with intermediate specifications, e.g. 7ft 6ins wide chassis with 8ft wide bodies, though none were of direct relevance to *Thames Valley*. However, this did lead to the decision that PS1-type Car 169 (LWL 995) would have an 8ft wide body on its 7ft 6ins chassis, the option to fit wider axles not being considered. Although the War had been over for 5 years, all staff were still reminded of the need to do their best to achieve economy in operation, as many materials were still in short supply. Indeed, for those who wcrc not around then, it is worth noting that even food rationing did not actually end until 1954!

Once the Bristol KS6B arrived in numbers they were to be found further afield. Car 589 (FMO 971) is seen at Great Missenden Station on Route 27.

58

Although new buses were coming through, Leyland 'Titan' TD1's could still be seen on some of the longer routes. Car 412 (HF 6041) was obviously a good buy, originating with Wallasey Corporation but later with Alexander's in Scotland before being acquired in 1941. Subsequently given a Gardner 5LW oil engine, it also had a body refurbishment by ECW, changing its appearance from the piano-front, unlike Car 223 (RX 6343) seen behind it on Stations Hill, Reading as it prepares to depart for Newbury.

An interesting aside to austerity was the advert in the Summer 1950 timetable for the Mount Hawke Guest House, near Truro in Cornwall, complete with photos and details of public transport, placed in there by Mr. John B. Hewitson 'late of the Thames Valley Head Office Staff'.

August saw further withdrawals of old stock, though sales were by no means a foregone conclusion, so some vehicles languished at the Colonnade for some months since last turning a wheel, some with parts taken off as time went by. The final 'Lion' LT1 Car 10 (RX 5575) was cleared, along with 'Titan' TD1's 220 (RX 6111) and 236 (RX 8169). Bob Crawley saw these leave the Colonnade, with the 'Lion' towing the 'Jeep' that the purchasers had arrived in – it was all over the place and looked a highly illegal practice! On the last day of that month TD1 Cars 200 and 207 (RX 5562/9), 'Tiger' TS7 saloons 307/8 (JB 8346/7) and 'Tiger' TS8 saloons 365/7 (ARX 987/9) were all taken out of service. The Gardner 5LW engine from Car 200 was sold to local brewers H. & G. Simonds of Reading, who had a well-presented fleet based in Mill Lane, next to the Corporation premises. There were a number of instances where TV spares made their way to that operator going back to the Thornycroft era.

However, the next vehicle taken out of service was due to an unplanned event, when the seemingly ill-fated Leyland 'Titan' TD4 Car 272 (JB 5851) was overturned. It will be recalled that this bus had received an ECW body after a fire in 1940, but its bad luck struck once again on 8th September whilst the bus worked its regular run on the 6.51pm Route 4 between Reading and Camberley, leaving the road by the entrance to Warbrook Lodge at Eversley. Fortunately there were few passengers on board, and of the dozen or so, only one lady required hospital attention, quite a mess was made of the bodywork, so it was a lucky escape indeed. The bus was raised the following day by TV's Recovery Wagon with some assistance from REME from Arborfield Garrison, all afterwards taking a well-earned pint in the 'Tally Ho' pub before towing 272 back to Reading. In view of the extensive damage, it was sold un-repaired later that month. It is interesting also to note that, although this bus was on daily duty in and out of Reading Stations on major bus routes for 10 years, no photos have come to light of it bearing the ECW body!

September also saw the sale of Leyland 'Tiger' TS7 308 (JB 8347) and TS8's 365/7 (ARX 987/9), all of which followed tradition and went to showmen, which resulted in some of them regularly revisiting the area.

Following the loss of Bob Hepburn, his place as Works Superintendent was taken by W. G. Foulke, with T. R. Shepherd as his deputy, effective from 1st September. However, over at Newbury, Sid Taylor was not happy with the new regime, so he left and set up *Enterprise Coaches* instead! His assistant Reg Hibbert then took charge of the Newbury maintenance, aided on the Oxford front by the existing Foreman Mr. Bessell.

The stands on Stations Hill were used by routes heading north-west out of Reading. Here are Bristol L-type Car 485 (DMO 689) on Route 5b to Yattendon, followed by a LL-type on the new Route 50 to Abingdon, with an N&D Duple-bodied. AEC 'Regal' at the rear on the service to East Ilsley. The large shed behind was part of the Vincents coachworks and, much later on would be the site of the awful semi-underground Bus Station with Bingo Hall above it.

Leyland 'Tiger' TS7 saloon 307 (JB 8346) lingered on at the Colonnade until it found a buyer in November, and was the last PSV sold that year. Also based at the Colonnade was Route Servicing 'Titan' TD1 No.29 (RX 1758) which, by 13th September, had received a Gardner 5LW engine and had been repainted in all-over green with simplified lettering. A number of staff cars were also disposed of in September, these being 1938 Austin 7hp BBL 443 and Austin 10hp ELT 722, 1939 10hp FLY 286 and similar 1941 car CJB 670.

New vehicles received during September were a further pair of Bristol KS6B's with ECW L27/28R bodies which became Cars 587/8 (FMO 969/70). TD1 Car 201 (RX 5563) was given a reprieve and returned to service from 22nd September, due partly because a pair of K5G's was transferred to Wycombe Marsh to allow that garage to double-deck Route 27 to Great Missenden. On the following day a new service commenced between Reading and Abingdon, which was worked jointly with *City of Oxford*. This was given the number 50, which fitted in with other routes in that general direction in the '5 series', though the Oxford company used Route 40 instead! Indeed, whereas TV's Oxford service was the 5, COMS used 34 for that route, and these facts were noted in the timetables, though they seem unnecessarily confusing in hindsight. Six return runs were worked on weekdays and Saturdays, with a lesser service on Sundays. From TV's perspective this also improved the service between Reading and Purley in response to

calls from residents, whilst COMS also provided some short-workings between Abingdon and Dorchester. It should of course be recalled that the *British* buses had reached Abingdon in October 1915, but had been withdrawn the following Spring as a fuel economy, so it is perhaps strange that so long went by before the link was again covered.

Also during September the zoo at Billy Smart's Circus base at North Street, Winkfield was re-opened to the public, and conductors on Routes 2 and 2b were reminded of the location and the need to announce the stop. Indeed, one well-known Ascot-based Conductor, Ted Rance, had his own names for many of the stops – 'Reading Underground' for Cemetery Junction, also referred to as the 'Dead Centre of Town', 'Galloping Gee Gee' for the Running Horse on London Road, Bracknell, 'Leg of Lamb' for the Shoulder of Mutton at Popeswood, though on another tact he always announced Mill Lane, Earley as 'Mill Lane, Gipsy Lane, Meadow Road and Pond Head Road' in full!

Seen outside yet another shopping name from the past is ECW-bodied Bristol LL6B Car 560 (FMO 942). It is working a Route 28 'short' to Marlow Common and is emerging from the Frogmoor terminus.

The decorated Windover-bodied Bristol L-type coach for publicising the Festival of Britain and coaching in general, photographed at Caversham Promenade, one of a number of photos taken in-house by the Reading Stores Superintendent Jimmy Lewendon, some of which were used in Company publications.

In those days local transport observer Bernard Lewenden lived by the King George V pub on the London Road in High Wycombe, noting that for one hour between noon and 1pm on a weekday there were 16 buses passing towards town and 17 the other way! This frequency was made up of a combination of TV Routes 20 (High Wycombe – Windsor), 25 (High Wycombe – Flackwell Heath) and 42 (West Wycombe – Loudwater), *London Transport* Routes 441 (High Wycombe – Staines) and 455 (Uxbridge – High Wycombe), *Green Line Coaches* Route 711 (High Wycombe – Reigate) and *City of Oxford* X8 express route (Oxford – London).

During September consideration was given to the fact that buses might be expected to replace trains should the Lamborn Valley line be closed. It was considered that out-stationing at Lambourn would need to be increased to 8 vehicles, preferably at the station yard, but protracted dealings with the railways over who would fund surfacing improvements rumbled on. Up in town, congestion around Victoria Coach Station led to the Metropolitan Police insisting that laid-over coaches be parked further afield, so TV and SM ones were changed from Ebury Square to Lombard Street, some 2.5 miles away in Battersea, with effect from 16th October.

Another long-serving employee died on 20th October, when Miss Chitty did so after 30 years service, the last 15 as the General Manager's Secretary.

On a brighter note, the Nation looked forward to the following year and the Festival of Britain, conceived to give the population a boost after all the years of austerity and sacrifice. The main focus of attention was the rejuvenated South Bank of the Thames in London, though there were also touring exhibitions and many localised events too. This would therefore be a very busy year for TV and its subsidiaries, both on the coaching front and the London express routes. As part of the local publicity, Bristol L6B/Windover coach 550 (FMO 25) was fitted out as a mobile travel exhibition, embarking on a publicity tour on 27th October and spending a number of days at Reading, Maidenhead, Marlow and High Wycombe.

The increased capacity of the Bristol LL-type made them a popular choice for the longer trunk routes, and Car 566 (FMO 948) was sent to Crowthorne Dormy Shed to cover Route 3, and it is seen approaching the Camberley terminus

No new vehicles arrived in October, but November saw further Bristol LL6B/ECW B39R Cars 560-4 (FMO 942-6) delivered, along with ECW L27/28R-bodied Bristol KS6B's 589-94 (FMO 971-6). Car 560 joined similar buses at Newbury, whereas 561-3 were

Maidenhead's first 30-footers, and Car 564 initially was placed at Reading. Of the double-deckers, Reading also received 590/4, whilst Cars 592/3 went to Maidenhead and 589/91 went to High Wycombe.

Car 594 (FMO 976) was one of the Bristol KS6B's on the Reading allocation and in seen a couple of years later in Northbrook Street, Newbury, after Route 5b had been extended through from Yattendon. The KS had a prominent dash below the cab window as part of the additional overall length.

A new addition to the Service Vehicle fleet was the GM's replacement car, a Ford 'Pilot' V8 (FDP 101), which was generally driven by Mr. Hawtin who acted as part-time chauffeur and part-time garage hand, as Mr. Balls preferred usually not to drive. His erstwhile car, Wolseley 8hp (ELX 440) was duly disposed of in August 1951.

Work on the project to turn the 'ugly duckling' 'Tiger' PS1 coach into something more elegant started with the disposal of the old body in November. This was the last example of a body being sold separately by TV and, although offered to staff at £30 (inclusive of delivery to an accessible site), there were no takers and it went for scrap for a tenner to the same yard at Darby Green that had saved embarrassment over the TD1's and little Morris lorries the year before. The chassis was taken to Reading Works and extended, which raised the question of whether it should be registered as new. TV naturally favoured treating it as new, but Berkshire CC Licensing disagreed, and Leyland even offered to produce new chassis plates if that helped! On 13th November the body for the AEC 'Regal' IV chassis was discussed at Duple of Hendon, the style being the centre-door 'Ambassador'.

Due to rising postwar costs of materials and fuel, a general fares increase came in on 17th November, but this caused some problems as half-pence fares could not be shown on the Setright Machines, so pre-printed tickets for that amount were issued as a supplement.

We have not heard much of the Leyland 'Beaver' tankers for a time, but they were working away on a daily basis, and at November 1950 those based at East Ham were No.5 (ABL 769, Driver Withers) and No.7 (ABL 770, Driver Smith), whilst those at Coley Goods Yard were No.9 (ABL 771, Driver Shaw) and No.11 (ABL 772, Driver Wyeth). The East Ham ones went to Maidenhead for servicing and those at Coley went to Reading Works.

During December further Bristol LL6B/ECW B39R buses arrived as Cars 565-9 (FMO 947 -51), of which 565/6 (plus 564 already in service) were sent to work at Crowthorne Dormy Shed as replacements for L6A-types 484-6 (DMO 688-90) on busy Route 3. Cars 567-9 were allocated to Maidenhead and mainly used on Route 22 and other workings where low bridges in the Slough area precluded the use of double-deckers.

Bristol LL6B Car 569 (FMO 951) on Route 22a.

In December a start was made on increasing the seating capacity of the 472-86 batch of Bristol L6A's, all of which had been received as DP31R, this being increased to seat the standard 35. The remaining KS-types (595-600) were receiving special bodies at ECW, so the next to arrive were Cars 601-3 (FMO 983-5), which were the first 8-ft wide Bristol KSW's for TV, 601 being the first 'decker of that width to leave Lowestoft on 15th December. 601/2 went to High Wycombe and 603 to Maidenhead, the trio often being seen on Route 20 (High Wycombe – Windsor).

TV buses were drafted in to cover operational problems on the Marlow- Bourne End railway and were in use from 26th December until 8th January 1951. With the expansion in area during 1950 the fleet now totalled 313 vehicles, which ran 11,776,479 miles and had carried 48,571,874 passengers. This represented an increase of 300% passengers, but only 62% in mileage and 33% in the total vehicles owned.

1951

No doubt as the result of recent contact between the Engineers of the respective concerns, some exchanges of vehicles took place between the *Wilts & Dorset*-controlled *Venture* fleet and TV's *Newbury & District* from 1st January 1951. All of the Guy buses that had been sent to the Basingstoke operator were transferred to N&D, comprising of a pair of 1943 'Arab' Mk11 5LW's which had been re-bodied in 1950 with Park Royal H30/26R bodies, originally in the *Red & White* fleet (EWO490/2, *Venture* Nos.100/1), which became N&D Nos. 173/4, plus a quartet of Duple H31/26R-bodied 'Arab' Mk111 6LW's received during May and June 1950 as *Venture* 103-6 (HOT 391-4), which became N&D Nos.175-8. A fifth member of the latter order had, of course, already reached the Newbury fleet direct as No.172 (FMO 517) during the previous May.

Above: Incoming Guy 'Arab' No.106 (HOT 394) seen on the Newbury to Oxford route. The advert for Simonds Beer was actually in place before the transfer, and note also that these buses received N&D fleetnames. Below: Outgoing AEC 'Regent' No.151 (EJB 521) seen later in Wilts & Dorset livery.

Venture had been originally due two further AEC 'Regent' double-deckers which had been diverted to N&D. No. 159 (HAD 745), which had also had a spell

More conventional fleet additions included Car 571 (FMO 953) seen at the Frogmoor parking ground between journeys on Wycombe Local Service 33.

in the *Cheltenham District* fleet, was passed to *Venture* when *Thames Valley* took control of the Newbury company a year previously, and that was now finally joined by No.151 (EJB 521), which meant that only single-deck AEC's were now in stock within the wider TV empire, whilst the Guys were added to those already delivered during wartime or inherited from N&D.

During January further Bristol LL6B's with ECW B39R bodies were delivered as Cars 570/1/3-5 (FMO 952/3/5-7), which were split between High Wycombe (570/1), and Maidenhead (573-5), and at each location their higher seating capacity saw them displace L-type 35-seater on intensive local services, which in turn were cascaded to replace withdrawn Leyland saloons. Indeed, 1951 was an unprecedented year for vehicle disposals, with a grand clear-out of old Leylands and the weeding out of the less-good N&D stock, and we will return to that subject a little later on.

A new 'THAMES VALLEY' sign was affixed to the front wall of the Reading Garage overlooking the yard in Lower Thorn Street during January, whilst discussions continued on the subjects of the coaching station at Maidenhead and a bus station at Reading. Plans for the new joint Rail/Road Enquiry Office in Stations Square, Reading were well advanced, though Driver Welch's attempt at a summary demolition of the old wooden structure, using Leyland 'Tiger' TS7 Car 268 (JB 5847) during February was nonetheless not entirely appreciated!

Basil Sutton recorded that 2 of the 1939 Harrington-bodied 'Tiger' TS8 coaches were given Leyland oil engines during January, but details of these are not known. All duly became oilers, so this seems to marks the start of a programme to convert the entire batch.

The AEC 'Regal' MkIV chassis was taken to Duple Motor Bodies at Hendon on 19th February, whilst the

Route 21 out to Woodlands Park served housing estates developed in post war years, also passing through Maidenhead's suburbs Boyn Hill and Cox Green. Car 574 (FMO 956) is seen in original form at the Maidenhead Bus Station.

now lengthened chassis of Car 169 went to ECW at Lowestoft on the 27th, the intention being to have both coaches added to the strength in time for what was going to be a very busy Summer. On the other hand, *South Midland* Leyland 'Tiger' TS3 No.28 (JO 1597), which had been withdrawn before the takeover, was finally disposed of that month.

The other new deliveries for January were the eagerly-awaited Bristol KS6B's with 'special' ECW bodies for use on Route B between Reading and London. The layout was CL27/26RD, and the bodies featured coach seating, rear doors, extra luggage space, and heaters (a feature not then standard on new buses!). As double-deckers were needed throughout on the busy service, these much improved passenger comfort over the bus bodies previously employed.

Bristol KS6B Car 596 (FMO 978) as new. Photos of these buses appeared throughout the Trade Press.

Cars 595-600 (FMO 977-82) were indeed very nicely appointed, and soon took up their duties on Route B, all being nominally allocated to Reading, though two were outstationed overnight at Samuelson's Garage in Victoria. Those Bristol K-types previously employed on the route were cascaded to oust older Bristol types, which in turn replaced the newer Leyland double-deckers, leading to further withdrawals of earlier 'Titans' during the year. As the year progressed, the Colonnade yard became the resting place of many a withdrawn bus, and a number were cannilbised as spare parts became scarcer, some losing headlamps, radiators or even engines.

On 30th January a derailment of a train in the Bracknell Station area resulted in a request to provide a shuttle service between there and Reading. Buses were run from 6.50am to 9.50am, covering 217 miles and conveying 658 passengers before the situation was rectified.

The inside of the London KS's featured coach seats and luggage racks above the nearside windows.

Seen on a wet day at Victoria Coach Station, Car 597 (FMO 979) has now received the painted adverts for Huntley & Palmer's Biscuits, and it was the practice for the London route buses to have painted adverts for a number of years.

During February the final pair of 7ft 6in wide saloons on order was received as Bristol LL6B/ECW B39R Cars 572/6 (FMO 954/8), the former going to High Wycombe and the latter to Maidenhead. A start was made on disposals that month, with 'Titan' TD1 Cars 200/2 (RX 5562/4) departing, along with 'Tiger' TS7 Car 299 (JB 7499). The latter went to *Reliance* over at Brightwalton, together with a spare set of seats, both items seeing further service.

Buses disposed of by Thames Valley often returned to the area whilst working for showman, but use for public service was a rarity locally. Former Car 330 (ABL 760), a 1937 ECW-bodied 'Tiger' TS7 was an exception, and is seen at Newbury Wharf awaiting departure on Reliance Motor Services Brightwalton route, repainted in brown and cream livery.

Heavier inroads into the Leyland ranks were made during March, marking the demise of 'Lion' LT2 Car 54 (RX 6248), 'Tiger' TS4 Car 245 (RX 9699), 'Tiger' TS7 Cars 265/9 (JB 5844/8), 296/8 (JB 7496/8), 302 (JB 8341) and 327 (ABL 757), as well as 'Tiger' TS8 Car 377 (BBL 563). 'Tiger' TS7 Cars 268/70 (JB 5847/9) also departed around this time, though the dates are not recorded. Over at Newbury,

the trio of former *South Midland* 'Tiger' TS7 coaches 166-8 (CWL 953, BWL 349 and CWL 951) were also finally retired, having spent most of the previous year back working for their original owner. Also from the Newbury stable, the priority was to clear the hybrid AEC 'Regal' 0642/5LW's with 1936 bodies, with February seeing the departure of Car 123 (FS 8562), followed during March by Cars 122/4-30 (FS 8560/67/76/72/66/74/75/65).

The prototype Bristol 'Lodekka' LDX-type seen after being sent onto Westcliff-on-Sea for evaluation. Note the trolleybus overhead wiring for the Southend fleet. and also the chrome-plated radiator and coach-style front bumper.

A highlight of early March was the loan of the 'Lodekka' prototype from Bristol Commercial Vehicles, the example supplied being the one wearing *Bristol Omnibus* livery and bearing its fleet no. C5000 (LHY 949). This revolutionary bus design, second only to the Leyland 'Titan' in the development of the lowheight double-decker, used an offset transmission, which allowed a flat floor in the upper saloon whilst retaining an overall low height. It was collected from previous trial with *Red & White,* a Newbury-based driver being sent to Chepstow (as presumably he'd been there before!), on 3rd March. After initial inspection and attention to a gearbox problem at Reading, it was set to work on the busy Route 2 (Reading – Ascot – Windsor) for two weeks. On 18th March it was collected by a driver from *Eastern National* for evaluation there and with the associated *Westcliff* fleet as it continued its extensive tour.

New deliveries for March were now to the revised 8ft width, as Bristol LWL6B/ECW B39R Cars 577-85 (FMO 959-67), and these were shared between Reading (580-5) and High Wycombe (577-9). It should be noted that, in order to distinguish between these very similar models of seven-and-a-half-footers and the eight-footers, the latter were supplied with white steering wheels, important since certain routes had restrictions against the use of the wider buses.

Car 577 (FMO 959) was put to work on the busy former Marlow & District Route 28 (Reading – Marlow – Henley – Twyford - Reading) and is passing through Marlow. The white steering can also be seen.

The Service Vehicle fleet was not neglected, with a new Bedford 10/12cwt Depot Van for Reading as No.31 (GJB 552). As a result of this the 1929 Austin 7hp Van No.6 (RX 3755) finally left in April, having seen a number of guises over its long career, originally as a Staff Car, converted for wartime servicing of gas trailers, then refurbished as the post - war Publicity Department runabout! The sale of this vehicle was again offered through the Staff Bulletin.

The early post-war period saw the railways considering the abandonment of a number of local branch lines in favour of replacement bus services, culminating as it did in the infamous 'Beeching Report'. And so it was that the replacement of the Watlington – Princes Risborough line was discussed by representatives of the Railway Executive, *Thames Valley* and *City of Oxford* during early 1951.

On the subject of joint participation, the Road/River Tours were again offered for the Summer months, but the ticket system became even more complicated! All agents were issued with colour-coded tickets, with yellow for steamer out and bus back, blue for bus out and steamer back, green for bus – steamer – bus, and pink for bus – steamer two ways – bus! Conductors had to issue the appropriate bus fare ticket and keep a portion of the ticket to go with the day's waybill. On another scheme introduced for that year, 'Holidays at Home', holidaymakers were encouraged to use the services of London Coastal Coaches express coach network for days out, e.g. coach to Henley, steamer to Boulters Lock and bus to catch coach at Maidenhead.

The only new vehicles received during April were an Austin A40 car (GJB 729) for the Accountant based at Reading, and a Vauxhall 'Velox' car (GJB 786) for the Traffic Manager, each of their old cars being initially cascaded for further use.

From 1st May a number of TV buses were sold to N&D (for a nominal £1 each), but unlike previous transfers these received fleet numbers in the Newbury series and *Newbury & District* fleetnames, as follows:

TV No.	Reg. No.	N&D No.	Type
342	AJB 814	179	Leyland 'Tiger' TS7
344	AJB 816	180	Leyland 'Tiger' TS7
372	BBL 558	181	Leyland 'Tiger' TS8
346	AJB 818	182	Leyland 'Tiger' TS7
379	BBL 565	183	Leyland 'Tiger' TS8
333	ABL 763	184	Leyland 'Tiger' TS7
343	AJB 815	185	Leyland 'Tiger' TS7
368	ARX 990	186	Leyland 'Tiger' TS8
420	CJB 139	187	Guy 'Arab' 1 5LW

1938 ECW-bodied Leyland 'Tiger' TS8 in its new role as Newbury & District Car 183 (BBL 565) and seen at the Wharf Bus Station in Newbury.

Bristol LL6B Car 576 (FMO 958) is seen turning into the Reading Stations Square terminus of Route 3 from Camberley. This photo was taken a few years after delivery, hence the white fleet numbers and Aldershot & District saloon in the background.

This rear view of Bristol LL6B Car 560 (FMO 942) shows off the typical style of the Eastern Coach Works bodies of the period, with conductor-operated sliding rear door, full-width rear window and destination apertures. For some reason, adverts for tobacco often featured on these saloons.

The Summer of 1951 was to be a busy time for the Nation as a whole, and *Thames Valley* would be no exception. It was also the first time that all the *South Midland* and *Newbury & District* operations were included in the timetable book, which as a result was expanded from 168 to 188 pages! Looking back through that book, it was indeed the zenith of travel by bus and, surely if the residents of those places were to see it now, they might well wonder what the past 50 years has really achieved? Indeed, even in the remoter parts of the TV network, services linked virtually every village to towns, many of the routes owing their origins to the Country Carriers or local pioneer bus operators.

Apart from the actual timetables, the booklets also provide such information as parcel agents, the market days in the district and hints for days out, whilst one can sense the fun had in the Publicity Office thinking up those little slogans to fill the odd gaps on pages –

my favourite being '*an umbrella in the hand is worth two in the lost property office*'!

During April a further decimation of older types took place, some having not seen use for a number of months, with Leyland 'Titan' TD1's 203/4/7/8 (RX 5565/6/9/70), 219 (RX6110), 222/3 (RX 6242/3) and 237 (RX 8170) all sold off, along with 'Tiger' TS4 Car 246 (RX 9700). May saw only one departure, that being 'Tiger' TS8 Car 347 (AJB 819).

However, the Nation's main focus that year was on the Festival of Britain, which opened on Thursday 3rd May, which coincidently was the author's birthday! The festival had been contrived to cheer the populace up after all the years of war and austerity, offering hope for a future of progress and modernity. The main focus was the South Bank of the Thames, where the former bombsite had been re-constructed as a complex of modern concert halls and galleries, of which the Royal Festival is perhaps the best known. Apart from the main event opened by King George VI, there were other local and national events, all of which certainly boosted coaching work that year. As *Thames Valley* and *South Midland* already had express routes into London, loadings were enhanced, whilst there were numerous excursions to the South Bank Exhibition, the Naval Review at Spithead and other events, so the coach fleet was very busy. This period also marks when it became necessary at times to provide double-deck reliefs on London Route A, as the Bristol L-type coaches could not cope. The F-o-B logo could be seen on all Booking Offices, whilst the Lower Thorn Street Offices were decorated with flags and bunting stored since the 1937 Coronation.

Interior of the Colonnade Booking Office, which was kept busy throughout 1951, with excursion bookings, tickets for Associated Motorways coach network and the South Midland extended tours.

The one fly in the ointment was that the new coach body of Leyland 'Tiger' PS1 Car 169 (LWL 995) was not completed in time for the opening of the Festival, being collected from Lowestoft on 6th June, complete with *Newbury & District* fleetnames!

The ugly duckling turns into a swan! Car 169 (LWL 995) resplendent with its new Eastern Coach Works 8ft-wide body seen by the River Thames at Caversham Promenade. The body was of the same style as being constructed on Bristol LWL-type chassis, though in this case the Leyland radiator remained exposed. The radiator is seen decorated with the Festival of Britain logo and Union Jacks, whilst the cream livery was relieved by red mudguards and radiator grille.

There was, however, continued disappointment over the body for the underfloor-engined AEC 'Regal' IV chassis, as no progress at all had been made with it, so Duple accepted cancellation of the order on 16th May. As there were already some underfloor-engined Bristol coaches in the pipeline, the AEC chassis was added to that order at ECW, though delivery was now scheduled for March 1952! The chassis was collected from Hendon on 21st May and taken to Lowestoft two days later.

A notable retirement took place on 24th May, when the Tyre Repairer Mr. T. Cserwenka finally hung up his vulcanising kit at the age of 74! He had been in the Company's employ for 36 years and, along with Basil Sutton, had been instrumental in taking TV's tyre policy to near cult status. The Company efforts had resulted in mileages achieved well above comparable concerns, the secret being accuracy of records and the frequent inspection and timely repair of tyres. Early contact with the fledgling operator had actually stemmed from the fact that Cserwenka had originally been gardener to Emile Garcke, whilst the family tradition had continued when his son became the tyre man at Maidenhead Garage, latterly working on behalf of Firestone Tyres. He duly replaced his father at Reading Garage with effect from 8th December.

With the death of the Assistant Foreman Mr, J.J. Metcalfe, his place was taken by Mr. J.F. Dickenson in May, whilst his former position of Charge Hand passed to Bob Elder.

As though the Summer was not busy enough, the first takeover of an independent operator for some years took place on 1st June, with part of the business of R.E. Jackson based in St. Andrews Crescent, Windsor and trading as *Crescent Coaches*. The purchase was a joint venture with *London Transport*, who took over the Windsor – Slough service, whilst *Thames Valley* acquired the Slough – Cippenham route. TV's share was £6750, which also included 5 vehicles, the latter being a fairly rum collection which were not operated.

Two of the former Jackson Bedford buses await their fates in the Colonnade yard. Despite their rather indifferent condition some found further PSV owners.

68

Windsor had, in earlier times, hosted numerous independent operators, but most had succumbed to either Thames Valley or London Transport. Bristol KSW6B Car 603 (FMO 985) works a' short' on Route 20 to Dedworth inherited from the Pixey Bus Service as it passes Wren's ornate Guildhall building.

The vehicles acquired from Jackson were as follows:

Reg. No.	Chassis	Bodywork	New
JB 7289	Bedford WLB	Duple C20F	10/35
JB 9860	Bedford WTB	Duple B26F	8/36
BJB 580	Bedford WTB	Duple C20F	10/38
CRX 333	Bedford OWB	Duple UB26F	1/45
EBL 967	Bedford OB	Mulliner B26F	12/47

All of the above were disposed of within the same month, whilst the service became TV Route 62. Route number 61 had already been earmarked for a new service starting with the Summer timetable on 16th June, operating between Summerleaze Road in Maidenhead and Pinkneys Green (Waggon & Horses) by way of Ray Mill Road West, Bridge Avenue, King Street, Marlow Road Corner, All Saints Avenue and Sealeys Stores.

Other timetable changes at that time saw some journeys on Route 35 (High Wycombe – Downley) extended onto Downley Common, whilst Wycombe local Route 42 was extended to run through Booker Hill Estate, then re-emerging onto New Road.

As already noted, the elegant suspension bridge over the River Thames between Bisham on the Berkshire bank and Marlow on the Buckinghamshire side, had long been subject to weight restrictions, something that had a played a significant part in shaping the erstwhile *Marlow & District* operations, and indeed had caused TV to purchase special smaller buses.

From time to time significant works were required in order to keep the bridge safe, which meant that the bus service over the bridge could not run. There was of course also Route 60, which joined Maidenhead and Marlow by way of Bourne End, but that was a relatively long way round and only had two return trips per day. A restriction came into force in June 1951, resulted in Route 18 having to terminate in Bisham at Quarry Wood Road, passengers having to walk over the bridge. At the time no one seemed to know how long the restriction might remain in place, so it is perhaps rather surprising that the trio of little Leyland 'Cubs', Cars 337/8 (ABL 767/8) and 411 (FM 7455), survived the general cull of older types during the year. Even the Bedford OB Cars 437/8 (CRX 546/7) had only odd relief runs to occupy them during that time. Also the school children for Borlaise School in West Street had to walk over the bridge, but that had been the case ever since a double-deck had been necessary, whilst those from the High Wycombe area were luckier, as their 'special' used the Quoiting Square lay-over point near to the school.

Leyland 'Cub' KPZ2-type Car 338 at Maidenhead.

Apart from the express services *South Midland* had also developed, under *Red & White* management, a selection of extended tours. These continued to be expanded under *Thames Valley* control, whilst there were also new ventures such as joint operation on links to the South Coast with *Southdown* and *East Kent*. However, as David Flitton's excellent book on *South Midland* fully covers all aspects of that concern's history, the reader is recommended to read the full account, as from this point only fleet details will be included within this volume.

Despite heavy inroads into the 'Tiger' TS7's some of the older examples survived, such as 1935 Car 266 (JB 5845) seen in late 1951 at Slough Station.

Bus crews invariably got to know their regular passengers, and in some cases the entire population of smaller locations, so a letter published in the Staff Bulletin of June 1951 is worthy of note. A blind man who usually travelled from his home in Hurst to work in the Orts Road area of Reading, had contacted the Company to thank the bus crews for kind assistance over the past 3 years. This had come about after crews had noticed his absence and called at the cottage to check if he was alright. As it was, his landlady could confirm he was actually taking a holiday, but the incident served to highlight the level of care, and also the good general practices like assisting the young and elderly passengers across the road were also praised.

With the Summer timetable of 16th June and general pressure on London Route A, it had been hoped to field the additional double-deck coaches, but delivery had been delayed. In the meantime, other double-deck deliveries were pressed into use, which resulted in yet another flurry of newer Leylands resuming full-day turns on some of the longer routes. The Windover-bodied Bristol L6B coaches previously on the route, Cars 487-91 (EJB 209-13) were overhauled and re-assigned to the coaching fleet, with 487 going to High Wycombe, 488 to Ascot and the remainder going to Reading.

'Titan' TD5 Car 369 (ARX 992) on Route 4a loads with Holt girls in Wokingham's Broad Street under the watchful eye of the Inspector Shackleford.

The allocation of a coach at Ascot started a trend that persisted for some years, as it seems that quite a lot of private hire emanated from that area. Apart from that, space in the other garages was at a premium, and Ascot had both the facilities and the geographical position to make it a useful roosting place.

Over at Oxford the Service Vehicle fleet required renewal, so in June 1951 a Bedford 10/12cwt van (RWL 71) and a Vauxhall 'Wyvern' car (RWL 72) were delivered. Apparently the van was later given the number 35, though no one apparently noticed that TV already had a lorry with that number, so later still it was re-numbered as 27 (after the original vehicle bearing that number was sold in August 1956!). These vehicles resulted in the disposal of the 1938 Austin car (EUW 584) and 1939 Morris 8hp car (EGK 623).

Another shot of ECW-bodied 'Titan' TD5 Car 369 (ARX 992) at Reading Stations on relief duties.

Only one new service bus arrived during June, Bristol KSW6B/ECW L27/28R Car 634 (GJB 272), followed by identical Cars 635/6 (GJB 273/4) in July. These went one apiece to Newbury, Maidenhead and Wycombe respectively, the Newbury one representing that garage's first 8ft wide double-decker.

The first completely new 30ft long coaches were on Bristol LWL6B chassis with ECW 'Queen Mary' style fully-fronted bodies. Car 608 (GBL 872) is seen on an outing, the livery was cream with maroon mudguards.

The real show-stealer for June was the re-bodied PS1-type Leyland 'Tiger' inherited through *South Midland* and rebuilt to 30ft long. The new body was to that full length and also to 8ft width, though the chassis was still at 7ft 6ins, and the body was the same style as the Bristol LWL shown above, though the radiator was still exposed. Car 169 (LWL 995) returned to Newbury, where the staff had a great pride in it, and it enjoyed a long and interesting career.

The interior of one of the LWL coaches, showing the clean lines and monogrammed headrest covers. The seating for only 35 made these comfortable vehicles.

Delivery of the Bristol LWL6B coaches was a little later than desired, as they only arrived in July as Cars 607/8 (GBL 871/2) and the rest in August as Cars 609-12 (GBL 873-6). These were allocated to Reading

(610-2), to Maidenhead (609), and Desborough Road (607/8). Not long after they had been delivered a number of rear tyre fires occurred on similar coaches in other fleets, so the rear wheel arches were modified to allow tyres better ventilation.

A pair of 1929 Leyland 'Titan' TD1's, Cars 184/7 (RX 4346/9) were give a reprieve and re-licensed for 3rd July and used on relief work, as already noted there had been a need to put some Bristol double-deckers on the London A Route. Also during July or August the London-based Petrol Tankers were re-located to the yard of Mr. E.L. Berry at 139 Ranelagh Road, East Ham, London E6. During July 'Tiger' TS4 Car 255 (RX 9709) was sold, followed by TS7 Car 311 (JB 8350) in August. At this time it was still commonplace for showmen to buy old buses for use as living vans, and *Thames Valley* had, through Basil Sutton, earned a good reputation amongst that group as providing well-maintained vehicles for that use.

The slightly older Bristol L6B coaches were also kept busy, and Car 553 (FMO 935) is seen on Marine Drive in Brighton. These stylish coaches were indeed kept busy, but ultimately their appearance became dated, resulting in them being rebuilt and rebodied as service saloons in due course.

Some of the 'Happy Ascot' crews of the day, with left to right back row: Tommy Watson, Bert Smith, Norman Lovejoy, Peter Sargeant, -?- Ritch, Inspector Frank Williams, George Johnson, Sherly Hall (at rear), Peggy Turner and Inspector Arthur 'Nobby' Clarke; front row left to right: Mick Hoptroff, Freddie Hitchins, Johnny Reader, Irving Chapman and Bert Woods. Peggy was a 'clippie' for 16.5 years and married another Hoptroff driver in 1954. Bert Woods later became an Inspector. Note the L coach behind.

From 31st August Mr. C.E. Lewis became Assistant Traffic Superintendent for No.2 Area, taking the place of Mr. F.H.H. Robinson who had resigned. During September it was agreed to set up a temporary enquiry office in the Southern Railway yard at Reading and for the demolition of the old wooden one. Once the new joint road/rail office was ready, the building would then become a staff canteen.

It was also agreed that an inspection pit would be constructed in the Ascot Garage workshop area, which helped keep that garage largely self-sufficient. Ascot was also noted for its 'family feel', as a lot of the crews went back to the large expansion of 1924, and many were related to each other by family or marriage. 'Newcomers' Peter Sargeant and Norman Lovejoy both joined around this time, and both have recalled the excellent spirit that existed there, though Norman did leave the regular bus work to drive the coaches of *S.R. Gough (Gough's Garage)*, over in Bracknell in due course. The very active Social Club was an essential element of this camaraderie, such activities at *Thames Valley* never suffering from any demarcation between the ranks. Activities ranged from darts to horticultural, Ascot being particularly competitive over the latter, whilst the bowls section flourished under captaincy of Ernest Jeffries, No.2 Area's Superintendent and originally at Marlow.

The wartime restrictions had certainly left the public hungry for travel, so a joint road/rail outing on Sunday 2nd September saw 62 passengers taken to Oxford by train, where they decanted to a pair of *South Midland* coaches for a tour to Bourton-on-the-Water and back.

The *Newbury & District* conductors had new Setright Ticket Machines in place of the Automaticket Machines on 10th September, whilst the Board agreed that all the Setright Machines then on hire from the manufacturer would be purchased. It should be noted that maintaining these machines was quite a task, with fairly frequent overhauls being required. It is even said that some devious conductors could disassemble one, turn back the register wheels and profit as a result, but they have only been canteen chatter! On another tact, the Company now decided to pay Conductors commission of 1 shilling and 6 pence for each dozen timetable booklets sold. Although the enlarged issue of Summer 1951 stayed at 6 pence, the following issue was charged at 9 old pence.

At the western end of the Thames Valley area, the old N&D Enquiry Office in the ancient granary building at The Wharf remained the public focus of operations.

With the Summer over, September saw further inroads into the ranks of elderly Leylands, with the demise of 'Titan' TD1's 201/6 (RX 5563/8), 221 (RX 6112) and 234 (RX 8167), along with 'Lion' LT2's 46 and 50 (RX 6245/6). During October TD1's 199 (RX 5561) and 232 (RX 8165) followed, along with 'Tiger' TS4 250 (RX 9704), plus 'Tiger' TS7 294 (JB 7494). TS4 Cars 247/56 (RX 9701/10) followed in November, whilst the N&D fleet also lost older types during this period. October saw the last of the Bedford OWB's 94-6 (CMO 523/624/657), plus the final AEC 'Regal' 5LW-engined 0642-type Car 121 (FS 8582), along with other rebuilt 'Regals' 153-5 (AGX 455, TG 1819 and AGP 841).

There were still a number of N&D vehicles in the Red & White style livery in 1951, though repaints would see the fleet gradually assimilate into the TV scheme with a couple of years. Duple-bodied Guy 'Arab' III Car 170 (FMO 515) is seen at The Wharf.

TV's own Guys were still kept busy on high-capacity local services in Maidenhead and High Wycombe, and Car 419 (CJB 138) is seen at Maidenhead.

Despite the heavy depletions of Leyland vehicles during the year, a number were still active, and the revised working arrangements from 22nd September provides an interesting snapshot of the duties they were being used on:

Two of the surviving Leylands at Slough, with 'Tiger' TS8 coach 388 (BMO 987) and 'Tiger' TS7 saloon 324 (ABL 754) on the former Crescent Coaches route.

Double-deck Leylands based at Reading –

No.	Seating	Duties
3	L52R	Reliefs, Mondays to Saturdays
3	L51R	Reliefs, Mondays to Saturdays
4	L48R	Reliefs, Mondays to Saturdays
5	L51R	Contracts TV1 to 5*

* TV1, TV2, TV4 and TV5 all Reading - Aldermaston
TV3 Reading – Bramley (Cohen's)

Double-deck Leylands based at Maidenhead -

No.	Seating	Duties
2	L51R	Reliefs, Mondays to Saturdays
2	L48R	Reliefs, Mondays to Saturdays
1	L48R	Route 22 Maidenhead – Slough

Double-deck Leylands based at Newbury -

No.	Seating	Duties
3	L51R	Reliefs, Mondays to Saturdays
2	L51R	Contracts to AWRE Aldermaston

Single-deck Leylands based at Reading –

No.	Seating	Duties
1	B35R	Route 9a Reading – Tadley
5	B32R	Reliefs, Mondays to Saturdays
1	B35R	Reliefs, Saturdays, otherwise spare

Single-deck Leylands based at Maidenhead –

No.	Seating	Duties
2	B32R	Route 17 Maidenhead – Henley
1	B32R	Route 21 Maidenhead – Waltham St. Lawrence
1	C33F	Route 60 M'h – Bourne End – Marlow
1	B32R	Route 61 M'h – Pinkneys Green
2	B35R	Route 62 Slough – Cippenham
3	B32R	Reliefs, Mondays to Saturdays
3	C33F	Reliefs, Mondays to Fridays

Single-deck Leylands based at High Wycombe –

No.	Seating	Duties
1	B32R	Route 27 HW – Gt. Missenden (shorts)
1	B32R	Route 28 HW – Marlow (shorts)
1	B32R	Route 33 High Wycombe Local Service
1	B35R	Route 34 High Wycombe – Speen
1	B32R	Route 36 High Wycombe – various points
1	B32R	Route 42 West Wycombe – Loudwater
1	B32R	Route 80 High Wycombe – Aylesbury
4	B32R	Reliefs, Mondays to Saturdays
1	C33F	Reliefs, Mondays to Fridays

Single-deck Leylands based at Newbury –

No.	Seating	Duties
1	C33F	Route 113 Kintbury – Shaw Factory shorts
1	C33F	Route 114A N'b – West Woodhay (Th/Sa.)
1	C33F	Route 116 Schools and short-workings
8	B32R	Contracts from Newbury*

* Contracts 944/87 Kintbury – Didcot, 944/85 N'b Wharf – Milton A, 944/79 N'b Wharf – Milton B, 944/68 N'b Wharf – Didcot A, 944/86 N'b Wharf – Didcot B, NC/1 Camp Close – Harwell, NC/2 Henwick Lane – Harwell, NC/3 N'b Regal - Harwell

Single-deck Leylands based at Outstations (in bold) –

No.	Seating	Duties
2	B32R	Contract 944/87 **Lambourn** – Harwell
1	C33F	Contract 944/68 **West Ilsley** -Didcot

One of the Bristol LWL6B's, Car 614 (GJB 252) is seen in later years in Hambleden in typical Chiltern village scenery as served by routes in the High Wycombe area. Route 37 ran from the latter to Henley and buses were outstationed at Fingest Dormy Shed.

As coaches were delicensed for the Winter, the initial batch of Bristol L6B's with Windover and Vincent bodies had their rear seat modified to take 5 persons to increase the overall seating capacity to 33 in line with the later batches.

Bristol KSW6B Car 645 (GJB 284) at Reading for the busy Route 2 to Windsor via Wokingham and Ascot.

October saw the replacement van for the Publicity Department take the road as No.33 (GMO 943), an Austin A40 based at Reading.

A further pair of Bristol LWL6B/ECW B39R saloons entered service in October as Cars 613/4 (GJB 251/2), and both were allocated to Reading. Standard Bristol KSW6B/ECW L27/28R double-deckers also received

were Cars 640-2 (GJB 278-80), all of which were sent to Ascot as the start of replacing the Strachans utility-bodied Bristol K6A's which had faithfully served that garage since 1945. November saw further KSW6B's as Cars 643-7 (GJB 281-6), and all but the latter went to Ascot to continue the replacement programme, the other being sent to High Wycombe. That left only K6A Cars 433/4 (CRX 544/5) still at Ascot to cover Routes 2a and 2c between Ascot and Sunningdale. It was not, however, the end of the road for that type, as they were cascaded onto relief duties at Maidenhead and Reading, and in due course became the mainstay of the Reading contract workings.

The other Bristol KSW6B's received in October were the ECW-bodied CL27/26RD 'specials' for use on the London A Route, which became Cars 637-9 (GJB 275-7), all of which were based at Reading.

Outwardly there was little to distinguish the bodies of the 'London KSW's', other than glimpsing the higher seating. Car 637 (GJB 275) is seen leaving London.

Above: Reg Hibbert inspects the extensive damage to Car 634 on the following morning, and no doubt he had some interesting comments to make! Below: The interior of the lower deck looking forward. It was very lucky that the vehicle was only lightly loaded and no one was occupying those front offside seats.

However, the new deliveries were somewhat marred by a bad smash involving Bristol KSW Car 634 (GJB 272) on 11th October, the bus having only been sent as new to Newbury in June (and not even having received adverts yet). The incident occurred on the Bath Road approaching Thatcham from Newbury at 9.15pm, after the driver decided to overtake and collided with a lorry coming from the opposite direction. The driver admitted to being at fault, a fact that haunted him throughout his otherwise careful and long service with the Company. Apparently ever since the advent of the 1939 Bristol K5G's, with their 5th 'overdrive' gear, the crews on Route 10 between Reading and Newbury had become accustomed to bowling along the Bath Road, particularly during wartime when other traffic was much less. However, that famous road remained the main arterial route to the west, and since the war ended had become very busy again. The driver's bad judgement was costly, but it was indeed fortunate that the cost was in terms of vehicular damage rather than human life. Newbury Engineer Reg Hibbert was soon on the scene, as he lived close by in Roman Way, and on the next morning the bus was taken to Reading Works. Just a fortnight later, one of the Crowthorne Shed drivers managed to hit a lorry with Bristol LL6B Car 566 (FMO 948), adding yet another bus for urgent unscheduled attention in the Works!

A further old faithful Service Vehicle was finally let go in November, when 1934 Austin Van No.8 (JB 4217) left. It had started life as a Staff Car, later being converted for use as the Engineering Department van based at Reading.

During November the purchase of land for the Coach Station at Maidenhead was finalised, and a start was made on the groundwork, the plan being for a perimeter road around an elongated oval central grass area, which was well over the size actually required but would allow further development if required. The outstanding improvements to the Bus Station nearby were also approved. The materials for the new café were now available, so that went ahead, whilst the Tilling Group architects designed a new Enquiry Office to be constructed on the east side of the staff canteen bungalow at 'Yorkstream'. Approval was also given for an extension to the east side of Maidenhead garage, though a plan to lower the floor at the Colonnade in order to take double-deckers was found to be impractical once an inspection had taken place. In December a further extension at Newbury was agreed, though the work at Maidenhead garage was actually delayed for some time as steel was still hard to obtain, and was in effect still rationed according to priority of purpose.

It is interesting to note that 5 Leyland 6-cylinder petrol engines were sold to a single purchaser during December at £6 apiece. When the engine numbers of these are examined it is found that all originated in 'Titan' TD1's converted to oil engines in the late 1930's, their petrol engines then being re-used for the 1939 'Tiger' TS8 coaches. As all the latter were with oil engines by the end of 1951, this would seem to confirm the process was completed around this time.

Car 634 after being stripped in the Reading Works to assess the extent of damage. Fortunately the typically robust Bristol chassis was unharmed, whilst the ECW composite body made repairs fairly easy to achieve.

The new café building at Maidenhead Bus Station was duly completed and was a well-lit and modern facility offering hot food and snacks from early morning to 10pm each evening. The toilet blocks were built in the wings and could be accessed from both the café and directly from the bus station. A group of Omnibus Society members are seen admiring the building on a tour of the Thames Valley, whilst 1948 Bristol L6A Car 483 (DMO 687), re-seated for normal service work awaits departure on Route 17 to Tittle Row. The site of the new Enquiry Office is behind the other bus.

At a meeting on 7th December, Mr. Wilkins of *Hants & Dorset* had informed Basil Sutton that he could supply parts that would allow the bus washing machines to be easily adapted for use by 7ft 6ins and 8ft vehicles alike. This was followed up by a visit by Messrs. Foulke and Campbell to Southampton on 14th December. The latter also returned to his old haunts at Norwich on 27th of that month, when he managed to secure seating from *Eastern Counties* to convert two Guy 'Arab' double-deckers still with wooden utility seats to red and black moquette-covered comfort, the lorry of the East Anglian operator delivering them on the following day.

Cemetery Junction, where the A329 and A4 meet to the east of Reading, was a favourite spot for bus photographer Bill Haynes, offering a variety of Company and Corporation routes, plus coaches passing through - Car 540 (FMO 15) is on Route 3a.

Mr. Woolf, the Sub-editor of Commercial Motor paid a visit to the Reading Offices on 12th December, where he interviewed officers of the Company about an article he was preparing on its activities. A proof was duly sent and after amendments formed an accurate and interesting article which appeared in the issue of 4th January 1952, painting a good overview of the area of operation and the history of the *Thames Valley's* development over 3 decades.

Still active were the 1942 ECW-bodied Bristol K5G's, and Car 415 (CJB 134) was on the Mortimer Route 9.

Consideration was still being given to improving the Works facilities in Reading, so on 29th December, Mr. Sutton and Mr. Campbell met to discuss the possible use of sites in Cardiff Road, Chester Street , Oxford Road and the Basingstoke Road with the Assistant Borough Surveyor.

As already noted, the underfloor-engined chassis was coming into vogue, so it was decided to amend the 1952 vehicle programme so that the last 5 LWL-types on order would be of the new Bristol LS (Light Saloon) instead. In respect of the other outstanding underfloor-engined coaches, discussions were held at Lydney on 10th December to see if standard ECW seat frames might be used, but the cost precluded their use.

76

1952

The issue of making fuller potential of the Colonnade premises was partly resolved in early January, when it was decided to erect a steel and timber Bodywork and Paint Shop measuring some 63ftx40ftx16ft. Also some consideration was given to the Oxford premises, as the Iffley Road garage was rather sub-standard for the purpose, even allowing for all major dockings being handled over at Newbury. Through their BTC connections Messrs. Sutton and Campbell went to view the old *London, Midland & Scottish Railway* station in Oxford, with a view to adapting it for use as a garage and coach station, particularly as it was situated between the main Oxford railway station and Gloucester Green bus station. However, as we shall soon see, other events provided a different solution.

Above: The Company offices in Frogmoor continued to be the focus for bus information, coach and tour bookings, plus the Parcels Service. Below: The Enquiry Office at Maidenhead Bus Station was a rather more modern affair, being purpose designed by the Tilling Group architects, and two of their technicians pose as customers in the doorway.

From 1st January a new Management Agreement was set up between *Thames Valley, Newbury & District* and *South Midland*, based largely on the experiences of the previous year. The SM coaches bore that title on the legal lettering panel, followed by the Reading address.

Newbury & District Guy 'Arab' MkII Car 100 (CRX 280) was still wearing the full livery of the Red & White era, but this soon began to disappear as buses were repainted into the Thames Valley scheme. Note the small headlamps supplied with these utility buses.

Those vehicles actually owned by N&D continued to carry that title on the legal lettering, followed by the Reading address, the last examples through to 1968, whilst all other allocations to Newbury carried the standard TV details. The N&D and SM Registered Office plates were affixed to the front of 83 Lower Thorn Street, making use of the old screw holes vacated by the erstwhile *Ledbury Transport* plate. The *South Midland* name continued in use throughout the next two decades, whereas the *Newbury & District* name faded as 1952 wore on and the stock of transfers was used up.

As further old N&D vehicles were withdrawn, their places were taken by standard Bristol/ECW types from the parent fleet, including K6B Car 454 (DBL 162) seen at the Wharf on Route 116 to Hungerford.

On the saloon front, some of the earlier Bristol saloons were drafted into Newbury, including 1947 L6A-type Car 458 (DBL 166), also seen laid over at The Wharf for Route 103 to Ecchinswell. Note that the side destination indicator, situated in the bay forward of the rear entrance, is already out of use.

It is perhaps a fitting tribute that the last vehicle to bear the *Newbury & District* fleetname was Car 169 (LWL 995), the re-bodied Leyland 'Tiger' PS1 coach, which was also the last Leyland in service. As the name also featured on the destination blinds, nostalgic drivers often took the opportunity to display it, which must have puzzled many a bus spotter when it roamed farther afield on *Associated Motorways* duties!

On 15th January Mr. Campbell went out with a representative of the Traffic Commissioner to see how a 30ftx8ft Bristol saloon might cope with certain of the rural routes in the Newbury area, with a view to supplying some new saloons to that location. However a similar bus had disgraced itself by colliding with the inn sign of the Iron Duke in Crowthorne High Street, so the Route Servicing Crew went out to effect repairs by way of amends. Always kept busy, the gang also dealt with repairs to Fingest and Princes Risborough Dormy Sheds that same month.

TV's Service Vehicle fleet was also called upon on 19th January, when *Kemp's Motor Services* ditched one of their AEC 'Regent' double-deckers near Hatch Gate, the pair of Ford V8 Recovery Wagons making light work of the task.

Between 18th and 24th January the 4 Guy underfloor-engined chassis were brought down from the works at Wolverhampton to the Lydney Coach Works in the Forest of Dean, where it was hoped they might be completed in time for Easter. On 23rd January an exhibition of coaches was held at Victoria in the Samuelson's Garage, where TV's Bristol KSW coach 639 (GJB 277) caused quite a lot of attention, being the only double-decker on display.

Basil Sutton attended the 29th January meeting of the Vehicle Design & Maintenance Committee held at ECW's Lowestoft works, the main feature of the event being inspection of the prototype body on the semi-chassisless Bristol LS-type underfloor-engined model. TV's own examples were to be painted cream with black mudguards, so in preparation for the 1952 season the LWL6B-type coaches 607-12 (GBL 871-6) had their mudguards repainted from red to black.

The newer AEC 'Regals' inherited from N&D were fine machines, and Car 134 (DMO 323) was seen at Winchester Coach Station on an outing in 1952.

January saw the departure of Leyland 'Tiger' TS4 Car 252 (RX 9706) and former N&D AEC 'Regal' rebuild 152 (AGJ 929), the latter being disposed of without an engine, gearbox or differential.

A little earlier, on 26th January, saw the Company as host to 30 boys from the London Section of the Ian Allan Bus Spotter's Club, and they were treated to a tour of the Reading Works. Later they were taken to Maidenhead to view the bus station, where they had a canteen lunch before the complimentary coach returned them to Reading Stations.

On the final day of January the Reading Works suffered a sad loss, when R. H. Nicholls died after an operation. He had served as a Skilled Engine Fitter at the *'Valley'* since 1936, so he had worked through the dieselisation of the late '30's, as well as the various trials and tribulations of the war years. There was a further tragedy on 6th February, when *South Midland* AEC 'Regal' coach was involved in a fatal accident with a cyclist. The speed of the coach was reported and the driver summons, though at 10.10pm other factors may have contributed to the unfortunate event?

Maidenhead's Car 649 (GJB 287) was put to work mainly on trunk routes, but when seen at Mackenzie Street in Slough it was on the busy Local Service 22b serving the housing estates of Cippenham. The KSW's gave excellent service and lasted through to the end of the '60's, some surviving longer on driver-training.

Newbury Car 648 (GJB 286) is seen soon after being delivered, working on the joint service 112 to Oxford, where it lays over at Gloucester Green Bus Station.

New buses delivered during January were further of the large batches of Bristol LWL6B/ECW B39R, Cars 615-21 (GJB 253-9), and the Bristol KSW6B's with ECW L27/28R bodies, Cars 648-50 (GJB 286-8). The saloons were split between Reading (615-7) and High Wycombe (618-21), whilst double-decker 649 went to Maidenhead and 648/50 became Newbury's first 8ft-wide buses. February saw further LWL6B saloons, as Cars 622-7 (GJB 260-5), which were shared as 622-4 to Maidenhead and 625/6 to High Wycombe.

During February internal alterations were carried out at the Company premises at 35/37/37a Frogmoor, in order to give access between the Booking Office and the Traffic Office, the premises being variously listed as 35 or 37 in Company publications!

Over at Oxford plans were being made to transfer the Oxford – High Wycombe – London express service from *United Counties* in the interests of rationalisation as it could now be covered by *South Midland*. The transfer date was set at 1st May, which would include the vehicle allocation and the garage at Botley Road, and the latter was inspected by Messrs. Campbell and Sutton on 15th February, in the company of UCOC's Chief Engineer Mr. Lindsay. On that same day Ascot garage had a bus with a gearbox fire at Cranbourne, though it should be noted that failures in service of cars based there was indeed a rare event, as Foreman Stan Tucker and his crew were a dedicated bunch.

The Bristol LWL saloons were equally hard-worked and many of them had long careers, and could be found all over the area, particularly on the varied workings from Reading. Car 584 (FMO 966) awaits departure from Station Hill on Route 5a to Chilton.

A number of TV buses, including Leyland 'Titan' TD1 Car 182 (RX 4344) and TD5-type Car 339 (AJB 811), were seen on a contract or at some special event.

By February a new daily contract had commenced between Maidenhead and the ICI Research Station at Jealotts Hill, some halfway between Maidenhead and Bracknell. For many years before, and indeed after, a number of operators had endeavoured to provide such a link to the relatively remote site with varied success.

March saw the disposal of only one bus, 'Titan' TD1 Car 205 (RX 5567), new in 1930 and rebuilt by ECW during the war years. Incoming buses that month were a further trio of Bristol LWL6B's with ECW B39R bodies, Cars 628/30/1 (GJB 266/8/9), the first going to High Wycombe and the other pair to Reading.

Fuel consumption reports from this period also confirm that no petrol-engined cars were operated. As already noted, the Marlow Bridge route could not be worked through, so the trio of Leyland 'Cubs' Cars 337/8 (ABL 767/8) and 411 (FM 7455) and Bedford OWB's 437/8 (CRX 546/7) were all in store, as were the dual-purpose bodied Bedford OB Cars 510-2 and 520 (EJB 232-4/42). As a number of the 'Tiger' TS8 coaches were active at this time, this seems to offer further proof that conversion to oilers was completed.

With snow on their roofs, Leyland 'Tiger' TS7 buses 295 (JB 7495) and 321 (ABL 751) sit in Lower Thorn Street yard, both then allocated to relief and contract duties.

During March a new Essex Bus Washing Machine was installed at Newbury Garage, Fitter Potter of Reading having been trained to undertake the work. On 3rd March all the Garage Foremen had the chance to inspect one of the Bristol LS-type chassis when it called into Reading from the Bristol works. After that it also called at *Eastern National* before completing the journey to Eastern Coach Works at Lowestoft.

However, there was some concerns over the delivery programme for the LS-types then on order for both the *Thames Valley* and *South Midland* fleets, as well as the outstanding body on the AEC 'Regal' MkIV coach entrusted to ECW, and also the quartet of Guy coaches still awaiting completion. In respect of the latter, the situation at Lydney had deteriorated to such an extent that the supervising officer sent in by ECW, who had been dispatched to oversee completion of bodies there, advised on 18th March that he was going to transfer them to the BBW works at Brislington for completion instead.

Seen at the Frogmoor parking ground, with the railway embankment in the background, is Car 517 (EJB 239), a 1949 ECW-bodied Bristol K6B-type on Route 30 to Aylesbury.

With such uncertainties regarding new coaches, it soon became evident that the Harrington-bodied TS8 'Tigers' would need to be retained for yet another season. There had recently been some contact with Mr. Wallis, the Engineer at *Hants & Dorset* over the issue of vehicle refurbishments, that operator having undertaken extensive work on its own fleet. TV asked them if they could undertake the re-trimming of these coaches, so H&D agreed to take the 6 selected for such attention, covering the seat tops and backs with blue leather and undertaking re-painting.

Another Bristol K6B, Car 518 (EJB 240), stands in the Micklefield Road side of the garage at Wycombe Marsh before embarking on the busy Local Service Route 26, which was worked jointly with Route 326 of London Transport. Note the Milward's advert placed somewhat forward on the side panels.

A programme was worked out for the TS8 coaches, with the first trio departing for Southampton on 15th April, Car 385 (BMO 984) returning on 30th April, followed by Cars 388/9 (BMO 987/8) on 2nd and 6th May. As they returned, the others were taken in their place, with Car 384 (BMO 983) returning on 8th May, then finally Cars 382/6 (BMO 981/5) came back on 12th May. All of these, plus those repainted at Reading were put in a scheme of all-over red other than the side flash which was in cream.

As delivery of the Guy coaches for Summer use now seemed unlikely, the Manager of *Red & White* had offered to loan up to four coaches from those nearing completion at Lydney, and we shall hear more of this interesting development a little later.

Indeed, there had also been some negotiations regarding the orders for Bristol LS chassis, and TV forewent 6 of the chassis due to be bodied as saloons in favour of bringing the completion of coaches for *South Midland* forward, these originally due to become Cars 71-6, though other events would change that allocation of numbers. It was also decided that the LS chassis destined to be TV's Car 686 would receive a 5-cylinder Gardner engine for evaluation, there being no Bristol alternative then available. It is also worth noting that the vehicle programme discussed in February also proposed that 8 of the 1939 Bristol K's should be re-bodied by ECW. In fact, this was never to occur, though some were rebuilt in due course.

On 27th March the TV Recovery Wagons were called upon by Mr. Evans, General Manager of *Reading Corporation,* after its AEC trolleybus 126 (ARD 689) overturned on the Oxford Road by the junction of Cranborne Gardens. One of the Fords and the 6-wheel Dodge attended, and they were further aided by an Army AEC 'Matador'. The trolley was duly righted after about 80 minutes, though it never ran again due to a twisted chassis. Only three days later the Corporation once again called for assistance, though it was only to remove a fallen tree near Tilehurst church, an easy job for one of the Fords.

As noted previously, there had been talk of replacing the trains on the *Lambourn Valley Railway* with buses, but by April it had been decided to keep the line open. The resignation of Wycombe Marsh Charge Hand E. Denton led to his replacement by G. Pitfield from 26th April, whilst during that month it was agreed to issue the Petrol Tanker Drivers with full *Thames Valley* uniform.

Windover-bodied Bristol L6B coach 546 (FMO 21) is seen on a private hire to carry the Sainsbury Singers to an event.

1952 is regarded as the peak year for passenger travel by bus and coach in the UK. Although the number of rail passengers had remained basically static at 1938 volumes, bus and coach travel accounted for 75% of all land travel mileage. To meet this challenge, the TV coach fleet was also at its peak, with Bristol L6B's 460-5 (DMO 664-9), 487-91 (EJB 209-13), and 545-55 (FMO 20-6 and FMO 934-7), plus Bedford OB's 164/5 (LJO 756/7) and 604-6 (FRX 313-5), Bristol LWL6B's 607-12 (GBL 871-6), as well as the TS8 Leyland 'Tigers' 381-90 (BMO 980-9) and coaches available from the Newbury and Oxford contingents.

Three new service saloons arrived in April as Cars 629/32/3 (GJB 267/70/1), and all were ECW B39R-bodied Bristol LWL6B's. These were the last of this type and all were allocated to Reading, the outstanding 5 chassis being taken as LS's instead.

Above: Bristol LWL6B Car 629 (GJB 267) emerges from the bus wash at Reading Garage. Note the duty boards and the offices of the Engineering Department on the south side of the premises Below: The same bus seen a little later when working on Route 38 from High Wycombe.

During April the laid-up ex-*Crosville* Leyland 'Cub' Car 411 (FM 7455) was officially withdrawn, as was

TV's original pair of that type, Cars 337/8 (ABL 767/8), all of which were to be advertised for sale.

'Cubs' 337/8 and the former Wallasey Corporation 'Titan' TD1 Car 412 (HF 6041) await their fates in the Colonnade yard.

There was still an acute shortage of skilled fitters, so the local representative of the Labour Exchange asked *Thames Valley* if they would consider employing three Dutch applicants, though in the end only one actually materialised.

Transfer of the *United Counties* route from Oxford to London, actually inherited from *Varsity Express,* took place on 1st May, giving *South Midland* a second way between the two towns, as well as fitting in nicely with TV's general coverage of the High Wycombe area. The Botley Road garage was included and had already been extended by UCOC, making it preferable to the rather basic premises at Iffley Road. Along with the fully equipped garage came a Morris 8hp car (VV 8163), plus a modern collection of coaches of types already familiar to the parent fleet, as detailed below –

F. No.	Reg. No.	Chassis	Body	New
71	EBD 234	Bristol L6B	ECW DP31R	8/48
72	EBD 235	Bristol L6B	ECW DP31R	9/48
73	EBD 236	Bristol L6B	ECW FC31F	5/50
74	EBD 237	Bristol L6B	ECW FC31F	5/50
75	FRP 832	Bristol LL6B	ECW FC37F8	2/51
76	FRP 833	Bristol LL6B	ECW FC37F8	2/51
77	FRP 834	Bristol LL6B	ECW FC37F8	2/51
78	FRP 836	Bristol LL6B	ECW FC37F8	2/51

These vehicles were formerly *United Counties* Nos. 807-10/32-4/6. The first pair were of the 'express' type, with a bus shell and coach seating, whilst the 4 LL6B's were of the interim type with 7ft 6ins chassis fitted with 8ft wide fully-fronted 'Queen Mary' bodies. The coaches were in cream livery with green mudguards, which were repainted black in due course. The two 'express' examples had a side beading with a green painted area, which was initially retained.

The trio of Wilts & Dorset 'Titans' are seen awaiting sale at the Colonnade yard, together with TV's 'Tiger' TS4 Car 249 (RX 9703) and 'Titan' TD1 Car 186 (RX 4348). Note that the frontal profile of each of the TD1 buses had been modified during the wartime period.

As noted earlier, *Red & White* had offered to loan some new coaches in lieu of those outstanding from the orders it had placed with Lydney Coach Works, as they must have felt some embarrassment regarding the choice of bodybuilder? So a pair of Leyland 'Royal Tiger' PSU1/13's with Lydney C41F bodies, bearing R&W fleet numbers UC951 (JWO 213) and UC2051 (JWO 546) were collected from Chepstow on 2nd May and sent to work from Oxford.

A transfer of an altogether different kind occurred on 8th May, when a pair of *Wilts & Dorset* Leyland 'Titan' TD1's were brought to the Colonnade. It would seem that Basil Sutton had gained a reputation for shifting the impossible, and it hoped he could sell these on behalf of their owner. A third one arrived by June, when the trio became W&D Nos.96 (MW 8753), 38 (TK 2592, ex-*Hants & Dorset*) and 218 (CK 4278, ex-*Ribble Motor Services*). Sutton got £250 apiece for them, so one hopes he was on commission over the sale!

The L6B coaches inherited from United Counties had a style of body similar to that applied to the rebodied Newbury & District Leyland 'Tiger' PS1, leaving the Bristol radiator exposed. Car 74 (EBD 237) is seen on the Oxford Colleges & Blenheim Palace tour shortly after changing ownership. This pair of coaches duly became the regular choice for extended tours where narrow roads were encountered.

May saw a few more old buses departing, with 'Titan' TD1 Cars 185 (RX 4347) and ex-*Wallasey CT* 412 (HF 6041), together with 'Tiger' TS7 Car 306 (JB 8345), the latter being sold to Douai College over at Woolhampton, but without its seats, engine and transmission, for use as a changing room. June saw only one further sale, with the departure of 'Tiger' TS7 Car 271 (JB 5850), though the Colonnade remained full of redundant vehicles.

A topic that has not been particularly noted before was the way in which duties were allocated to crews, the Company's main aim being to fully utilise crews during their hours of duty. The Union, however, strove to ensure crews got breaks, time allowances for transfers and enhanced rates for overtime working. A number of crews were basically stuck on certain runs, in particularly where Dormy Sheds were involved, but others did enjoy a greater variety. Probably the best example was the 'Reading single-deck' duties. In order to meet the aims of both Company and Union, various duties were arranged which mixed shorter and longer journeys, and of course offered some changes of scenery. Thus the infrequent Route 6b to Bramley was inter-worked with Route 8 (Reading – Binfield Heath – Henley) every couple of hours. By the same token the crews had to learn routes that might only be worked occasionally!

On the Union front, one of the strongest protagonists was Ted Tapper, a driver based at Wycombe Marsh. He had previously been a test driver for the Gilford Motor Company when they were based in the town, later becoming a driver with *City of Oxford* at Stokenchurch and passed to TV with the operations there in 1937. To be fair to Ted, conflict at Wycombe was never far away, partly because so many crews had come from absorbed concerns, and also the presence of the *London Transport* garage in the town, with its better rates of pay and conditions of service.

The town of Windsor had featured in the Company's routes for many years, though no garage was ever used there, with buses working to there from most of the other garages. However, London Transport did have a sizeable garage opposite the King George V Hospital, and Thames Valley's Ascot-based Bristol K6A Car 439 (CRX 548) passes it by on Route 2b (Winkfield – Bracknell – Easthampstead).

Another daily aspect of operation, and all too easy to overlook, was the constant maintenance of tyres. For many years TV's Engineer had strongly advocated a policy of tyre ownership and used a well-equipped tyre shop to maximise the mileages achieved before a tyre required scrapping. However, that policy had given way to awarding tyre contracts on a mileage rental basis, whereby certain suppliers provided both the tyres and maintenance. The Dunlop Company had the contract for Reading garage, along with Ascot and the two High Wycombe garages, whilst Firestone had Maidenhead and Newbury, and Goodyear looked after the Oxford allocation.

Over at Maidenhead arrangements were being made for the opening of the new Coach Station, and it was agreed to employ two Coach Park Attendents from June. They would be on duties which covered the hours between 7am and 10.30pm, and they would be responsible for issuing tickets to coaches wishing to park there during the day, as well as noting the details of service coaches working through for re-charging. The new coach station would also host TV's Route B to London, plus the Sundays-only Southsea express, as well as the *South Midland* London, Oxford, Worcester, Brighton, Eastbourne and Margate routes. It was also the departure point for SM's extended tour coaches to South Devon, North Devon, the Welsh Coast, Heart of England and three Wye Valley tours.

A rather unexpected bus to feature on London Route B during June 1952 was Brush-bodied Leyland 'Titan' TD5 Car 339 (AJB 811), one of a trio purchased to take over the Stokenchurch operations in May 1937.

Other operators using the Maidenhead Coach Station were *Associated Motorways* express services between London, Cheltenham, Gloucester, South Wales and the West of England, *Royal Blue* and *Bristol Greyhound* between London, Bristol and Weston-super-Mare, and the Scottish Omnibuses route to Edinburgh. The café nearby at the Bus Station was open 7 days a week between 8am and 10.30pm and was used as a layover on many journeys.

Thames Valley had an extensive programme of tours from the town, including Ascot Races, Blenhiem Palace & the Berkshire Downs, Bognor, Burnham Beeches, Bournemouth, California-in-England, Epsom Races, Hawthorn Hill Races, Hayling Island, London Olympia & Tower Pier (for boat cruise), London Zoo, Newbury Races, Southampton Docks, Southend-on-Sea, Southsea, Windsor and Whipsnade Zoo.

In order to provide accommodation for the Inspectors on duty at the Coach Station, two Leyland 'Tiger' TS4 saloons were parked up and connected to the phone. Car 244 (RX 9541) occupied the easterly entrance road, whilst 249 (RX 9703) was in the westerly road.

Above: The 1939 Bristol K5G's could still be found working on scheduled Relief runs, and Car 398 (BRX 914) is laid over at the parking ground between Reading's twin railway stations. Biscuits were another stable daily product considered worthy of advertising then. Below: Car 405 (BRX 921) works on the busy, but relatively short, Route 1a to Woodley, unaware that it would outlast all others of that type by a number of years, albeit in another role.

The Summer timetable commenced on Saturday June 14th and brought with it a number of changes. Firstly, Wokingham Borough Council had been agitating to ease congestion around the Town Hall, a triangular site where TV's buses used the shelters provided on the east and west sides. As a result, it had been agreed that Routes 4a (Reading – Arborfield – Wokingham) and 21 (Maidenhead – White Waltham- Binfield – Wokingham) would both terminate at Wokingham Station, adjacent to the Railway Tap pub. At that time the 21 was worked by a 39-seater Bristol LL6B and the 4a was covered by Bristol KS6B or KSW6B 55-seaters. As a result of this both routes were extended on from the Town Hall by way of Denmark Street and Wellington Road for journeys in either direction.

Route 18 was reinstated back through to Marlow, the buses again working over the bridge. The duty was now assigned to the Beadle-bodied Bedford OB Cars 510-2/20 (EJB 232-4/42), which had their seating

layout slightly modified to suit their new role, the seats over the rear wheel arches being turned to face inwards in order to give more circulation space.

The older Duple-bodied Bedford OWB Cars 437/8 (CRX 546/7) were officially retained as spares buses for that duty, though they were also used on some Local Reliefs and school runs from Maidenhead.

All other changes in the Summer timetable related to the Newbury area, following two years experience of those operations. Route 5b (Reading – Yattendon) was projected through to Newbury, replacing the need for Routes 119/119a (Newbury – Yattendon). Route 106 (Newbury – Lambourn) was extended to Swindon and the separate Route 107 journeys between Newbury and Swindon were deleted. Route 102 was extended to run as West Ilsley – East Ilsley – Reading, covered by the Guy 'Arab' double-decker outstaioned at East Ilsley, which could be seen laid over during the day in Reading. Route 129, which had a few journeys between the Broadway and Hambridge Road disappeared, but a new Route 110a (Hambridge Road – Thatcham Station) was introduced, several buses being saved as a result of these changes.

However, something of a set-back occurred at Newbury in early June, when a driver attempted to enter the low-height area of the garage with one of the Guy 'Arab' double-deckers! The bus was damaged, as was the garage, and no doubt Reg Hibbert muttered a few suitable words through his 'Capstan' that day.

East Ilsley-based Guy 'Arab' Mk1II Car 176 (HOT 392), with 57-seater Duple highbridge body is seen in the Southern yard between turns on Route 102. Note that the route number is still showing as 2, the blinds not having yet been modified – let's hope no passengers for Ascot or Windsor was tempted to board it! Note the Indian Head radiator mascot fitted to Guy buses, whose motto was 'feathers in our cap'.

Bedford OB Car 512 (EJB 234) emerges from Bridge Avenue on Route 18 to Marlow, with the Rialto Cinema behind to the right and the new Enquiry Office to the left. These vehicles generally carried painted adverts for coach hire or the London services. The young lady to the right anticipates the future by pretending to hold a mobile phone to her head.

The experiments in the use of light lubricating oils had continued, and attracted a considerable interest from other bus company Engineers, so it was appropriate that P.M.A. Thomas, Technical Editor of Bus & Coach Magazine (and friend of Basil Sutton) should pen an article on that subject for July's issue.

From the introduction of the Summer schedules, the Ascot allocation was changed to Bristol K6A/ Strachans UL27/28R Cars 433/4 (CRX 544/5), Bristol K6A/ECW L27/28R Cars 439-42 (CRX 548-51), Bristol KSW6B/ECW L27/28R Cars 640-6 (GJB 278-84), plus the Bristol L6B coach 488 (EJB 210) with Windover C33F body. The utility-bodied K6A's remained on the 2a/2c links between Ascot and Sunningdale, whilst one of the postwar K6A's covered the 2b between Windsor and Easthampstead, and all the others worked Route 2 (Windsor – Ascot – Bracknell – Reading).

As a result of the changes on Route 18 workings, the 3 Leyland 'Cubs' were advertised for sale on 16th June, this being done through the local press as it was considered they might make a new role as mobile shops or caravans – but there was no rush of purchasers for them. It was also decided that 9 of the 1929 Leyland 'Titan' TD1's and 5 of the older 'Tiger' saloons would be withdrawn by the end of the, also resulting in a decision not to accept any more contracts requiring double-deckers. A general clear-out of the accumulated materials stored at the

Colonnade was ordered, the place having become a veritable Alladin's Cave over the years.

During June the new underfloor-engined coaches on Bristol LS6G chassis began to arrive from ECW, there being orders for both the TV and SM fleets. Those for *South Midland* were Cars 79-81 (SFC 565-7), which had 37-seater bodies, whilst Car 671 (HBL 73) for *Thames Valley* had a 39-seater layout and was allocated to Desborough Road. As already noted, these coaches were delivered later than had been anticipated, mainly because the supply of chassis had been slow. TV's Cars 672/3 (HBL 74/5) followed in July and were sent to Reading and Newbury respectively.

The interior looking rearwards of LS coach 671 (HBL 73). The glazed cant-rail panels made these vehicles appear brighter on the inside. The seating had shaped headrests and real leather trim, but soon showed signs of adverse wear, which was partly attributed to condensation dripping from the stainless steel luggage racks. The rear windows are notably rather narrow even when compared to those on the previous LWL's.

The style of bodywork by Eastern Coach Works on the Bristol LS chassis was both attractive and practical. Note the glazed panel in the entrance door to aid the driver, and also the slot for the arms of the semaphore traffic indicators. Car 674 (HBL 76) is seen at Gloucester Green, Oxford in the original cream and black livery, the latter areas being repainted red for the following year.

South Midland's other LS's, Cars 82-4 (SFC 568-70) did not appear until October, and they were even beaten by the example on AEC 'Regal' IV chassis inherited from *Red & White,* and we shall hear more of that soon. Although the new coaches were a welcome addition, their first few months of service were marred by a high incidence of problems with the horizontal engines and gearboxes. All new models tend to experience some teething troubles, but the LS was dogged with problems, and one of the *South Midland* examples was forced to limp into the Chepstow works of *Red & White* with gearbox trouble, whilst Wycombe Marsh had to deal with a similar problem with a *Crosville* coach with the same fault. The other common problem related to road grit making its way into the engine and gearbox casings.

Despite the change in general configuration of single-deck chassis, the double-decker remained firmly front-engined, and even the revolutionary Bristol 'Lodekka' had not inspired *Thames Valley* to place an order other than further KSW-types.

July saw the arrival of KSW6B/ECW L27/28R buses 651/2 (HBL 53/4), followed by Car 653 (HBL 55) in August and Cars 654-8 (HBL 56-60) in September. Of those Reading received 653-6, Maidenhead had 651/7 and 652/8 went to High Wycombe.

As well as having sold the *Wilts & Dorset* 'Titan' TD1's, TV's own Cars 184/6 (RX 4346/8) were disposed in July, though the little 'Cubs' had not fared so well and languished at the Colonnade. Pressure on that site had been so severe that other buses were sent to be dumped behind Newbury garage, much to the annoyance of Reg Hibbert, who sent regular reminders to Basil Sutton of those vehicles still languishing there!

Car 184 (RX 4346) ended up dumped at Newbury awaiting disposal. It features yet another in the series of Milward's adverts, whilst the destination blind is rather optimistically set on 'Excursion'! The bodywork originally by Leyland had been re-built by Beadle of Dartford during the war years.

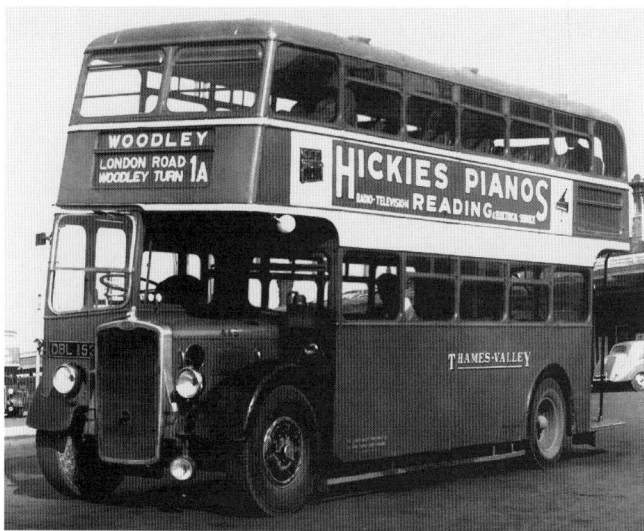

As the 8ft wide double-deckers took over the main trunk routes, the earlier postwar Bristols were put on the more intensive local routes. _Above:_ On Route 1a to Woodley is K6A Car 445 (DBL 153) seen at Reading Stations, whilst _Below:_ KS6B Car 593 (FMO 975) is seen in Slough on Route 61 to St. Andrews Way. Note the out of use side indicator on 445, whilst the adverts are typical of those on the 'Valley buses.

With so many inroads into the ranks of Leyland vehicles, it would be useful to examine what the remaining ones were being used for at 1st July:
Note: A full fleet allocation for July 1952 appears in Appendix 6.

9 Double-deck Leylands based at Reading –
Leyland 'Titan' TD1 Cars 183 and 235
Leyland 'Titan' TD4 Cars 273, 335 and 336
Leyland 'Titan' TD5 Cars 340/1 and 369/70
4 were used on Local Reliefs, and 4 on Contracts TV1, TV2, TV4 and TV5 to AWRE Aldermaston, 1 as spare

8 Single-deck Leylands based at Reading –
Leyland 'Tiger' TS7 Cars 321-4 and 334
Leyland 'Tiger' TS8 Cars 371/3/8.
7 of these were on Local Reliefs and 1 on Contract TV3 to Cohen's Yard, Bramley Camp

5 Double-deck Leylands based at Maidenhead –
Leyland 'Titan' TD1 Car 182
Leyland 'Titan' TD4 Cars 274/5/7 and 339
These cars were for Local Reliefs and reserve stock

9 Single-deck Leylands based at Maidenhead –
Leyland 'Tiger' TS7 Cars 266, 295, 305 and 325/8
Leyland 'Tiger' TS8 Cars 345, 374/5 and 380
Cars 266 and 295 were in reserve, 5 were used on Local Reliefs and the other 2 were spare.

10 Single-deck Leylands based at High Wycombe-
Leyland 'Tiger' TS7 Cars 303/9, 326/9 and 332/4
Leyland 'Tiger' TS8 Cars 348, 363/6 and 387 (coach)
2 TS7's were used on Routes 36/37 and based at Fingest,1 TS7 was in reserve and rotated with Fingest cars, 2 buses were on Local Reliefs from Desborough Road, 4 were on Local Reliefs from Wycombe Marsh, and 1 worked shorts on Route 27 from the Marsh.

5 Double-deck Leylands based at Newbury –
Leyland 'Titan' TD1 Cars 179, 180, 181, 187 and 190
All used on Local Reliefs

12 Single-deck Leylands based at Newbury –
Leyland 'Tiger' TS7 Cars 262/4 (coaches) and 333
Leyland 'Tiger' TS8 Cars 342-4/6, 361/2/8 and 372/9
8 were used on Contracts from Newbury: N/C1 Camp Close – Harwell (AERE); N/C2 Henwick Lane – Harwell (AERE); N/C3 Regal – Harwell (AERE); N/E1 Regal – Didcot (via East Ilsley); N/E2 Regal – Didcot (via Hampstead Norris); N/E5 Kintbury – Didcot; N/E7 Regal – Milton Depot (via Hampstead Norris); N/E8 Regal – Milton Depot (via Chieveley).
3 were used on Contracts from Lambourn outstation: N/C4 Lambourn – Harwell (AERE); N/E3 Lambourn – Didcot (via Wantage); and N/E4 Lambourn – Didcot (via Childrey).
1 was based at East Ilsley outstation and used on Contract N/E6 West Ilsley – Didcot.

This slightly later view of one of the Bristol KSW's new in the Summer of 1952 shows Car 656 (HBL 58) picking up in Denmark Street at the shelter by the Town Hall, with the Red Lion pub to the left.

Another busy annual event for the Company buses was the Marlow Regatta, which has always been a more family affair than the rather snobbier one held a few miles up river. Local resident and transport observer John Boot recalls how spare relief buses were parked up near Quoiting Square in the entrance to the Riley Recreation Ground. These ageing saloons were from the Wycombe allocation and did not normally venture into Marlow. To save fuel they were left there during the day, with crews returning on Route 28 service buses. In the very early 1950's these included examples from most batches of 'Tiger' TS7 and TS8 types, including the Harrington-bodied ones. John also recalls that crowds of Reading Football Club supporters would use Route 28 to home matches on a Saturday. Other former *Thames Valley* buses appeared regularly with showman on the parkland in Wethered Road. He also reminds us of the notice that once stood at the narrow hump-back bridge on the Wargrave road that read 'Conway's Bridge is quite a ridge, so single file for a while'.

Alf Button and his machine from a paper cutting.

Bus crews in those could rarely afford to run a car, so most therefore walked, cycled or ran a motorbike for the journeys to and from work, particularly as these were often outside operating hours for public transport. One Reading-based Conductor ran a nifty 'Cyclemaster', a normal push-bike adapted with a small petrol engine attached to the rear wheel. The manufacturers claimed that it would do 40 miles to the gallon, and Alf Button mentioned to his workmates, who were dubious about that claim. However, Alf decided to prove them wrong, and set off one Summer's day from London Street at 5.30am astride his machine (GDP 277) and in full *Thames Valley* uniform, bound for Cornwall! Maintaining a steady 20mph, and allowing for meals breaks, he averaged 15 miles per hour, out through Newbury, Andover, Sherborne and Yeovil, reaching the halfway point at Chard, where he sent a telegram reporting his progress. He had to dismount climbing out of that town, but otherwise all went to plan, Honiton, Exeter and Launceston all surrendering to his progress, the

16-hour epic journey ending in Camborne at 9.25pm! Alf achieved the trip on 5 shillings (25 new pence) on fuel and certainly silenced his critics. Alf's decision to wear his uniform may have been for its hard-wearing qualities, though perhaps he also used it as a passport to the various bus canteens along his route?

The Bristol K6A's of the wartime era were still kept busy on various duties, including Car 432 (CRX 543) on Maidenhead Local Service runs to Furze Platt. As can be seen, it was still kept in good condition.

During July the Crowthorne Dormy Shed was given a refurbishment, with doors repaired and repainted, almost certainly the first time since it opened in 1926. Work on the Body & Paint Shop at the Colonnade got underway, though the old Torpedo Test Tank needed to be filled in. Alterations of another kind were made when the driver of Guy 'Arab' Car 101 (CRX 281) swung round at Colthrop Mills when working a contract and hit an overhanging roof! The damage was extensive enough to warrant it coming to Reading Works on 1st August, and it also had to avoid the low bridge of the Didcot, Newbury & Southampton Railway over the Bath Road coming out of Newbury.

Still going strong despite heavy withdrawals of buses of the same vintage, were the surviving pair of 'camel-back' Duple-bodied Leyland 'Tiger' TS7's. Car 262 (JB 5841) is seen on hire to South Midland in London, and the pair went on for another couple of years. The third member of the trio disappeared on war service.

Bristol LWL6B Car 585 (FMO 967) was one of the large batches ordered to replace the war-weary buses, and it is seen on Stations Hill awaiting departure on the 30-mile journey to Abingdon on Route 50. All such buses were of course crew-operated, though the Conductors also had to manage the Newspaper and Parcels traffic, which were still quite significant.

On 24th July progress of the work at Brislington on the Guy coaches was inspected by Messrs. Sutton and Campbell, who closely examined the most complete shell. However, they considered the construction of the roof to be unsatisfactory, and noted that it did not conform to the standards of ECW bodies. The pair also took the opportunity to discuss the recent issues with the LS chassis at Bristol Commercial Vehicles.

As noted previously, a number of vehicles awaited disposal at the Colonnade during the early 1950's. In this view we see Leyland' Titan' TD1 Car 181 (RX 4343) with engine removed. Next to it is the chassis of 'Tiger' TS7 Car 267 (JB 5846) bearing the body from Leyland 'Tiger' TS8 Car 375 (BBL 561), the two buses having exchanged bodies around July. The TS7 never ran again in service, though the TS8 did so in its new form, though it all seems a lot of effort to do and, curiously, the swap is not recorded officially.

During July a further pair of 'Titan' TD1's departed, being Cars 184/6 (RX 4346/8), and they were followed in August by similar Cars 182/3 (RX 4344/5). Also disposed of that month were 'Tiger' TS4 Car 248 (RX 9702), 'Tiger' TS7 Cars 266 (JB 5845), 295 (JB 7495) and 304 (JB 8343), along with 'Titan' TD4 276 (JB 5855). August also saw 'Titan' TD1 Car 181 (RX 4343) taken from Newbury and de-licensed at Reading, its place at Newbury being taken by 1948 Bristol K6B Car 468 (DMO 672). Car 181 did, of course, have the distinction of being the first TV bus converted to a diesel engine way back in 1933, but despite that had retained the original 'piano-front' profile.

The recent clear-out at the Colonnade had revealed a number of old radiator types, so 11 were sold to the well known dealer J. Remblance of Hornchurch, Essex for £55. Also during August the Gardner 5LW from Car 181 was sold for further use by the Reading brewers H&G Simonds for £150.

On 26th August the long-awaited AEC 'Regal' MkIV coach was collected from Lowestoft, carrying a C37F body almost identical to the contemporary Bristol LS-type coaches for the *South Midland* fleet. Apart from the necessity to place access flaps for radiator water and the fuel tank, the only external pointers were the AEC roundels on the wheel centres and the chrome nut-guard rings on the front wheels. Oddly, no use was made of the blue triangular AEC badge that was usually found on all such chassis, even though it could have fitted in well with the existing ECW 'wings' on the front panel. This coach became SM Car 85 (SFC 571) and, despite being very much the odd one out in the fleet (especially once all other AEC types had gone), it ran its full life through to the Autumn of 1967. Casual observers would have not even suspected it was 'different', and I recall that once I caught up with it, I was sorry to find it was so normal!

90

Spot the difference! – <u>Above:</u> AEC 'Regal' IV coach 85 (SFC 571) in original condition and parked outside Samuelson's Garage in Victoria. The split windscreen was the only visible feature when seen from a distance. <u>Below:</u> The standard ECW/Bristol LS-type in the form of Car 79 (SFC 565), seen at Gloucester Green, Oxford, also in original livery

Three new routes were introduced in September, even though the Winter timetable did not come into force until Saturday 8th November. The first was a new Local Service in response to housing developments off Shoppenhangers Road in Maidenhead, Route 63, which ran as Bus Station – Railway Station – Shoppenhangers Road – Larchfield Avenue – Reid Avenue – Norreys Drive (Curls Lane Estate). It had a 25/30 minute headway throughout the day and was covered by one Bristol K-type 55-seater.

The second new route was to serve further housing at Booker, Route 81 running as Frogmoor – Worleys Garage – Deborough Avenue – Cressex Road/Marlow Road Junction – Booker (Turnpike Corner), which operated a 40-minute headway and initially called for 35-seater Bristol L-types. However, the need for frequent relief buses soon saw the route converted to 55-seater double-deckers.

Over in the Newbury area, the earlier demise of Route 119a had left a gap, resulting in the provision of a Thursdays and Saturdays-only Route 120a, with three daily return journeys covering Newbury – Shaw – Hermitage – Hampstead Norris – Ashampstead – Aldworth (The Bell), which also had a later return run

added for Saturdays, which must have been much appreciated by the locals. This route was placed in the hands of a 35-seater Bristol L-type, a number of which had been transferred to Newbury to take the place of outgoing older types.

During September Messrs. Sutton and Campbell made two further visits to Brislington to iron out issues on the bodies on the Guy coaches, all hope of delivery for 1952 having now faded! Despite that news, the pair of Leyland 'Royal Tigers' on loan from *Red & White* were released back to them on 4th November, and they had certainly been a useful stop-gap.

The trio of little 'Cubs' finally found a buyer on 1st September, though only at £25 each, whereas most of the sales at that time achieved £100! Although sold to a dealer, Car 338 (ABL 338) did become a mobile greengrocer's shop, with fruit symbols on the blind!

Bristol K6B Car 470 (DMO 674) was doing the honours on new Route 63 to the Curls Lane Estate. Note that the side destination indicator over the entrance has been panelled over during re-painting.

The Bristol KSW6B's were widely used and proved to be very reliable buses. Car 647 (GJB 285) is shown at Frogmoor parking ground awaiting its turn on the busy Route 81 to Booker (Turnpike Corner), one of the housing developments west of High Wycombe.

A further 5 Dutch Fitters were put forward by the Ministry of Labour during September, though only two actually made the move to Reading. Also, on 27th of that month, Derek Nobes joined Newbury Garage as a Fitter following demobilisation from the RAF. He was the son of Ernest Nobes, the independent operator running out of Lambourn Woodlands who had joined forces with *Newbury & District* in July 1938. Derek therefore kept in touch with local bus operations through his father, though the latter was sadly killed in a tragic accident at Didcot on 1st October 1943, when the Dennis 'Ace' bus he was driving was struck by an unsupervised shunting train at a goods yard crossing.

Variety at Oxford in the Summer of 1952, with 'Tiger' TS8 coach 388 (BMO 987) and Red & White 'Royal Tiger' UC2051 (JWO 546) both on loan to South Midland and covering the London routes.

During the Summer of 1952 some of the 'Tiger' TS8 coaches 381-90 (BMO 980-9) had served as reliefs on *South Midland* routes, complete with painted on-hire boards across the radiators, as were the pair of Duple-bodied 'Tiger' TS7's 262/4 (JB 5841/3). However, in September Cars 381-6 were transferred to Newbury to be used on contract runs. The TS7 coaches were also transferred for that purpose, which saw 264 running out of Lambourn – the very village it had received its complete body refurbishment in!

Leyland 'Titan' TD1 Car 179 (RX 4341) had been treated to a modernised front end when rebuilt by ECW during the war. It is seen in its last days when working out of Newbury. Despite that it shows no outward signs of body problems unlike some others.

At the end of September the remaining 'Titan' TD1's at Newbury were delicensed, Cars 179, 180, 187 and 190 (RX 4341/2/9/52) all four being sold during the following month. Also concerning Newbury was the decision to transfer the quartet of Bedford OB/Beadle buses 510-2/20 (EJB 232-4/42) there, the intention being to try them out on some of the restricted local roads. Route 18 to Marlow was rather over-subscribed with buses, so it was considered that Bedford OWB's 437/8 (CRX 546/7) could handle the lighter Winter traffic. However, Cars 511/2 had returned to Maidenhead by Christmas, and the others duly followed, ending the trial in the Newbury area. On the vehicle front, a demonstration of one-coat paint at the Colonnade had failed to impress Basil Sutton, so the representative left without an order on that occasion.

Further disposals of Leylands took place during September, with 'Tiger' TS7 Cars 309 (JB 8348), and 324/6 (ABL 754/6), 'Tiger' TS4 253 (RX 9707), and TS8 Car 362 (ARX 984) all departing. In October in addition to the four 'Titan' TD1's already noted, more inroads were made into that make, with 'Tiger' TS7 Cars 267 (JB 5846), 303/5/8 (JB 8342/4/7), 321/9 (ABL 751/9), as well as N&D's Car 184 (ABL 763 ex TV Car 333)). Other double-deckers departing that month were 1931 'Titan' TD1 Car 235 (RX 8168) and former *Plymouth CT* 'Titan' TD2 Car 436 (DR 9846), the latter sold without the new seating it had received in 1946. These changes left only one 'Titan' TD1 in the fleet, albeit withdrawn and engineless, in the shape of Car 181 (RX 4343). Only one further bus went that year, with 'Tiger' TS7 Car 331 (ABL 761) going in November.

As the Leylands departed Bristol saloons took over many former duties. LWL-type 619 (GJB 257) is seen on a Route 28 'short' to Marlow, whilst L6A-type Car 473 (DMO 677) had seen demotion from the longer runs it had previously been used on, and is covering Route 31 to either Walters Ash or Lacey Green.

New arrangements were made over at Oxford for the responsibilities now spread over two garages. From 1st October Mr. Sanders at Botley Road would undertake operation of the Oxford servicing and light repairs, whilst Mr. Bessell at Iffley Road would cover periodic inspections to take pressure off the Reading Works.

November saw the delivery of further Bristol KSW's and Car 662 (HBL 64) waits in the picturesque West Wycombe village prior to returning to Loudwater on Route 42.

Progress with the new Road & Rail Enquiry Office at Reading Stations was rather slow and, at the joint meeting held in October, *Thames Valley* officials were frustrated to note that the railway representatives did not seem to know much about the project, nor had any authority to make decisions! The temporary office building was delivered to the site in the nearby yard on 20th October, so Mr. Abberfield and his gang set about erecting it on the base they had prepared.

Bristol LWL6B Car 632 (GJB 270) had been away at the FVDRE from 17th October for further trials on light oils in collaboration with Esso Petroleum, and it returned to Reading on 3rd November. However, the Bristol LS's were still giving some headaches, as two further issues had raised their head now the days were drawing in. Firstly, drivers complained of excessive reflections on the large front windscreens, whilst the saloon heaters were found to be inadequate for the task, and this resulted in the whole *South Midland* lot being delicensed pending rectification of the issues – rather ironically their places were taken by 'Tiger' TS8's delivered way back in 1939!

The Company was starting to experience rising costs in both the areas of staff wages and materials. All of the Union Representatives were invited by the General Manager Mr. L.H. Balls to the White Hart at Sonning, where he talked to them about the need to avoid damage to vehicles and unwarranted tyre wear. On the other side of the coin, he stated that it might prove necessary to abandon uneconomical routes or consider the introduction of one-man-operation unless co-operation could achieve the necessary economies.

Considering those remarks, it is interesting to note that the next new vehicles to arrive in November were the first of the Bristol LS6G saloons with ECW B45F bodies, though all such buses were crew-operated when new. These were Cars 677/8 (HBL 79/80) and both were allocated to Reading for use on Route 5 between there and Oxford.

Car 677 (HBL 79) leaves Gloucester Green Bus Station for Reading on Route 5. Note that as new these buses lacked the Bristol-ECW badge, fleetname or fleet numbers on the front panel, making it appear very plain. The central fog lamp proved ineffective and was moved to below the nearside head lamp.

Other new buses received were further Bristol KSW6B-types with ECW L27/28R bodywork, as Cars 659-62 (HBL 61-4), which were distributed between Reading (659/60), Maidenhead (661) and Desborough Road (662).

On 6th November discussions were held at Newbury Borough Council, which desired that a Coach Station might be built nearby the Wharf. The area did indeed get very busy at times with coaches on express routes and excursions, or those just taking a break en route.

Another view of Car 677 (HBL 79) crossing the bridge near Magdelaine College in Oxford. Note the position of the filler caps for fuel and water on the offside, which were not fitted with flaps.

On 11th November a request was considered from the Regent Oil Company, who wished to take over direct employment of the four Petrol Tanker Drivers. The terms offered were not favourable to either the drivers or the Company, so the offer was rejected.

Over in the Newbury area, Routes 103 (Newbury – Ecchinswell), 104 (Newbury – Headley – Kingsclere) and 104a (Newbury – Ashford Hill) all required some re-routing from November, this being due to the closure of the section of road between Greenham and Knightsbridge. This had been caused by the extension of the runway to Greenham Common Air Base in order to accommodate larger United States Air Force bombers being stationed there under the Cold War. At the time this was regarded as a 'temporary' closure, though history would prove otherwise! Buses were routed out of Newbury by Newtown Road in order to skirt the enlarged site.

On 28th November yet another long service employee retired, as Mr. E. Lucas one of the Night Fitters at Reading hung up his tools after 35 years. He had begun as a Driver way back in October 1917, when the Belsizes were the order of the day, becoming part-Driver, part-Fitter between 1920 and 1922, when the re-building of ex-War Department Thornycrofts was at its peak, then after that he was fully involved in the Works.

December started badly with the dense fog that often clothed the Thames Valley, resulting in numerous minor collisions. Indeed, the task of driving buses

in such conditions should not be underestimated, as even the 'mainline' routes were often affected, as Route 1 (Reading – Maidenhead), Route 2 (Windsor – Reading) and Route 10 (Reading – Newbury) all passed through particular blackspots. However, there were no widespread cancellations of services, even though in some cases the conductors found it necessary to walk in front of the bus with a torch in the worst patches!

On 27th December 20 of the Works and Garage staff were taken by 'Tiger' TS7 coach 264 (JB 5843) to the Bristol Commercial Vehicles works at Brislington to see the production of chassis, though the LS's were still causing concern as several had jammed in gear on coming to a stop and could not be released by drivers!

Bristol KSW6B Car 661 (HBL 63) at Windsor Castle.

1953

Work on the Colonnade Body & Paint Shop was still frustratingly slow, due to the national shortage of building materials, even though it was over 7 years since the War had ended. The Maidenhead Enquiry Office was faring better and nearly ready, whilst during December 1952 a good start had been made on the Road & Rail Enquiry Office at Reading Stations.

After their brief spell at Newbury, the four Beadle-bodied Bedford OB's returned to the Maidenhead – Marlow Route 18. Car 520 (EJB 242) rests in Bridge Avenue in the sunshine, whilst the rear shot of Car 510 (EJB 232) was also taken at the same spot.

This would be another very busy year, and a bumper one for the coaching activities, particularly in respect of the Coronation of Queen Elizabeth II, excursions running from throughout the area.

Following the resignation of Mr. L.H. Grimmett as Traffic Superintendent at Oxford, Mr. W.R. Francis took over that role from 1st January. Mr. J.E. Bessell was Foreman covering both Iffley Road and Botley Road, though based at the latter, with Mr. J. Sanders as Chargehand at Botley Road and Mr. J. Tobin at Iffley Road. However, some of these changes caused some discord, resulting in further adjustments to the local structure later that month. All drivers were also reminded that if assistance was required at Oxford, they should contact Botley Road rather the previous arrangements made with *City of Oxford*.

On 5th January Mr. Campbell attended a meeting in London with the Chairman, where he was charged with heading a study into identifying a suitable light-weight bus for use in BTC fleets. His experiences on that topic whilst with *Eastern Counties* may well have been of relevance, but he travelled widely to discuss such requirements and to view the types already in use.

On 16th January, a serious accident had occurred when Wycombe-based Bristol LL6B-type Car 578 (FMO 960) ran out of control whilst descending Marlow Hill into the town. It eventually collided with a lamp-post, and it was indeed fortunate that personal injuries were minimal, as much damage was done to the bus. The driver had claimed to having been overcome by fumes, though tests on the engine and braking system back at Reading found no evidence to support either as the cause of the accident.

Further experiments with one-coat paint took place, with Bristol LWL6B Car 581 (FMO 963) being so treated on 16th January. The Vulcan paint used was not found to be satisfactory, so a redundant saloon was sent to ICI Paint Works at Slough, where it was 'hot-sprayed', but again the results were not good.

However, January was itself a milestone in *Thames Valley's* history, with the disposal of the last Leyland 'Titan' TD1 from the passenger fleet. 49 of that type had been owned since 1928, though a pair was lost in the formation of *London Transport*, whilst two others had perished in fires. Car 181 (RX 4343) had latterly languished at Newbury, engineless, and in that form it was sold for £50, being towed to its new owner over at Lambourn on 23rd January. Considering how many of the TD1's had been heavily rebuilt, it was perhaps unexpected that it should be one of the buses with the least altered appearance that marked the end of an era.

Bristol K6B Car 505 (EJB 228) was one of the buses regularly working from Stokenchurch Dormy Shed, and it is seen laid over at the Frogmoor Parking Area between turns on Route 40 out to Radnage. Tizer was a very favoured 'pop' drink of the period!

With new coaches now available for the *South Midland* fleet, it was decided to transfer the pair of 'express' bodied Bristol L6B's to the TV fleet, though they retained their original fleet numbers 71/2 (EBD 234/5). They were re-painted in the standard saloon livery, without regard to the side beading. As they had the single-aperture style of destination box, they were also equipped with hinged plates bearing the legend 'relief' and situated beneath the nearside canopy. As both lasted until 1959 it is perhaps surprising that the front aperture were never rebuilt to the standard format for the fleet. After re-painting 71 was sent to Maidenhead, but once 72 was completed in February, both were allocated to High Wycombe, one often being found on the Aylesbury 'by the pretty way' Route 80. It is also worth noting that certain journeys on that route allowed the crew breaks to drive round to the nearby *United Counties* garage and make use of the canteen, so it perhaps strange that joint operation was never considered?

Bristol L6B Car 71 (EBD 234) after transfer to the TV fleet and enjoying a trip to the races.

It will be noted that the Bristol LS-types so far received had the relatively powerful Gardner 6-cylinder engine, as there was no Bristol unit on offer at that time. However, in connection with the need to achieve more economic operation, it was decided that one of the chassis on order for bus work would receive a 5-cylinder Gardner engine for evaluation. As already discussed, there had been quite a few problems with the initial LS's received, but other issues concerned their handling by drivers. Being rather more box-like in structure, they were prone to knocks and scrapes, particularly as some drivers had problems with the concept of the front overhang, whilst their 11-foot height also caused damage where older types had safely passed by!

On 20th January Mr. Campbell paid a visit to *Brighton, Hove & District* to see how they had dealt with their Essex Bus Washing Machine to accept both 7ft 6ins and 8ft-wide buses. Their General Manager, Tom Pruett hosted the visit, after which the *Thames Valley* machines received similar modifications. Plans were also being made that month to extend the Botley Road garage, the ultimate aim being to house all the Oxford-based fleet under one roof.

1950 Bristol K6B-type Car 530 (FBL 32) emerges from Bridge Avenue on Maidenhead Local Service 19 to serve the estates westwards to Sealey's Stores, the route having its origins with Marlow & District.

New vehicles delivered in January consisted of one further Bristol KSW6B/ECW L27/28R Car 663 (HBL 65), which went to Reading, plus another of the Bristol LS6G/ECW B45F service saloons, Car 679 (HBL 81) allocated to High Wycombe.

During February the plans for extending Maidenhead garage were agreed, and a start was made in clearing the area of trees and re-locating the cycle shed, which also resulted in the loss of the rear parking area. There was still a chronic shortage of Skilled Fitters, the Newbury area now suffering with competition from the better wages on offer at the AERE and AWRE sites. This resulted in a number of vehicles having to be sent to Reading Works for major dockings.

Bristol LS-type Car 681 (HBL 83) was put to work on the long Route 28 (High Wycombe-Henley-Reading), and is seen at Cemetery Junction soon after delivery.

Only one new bus arrived in February, being a further Bristol LS6G/ECW B45F saloon, Car 681 (HBL 83), which was allocated to High Wycombe. Further of the type were received during March as Cars 680/2 (HBL 82/4), the former also going to Wycombe, whilst 682 was added to the Reading allocation.

High Wycombe's new Bristol saloons also covered shorter journeys such as the 35 to Downley Commom, where their 6-cylinder Gardner engines were put to good use on the steep Plomer Hill (or 'Downley Pitch', as it was known locally). This scene includes a delightful rustic bus shelter at the rural terminus.

In the meantime the troublesome Guy coaches were slowly shaping up at Brislington, resulting in Car 88 (SFC 503) being presented to the Certifying Officer at Bristol on 16th March. After that it returned to the Guy Works in Wolverhampton for pre-delivery checks on 19th, and it was finally delivered on the last day of that month, an event that had increasingly seemed never likely to ever occur! The C41C bodywork was largely based on the rather angular Leyland design for 'Royal Tiger' chassis, with a raked front windscreen and a high waistrail, the result looking heavyweight – a fact borne out on the weighbridge where they totalled 8tons 5cwt 3qtrs, against a Bristol LS coach at a mere 7tons and even a KSW double-decker at 7tons 17cwt!

Guy 89 (SFC 504) entering Victoria Coach Station.

It will be noted that the Guy coaches retained the 1952 registration numbers booked for them, with further examples arriving as Cars 86/9 (SFC 501/4) in April, all of the quartet being allocated to Oxford for express duties in the main. Deliveries from ECW were also still subject to delays, and TV accepted that it would have to accept some Bristol LS chassis originally for saloon bodies as coaches if delivery dates were to be met, resulting in some only having 30-gallon fuel tanks, in place of the 'touring' capacity of 50 gallons when first received (though these were later changed).

This rear shot at High Wycombe Station also shows Car 680 (HBL 82) on Route 35 duties. Note that these buses had full destination screens as new, though they were of course also crew-operated at that point.

Mr. Campbell continued his research into lightweight buses by visiting *Western National, Southern National, Eastern Counties, Eastern National, Hants & Dorset* and *Lincolnshire Road Car* before finalising his report in March.

A pair of older double-deckers were disposed of during March, each eliminating a particular type from the fleet. Former *Plymouth CT* Mumford-bodied

Leyland 'Titan' TD2-type Car 435 (DR 9636) and Brush-bodied 'Titan' TD4 Car 275 (JB 5854) were sold, whilst April saw the demise of N&D 'Tiger' TS8 Cars 179 (AJB 814, ex-TV 342) and 182 (AJB 818, ex-TV 346). New stock received in April was another Bristol LS6G/ECW B45F saloon allocated initially to Reading as Car 683 (HBL 85).

Car 683 was later one of the LS buses transferred to the Crowthorne Dormy Shed for Routes 3 and 3a, and it seen on the latter at Cemetery Junction in Reading.

In preparation for the move to the Colonnade of the Body & Paint Shop, a new recruit was taken on from 7th April as a Learner Bodybuilder. He already had some *Thames Valley* pedigree, as young Ken was the son of Dick Peddell, a long-serving Conductor at the Stoke Row Dormy Shed. The remainder of the staff were re-located to there from 4th May, and over the following decade they undertook some extensive work on several generations of Bristol double-deckers under the supervision of Mr. G. Bucksey. Shortly before this the same team had obliged with the re-painting of a trio of ECW-bodied AEC 'Regal' coaches on behalf of *Tillings Transport*.

Although the underfloor-engined saloons were taking over some longer routes, the Bristol L-series were still to be found very widely. Car 633 (GJB 271) was the final half-cab example delivered as new, and it awaits duty in the parking yard between the Reading stations. The need for a relief on the 3a seems remarkable!

The active fleet of Leyland-built vehicles continued to dwindle as newer buses arrived, and with the Summer schedules from 16th May their duties were as below:

Double-deck Leylands based at Reading –

No.	Seating	Duties
1	L48R	Contract R/C2 Aldermaston (AWRE)
1	L52R	Contract R/C4 Aldermaston (AWRE)
1	L52R	Contract R/C5 Aldermaston (AWRE)

Double-deck Leylands based at Maidenhead –

| 1 | L48R | Route 23 to Cookham Dean |
| 1 | L52R | Route 23 to Cookham Dean |

Single-deck Leylands based at Maidenhead –

| 6 | B32R | Used on Local Reliefs |
| 1 | C33F | Used on Local Reliefs |

Single-deck Leylands based at High Wycombe –

| 5 | B32R | Used on Local Reliefs |

Double-deck Leylands based at Newbury –

| 1 | L52R | Contract N/C1 to Harwell (AERE) |
| 1 | L52R | Contract N/C7 Aldermaston (AWRE) |

Single-deck Leylands based at Newbury –

3	C33F	Used on Local Reliefs
1	C33F	Contract N/E5 Kintbury – Didcot
1	C33F	Contract N/E7 to Milton Depot (via Hampstead Norris)
1	C33F	Contract N/E8 to Milton Depot (via Chieveley)
1	C33F	Contract N/E20 Aldermaston (AWRE)
1	C32F	Contract N/E17 Frilsham – Harwell

Single-deck Leyland based at Lambourn –

| 1 | C33F | Route 106/106a and school journeys |

Car 340 (AJB 812) at Newbury on contract duties.

At this point of time the Leylands based at each location were as follows:

Reading – 'Titan' TD4 Cars 335/6, TD5 Cars 341/70, plus spare 'Tiger' TS8 Cars 344 and 371-3

Maidenhead – 'Titan' TD4 Car 274, TD5 Car 339, 'Tiger' TS8 Cars 345/8, 374/5/9/80 and TS8 coach 388 or 389 (the other one being based at **Lambourn**)

High Wycombe – 'Tiger' TS7 Car 332 and TS8 Cars 361/3/6/8 and 378, plus TS8 coach 390 as a spare

Newbury – 'Titan' TD5 Cars 340 and 369, 'Tiger' TS8 coaches 381-7 and one TS7 coach in use and the other of that type as a spare vehicle

As the numbers of Leyland saloons declined, more of the contract runs and relief duties fell to the older batches of Bristol L-types. One of the 1948 examples with high-backed seats takes a rest whilst the crew partake of a tea break at the popular Frank's Café at Loddon Bridge. Also note the damaged side panels!

Sharp-eyed readers may note that several of the TS8 saloons mentioned above that had for a time carried N&D fleet numbers had, by this point, reverted to their original numbers, as did Guy 'Arab' 420.

Further Bristol LS6G/ECW B45F saloons arrived in May as Cars 684/5 (HBL 86/7), which were initially allocated to Reading, though they were earmarked for conversion of Route 3 to that type once sufficient of them were available. The final Guy coach also arrived that month as Car 87 (SFC 502) and went straight to Oxford. A further trio of Bristol KSW6B's with ECW L27/28R bodies were delivered that month as Cars 664-6 (HBL 66-8), the first pair going to Reading and the third one to Maidenhead.

Bristol KSW6B Car 664 (HBL 66) was seen on Route 9, which had workings between Reading and Mortimer, plus a number of journeys onto Tadley, and used a bus was based at the Tadley Dormy Shed.

A new addition to the Service Vehicle fleet in May was a Ford 'Anglia' 8hp car (HDP 401), which was obtained for Inspector's use at High Wycombe, the cost being £452 10s 6d (less fleet discount of course!).

One of the Leyland double-deckers nearing the end of its working life with Thames Valley was ECW-bodied 'Titan' TD5 Car 369 (ARX 991) seen by the Head Office building in Lower Thorn Street.

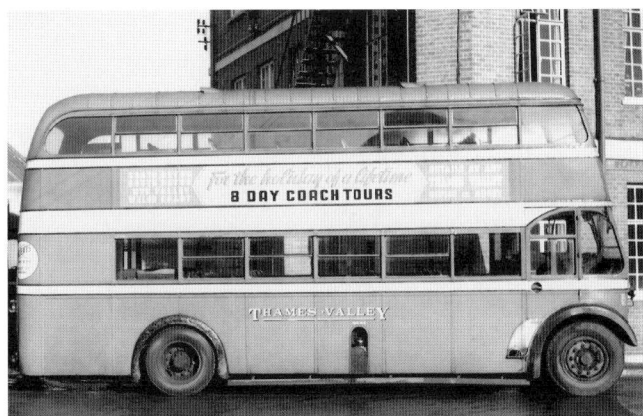

There were a number of changes with the Summer timetable of 16th May, mostly affecting operations in the Newbury area. However, the exception was Route 29 (Marlow – Marlow Common), which became just a short-working of Route 28. The hourly headway was maintained and the duty covered by a 39-seater LL6B-type Bristol based at Wycombe Marsh.

Over at Newbury, Route 101 (Newbury – Chilton) was altered to run through Stanmore, whereas the Tuesday/Thursday/Saturday-only service on Route 101a (Newbury – Peasemore – Stanmore) was cut back to run as far as Peasemore only. Route 104 (Newbury – Headley – Kingsclere) lost its separate identity, being incorporated into new Route 122 from Newbury through to Basingstoke. This was worked jointly with *Wilts & Dorset,* though the Kingsclere-based Guy 'Arab' bus continued to contribute to the service, along with a Newbury based vehicle and the W&D bus working from Basingstoke.

This new through route operated hourly, with a 56-minute scheduled time over the 17-mile journey. It is perhaps strange that this had not been a joint operation before then, as *Venture* had reached Newbury in October 1937, when it purchased *Bill Kent's* services based in Baughurst. *Newbury & District* purchased his mother's *Kingsclere Coaches* that same April, though they continued to work her routes to Kingsclere and Ashford Hill without any apparent thoughts on running through to Basingstoke (though she had in fact done so). Even when both those operators came under *Red & White* control, the link was not made, and even *Thames Valley* and *Wilts & Dorset* took 3 years to finally get around to it!

The vehicles of the Red & White era were still quite evident. Above – Duple-bodied AEC 'Regal' coach 145 (EBL 736) was still in fine condition when seen at the Bath depot of Bristol Omnibus when on a day trip. Below – One of a trio of Lydney-bodied AEC 'Regals', Car 162 (FBL 920) is seen on contract work, where these were often to be found. The cab window arrangement is unusual, but the overall look is very typically of the Red & White style.

At the same time Route 104a (Newbury – Ashford Hill) was extended onto Wolverton and Hannington, though it still only ran on Wednesdays, Thursdays and Saturdays. It should be noted that *Wilts & Dorset* had acquired the services of *S. Huntley & Son* of Oakley, so the Kingsclere – Basingstoke route (originally *E.G. Kent*), also Basingstoke – Hannington and Kingsclere – Hannington routes, which doubtless directly influenced the changes in that area.

Route 110 (Newbury, Western Avenue – Thatcham Station) was also extended to run as Newbury, The Wharf – Thatcham Station – Brimpton – Baughurst – Aldermaston – Tadley, which gave a direct workman's service to the AWRE site, whilst there were early-morning 'shorts' to Thatcham Depot. The latter did actually feature on the previous schedule, but other projections from Newbury and Hambridge Road were dropped. With the extension it also made a connection with *Wilts & Dorset* Route 137 for travel onto Basingstoke, though that was not mentioned in the timetable.

One completely new route was a Sundays-only 129 (Newbury Station or Wharf – Shaw – Hermitage – Hampstead Norris – Compton – East Ilsley – Chilton – Upton & Blewbury Station – Didcot Station), though it only featured two return journeys. This had been put on in place of the Sunday operation of trains on the Didcot, Newbury & Southampton Line.

Also following on from the previous Road/Rail/River Tours of the year before, further trips were arranged for rail passengers from Cardiff and Southampton, who travelled to Reading for a steamer trip to Henley-on-Thames and returned to Reading by bus.

Former Thames Valley buses remained popular with showmen, and Car 378 (BBL 564) is seen still in full TV livery, but with a few structural additions!

May saw the end of the road for Leyland 'Titan' TD5 Car 369 (ARX 991), and its place on contract duties was taken by one of the utility-bodied Bristol K6A's. During June Leyland 'Tiger' TS8 Car 378 (BBL 564) found further employment on the fairgrounds, but that still left a number of Leyland buses languishing behind the Newbury shed, of which we shall hear more about in due course.

The Company lost another old faithful servant with the death of Mr. H.H. Robinson on 8th May. He had been a respected Fitter at Reading Works since June 1927, when the Tilling-Stevens B9A's were arriving!

The Newbury scene in respect of double-deckers also changed during the early 1950's, as standard Bristol types joined the native Guys, which were duly joined by others of that make drafted in from the TV fleet, a good selection of which are in this view of The Wharf.

There was quite a flurry of activity in painting up the Head Office, the Colonnade Enquiry Office and even Fingest Dormy Shed, some of which was inspired by the forthcoming Coronation. Additional signs were made and erected at the Maidenhead Bus and Coach Stations, and also at the bus shelters in Mackenzie Street in Slough, whilst the signs at the entrance to the Colonnade were updated. At Slough the TV buses met with three *London Transport* routes, as there had long been a joint arrangement over that town. Over at High Wycombe LT buses worked alongside TV's on the busy cross-town Local Services 26/26a (LT 326/326a) and at times the latter's buses could be seen laid over on the forecourt of Desborough Road Garage, saving dead mileage out to its premises at the foot of Marlow Hill. Over at Maidenhead at strike broke out on 16th May, after a crew refused to take a bus over which they considered had insufficient route indication, but the dispute was not backed by other garages and was soon over!

As preparations were made for the Coronation, all the coach fleet received attention, and Bristol L6B Car 490 (EJB 212) emerges from a full repaint.

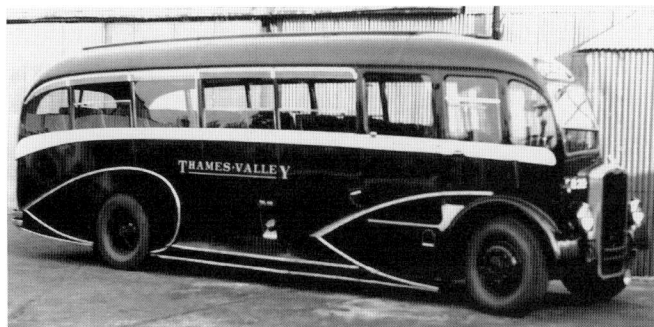

On 20th May Bristol KSW6B Car 643 (GJB 281), one of the Ascot allocation working on Route 2, was ditched at Farley Hall, near Binfield after the driver had to take action to avoid colliding a cattle lorry. However, there were no injuries, and the pair of Ford Recovery Wagons soon had the bus back on the road, the damage not being major.

Coaches of the N&D fleet were still to be seen widely, often providing assistance to South Midland, where only the sharp-eyed would notice their ownership.

The big news for June was of course the Coronation, and special red, white and blue leaflets were produced to highlights travel arrangements. On Coronation Day, 2nd June, additional early-morning coaches left Oxford at 5am, arriving at Victoria Coach Station at 7.55 am, running via the Henley road. Throughout the day both the routes between Oxford and London, via Henley or High Wycombe, had journeys every hour on the hour, with extra coaches drafted in from Newbury and High Wycombe. For viewing the illuminations, an extra departure left from Victoria at midnight, running daily between 26th May and 16th June, via the Henley route. The actual procession route could be toured on a special *London Transport* route leaving from nearby the Coach Station at Elizabeth Bridge, and ran every few minutes. The event was highly popular, as another opportunity to shake off the post-war austerity.

Events related to the Coronation continued for an extended period, resulting in excursions to view the Coronation Fleet Review, which could also be reached by the express service of *South Midland* between 11 and 16 June. In addition, there was a journey to Lee-on-Solent to view the fleet on 14th June, whilst on 15th a later journey left Southsea at midnight in order to see the fleet illuminated, and all of these journeys required 3 or 4 coaches to meet the demand. As usual the loadings from the Newbury area were catered for by coaches based at that garage, whilst the other towns served by *Thames Valley* were also provided with excursions for the same events.

As well as the Coronation, there was the usual peak traffic for Royal Ascot Races, a time when unfamiliar types reached the Grange Parking Ground at Ascot. Above – Harrington-bodied Leyland' Tiger' TS8 Car 389 (BMO 988) and, Below – TV's prototype Bristol K5G Car 391 (BRX 656) with ECW body, both being delivered during 1939.

Both of the London express routes from Reading also experienced exceptional loadings during this period, resulting in numerous relief vehicles being added, and even some quite aged types and more recent service cars were to be seen on both the A and B routes. The relative lack of disposals during that Summer is partly explained by these peak needs, though there were a number of vehicles out of use that were not worthy of the work that would be required to return to service, and there was also a downturn in demand for sales.

From the outset Desborough Road Garage was used to serve routes leaving the town to the west and north, as well as the cross-town Local Services, saving a lot of dead miles had Wycombe Marsh cars been used. By June 1953 the garage was responsible for, or provided a contribution to, the following routes:

Route	Service	Covered by
27	HW – Great Missenden	3 Bristol L55R
31	HW – Lacey Green	2 Bristol B39R
33	HW – Desborough Castle Est.	4 Bristol B39R
34	HW – Speen	1 Bristol B35R
38	HW – Booker	2 Bristol L55R
42	Loudwater – W. Wycombe	2 Bristol L55R
42	Loudwater – Booker Hill Est.	2 Bristol B39R
80	HW – Aylesbury	1 Bristol B35R
81	HW – Booker	1 Bristol B35R

The shiny new Western National Bristol 'Lodekka' 1863 (OTT 2) was caught on camera by young Les Hollingsworth who found it outside his parents shop and Spinning Wheel Café in Bracknell High Street.

It will be recalled *Thames Valley* had sampled the prototype 'Lodekka' back in 1951, but no order had been forthcoming, which seems rather surprising when one considers how enthusiastically Basil Sutton had reacted to the Leyland 'Titan' at the 1927 Show, the two buses representing the most significant events in double-deck bus design! For this second trial, BCV sent one of the 'pre-production' examples destined for *Western National*. It was used from 16th June, the 58-seat capacity being put to good use during Ascot Week, and it spent until 29th June working Route 2 (Reading – Ascot – Windsor) from Ascot Garage. The staff there, along with passengers were asked for their comments, Messrs. Sutton, Campbell and Cross trying it out on 27th in service, though it would be a further 3 years before TV actually took delivery of any!

Bristol LS6B coach 92 (TWL 57) was for the South Midland fleet and is seen at Oxford when new.

However, deliveries in June were of familiar types, and consisted of further ECW L27/28R-bodied Bristol KSW6B's, Cars 667-70 (HBL 69-72), plus another LS, but this time fitted with a Gardner 5HLW engine, as Car 686 (HBL 88). The KSW's were allocated to Reading (670), Maidenhead (667) and Newbury (668 and 669), whilst the saloon went initially to Reading. Also received were 3 of the Bristol LS coaches of the *South Midland* order, as Cars 90-2 (TWL 55-7), fitted with horizontal Bristol AVW engines and ECW C37F bodies primarily intended for express work.

Bristol KSW6B Car 670 (HBL 72) on the Station Hill stand for Route 9, awaits the departure for Mortimer Station. Note the Langstons advert, a traditional shop on the corner of Friar Street and West Street selling a wide variety of country casual and working clothes.

As previously noted, one of the Windover-bodied L6B coaches was at Ascot, that being Car 488 (EJB 210) up to March 1953, went it went to Reading for overhaul. Its place was initially taken by similar coach 548 (FMO 23) through March and April, which was replaced by identical Car 545 (FMO 20) in May. That vehicle remained active until delicensed in December, when it was placed in store at Ascot, and the active role passed to Car 546 (FMO 21) until 545 came out of store in March 1954.

Loss of parking space at the Colonnade and behind the Maidenhead Garage led to Newbury becoming a veritable dumping ground of redundant vehicles from May 1953 onwards, much to the annoyance of Reg Hibbert! Little progress was made on selling many of these vehicles, some of which had parts taken from them as time went by. By 22nd July the area behind the erstwhile TV Dormy Shed was host to the following:- Leyland 'Tiger' TS4 Cars 244/9 (RX 9541 and 9703), 244 being without an engine; 'Tiger' TS7 Cars 322/3/5/8/34 (ABL 752/3/5/8/64); 'Tiger' TS8's 343 (AJB 815), 368 (ARX 990) and 372 (BBL 558); along with 'Titan' TD4 Cars 274/7 (JB 5853/6) and TD5 Car 341 (AJB 813).

With such a rural area to cover, mishaps occurred to buses from time to time, and Maidenhead's 1939 Bristol K5G Car 403(BRX 919) landed up in a ditch on a wintry road, requiring rescue by one of the Ford V8 Recovery Wagons.

Details of the vehicles dumped at Newbury were also circulated to associated companies, but there were no takers! By 28th August Car 249 had also lost its engine, whilst the quintet of TS7's had been sent back to Reading. TD4-types 274/7 also returned there, though the latter was back at Newbury in due course. However, other buses were sent to those still awaiting disposal, with former *Newbury & District* AEC 'Regal' rebuild Car 157 (FAX 349) and Leyland TS8 Cars 344 (AJB 816) and 379 (BBL 565) being added by then. A number of other double-deckers were also present at times during the period July to August, either sold from Newbury or returned to Reading, with 'Titan' TD4 Cars 273 (JB 5852) and 335/6 (ABL 765/6) and TD5 Cars 339/40 (AJB 811/2) all making appearances. It should also be noted that 'Tiger' TS4 Car 244 had served as a temporary Inspector's Office at Maidenhead Coach Station, along with similar Car 249 (RX 9703), each linked to the telephone and with one being situated on either side of the large oval central grassed area.

Reg Hibbert's other big concern at that time was the condition of many of the utility bodies on the Guy buses, both from the original N&D fleet and those now transferred from *Thames Valley*. Leaking cabs were a frequent entry on the Driver's Defects Sheets, and Reg would resolve where the work was required by driving the bus into the Bus Washing Machine and he would sit in the cab noting the results of his 'water test'! The detailed records made by him survive, so I will quote the results of his inspections:

Car 100 (CRX 280) – *Floor weak in centre gangway of lower saloon forward of gearbox trap door. Staircase has split and two rear seats in lower saloon require re-upholstery. Top deck rear window near side leaks, panels above platform leaking, as are nearside and offside panels. Water-tested 13th August, windscreen requires re-fitting, leaking across top in several places. Nearside front bulkhead window leaking badly into the lower saloon, leaking centre pillar above front destination box, glass of box not watertight, top deck first nearside and offside windows both leak, second and fourth nearside and first and fourth offside in the lower saloon all leak, roof cracked in lower saloon at grab-rail fixing.*

Duple-bodied Guy 'Arab' Car 419 (CJB 138) is seen after transfer to Newbury, though it was evidently one of those in better condition. Note that it still retains the un-glazed upper-deck rear emergency door which was one of the utility features.

Car 101 (CRX 281) – *General condition very fair, timber good, emergency door glazed, signs of body movement, panelled inside and upholstered in red and black ex-TV seating which is in very fair condition.*
Car 106 (CRX 596) - *This was sent to Reading Works in November as a result of inspection, though Reg did not even attempt to list its numerous problems!*
Car 421 (CJB 140) – *Glass fitted to rear emergency door, soft timber in roof of upper saloon, though in general good condition, upholstery blue and yellow in poor condition.*
Car 423 (CMO 653) – *General poor condition, blue upholstery in poor condition, no glass in emergency door. General body movement, not panelled inside,*

soft timber above rear platform, front centre upper deck pillar in poor condition.

The Strachan utility bodies on the Bristol K6A's were in much better shape than the bodies on the Guys, and Car 427 (CRX 197) is seen working at Maidenhead after being displaced from Ascot by newer types.

With the above aspects, it is little wonder that there was a feeling amongst the Newbury maintenance staff that they had been 'dumped' on! However, on the other hand, they soon got adept at fitting rubber sealing to offending windows. Also suffering from leaks were the rear boot panels of the Bristol LS coaches, a number of passengers on *South Midland* having complained about damp luggage, so the ECW representative was summoned to resolve the problem. If that wasn't bad enough, marks started to appear on the moquette of the seats on that type, which were caused by dripping condensation from the overhead metal luggage racks.

A pair of Bristol L-types at High Wycombe Station, with Car 521 (FBL 23) on Route 35 to Downley and Car 478 (DMO 682) on Route 32 to Bledlow Ridge.

Leaks of another kind necessitated notices in the Staff Bulletin in July 1953. The first concerned a reminder to crews at the Tadley Dormy Shed not to use the land adjacent to Allen's Garage as a toilet, whilst crews on the notorious 'drinker's bus', the 10.35 p.m. departure

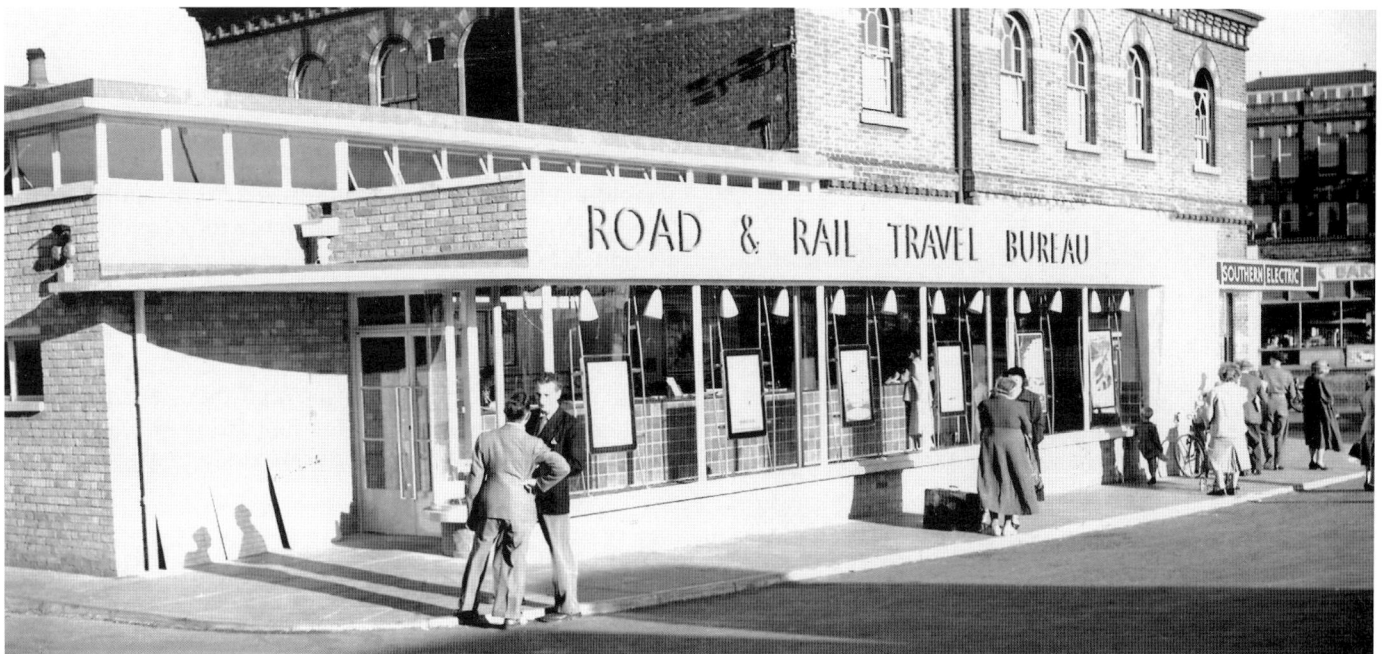

The new Road & Rail Travel Bureau adjacent to the Southern Railway Station. Note the wall-mounted bell to summon the Duty Inspector to the phone seen on the wall of the new Staff Canteen.

of Route 9 from the Three Firs pub in Burghfield Common, that the customary 'comfort stop' must be taken in open country so as not to offend residents!

At Reading the new Travel Bureau was opened on 6th July, though the railway representatives had wanted to wait for a formal opening ceremony. The new affair was indeed smart and modern, and it certainly offered more elbow room than the old wooden hut that had served in that capacity for many years. At the same time the works at the Colonnade were completed.

South Midland Bristol LS6B coach 90 (TWL 55) ran with the ECW 'wings' on the front panel painted black for a short time, and appears to be the only one so treated, though some other operators did favour that.

However, in connection with the works planned at Botley Road, it was acknowledged that there would be an accommodation problem over the Winter months. Therefore, it was decided to make Iffley Road garage an operational base again, though the Bristol coaches would need to remain at Botley Road as they were too

high to enter the Iffley Road buildings. The active fleet at Oxford was reduced by 3 cars to 32, and some delicensed coaches for storage went to other locations.

On 9th July Basil Sutton attended the Southern Area Sub-committee of the Vehicle Design & Maintenance Committee hosted in Southampton by Mr. Wallis of *Hants & Dorset*. Whilst there he inspected the heating system developed Wing-Commander Cave-Brown-Cave and Southampton University, which was fitted to 1940 Bristol K5G-type 1068 (APR 423), a system that was fitted to Bristol 'Lodekkas' in due course.

Further new deliveries for July were another Bristol LS6B coach with ECW C37F body for *South Midland* as Car 93 (TWL 58), plus Cars 694/5 (HMO 840/1) on Bristol KSW6B chassis with ECW L27/28R bodies which were both allocated to Wycombe Marsh. These buses introduced staggered seating on the upper deck, which made leaving inside seats a little easier.

Car 695 was put to work on the busy 18-mile Route 20 between High Wycombe and Windsor.

Although a number of former Thames Valley buses saw service with showmen, few others saw further use from those sold in the early 1950's. An exception to that was Car 336 (ABL 766), a Leyland 'Titan' TD4 new in 1937, which was kitted out as a mobile caravan, remaining in use until the early 1960's and still retaining its old livery. Saved for preservation, it sadly was a project that never made it to fruition.

Another engine was disposed of to H&G Simonds, the Reading-based brewers in July, this time being a Leyland 8.6 litre 6-cylinder oiler, though sold with a broken crankshaft. During the following month two similar engines were sold to *Brimblecombe Bros.*, based in Wokingham, whilst a further pair of incomplete examples went to a dealer in Stratford in East London.

Sales of whole vehicles were, however, in complete doldrums, so the Chairman suggested submitting some to the auction sales held regularly at the old-established London Horse & Motor Repository at the Elephant & Castle in South London. 'Tiger' TS7 Car 334 (ABL 764) was sold there on 30th July for £154 18shillings (after commission), so further buses were selected. However, identical Car 323 (ABL 753) only realised £130, whilst 'Titan' TD4 Car 277 (JB 5856) didn't even reach its reserve price, the latter being taken back and sold at Reading 4 days later for less than its book value! There was of course something of a glut of old buses around this time, whilst frankly many of these on offer from TV were past further use.

Other buses sold during July were the engine-less TS4 'Tiger' Car 244 (RX 9541), 'Titan' TD5 Car 341 (AJB 813) and 'Tiger' TS8 Car 343 (AJB 815). Also disposed of during August were the last 'Tiger' TS4 Car 249 (RX 9703), again without an engine, the last

of the 'Titan' TD4's 273/4 (JB 5852/3) and 335/6 (ABL 765/6) as well as 'Tiger' TS7 Cars 322/5/8 (ABL 752/5/8).

Once the Body & Paintshop had been relocated to the Colonnade, further inspection pits were added in the expanded Reading Works which took over the old bodyshop. Further experiments with one-coat paints took place, and Bristol LWL Car 613 (GJB 251) was so treated during August.

The Annual Horticultural show of the Thames Valley Social & Athletic Club (Reading Branch) was held in Reading Garage on 22nd August, the 1st Prize for the best onions being 7 shillings.

Two further Bristol LS's arrived during August, one being LS6B/ECW C37F-bodied coach 94 (TWL 59) for the *South Midland* fleet, whilst the other was an LS5G-type with ECW B45F body which, as Car 687 (HBL 89) was earmarked for Crowthorne Dormy Shed in due course.

Above - Car 687 (HBL 89) was Maidenhead's first example of that bus type, though it was really intended for other duties as noted. It is seen leaving Maidenhead Bus Station on Route 16 to Tittle Row, the opportunity being taken to try the type out on various local routes. Below – Bristol LS Car 682 (HBL 84) was the regular exchange bus for when any Crowthorne examples were in for servicing, and it is seen on Route 3 arriving at Stations Square.

The intention had been to Replace Bristol LL6B Cars 564-6 (FMO 946-8) at Crowthorne Dormy Shed with

106

Bristol LS6G's 684-6 (HBL 86-8) on Route 3 (Reading – Crowthorne – Camberley), and for Bristol LS5G Car 687 to replace L6B-type Car 540 (FMO 15) on the 3a (Reading – Wokingham – Finchampstead). However, when one of the type was taken over to the shed on 22nd October, it was found that although there was just enough headroom, the hinged doors were not ideal, and they were replaced in due course. Car 540 had already been replaced by mid-September, being re-allocated to serve at the Tadley Dormy Shed on Route 9a (Reading – Grazeley – Tadley, though the exact date of the transfer of the other 3 LS's is not recorded.

A further trio of standard Bristol KSW6B buses with ECW L27/28R bodies arrived in September as Cars 696-8 (HMO 842-4), and the first pair went to Reading. The arrival of further new double-deckers and the sale of the old Leylands resulted in what was left of the latter, plus older Bristol types, being cascaded onto relief and contract duties.

Bristol KSW6B Car 698 (HMO 844) was allocated to Maidenhead and is ready to act as a relief on the busy Route 22 along the Bath Road to Slough.

Car 702 (HMO 848) went to Newbury and is seen at The Wharf Bus Station for Route 112 to Oxford.

On 17th September about 40 members of the Institute of Road Transport Engineers spent the afternoon touring the Reading Works and the Colonnade Body & Paintshop, before travelling on one of the Bristol LS coaches to Monkey Island Hotel at Bray for tea and a later tour of the Maidenhead garage, bus and coach stations.

Bristol LS coaches for Thames Valley included Car 690 (HMO 836), although on this occasion it is shown on hire to West Yorkshire for some unrecorded use.

More KSW6B-type buses followed in October as Cars 699-702 (HMO 845-8), 699 going to Maidenhead, 700 to Wycombe Marsh, 701 to Reading and 702 to Newbury. On the single-deck front, a further pair of Bristol LS5G's with ECW B45F bodies, Cars 706/7 (HMO 852/3) were received and both sent to Wycombe Marsh and put to work on the long Route 28 (High Wycombe – Henley – Twyford – Reading).

The delayed Bristol coaches for *Thames Valley* were received in October as Cars 688-90 (HMO 834-6), the first going to Reading and both the others to Newbury. These were LS6B chassis and had the maximum seat layout of C39F, whereas the other LS6B delivered that month was for *South Midland* as Car 95 (TWL 60), which had 37 seats for express duties. The latter was actually the last vehicle to be numbered in the old SM series, as after that all coaches were within the main *Thames Valley* scheme.

Problems had been experienced with the ventilation on the Guy coaches, so Car 86 (SFC 501) was fitted with a roof vent as an experiment during October. In general there was still a shortage of Skilled Fitters, with Newbury and the High Wycombe garages worst affected. One Dutchman was successfully recruited in October, but others did not accept the offer. Two new passenger shelters were erected at Lane End that month, and Mr. Abberfield and his gang were kept busy around this period, having to deal with snagging issues at Maidenhead Enquiry Office following the liquidation of the original contractor! It should be noted that some shelters were supplied by the Company, others being provided by Local Parishes.

AEC 'Regal' rebuild 157 (FAX 349) had mysterious origins, having been re-registered by Red & White in March 1946 but quoted as having a chassis number already claimed elsewhere. The utility-style body was by Burlingham, and like other rebuilds of the time it received a Gardner 5LW oil engine.

With further new stock, the ranks of the older buses took a hammering, with the withdrawal on October 14th of 'Tiger' TS8's 344 (AJB 816), 368 (ARX 990) and 379 (BBL 565), all of which had latterly been with N&D, plus that fleet's own AEC 'Regal' 157 (FAX 349). Two days later 'Tiger' TS7 Car 332 (ABL 762) followed, as did TS8 Cars 348 (AJB 820) and 361 (ARX 983), all of which went to Newbury dump. The sale later that month of 332 eliminated the TS7 model from the service bus fleet, the first having arrived in June 1935.

TS8 Car 348 went in October, as did 'Regal' 157, which is believed to have been new in 1931, having been purchased through the Ministry of Supply. TS8 Car 375 (BBL 561) went in November, followed by similar buses 361, 368 and 379 in December.

Another AEC 'Regal' was involved in a fatal crash, as *South Midland* coach 59 (NFC 130) collided with a motorcyclist who was overtaking on the wrong side of the road, though the driver was unable to avoid him. The re-bodied 'Tiger' PS1 coach 169 (LWL 995) received a thorough overhaul at Newbury during November, and it certainly repaid the investment of the new body. Indeed, it was always well kept and very much liked by the drivers there.

On 2nd November a set of bus seats were sold to the Yattendon & Frilsham Social Club, a not uncommon situation for resolving a seating requirement. Indeed, the author recalls going into The Cricketers in Yateley to find former *Royal Blue* coach seats in use, complete with seat numbers, and there were other examples of coach or even aircraft seating being reused that way!

Further old cars joined the Newbury yard during late October and early November, and apart from those listed above as sold in those months, these were now 'Tiger' TS8's 345 (AJB 817), 361/8 (ARX 983/90) and 372/3/9 (BBL 558/9/65), 'Tiger' TS7 coaches 262/4 (JB 5841/3), though 264 would return to use,

'Titan' TD5 Car 370 (ARX 992) and Bristol K5G's 395/6/8, 403/8 (BRX 911/2/4/9/24) and 413 (CJB 132). These were joined shortly afterwards by Guy 'Arabs' 421-3 (CJB 140/1 and CMO 653), though the Guys all returned to service again. Two further Bristol LS5G's with ECW B45F bodies arrived during November, as Cars 708/10 (HMO 854/6), the first going to Reading and the second to High Wycombe. During December identical Car 709 (HMO 855) was received and allocated to Reading, whilst new Bristol KSW6B/ECW L27/28R 'deckers 703/4 (HMO 849/50) were sent to Ascot and Newbury respectively. Ascot's Bristol K6A-type Car 439 (CRX 548) was displaced by the new bus and was re-allocated to Newbury.

Wycombe Marsh's Bristol LS Car 706 (HMO 852) is seen waiting on Station Hill in Reading on Route 28.

Work continued on the Botley Road extension during December, sweeping away the old air raid shelter. The Nissen hut in the Southern Railway Yard at Reading was also disposed of that month, now the new canteen was open. Some very cold weather that month also had a detrimental effect on operations, and the Guys once again showed their weakness to radiator bursts!

The cold weather also revealed another issue on the LS-type saloons, as the nearside windscreen tended to mist up, a problem not encountered on half-cab buses. Various experiments with ventilator grilles were made but drivers also complained of excessive reflections from interior lights, leading to the fitting of blinds for lowering in the hours of darkness, these being made of a dark green material.

On 30th December a snowy lorry arrived at Reading from Norwich, as TV had agreed to exchange three Gardner 5LW engines for the same number of Bristol AVW units from *Eastern Counties*.

From December Harrington-bodied 'Tiger' TS8 coaches 381-6 (BMO 980-5) remained allocated to Newbury, whilst 387 (BMO 986) was transferred to Reading, 388/9 (BMO 987/8) were at Maidenhead, and 390 (BMO 989) was still at High Wycombe, all of these vehicles being in constant use. It is true to say that these vehicles worked hard all their long lives, as after only a brief spell on their intended coach duties, they had been plunged into use as buses during the war, then refurbished and kept busy ever since!

1954

Vehicles deliveries for this year had originally been intended as 12 Bristol KSW6B's and 12 Bristol LS5G saloons, but the latter were cancelled and a full order for 24 KSW's taken instead. Eastern Coach Works did indicate that the final 5 would have to be programmed for 1955, whilst 6 were specified with coach seats and doors for the London services. Given the recent trial of the 'Lodekka', it seems surprising that TV ordered such a large batch of the previous model.

During January a smaller and un-shaded fleetname was applied to buses, with KS6B-type Car 600 (FMO 982) being the first to be so treated. It should also be noted that the LS-type saloons lacked a fleetname on the front panel when new, so they looked very plain, though over the years the addition of fleetnames, fog lamps and pay-as-you-enter signs all filled the space.

Bristol LS6B Car 714 (HMO 860) leaves Bridge Avenue on Route 24 to Cookham Dean. The front end is still in the original style, with central fog lamp, but the side fleetnames are of the new thinner type.

As noted back in October 1953, the poorer examples of the 1939 Bristol K5G's had been withdrawn, but the better ones passed through the Colonnade Shops over the Winter months for further service. Re-paints were now being achieved at a much higher rate, whilst the Newbury was once again undertaking full repaints following improvements to staffing there, the latter easing the pressure on the Reading facilities. Newbury was also self-sufficient in PSV Driving Tests, all being personally conducted by Reg Hibbert. The candidate would set off in one of the older service cars on a trip out to Camp Close, with Reg sitting behind him in the lower saloon. If all went well, the driver was passed, but if Reg was not happy with the outward journey, he would take over 'before he bent the bloody thing' and the candidate was rejected. All these tests were recorded in a little notebook, though some comments are unprintable! Another aspect of the working of Newbury Garage was 'Ginger', very

much Reg's right-hand man and very good engineer, who formed an essential buffer between Reg and the other staff, as he could gauge when it was safe to talk to Reg - only when smoking his Capstan full-strength cigarette. Actually, Reg could also be very kind if he took a liking to you, but I still recall the dressing down he gave me when he first caught me skulking round Newbury Garage, though after that I was given a mug of tea and allowed to look at his photos in his drawer – and I was always welcome to call in again.

Above - One of the photos from Reg's desk drawer recorded AEC 'Regal' Car 137 (DMO 329) after collision with a telegraph pole. Below – This device was used at Reading Works for manouvering vehicles in and out of the shops. Bristol L6B Car 540 (FMO 15) was usually allocated to Tadley Dormy Shed as the destination blinds clearly indicate.

Several vehicles were subjected to experiments during February, with LS-type Car 686 (HBL 88) receiving modified road springs to improve handling. Bristol KSW6B Car 705 (HMO 851) was fitted from new with a different type of front ventilator on both decks and was sent to the FVDRE at Chobham for testing in the wind tunnel alongside standard issue Car 701.

The surviving Leylands were rarely used on service runs by this time, though 'Tiger' TS8 Car 371 (BBL 557) was sent out on Route 3 to Camberley.

As noted above, Bristol KSW6B/ECW L27/28R Car 705 (HMO 851) was received during February and was allocated to Reading. Also delivered during that month were further Bristol LS6B/ECW B45F saloons 711-4 (HMO 857-60), allocated to High Wycombe (711/2) and Maidenhead (713/4). The remaining trio of LS6B/ECW C39F coaches were also delivered as Cars 691-3 (HMO 837-9), with the first two going to Maidenhead and the third to Desborough Road.

The month of March started badly when Desborough Road Fitter Johnson noticed that Bristol LS Car 680 (HBL 82) had disappeared from the forecourt at 11.15pm. The matter was reported to the Police, who a little later heard from a lorry driver at Stokenchurch that the bus had collided with him then driven off. It was eventually found at 5.30am the next day and was badly damaged, two men later being charged with the various offences.

Over at Newbury there was mixed news during March, with Arthur Waldron becoming Assistant Traffic Supervisor from the 15th, a job he did very well and one that fostered harmonious working within the workforce there. There were still many employees there who traced their roots back to the constituent operators of the old *Newbury & District*, and still had a considerable pride in a job done well. Indeed, he was aided by Inspector Ralph Revell, who had been a driver for N&D. On the other hand, a suggestion at a meeting on the 19th that the Newbury bodyshop work be transferred to Reading received a short sharp 'no' from Reg Hibbert, who had now managed to get a very good team together!

Also on the 19th a *British Road Services* lorry was involved in a fatal accident at the notorious Royal

Hotel crossroads by Ascot Racecourse, so one of the TV Ford Recovery Wagons attended. Another example of co-operation between the bus company and the nationalised haulier had occurred earlier that month, when the BRS Depot Manager at Reading had asked if TV would be interested in employing fitters who might become redundant if their depot closed.

On the last day of March Bristol KSW6B Car 670 (HBL 72) was overturned near the Magpie & Parrot at Arborfield when its driver was forced to use the grass verge to avoid an overtaking lorry. The inexperienced driver soon found the verge to be soft, and the bus then fell sideways into the deep ditch. There were no serious injuries, though the bus was badly damaged and quite difficult to recover. The incident was identical to that befalling Leyland 'Titan' TD4 Car 270 back in 1950, though the roof stayed intact.

Above- Car 670 where it came to rest at Arborfield and, *below-* the recovery half completed, with winches to the upper deck and baulks of timber shoring up the nearside.

During March the last active Leyland at Maidenhead, 'Tiger' TS8 Car 374 (BBL 560), was withdrawn and ended the association between that garage and Leyland vehicles that had existed since 1928. Indeed, the town had seen the make even earlier, as the first route operated by *British* in the area had reached there with former *Barnsley & District* Leylands in July 1915. 'Tiger' TS8 Cars 372/3/4/80 (BBL 558/9/60/6) were all disposed of during that month.

April saw a start being made on removing the old Leyland 'Tiger' coaches, with TS7 Car 262 (JB 5841) and TS8 Cars 382/5 (BMO 981/4), all departing now that the other Bristol LS-types were in stock. The one remaining TS7 coach 264 (JB 5843) returned to service, as did the other 'BMO's, and all remained in use throughout the Summer, with some returning to Oxford again to assist *South Midland*.

Harrington-bodied 'Tiger' TS8 Car 381 (BMO 980) was helping out at Ascot Races in June.

The only service buses disposed of during April were 6 Bristol K5G's which *Eastern National* had decided to purchase for contract duties. The type was standard to its fleet, which required further buses for building projects in that area. Cars 395/6/8/9 and 403/8 (BRX 911/2/4/5/9/24) became EN Nos. 1002-7 and they were collected by the Essex drivers two per day between 21st and 23rd April. Their new owner used them on the Tilbury Power Station contract for 3-4 years, and local transport correspondent Peter Snell noted that two carried the associated *Westcliff-on-Sea* company fleetnames, whilst 3 were apparently not used at all. Even more curious was the fact that those 3 returned to TV again as we shall see in due course.

Car 408 (BRX 924) repainted into the green and cream livery of Eastern National with silver radiator.

In the meantime a completely new bus service had commenced on 5th April, linking the towns of Reading and Guildford for the first time. Route 75 travelled as far as Bracknell parallel to Route 2, offering yet more journeys over that road, but was worked jointly with *Aldershot & District*. Considering the very similar origins of the two concerns, with the same Directors and even Chairman, very little active co-operation had taken place between them. The new venture ran every 2 hours, the first TV bus leaving Reading at 7.25am and the first A&D journey left Farnham Road Bus Station in Guildford at the same time. The route was 28.5 miles long and after Bracknell it ran by way of Bagshot – Lightwater – West End – Bisley – Brookwood – Worplesdon and Stoughton, the journey time being 1hour and 45 minutes. The final evening journeys left at 9.25 and the TV bus reached Reading at 11.07, and it is worth noting that the operation took place on seven days a week at the same headway.

Bristol LWL6B Car 613 (GJB 251) was the first bus on new Route 75 and is seen at Reading Stations. The Aldershot Company used Dennis 'Lancet' saloons.

Work on the construction of the Maidenhead Garage extension finally got underway on 20th April, though problems with groundwater from the adjacent stream caused some difficulties. Also, over at Frogmoor, a lot of activity took place that Spring tidying up buildings owned by TV. Some were rented out, whilst others were demolished as the site was increasingly used for bus parking, However, services continued to pick up and set down at the Frogmoor Gardens bus stands.

Rising fuel costs and low income from some of the rural routes invariably led to bus company managers to consider one-man-operation, something that was (ironically) common amongst those independent firms taken over. This topic at TV also became allied to the thoughts on lightweight vehicles, which could be used economically on restricted roads and without separate conductors. *Thames Valley* therefore discussed during the Spring the possibility of converting Bedford OB's to one-man-operation. The Company had 5 with coach bodies, Cars 164/5 (LJO 756/7) and 604-6 (FRX 313 -

111

Above- The lowbridge pair of Duple-bodied Guy 'Arab' 111's were the usual performers on Route 106 (Newbury – Lambourn). Car 171 (FMO 516) is seen parked at the Lambourn terminus. Below- The perils of the rural operations in the Newbury area are shown by another of Reg Hibbert's photos. This AEC 'Regal' Car 134 (DMO 323) had been abandoned in a snow drift near Chaddleworth and passengers taken to safety by Land Rover. On 29th January Reg and his lads could finally reach it and return it to Newbury.

5), as well as bus-bodied examples 510-2/20 (EJB 232-4/42), which covered weight-restricted Route 18 between Maidenhead and Marlow. The Certifying Officer was asked to comment, but the work required to convert the coach-bodied examples would include a driver-operated door and removal of the pair of seats forward of the door, so none of those were converted. He did, however, approve one of the bus bodies converted to a 27-seater by making the rear seat for five instead of four, and by placing seats for three longitudinally over the wheel arches. The revised seating was of a tubular - framed bus - type, and still it

could traverse Marlow Bridge within the 5 ton weight limit. All four were so converted, though they remained crew-operated for the meantime.

Bedford OWB's 437/8 (CRX 546/7) had become spare by that time, but were retained for odd school runs and reliefs locally around Maidenhead. One was used regularly to Borlaise School in Marlow, but the boys soon found how to turn the petrol supply off and make the bus fail!

An interesting meeting took place during the Spring, when a representative of the Dunlop Rubber Company came to discuss tyre repair techniques at Reading. He had heard that, although repairs from the Dunlop shop had often failed, resulting in the scrapping of the tyre, such failures on tyres repaired by *Thames Valley* were unknown. At Reading he met Basil Sutton, who took him to see the Tyre Repairer, Mr. N. Cserwenka, and there he saw the methods of layering and plugging used. This of course fully vindicated the reputation TV had built up over the years for remarkable tyre life, and Sutton was evidently proud to agree to share their experience with the Dunlop Tyre Repairers!

The use of Depot Codes had started at some time not recorded, though there is no evidence of their actual use pre-war. Certainly they were shown as car running numbers on the Scheduled Working Arrangements from 1951 onwards. The use of running number plates in the early 1960's is recorded by the author, notably at Maidenhead and High Wycombe, though none are recalled at Reading, whilst some Newbury cars were noted with numbers chalked on in crayon.

On 1st May another joint enterprise with *Aldershot & District* commenced, though this time the roads had previously already been served by buses of the two concerns. TV's buses had run as far south as Hartley

Row (The Swan) from Reading on Route 6c, whilst A&D had run up from Aldershot to Reading through Hartley Wintney, and then basically the same road as TV into Reading (though they omitted Swallowfield village). The new joint route was given the number 12, which was already as used by A&D but, coincidentally, not then allocated by TV. The first departure from Reading was at 8.15am and from the Aldershot end at 8am, with an hourly headway, and the last buses left Aldershot at 10pm and Reading at 10.30pm, with a journey time of 1hour 16 minutes and a route length of 22 miles. A number of early morning 'shorts' operated between Reading and the Wellington Monument at Heckfield Heath, as had long been the practice, whilst passengers along various points of the Basingstoke Road could also catch buses on Routes 6 (to Basingstoke), 6a (to Odiham), 6b (to Bramley) and 9a (to Tadley), which meant that a resident in Three Mile Cross had some 50 buses per day! As with the 75 a service was provided on 7 days per week, and A&D used Dennis 'Lance' double-deckers.

Strachan-bodied Bristol K6A Car 426 (CRX 196) is seen awaiting relief duties at Reading.

Thames Valley used Bristol KSW6B's on Route 12, and Car 705 (HMO 851) is seen on the inaugural run from Reading Stations Square.

For the Summer months of 1954 some of the 'Tiger' TS8 coaches were once again helping out at Oxford, though only Car 386 (BMO 985) was regarded as an actual allocation, the rest being nominally based at Newbury. Disposals for May saw the passing of the last Leyland double-decker in the passenger fleet, 'Titan' TD5 Car 370 (ARX 992), along with Leyland 'Tiger' TS8 Car 371 (BBL 557). The TD5 could, however, still be seen locally, as it went to a contractor working on the New Town expansion of Bracknell. The only new buses received in May were Bristol LS6B's with ECW B45F bodies, Cars 715/6 (HMO 861/2). The first went to Maidenhead, whilst the other became Newbury's first underfloor-engined saloon. A new Inspector's car for Newbury was also ordered that month, being a Ford 'Popular' 10hp (JRD 479) as replacement for the Morris 8hp car (ELJ 27) used at that location. The latter was offered for sale to staff and went to Conductress Restrick of Maidenhead, but the new car did not actually arrive until December for some reason.

The interior of Bristol LS6B Car 713 (HMO 859).

Also from 1st May, the Ascot – Sunningdale services were re-organised in response to local representations, becoming the 2a (Ascot, Horse & Groom – The Wells Hotel – Sunninghill Schools – Sunningdale Station), and 2c (Ascot, Horse & Groom – Ascot Station – The Marie Louise Club – Sunninghill Schools – Sunningdale Station). A few journeys on Route 2a were also diverted via Cheapside (Post Office) and both routes were covered by the remaining pair of utility-bodied Bristol K6A's on the Ascot allocation, Cars 433/4 (CRX 544/5). The others of that type had been demoted to relief duties at Maidenhead and Reading, then duly being switched to contract runs.

Bristol KSW6B Car 702 (HMO 848) loads for Route 110 at the position originally used by Thames Valley buses before the acquisition of Newbury & District. The sign above the shelter proclaims the services available at the Enquiry Office opposite in the Old Granary building.

From June 1954 the contracts running between Reading and Aldermaston (AWRE) needed revision, becoming known as RC/6 and RC/10, each running via various points to the establishment, and these were covered by utility-bodied Bristol K6A-types.

On 1st June the Company hosted a party of 10 men and 2 women from the London Transport Executive, who were initially taken on a tour of Maidenhead Bus and Coach Stations, then on by TV coach to Reading Works.

During June the idea was put forward of converting a Bristol K5G into a Stores Lorry, Car 402 (BRX 918) being identified as the candidate. Enquiries were made by Mr. Campbell on 21st June with Brislington Body Works regarding building a body for that purpose but, as they were slow to respond, other quotations were also sought by local firms Vincents, Markhams and Ardler Coach Works. Only the latter showed any interest in the project, but their estimate was higher than the BBW one, so it was decided to purchase an ordinary lorry instead for that purpose. As a result of

that Car 402 was re-certified for PSV use towards the end of August, whilst Leyland 'Cub' Stores Lorry No.1 (WO 9157) had a brief reprieve.

Possibly arising from discussions held during the recent tour by LTE employees, a meeting took place on 16th July regarding the garaging the *South Midland* coaches out-stationed in London at one of its garages. Such arrangements had already been made on behalf of coaches for *Red & White* and those of *Scottish Motor Traction,* and the SM examples were placed at Stockwell Garage from 1st October.

Newbury saloon operations still had plenty of AEC 'Regals', and 1950 Lydney-bodied Car 162 (FBL 920) is seen at The Wharf.

A further pair of Bristol LS6B/ECW B45F saloons arrived during June as Cars 717/8 (HMO 863/4), the former being allocated to Reading and the latter to High Wycombe. On 14th July there was a 33-seater Commer 'Avenger' demonstrator brought by local agents Reading Garage. The 3-cylinder diesel engine and Eaton 2-speed rear axle created a lot of interest. It is also worth noting that the engines were made at the old Tilling-Stevens works at Maidstone, and although it created a favourable impression and was taken by some other large concerns, none were ordered by TV.

Above- Route 6b to Bramley Station was a pleasant 45-minute run, but only ran 4 or 5 times a day. Bristol L6B Car 542 (FMO 17) awaits the journey at Reading. *Below-* In contrast, many of High Wycombe's Bristol half-cab saloons rarely left the town, being employed on the Local Services. Car 574 (FMO 956) was an LL6B-type with ECW B39R body and is seen on the intensive Route 33, which drivers were not too keen on as almost every stop would be used, which meant an awful lot of gear-changes!

On 12th August Maidenhead Garage was asked to recover a Dennis dustcart of the Cookham Rural District Council which had overturned near Bisham, such tasks always providing an interesting diversion for the Fitters. As already noted, the Vocational Pre-Release Scheme for Army Personnel had been running for some years at Reading Works, so it must have been pleasing to note that one of the men took a position as a Fitter at Wycombe Marsh as a result of that, and indeed the scheme produced a number of Fitters and Drivers in due course.

Consideration was given to refurbishing 12 of the older AEC 'Regal' 0662-type coaches in the *South Midland* fleet, so a representative of Rowland Hartriel visited on 25th August with a sample of the seat they supplied for refurbishment of Duple bodies of that age, and it was agreed to approach ECW regarding undertaking the work over the off-peak months. As a result the following programme was carried out during 1954-5 (Car 39 not being included):

Car No.	Reg. No.	Date Out	Date Back
40	LWL 997	28.04.55	08.07.55
41	LWL 998	19.10.54	18.01.55
42	LWL 999	07.02.55	29.04.55
45	LJO 758	09.05.55	22.07.55
46	LJO 759	25.11.54	18.02.55
47	LJO 760	17.01.55	01.04.55
48	LJO 761	28.02.55	10.05.55
49	MWL 741	23.06.55	07.09.55
50	MWL 742	25.11.54	11.03.55
51	MWL 743	25.11.54	08.02.55
52	MWL 744	24.03.55	24.05.55
53	MJO 278	07.07.55	23.09.55

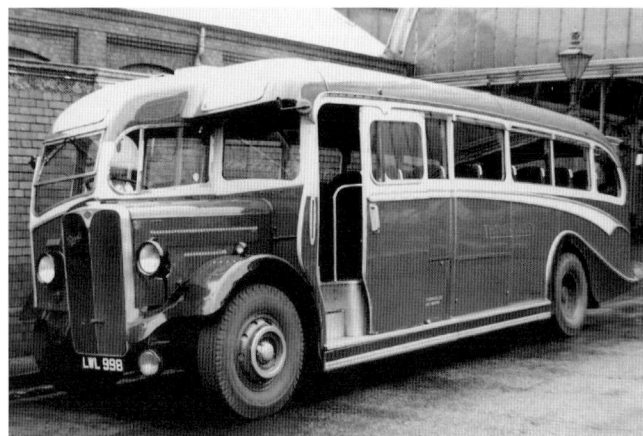

AEC 'Regal' coach 41 (LWL 998) received TV fleet names and is seen at Windsor for Ascot Race Week.

Also on the *South Midland* front, the work at Botley Road was completed and the remainder of the allocation returned there on 27th August.

Deliveries of new buses continued with Bristol KSW6B/ECW L27/28R Cars 726/7/9 (JRX 801/2/4), the first two for Newbury and the other for Wycombe.

Wycombe Marsh-based KSW Car 729 (JRX 804) stands on the bus park at Quoiting Square, where the short-workings terminated, and also used for school buses for the nearby Borlaise School.

Quotations were obtained for the new Stores Lorry from Reading Automobiles for an Austin, from Reading Garage for a Commer and from Gowrings for a Ford Thames, all being for a diesel-engined 3-tonner with a dropside lorry body. Gowrings were the successful bidders, and the lorry arrived as No.35 (KBL 963) during September and was allocated to Reading. Leyland 'Cub' Lorry No.1 (WO 9157) was sold to Twyford scrapyard owner Harold Goodey the following month, and it saw further use with him.

Car 729 (JRX 804) is seen once again, this time at Great Missenden Station on Route 27.

Further new buses arriving for September were Bristol KSW6B/ECW L27/28R Cars 728/30-7 (JRX 803/5-12), plus another batch of double-deck coaches to CL27/26RD configuration on the same chassis as Cars 738-43 (JRX 813 - 8). All the latter were for the busy

London services, whilst 728 went to Newbury, 730/1 to High Wycombe, 732-4 to Maidenhead and 735-7 to Reading. Cars 729-31 then became the trio of buses rotated each week to provide the pair out-stationed at Stokenchurch Dormy Shed.

At the Board Meeting of 14th September it was decided that the Road Service Licenses of *Newbury & District* and *South Midland* would be transferred over to *Thames Valley*. The remaining 'Tiger' TS7 coach 264 (JB 5843) and TS8 coaches 381/3/4/6-90 (BMO 980/2/3/5-9) all worked through to September, but time finally caught up with them. A little earlier Mr. Swartz of the Baker Street Trading Co. had visited in company with Mr. Stianovitch to see TS8 saloons 345 (AJB 817), 363/6 (ARX 985/90) and 371 (BBL 557) – all of which they purchased for export to Yugoslavia! When they returned on 6th October they also bought the 9 'Tiger' coaches noted above for same purpose. All the vehicles were fully serviced prior to departure for Harwich , forming a little *Thames Valley* enclave in a foreign land.

With side panels reminiscent of its days along the chalky Chiltern lanes, former TV TS8 Car 363 is seen in service in Yugoslavia. The livery appears unaltered, though the blind setting is none too good!

The increasing numbers of Bristol KSW's were found on a variety of duties, and Reading-based Car 736 (JRX 811) waits on Station Hill for departure on the 4a to Shinfield – Arborfield – Wokingham. Repaints later omitted the top cream band, as shown here.

With the departures abroad of the foregoing Leylands, only the 1947 'Tiger' PS1 coach 169 (LWL 995) remained to represent the marque in the passenger fleet. However, the older generation of 'Titans' was represented by the TD1 Route Servicing Vehicle No.29 (RX 1758), which coincidentally had been 169 as a bus!

The other disposals for September were Bristol K5G's 393/7, 404/6/7 (BRX 909/13/20/2/3), whilst identical bus 401 (BRX 917) followed in October and was the final disposal that year.

During October another Ford 'Popular' 10hp car arrived (JRD 982) and it was allocated to Mr. Chun, the Assistant Traffic Superintendent at Reading.

The remaining Bristol K5G's of the 1939/42 batches were now to be found mainly on relief duties, though Car 416 (CJB 135) is set for the 6-mile trip on Route 7 to Peppard.

The only new bus that month was the first of the final batch of 6 Bristol KSW6B's on order, Car 744 (JRX 819), which was allocated to Reading – though the 5 others could not be completed until 11 months later, perhaps both Bristol and ECW hoping that advice might persuade TV to take 'Lodekkas' instead? This batch was also specified as piped up for heaters, though not initially used, and it was around this time that the Union sought heaters in the cabs of the LS-types, the drivers no longer receiving heat from the engine!

Car 738 (JRX 813) was one of the batch for service on the London routes and is seen at Victoria Coach Station a little later, also minus the upper cream band. Note the painted Huntley & Palmer adverts and the rear platform door.

There was another spate of accidents in October and November, with that to LS-type Car 711 (HMO 857) on 19th October being the most bizarre. The saloon had suffered from engine trouble and the Fitters at Wycombe Marsh had started stripping it down, when shortage of staff dictated that it be transferred to the Reading Works. It was placed on tow and the vehicles were proceeding on the windy road above Flowing Spring Hill, near Binfield Heath, when a passing lorry struck the bus, causing extensive body damage. Also damaged on 3rd November were Bristol L6A Car 474 (DMO 678) and Bristol LWL6B Car 577 (FMO 959), which collided with each other, causing a few red faces, the two incidents depleting the High Wycombe allocations by 3 buses!

In the meantime over at Oxford, the extensions to the Botley Road Garage made the Iffley Road premises unnecessary from the operational standpoint, and all staff from the latter were re-assigned to the main site, whereupon they all resigned other than Mr. Bessell! The premises ceased operationally on 20th October, but were retained for storing coaches until sold 1960. It had also been hoped that the Maidenhead extension would be completed and in use by 1st November, but flooding of the nearby stream put paid to that, the pits remaining full of water through to 4th December.

Above- The impressive façade of the old Great Western Railway terminus in Windsor was the centre for the TV operations in the royal borough. A trio of Bristol KSW6B's can be seen on the various routes, whilst just to the right of the front one is the passenger way into the station. Just behind that is the ledge upon which the author sat awaiting his bus home from school in the early 1960's. *Below-* KSW-type Car 601 (FMO 983) is seen at the far end of the canopied area, before going into the open yard to turn around for the Route 20 journey back to its High Wycombe base.

Plans were also considered in November regarding a new garage to be sited in the expanding Bracknell New Town, which would replace the Ascot Garage and the Crowthorne Dormy Shed. Discussions with the Bracknell Development Corporation took place to earmark a site for premises to hold around 30 buses, though completion would not be for some years yet. The future of the Frogmoor site was also discussed by the Board on 5th November, with a view to siting the

proposed Bus Station there but, as the Old Cattle Market area was still not available, the scheme could not progress. The situation with Fitters at High Wycombe was also still very difficult, so a number of major overhauls had to be sent to Reading instead, though generally vehicles were worked between those points by way of Route 28, the exchanges usually taking place on Saturdays.

Seen on the former Borough Bus Service Windsor Local Service is Bristol KSW-type 644 (GJB 282), the terminus of which was relocated to the central station.

During early November the Board approved the takeover of *Borough Bus Service,* operated by *Frowen & Hill* of Windsor. This operator was one of the last of the numerous outfits linking Windsor and Slough in pre-war years, transferring their base to Windsor from Slough in due course and providing a local service instead. Their route ran in a circular fashion from the High Street in Windsor – Clewer Green (Hatch Lane) – Clewer Green (Prince Albert) – Windsor (Castle Hill), operating the 25-minute journey on a 30-minute headway on Mondays to Saturdays and on Sunday afternoons. The route was evidently worthwhile purchasing, as the Company paid £5375 without any vehicles, the service having been maintained by a 1947 Bedford OWB bus (DRX 296). TV took over the operation from 1st December , though the route was made a linear one operating as Windsor (Central Station) – Clewer Green (Prince Albert) – Clewer Green (Hatch Lane), and the 30 minute headway and days of operation remained the same. Ascot Garage was responsible for this new service, which was given Route No.51, and the allocation was increased by the transfer of Bristol KSW6B/ECW L27/28R Car 705 (HMO 851). The latter had pioneered the Aldershot Route 12, but that duty had now been re-assigned to coach-seated Bristol KS6B's demoted from the London routes. Route 51 therefore came under the watchful eye of 'Nobby' Clarke, who was the Duty Inspector at the Central Station, controlling the activities on Routes 2, 2b, 20 and 51.

Bristol LS6B Car 722 (HMO 868) is seen in later years when working from Reading Garage, passing from West Street under the trolleybus overhead to St. Mary's Butts on Route 6a to Odiham.

A further trio of Bristol LS6B/ECW B45F saloons arrived during November as Cars 719-21 (HMO 865-7), with the first pair going to Reading and the third one to Maidenhead. They were followed by identical Car 722 (HMO 868) in December, and that was sent to High Wycombe.

A number of buses had received repaints using the 'Vulcan' one-coat paint, and on 10th December their representative came to Reading to inspect the progress of Cars 535 (FMO 10), 540 (FMO 15), 581 (FMO 963) and 613/6/33 (GJB 252/4/71), but it was found that the red was fading to a pinkish bloom!

December was a bad month for accidents, and it is worth considering if there can be such a thing as an 'unlucky' bus? It will be recalled that Bristol KSW6B Car 670 (HBL 72) had already been fully ditched at Arborfield in late March, but found another at Play Hatch when working Route 8 around 6.10pm on the 16th, recovery being made the following morning.

Above- Car 721 (HMO 867) was Maidenhead's latest saloon and is seen in Bridge Avenue leaving on a Route 17 'short' to Tittle Row. Below- Many of the buses garaged at Maidenhead were used for services linking through to Slough by a variety of routes. The 22a took the back-roads past Clivedon Hospital, Taplow and Dropmore and had been originally worked by the B&M Bus Service of Philip Keep.

The other unlucky bus that month was Newbury-based Guy 'Arab' Car 101 (CRX 281), which it will be recalled hit an overhanging roof at Colthrop Mill a little earlier on, but this time the collision was rather more serious. The bus struck the low bridge where the railway line crossed the road near Boxford on the Lambourn Route 106, the driver having apparently misheard the Inspector when he had instructed him to take Car 171! Fortunately no one was on board the top deck at the time, but during the subsequent enquiry it was concluded that the highbridge double-deckers would need to be readily identifiable. Soon after that they were all re-numbered into a separate series pre-fixed by H, and notices were placed on the conductor's lockers stating that they must not be used on the Lambourn Route 106. The re-numbered buses were as follows:

Old No.	New No.	Reg.No.	Chassis Type
99	H1	CRX 279	Guy 'Arab' II 5LW
100	H2	CRX 280	Guy 'Arab' II 5LW
101	H3	CRX 281	Guy 'Arab' II 5LW
102	H4	CRX 282	Guy 'Arab' II 5LW
103	H5	CRX 283	Guy 'Arab' II 5LW
104	H6	FAD 253	Guy 'Arab' II 5LW
105	H7	CRX 595	Guy 'Arab' II 5LW
106	H8	CRX 596	Guy 'Arab' II 5LW
160	H9	EWO 484	Guy 'Arab' I 5LW
172	H10	FMO 517	Guy 'Arab' III 6LW
173	H11	EWO 490	Guy 'Arab' II 5LW
174	H12	EWO 492	Guy 'Arab' II 5LW
175	H13	HOT 391	Guy 'Arab' III 6LW
176	H14	HOT 392	Guy 'Arab' III 6LW
177	H15	HOT 393	Guy 'Arab' III 6LW
178	H16	HOT 394	Guy 'Arab' III 6LW

Duple-bodied highbridge Guy in its new guise as H13 (HOT 391) lays over by the canal at The Wharf.

On 16th December Mr. Campbell went over to Oxford to meet with Mr. Dobbs of the East Midland Traffic Area, and they discussed the making available of *South Midland* coaches in the event of a National Emergency for Inter-hospital transport, the Cold War

having now entered a rather 'warmer' phase with the threat of nuclear war and increased world tensions.

Operation of Route 75 was generally in the hands of a 39-seater Bristol LWL6B, and Car 616 (GJB 254) is seen at the Farnham Road Bus Station in Guildford.

Changes were also afoot at *Thames Valley*, as one week later Mr. Balls announced that he would be leaving to take up a similar position with the *Eastern Counties* company based in Norwich. His successor would be Tom Pruett from *Brighton, Hove & District*, though each man would only gradually transfer by mutual agreement between all parties. Mr. Pruett had also been the Engineer at *BH&D* so there had already been quite a lot of contact with him in that capacity.

Some mention has already been made regarding the social side of bus work, and indeed all such activities were fully supported by senior management and also attracted wide participation. The horticultural side was a particularly flourishing one, as shift-working did mean time to tend allotments. Darts were also very popular, and Jimmy Lewington's wife donated a fine cup to be awarded to the individual champion, he having been with the Company since 1923.

1954 had seen the fleet carry 52,721,278 passengers over 16,230,918 miles. The total route mileage was 1,283 and the scheduled fleet was 134 single-deckers, 189 double-deckers and 107 coaches, employing 498 conductors, 576 drivers and 583 other staff.

Bristol KSW6B Car 664 (HBL 66) leaves Reading's Stations Square on a short-worked Route 1 to Hare Hatch, passing the little parade of cafes and shops.

1955

Revised working arrangements which came into force from 1st January 1955 show that little had changed in the allocation of duties at Desborough Road since we reviewed them in June 1953. The pair of saloons now in use on Route 31 (High Wycombe – Lacey Green) was changed to Bristol LS-types, whilst Route 81 (High Wycombe – Booker) now warranted a 55-seater Bristol double-decker.

Over at Maidenhead it is interesting to note that Bedford OWB 438 (CRX 547) was only being used for odd reliefs and the Borlaise School run, whilst the other of that type, Car 437 (CRX 546), was described as not in use and in need of attention. This latter point is of interest because it replicates the pre-war status of former *Marlow & District* Karrier Car 16 (KX 8481), which was retained as 'spare' even though it was not fit for use, then exactly the same occurred with the ex-*Crosville* Leyland 'Cub' 411 (FM 7455), which barely turned a wheel in its latter days. There appears to have been an ongoing paranoia that there might be a need for cover on the Marlow Bridge route! *A full summary of the working arrangements for January 1955 will be found in Appendix 6.*

Also inactive at that point in time were Guy 'Arabs' H3/4 (CRX 281/2), the former with its smashed roof and the latter requiring serious body attention of the more general kind. The reserve fleet then comprised of K5G Bristols 391 (BRX 656) and 413/4 (CJB 132/3) and Guy 'Arabs' 418-25 (CJB 137-41, CMO 653-5), all of which were parked at Newbury. Many of the TV Guys were in poor shape, so buyers would not be easy to find. It is also interesting to note that when the author visited Reg Hibbert in the 1960's he had one of the Red Indian head mascots from a Guy in his office, all painted up in full colour!

A Newbury Wharf line up with AEC 'Regal' saloon and Guy' Arabs' 419 (CJB 139) and 425 (CMO 655).

Above - One of the better examples of Guys from the Newbury fleet was Car H2 (CRX 280), seen after receiving TV livery. The absence of an upper deck cream band and the very small front destination aperture combine to alter its general appearance, whilst the Red Indian head mascot can be seen on the top of the radiator. *Below –* Car H11 (EWO 490) on Route 128 to Bartlemy Close, but still displaying the former route number 38!

Whilst on the subject of Newbury, contract work in that area continued to be of high importance, and at January 1955 the following duties were being worked on Mondays to Fridays with dedicated vehicles:

Ref.	Route	Type	Base
N/C1	Camp Close – Harwell	'Regal' C35F	N
N/C2	Henwick Lane – Harwell	'Regal' C35F	N
N/C3	Woolton Hill – Shaw House	'Regal' C35F	N
N/C4	St. Johns – Shaw House	'Arab' H56R	N
N/C6	Black Boys – Aldermaston	'Regal' C35F	N
N/E3	Lambourn – Didcot	'Regal' B35F	L
N/E4	Lambourn – Didcot	'Regal' B35F	L
N/E5	Kintbury – Didcot	'Regal' B35F	N
N/E7	N'bury (Regal) – Milton)	'Regal' B35F	N

Ref.	Route	Type	Base
N/E8	N'bury (Regal) – Milton *	'Regal' B35F	N
N/E9	H'ford – Bedwyn – Harwell	'Regal' B35F	H
N/E10	Chilton Foliat – Harwell	'Regal' B35F	H
N/E11	H'f – Ramsbury – Harwell	'Regal' B35F	H
N/E13	Newtown – Harwell	'Regal' B35F	N
N/E14	Bucklebury – Harwell	'Regal' B35F	N
N/E16	Aldbourne – Harwell	'Regal' B35F	L
N/E17	Frilsham – Harwell	'Regal' B35F	N
N/E18	Valley Road – Aldermaston	'Arab' H56R	N
N/E19	Valley Road – Aldermaston	'Arab, H56R	N
N/E20	Valley Road – Aldermaston	K5G L51R	N
N/E21	Valley Road – Aldermaston	'Arab' H56R	N

Notes: These vehicles were based at Newbury (N), Hungerford (H) or Lambourn (L). The Shaw House runs were school journeys, whilst the remainder were works contracts to Didcot or Milton Depots, Harwell AERE or Aldermaston AWRE. * This bus was parked at Harwell during the day, where its part-time driver also worked.

Bristol LS6G Car 682 (HBL 84) is seen on the south side of Stations Hill awaiting departure on Route 5b (Reading – Yattendon – Newbury).

The use of Bristol LS saloons by January saw the following routes now covered, and these 45-seaters were credited by Traffic Manager John Dally as having reduced the need for relief vehicles:

No.	Route	Base	Qty.
3	Reading – Camberley	Crowthorne	3
5	Reading – Oxford	Reading	2
5b	Reading – Newbury	Reading	1
5b	Reading – Newbury	Newbury	1
6b	Reading – Bramley	Reading	1
24	M'head – Cookham Dean	Maidenhead	2
25	HW – Flackwell Heath	Wycombe Marsh	2
31	HW – Lacey Green	Desborough Road	2
35	HW – Downley Common	Wycombe Marsh	2
50	Reading – Abingdon	Reading	1

Over at Crowthorne, it is notable that an LS had been allocated to Route 3a (Reading – Wokingham – Finchampstead), but cover had reverted to a Bristol L-type because the rather box-like LS had picked up too many knocks and scrapes on the narrow local roads!

Desborough Road-based LS Car 684 (HBL 86) and Car 680 (HBL 82) from Wycombe Marsh both rest at the Frogmoor parking ground.

On the subject of suitable buses for rural routes, Mr. Campbell's recent study into lightweight types led to the loan of one of the prototype Bristol SC-types. The bus was destined for *Eastern National* as its Car 395 (724 APU), and it had a 35-seater lightweight body by Eastern Coach Works and used a Gardner 4LW oil engine. It was collected by a TV driver from *United Counties* on 9th January and ran on Route 1b (Reading – Hurst – Shurlock Row) from 10th-15th of that month. It was favourably received by crews and passengers alike, whilst Messrs. Sutton, Dally and Campbell rode on it in service to try the type out. On Saturday 15th it was cleaned and serviced prior to collection by a driver from *Wilts & Dorset*, and as a result of the trial the possibility of replacing the Bedfords on the Marlow route was discussed, though Sutton was not sure the type really suited that purpose. The difficulty would be meeting the weight restriction over the weak bridge, as the SC had an unladen weight of 3tons 18cwt, leaving only 22cwt for the driver, the conductor and passengers, which Sutton calculated would only allow 17 passengers to remain aboard on the bridge.

The Eastern National SC prototype 395 (724 APU) is seen later on its tour of operators when with the West Yorkshire company. The body incorporated a number of features to keep the weight down, whilst the front end design featured a scaled down Bristol radiator, a full-width cab (with one-man-operation in mind). Note the ECW badge on the radiator grille mesh, not found on production examples.

As noted above, Route 3 was re-equipped with Bristol LS saloons, and Car 718 (HMO 864) is seen when new at Reading Stations Square. Note the side advert for Wethered's of Marlow, one of many breweries on the Thames now lost through monopolistic takeovers.

Indeed, Sutton felt they should look at some of the chassis-less rebuilds that had been constructed for such operators as *Eastern National, Eastern Counties* and *Lincolnshire Road Car.* These had used running units taken from older types, so under that alternative option, the old Leyland 'Cubs' might have been stripped down and rebuilt into 'new' buses! As it was, Sutton was duly proven right, and a limit on passengers did in fact come in, though as they walked alongside the bus, it is hard to see what it really achieved in terms of safeguarding the bridge?

A little earlier another rather different type had also been tried out, when on 8th January the Royal Berks Motor Co, had brought round a Volkswagen 8-seater 'Microbus'. This now iconic type was taken on a short run with the Engineer aboard and, although he expressed his interest in it, no orders were forthcoming. Just prior to that, on 6th January, seasonal ice had put one of *Kent's Coaches* of Baughurst Bedfords in a ditch, so Mr. Cross and a Recovery Wagon were sent out to restore it to the roadway. *Kent's* were of course also heavily committed to AWRE contracts, as were nearby *Ford's* of Silchester, both fleets expanding in the post-war era to meet the demand.

January saw two of the Windover-bodied Bristol L6B coaches transferred to the *South Midland* fleet, as there were no longer any old TS8's to call upon for the Summer peak on the Oxford operations. Cars 548/53 (FMO 23, FMO 935) were given appropriate fleetnames, but otherwise were unaltered. Other loans to Oxford were frequent when bookings were high.

Further problems were being experienced with the underfloor-engined LS-types, as recent flooding had allowed silt to get into the crankcases of some, and this was brought to the urgent attention of Bristol Commercial Vehicles.

Bristol L6B coach 548 (FMO 23) with South Midland.

Route 28 (Reading – Twyford – Henley – Marlow – High Wycombe) was still being covered by Bristol LWL6B saloons such as Car 628 (GJB 266), though it was earmarked for conversion to LS-types once the outstanding deliveries were met.

Maintenance was still proving problematical, as skilled staff were hard to find, resulting in work that should have been dealt with at Newbury or Oxford having to be diverted to Reading. Indeed, one Fitter was engaged at Newbury from Scotland but, after failing to find economical 'digs' locally, he instead took a job in Bristol. Over at Wycombe, some work was re-scheduled for weekends, when there was not the pressure from workman's services, whilst it was hoped that Maidenhead could become self-sufficient.

On the double-deck front, <u>above</u> – it was not usual to find a K-type, such as Car 499 (EJB 221) on Route 1, though <u>below</u> – KS-type Car 588 (FMO 970) was the usual choice for the 7 to Stoke Row and other medium distance Reading-based routes.

Spells of bad weather during January resulted in a number of accidents, with Bristol L6B bus 71 (EBD 234) running through the crossing gates at Bourne End and hitting a stationary train. This was on the 19th January, when the bus was on the Borlaise School run, though fortunately no scholars were seriously hurt. On 22nd *South Midland* AEC 'Regal' coach 61 (NWL 878) was descending Bix Hill towards Henley when the propeller shaft broke, so Driver Leary had an anxious time bringing the vehicle to a safe halt!

Len Balls, the outgoing General Manager, thanked staff for their 10.5 years of service and loyalty as he prepared to leave, though he was still about much of January, interspersed with visits to his new employers in Norwich. Similarly, the incoming GM, Tom Pruett, issued an introductory message through the Bulletin. He also remained at *Brighton, Hove & District* for much of the month, with a number of visits to TV. He had already met many of the senior officers at the various liaison groups and, in particular there had been contact with the engineering side over a number of matters. Mr. Pruett had already been in the industry for 27 years, starting at the *Bristol Tramways & Carriage Company,* moving onto BH&D in 1944 as Chief Engineer, becoming GM & Engineer with the Nationalisation of the Tilling Group.

Tom Pruett

During February a number of improvements continued to be made to properties in the Frogmoor area, including the office used by Inspector Hammond, who oversaw activities at that location. In Maidenhead the Company had a demolition order served on it by the Corporation in respect of the cottages owned at 19/21 Forlease Road. However, in November 1955 the local portfolio was increased with the acquisition of Nos.15/17 Forlease Road and the Salvation Army Citadel, this being with an eye to future extensions of the garage or parking area.

On 3rd February a Leyland 'Tiger Cub' chassis, which had been fitted out as a lorry by Clayton-Dewandre called at Reading Works to demonstrate a number of technical features, including a power-operated radiator shutter, exhaust brake and air-assisted power steering.

Ascot-based Bristol KSW6B Car 644 (GJB 282) is seen about to pull out around The Guildhall, Windsor as it works the Local Service 51.

As a result of the visit of the demonstrator, Bristol LS Car 717 (HMO 863) was experimentally fitted with a Clayton-Oetiker exhaust brake during April.

Mr. Abberfield found himself having to make an entry in the Accident Book, after his Vauxhall car (ERX 580) skidded on ice near Sonning on 21st February, after which it went to Great Western Motors for some front end repairs.

Former Newbury & District AEC 'Regal' coach 147 (EJB 147) was still in the Red & White style livery, but with Thames Valley fleetnames, when caught by the camera parked near Manchester Piccadilly. The coach is evidently well cared for, and it was a Newbury routine to re- paint front wings regularly.

In March two of the *South Midland* AEC 'Regal' coaches, 61 (NWL 878) and 64 (NJO 218) received repaints into a scheme of all-over cream, with red mudguards and also initially the distinctive Duple side-flash. However, when Mr. Francis came over from Oxford to view the results, he asked for the side flash to be omitted, and this became the new standard livery for all the coaches in both fleets, excepting for the half-cab Bristol L6B's, which remained in the red and cream 'service' scheme. The existing batches had red mudguards in place of black, though in the case of the former *United Counties* examples, this was actually the third colour to date!

History was made on 7th March, when the Company employed its first Jamaican in the Works. Wilbert Flash was taken on as a Semi-skilled Fitter, and soon settled down to the work. However, it was a sign of the times that the Union was quoted as 'having no objection to the employment of a coloured man in view of the current labour shortage'.

One of Mr. Pruett's early meetings with Senior Staff resulted in the decision on 18th March to reduce the number of Staff Cars from 18 to 15, and as a result of this Austin cars UD 9244, EXY 823 and FHA 257 were all sold to a local garage.

As with all new GM's, Tom Pruett brought a number of new ideas with him, some of which were certainly novel for the area, and which we will hear more of in due course. However, if he had hoped for a Brighton Area type of agreement with *Reading Corporation* he would soon be disappointed! In Brighton, the agreement had fostered a good working relationship between the Corporation, the Tilling-owned BH&D and the BET-owned *Southdown Motor Services*.

Indeed, it had been a long-standing contention by TV that the town benefited commercial from the many passengers brought in, but no acknowledgement of that resulted in any willingness to co-operate from the Corporation.

The Strachans-bodied utility Bristol K6A's continued in use on contracts and relief duties, and Car 428 (CRX 198) is seen in the Southern Yard at Reading with the blind set for Compton and the permanent relief board in the front bulkhead.

However, at officer level relations between the two operators was much more cordial, and so on 1st April RCT's General Manager Mr. Evans invited Basil Sutton and others over to Mill Lane to see the Leyland rear-engined 'Lowloader' double-deck demonstrator (STF 90). The design used an engine mounted under the stairs on the offside rear of the chassis, which allowed normal headroom to be achieved on both decks within an overall height of 13ft 3ins. These factors certainly interested the TV Engineer, though the rather trolleybus-like Saunders Roe body to FH37/24R configuration did not impress him at all.

The Bristol LWL6B saloons had long working lives, though they retained the rear-entrance layout and were crew operated to the end. Car 630 (GJB 268) spent some time at the Fingest shed in the 1960's.

A new car for Mr. Pruett arrived on 21st April, as Vauxhall 'Velox' LBL 331, whilst a number of transfers took place in the ranks of the staff cars. Firstly, Morris 8hp VV 8163, Vauxhall 10hp DJB 685 and Hillman 'Minx' AMO 960, were withdrawn from Oxford (Traffic), Wycombe (Traffic) and Newbury (Engineering) respectively and offered for sale on 15th April. Vauxhall 10hp DRX 476 was transferred from Reading (Works) to Newbury (Engineering), and it was decided to replace Austin 16hp LFC 562 at Oxford with a new Morris 'Oxford', which was ordered and appeared in May as XFC 888. Cars for sale where usually offered to staff through the Bulletin, so Driver Shaw (one of the Reading-based Petrol Tanker Drivers) got AMO 960, whilst in July Driver Esaias of Princes Risborough bought the GM's old Ford 'Pilot' FDP 101 – which must has caused the odd stir when he visited Wycombe Marsh garage!

On the staff front, it was decided to offer interviews to a number of local school leavers in order to attract boys to be learners in the Fitting, Coach Building and Coach Painting Shops. Also, two of the Army personnel trained on PSV Driving Courses came into the *Thames Valley* ranks at Reading and Maidenhead, with others following in due course.

Bristol KS6B Car 594 (FMO 976) leaves the Stations Square, Reading for a short-working to Wargrave on Route 1. 'Corona' adverts featured on TV's double-deckers for many years.

At Maidenhead further improvements were made to the Bus Station during the Spring of 1955. The ice cream sales were moved into the café, whilst the former sales kiosk was converted for Inspector's use. Outside, the 9 double-shelters kept passengers dry, and also provided plenty of advertising space for services and excursions, whilst the bus station also featured clear alphabetical service guides and the shelters had metal plates displaying the route numbers. Over the year there were 233,428 scheduled departures on the service routes, whereas the adjacent Coach Station could handle 70 coaches at a time, the annual total of passengers on express journeys and on extended tours being around 10,000, whilst a full-time gardener tended to the vegetable and flower beds!

The bus stands in Mackenzie Street, Slough had been improved over the years, including the sign-written route information seen in this view of Bristol K6A Car 450 (DBL 158) about to depart to St. Andrews Way on Route 22b. Hickies Pianos were another firm regularly advertising on the fleet.

Distaster struck the last of the large batch of Bristol LWL saloons on Sunday 1st May, when Car 633 (GJB 271) was covering the 11.25 departure from Reading to Guildford on Route 75. At 12.37 the bus was at Bisley Heath when the Driver's attention was directed to smoke coming from the nearside rear wheels. Flames soon followed and the fire extinguishers from the bus, plus one from a passing *Aldershot & District* bus proved ineffective. Fortunately the Fire Brigade had been alerted and were soon on the scene, by which time the rear tyres, wheelarch and some of the panels above were damaged. Later investigation led to the conclusion that the brakes had been binding slightly and, as the route was rather longer than most, heat had built up in that area.

As more Bristol LS-type saloons were delivered, the type featured on further routes. Car 724 (HMO 870) is seen on Route 1b to Hurst - note the cream maker's badge flanked by air vents on these later examples.

The remaining trio of Bristol LS6B/ECW B45F buses arrived in June as Cars 723-5 (HMO 869-71) and they were allocated to Reading (723/4) and Wycombe (725), though after a time there were a number of re-allocations of the type as will be seen in due course.

Car 725 (HMO 871) is seen when new and was used to convert Route 28 to LS operation, though later the service was provided with double-deckers instead.

A prolonged rail strike ran from 29th May until 14th June, resulting in the cancellation of Royal Ascot Week, the loss of the lucrative traffic associated with that event, and also the chance for the crews to enjoy their off-duty time at the racetrack.

As will be recalled, Guy 'Arab' Car 101 (CRX 281) had been badly damaged in a low-bridge collision in December 1954. In June 1955 it was broken up, and in fact probably never received its new fleet number H3. The engine was retained, as were others taken from a number of Guys withdrawn in the same 12 month period, and these were reconditioned for further use as will be noted a little later.

Official disposal lists of the period note a number of buses, including the remains of Guy 101, as sold to Hibbert, Newbury. In reality this was a deal between Reg Hibbert at Newbury Garage and the Middle Wallop-based scrap dealer Mattia, whereby buses were driven down to the Hampshire yard, de-bodied and then the chassis was taken back to Newbury for stripping down, the two men sharing the scrap value once the body was scrapped. Former N&D Guys H8 (CRX 596) and H9 (EWO 484) also went through that process later, though the Company did not lose out as Mattia took the vehicles unlikely to attract a buyer.

Now with Thames Valley fleetnames, but still bearing Newbury & District legal lettering, the ECW-bodied Leyland 'Tiger' PS1 coach 169 (LWL 995) was seen at a West Yorkshire garage whilst in that area.

The reluctance to embrace the Bristol 'Lodekka' has already been aired, and strangely the same had been the case at Mr. Pruett's previous posting. However, he and Basil Sutton went to BCV at Bristol on 27th June to discuss vehicle deliveries for 1956. It was agreed to order 20 'Lodekkas', 10 to be fitted with Gardner engines and the others with Bristol AVW units. Mr. Heath of BCV also undertook to see if the 5 KSW6B chassis recently dispatched to Lowestoft for bodying could be diverted to another operator, in which case TV would take 25 LD, but that did not prove possible.

The Bristol KSW was for many years a real workhorse for TV, and Car 664 (HBL 66) is seen in Binfield Road, Bracknell en route for Reading via Binfield.

KSW-type Car 728 (JRX 803) was allocated to Newbury and is seen at Gloucester Green Bus Station at the Oxford end of Route 112. Note the LS saloon behind it from the Bristol Omnibus fleet, there also being a connection for the Stratford Blue service too.

Plans for a garage at Bracknell had been formulated with the Development Corporation by the Summer of 1955, the site being not far from the railway station at the High Street, though the Company was concerned about the high lease cost. As part of the plan the Ascot Garage and Crowthorne Dormy Shed would both close, which was not really welcomed by the crews there, as they were a tight-knit bunch. However, the expansion of the town would at least ensure that the TV buses in the area would be busy and employment therefore assured.

As previously noted, the Dormy Shed crews were a self-reliant body of men and women, so it is unusual to hear of dissatisfaction with their lot. However, the Fingest crews had lost their old faithful Leyland 'Tigers' in favour of a pair of Bristol L6A's, and after a while these began to smell rather musty, the situation being further worsened by the rather drab interiors. The Union brought these issues up, and as a result Car 473 (DMO 677) was taken to Reading in August for inspection. The darkness of the interior was acknowledged, and the number of lights was doubled, whilst the beige roof-lining was re-painted cream as far down as the roof-mounted luggage racks. It was also found that the lining of the body interior had become damp, which had caused the smell, so it was re-lined. Once that bus had returned to the shed, others of the type were also treated, and indeed the whole batch was similarly inspected and dealt with through normal overhauls.

From July Route 32 (High Wycombe – Routs Green – Bledlow Ridge) was extended onto Chinnor, though for some reason the extension was again temporarily suspended the following June.

Further Guy 'Arab' buses were sold on 17th August, when TV utility examples 418-20 (CJB 137-9) were actually sold back to Guy Motors who had a buyer for them for further service in the Canary Islands!

Perhaps anticipating the era of package holidays, the trio of Guys headed by Car 419 (CJB 138) heads from the gloom of Wolverhampton to the perpetual sun of the Canaries.

Those Guys were not actually collected for some weeks, and a number of others were laid up for some time before being disposed of. The next vehicles to be disposed of were Bristol K5G's 391 (BRX 656) and 413/4 (CJB 132/3), which went in September, then in October the former *Red & White/Venture/N&D* Guy 'Arab' buses H11/2 (EWO 490/2) were sold, but their engines were retained for re-use in Bristol LD-type chassis. October saw Guy 'Arab' Car 424 (CMO 654) disposed of, which concluded sales for this year.

Another long-service employee retired on 9th August, and Maidenhead Fitter J. Broadbent received a visit the following month when the GM and Engineer presented him with £25 in recognition of his 29 years service. However, that record was duly topped on 7th October, with the retirement of Coachbuilder Barker at Maidenhead after 33 years.

Another Newbury Guy was involved in a mishap on 23rd August, though this time the roof was not the problem. Car H8 (CRX 596) was arriving at Lambourn on Route 108 (Newbury – Speen-Wickham – Shefford Woodlands – Lambourn Woodlands – Lambourn) when a fire broke out under the seat cushions over the nearside wheel arch. This was promptly put out by the Conductor and it had been caused by a discarded cigarette butt. However, it was the fact that over-flowing tickets from the platform-mounted used ticket box had accumulated under the seat that had made that worse, so all that type had the area blanked off to avoid a repition.

With the coming of September the final pair of utility-bodied Bristol K6A's at Ascot, Cars 433/4 (CRX 544/5), were transferred to Reading for use on the Aldermaston contracts and relief duties. Bristol KSW Car 744 (JRX 819) was transferred from Reading to Ascot, and brand new buses of that type, Cars 745-7

(JRX 820-2) were also sent to Ascot as they arrived during September. This was also in connection with improvements planned for the Windsor Local Services, whilst the remaining new KSW Cars 748/9 (JRX 823/4) were both allocated to Reading that same month.

Although no TV 'Lodekkas' were due just yet, Recovery Wagon 21 (*112 DP*) was dispatched to recover a chassis of that type on 16th September which had been involved in a collision near Iver on its route to Lowestoft, such chassis in 'desert sand' paint and fitted with a temporary driving position being a common sight along the Bath Road then. It is notable that 25 other operators took LD-types before *Thames Valley,* but only 3 new ones did after that, one of which was *Brighton, Hove & District,* which remained loyal to the KSW until 1957!

The additional Bristol KSW6B's were widely used and had long working lives, and both these examples are seen a few years after delivery, by which time they had white fleetnumbers and had lost the top cream band. Above – Car 749 (JRX 824) enters Victoria Coach Station when helping out on London Route B, whilst below – Car 745 (JRX 820) is seen passing the old Heelas store in Wokingham whilst covering the busy Route 2 (Reading – Wokingham – Bracknell – Ascot – Windsor).

Another KSW on a long and well-patronised route was Car 654 (HBL 56), which was caught entering St. Mary's Butts from Bridge Street after the 16.9 mile journey from Camberley on Route 4 via Yateley.

Mr. W.G. Foulke, the Reading Works Superintendent, had been very ill and had undergone surgery, but he sadly passed away on 6th October. His funeral at St. Peter's Church, Earley was attended by many of his colleagues and senior managers on 12th October, and the vacancy was filled by the promotion of Mr. T.R. Shepherd from 1st November.

On 9th November Great Western Motors demonstrated a Bedford coach with a Duple 'Super Vega' body, and after a short run out by Company officials, they were suitably impressed. Although none were immediately purchased, examples of that combination of chassis and body did feature regularly over the next decade.

KSW-type Car 748 (JRX 823) prepares to leave on the 22-mile Route 12 to Aldershot Bus Station.

Mr. Campbell set about compiling a set of scale drawings of the operational properties, including the Dormy Sheds, particularly in view of all the changes since the pre-war set had been put together. At about the same time, the *Thames Valley* sign was removed from Fingest Shed, presumably so as not to advertise that buses full of fuel were left there overnight?

As previously noted, the Bristol SC-type was thought of as a possible replacement for the Bedfords on the Marlow route, and on 12th December Mr. Pruett visited the BCV works in Brislington and confirmed an order for 5 of them. This made TV the only firm outside of East Anglia to order that type by that time.

'Never mind the rain' seems to be the attitude of these jolly passengers who have dropped off Car 733 (JRX 808) somewhere on Route 20.

1956

The Reading Works lost another long-serving employee on 5th January with the death of Mr. A. V. Barton, who had started as a 'composite' (i.e. Driver/Conductor) back in February 1930, transferring to the Welding Shop in July 1943.

Drivers of the quartet of Oxford-based underfloor-engined Guy coaches, Cars 86-9 (SFC 510-4) found that the wipers were badly scratching the glass on the angular windscreens, which caused distracting reflections especially in the dark. Urgent action was taken to correct this and to polish away the marks.

The Guys of the double-deck variety inherited from Newbury & District continued to give excellent service, and Car 171 (FMO 516) is seen on a layover in Hungerford High Street on Route 113 to Newbury.

Due to rising operating costs and changes in vehicle design, bus companies started to consider introducing one-man-operation on rural routes. Officers from the Company visited *Wilts & Dorset* at Salisbury on 24th January to see the Bristol LS-type converted to B41F layout for o-m-o working, as well as some Bristol LWL-types modified to a front entrance and rebuilt to fully-fronted for the same purpose. As a result of this a meeting was held at 'Yorkstream' with representatives of the Maidenhead drivers to discuss the possibility of similar conversions, and Drivers Morgan and Mitchell were subsequently sent to Basingstoke to see the same types. On 29th February a notice was issued seeking Maidenhead Drivers to come forward if they were interested in o-m-o duties. However, the issue was initially dogged by a number of misunderstandings between the Management and the Union Representatives, even though TV had been totally open in its approach.

Indeed, another wrangle between the Company and the Union occurred during February, when the latter reacted to a reduction in overtime working by refusing to co-operate with the Vocational Training Scheme, which it suspected was being used as cheap labour. This was a personal blow to Basil Sutton, who had certainly enjoyed assisting the Military in that way, and in view of the number of good recruits who came into the TV ranks through that scheme, the Union was rather short-sighted in taking that view.

The LS-type was becoming more widespread, and Car 707 (HMO 853) was about to cover Route 75 through to Guildford, though it was still crew-operated.

Meanwhile on the services front, a number of changes came into effect on Saturday 21st January, all of them affecting operations from Ascot Garage. Firstly, the demise of *S.R. Gough's* bus operation between Winkfield and Crowthorne, led to TV extending the Windsor – Easthampstead Union Route 2b through to Crowthorne. As TV's it came from further east, it was altered to run as Brockhill Farm – Goose Green – Mushroom Castle – Chavey Down Road – Long Hill Road – London Road in order to cover the points of the *Gough's* route. However, Crowthorne Shed still did not contribute to the operation, which was covered by a 55-seater Bristol K based at Ascot.

Nearing the end of their working lives were the 29-seat Bedford OB coaches, of which Car 164 (LJO 756) originated with South Midland, passed to N&D, but is seen here with Thames Valley fleetnames.

Bristol LWL6B Car 581 (FMO 963) appears to be suffering from a bout of indecision, showing on its blinds an ultimate destination of Thatcham, but with the intermediate blind set to a short-working of the 9a to Three Mile Cross!

The other changes in the Ascot operations related to the Windsor Local Services, which improved the service taken over from *Borough Bus*, whilst also incorporating the short-workings of Route 20, these having their origins in the *Pixey Bus Service* taken over in 1933. The re-vamped services became Route 51 (Windsor Central Station – Hospital – Clewer Green, Hatch Lane), 51a (Windsor Central Station – Hospital – Clewer Green, Hatch Lane – Sebastopol – Clewer, Three Elms – Foster Avenue – Dedworth, The Wolf – Clewer, Three Elms – Windsor Central Station), and 51b (Windsor Central Station – Clewer, Three Elms – Dedworth, The Wolf – Foster Avenue – Sebastopol – Clewer Green, Hatch Lane – Hospital – Windsor Central Station).

In order to cope with these additions, Ascot's stable was increased, consisting of Bristol K6A's 441/2 (CRX 550/1), Bristol KSW6B's 640-6 (GJB 278-84), 703/5 (HMO 849/51) and 744-7 (JRX 819-22), along with Bristol L6B coach 545 (FMO 20).

Another low-bridge smash occurred on 1st February, when Bristol KS6B Car 587 (FMO 969) was driven off the route and became wedged under the railway bridge in Culver Lane, Reading. Damage to the roof was extensive, with almost all the upper-deck structure wrecked. As the body type was no longer in production, ECW was requested to make up parts in order to make this repair possible. No mention is made of the Driver in this case, but actions such as this invariably led to instant dismissal, as these events were both costly and bad publicity!

During February the Board gave approval for the new garage at Bracknell, though it would be a further 4 years until completion. It was also agreed to sell off land owned in Oxford Road, Reading, any thoughts of re-locating the Works having been put aside. An order was also placed for 10 electronically-operated Setright Ticket Machines with o-m-o conversions in mind.

The four-weekly Engineer's Reports that had been provided by Basil Sutton since the appointment of Mr. Balls had always been very informative, but with the issue of 26th March they came to a close. On the other hand, Mr. Campbell's reports were rather bland and offered none of the insights of the 'Sutton era'!

Thames Valley finally embraced the Bristol LD-type, and Car 754 (MBL 835) is seen in original condition at Maidenhead Coach Station on Route B. The long front mudguards were soon found to cause overheated brakes, so they were (literally) chopped down soon after delivery. Also note the painted adverts for Huntley & Palmers biscuits made in Reading.

The first of the Bristol 'Lodekkas' arrived in March as Cars 751-4 (MBL 832-5), with Gardner 6LW engines and ECW CLD31/25RD bodies for use on the London express services. Also received that month were three with service bus bodies of LD33/27R layout and fitted with Bristol 6-cylinder engines, as Cars 755-7 (MBL 836-8), and all the trio were sent to Maidenhead. The coach-seated vehicles were used to convert Route B from 1st April, though Route A would have to await further deliveries, which it was also planned to use two of that configuration on the long Route 112 between Newbury and Oxford. Some of the coach-seated Bristol KSW's were therefore cascaded onto Routes 6 (Reading – Basingstoke) and 12 (Reading – Aldershot) after being taken off Route B.

All three of Maidenhead's examples were initially used on Route 20 (Windsor – Maidenhead – High Wycombe), but as more arrived they also covered Route 22 to Slough via the Bath Road. Both Car 757 (MBL 838) <u>above</u>, and Car 755 (MBL 836) <u>below</u>, have had their front mudguards cut back. Both also still carry 'TV prefixes to their fleet numbers, an error caused when the prefixes were shown on a list to indicate which vehicles were destined for the Thames Valley or South Midland fleets!

Pictured with Basil Sutton on his retirement is John Dally Traffic Manager (left), John Pearmain, Company Secretary (right), and Len Balls, former General Manager (seated). The citation for Mr. Sutton's British Empire Medal can be seen on the wall above the Secretary, something he was very proud of.

On 6th April Basil Sutton, Thames Valley's only Chief Engineer since its formation, retired after exactly 36 years service. The special menu card for his retirement dinner at the Caversham Bridge Hotel on 10th April showed one of the Belsize saloons still in evidence when he joined just prior to the formation of the Thames Valley company, contrasted with one of the latest Bristol underfloor-engined LS coaches, a fitting tribute to the progressive development of the fleet under his guidance. Even the seating plan for the dinner read like a long-service roll, as Sutton had developed a very sound and loyal team of Works Staff and Garage Foremen, plus his teams keeping the vehicle records and maintaining the properties. He is recalled for his very precise ways, an often militaristic approach, and his efficient (but never over-bearing) hands-on management. There were official toasts, though the honour of presenting him with a camera and photographic equipment from the staff collection went to Mr. C.J. Withers, Workshop Foreman of a mere 29 years standing. The Company presented him with a retirement gift of £3000 (double his annual salary) in its appreciation of his dedicated service. It is true to say that an era had truly ended. Although I only met him the once, I soon understood all I had heard about him from various sources, and what a contribution he had made at *Thames Valley*.

Mr. Campbell became Chief Engineer from 1st April, and he of course already become familiar with the fleet. It is also worth noting that the General Manager was himself a very competent engineer, having also served in that capacity with the Brighton company, which meant that he took an ongoing interest in vehicle policy.

The Borlaise School buses waited for loading in the small bus park at Quoiting Square in Marlow, and young Peter Wilks caught this scene on his homeward journey in June 1956, with Bristol K6B Car 499 (EJB 221) and utility-bodied K6A Car 432 (CRX 543).

Over at Frogmoor the former *British Road Services* shed was used around this time for the storage of some TV vehicles, one of the Guy double-deckers and the trio of Bedford OB coaches 604-6 (FRX 313-5) all being noted there.

As previously noted, Route 112 was due to be equipped with coach-seated LD-types, and Car 763 (MBL 844) is seen at the Oxford terminus.

On 7th April the first of the Maidenhead routes to be converted to one-man-operation came into effect, these being the rather lightly-trafficked Routes 16 (Maidenhead – Thicket Corner – Knowl Hill – Warren Row – Crazies Hill – Remenham Church Turn – Henley) and Route 17 (Maidenhead - Thicket Corner

– Burchetts Green – Hurley – Remenham Church Turn – Henley), both of which had been inherited with the takeover of *Thackray's Way* in 1936. The timetables, which also included a number of short-workings, as far as Tittle Row or Hurley, called for 3 buses, and Bristol LS-types 714/5/21 (HMO 860/1/7) were so converted. Electronically-operated ticket machines were fitted on the driver's cab door, whilst the first two pairs of seats were removed to form a luggage pen area, the services of a conductor not being available (the LS actually having a rear boot, but its use was not approved for o-m-o working). On such routes the duties were not too onerous, whilst the layout of the underfloor-engined types made such conversions very easy, though no such work on the Bristol half-cab types was under consideration at that time. However, no one would have even considered having a large double-decker being operated in that fashion, yet alone on busy city streets!

Coach-seated 'Lodekka' 760 (MBL 841) is seen on Route B at London Victoria Coach Station on the regular stand used by TV's buses. At the time these were the only scheduled double-deckers working to that location, and attracted much publicity in the trade press, though being in a red livery most casual observers probably never noticed their provenance.

May saw the delivery of further Bristol LD-types, with Cars 750/61/3 (MBL 832/42/4), all with Gardner 6LW engines and ECW CLD31/25RD bodies, along with Car 758 (MBL 839) on the same chassis, but with standard LD33/27R bodywork. All the coach versions were initially placed on London Routes A and B, whilst the bus example was Wycombe Marsh's first one of that type and joined Maidenhead's LD's on Route 20.

Car 759 (MBL 840) was, in due course, another LD-type on the Wycombe Marsh allocation, and it is seen on Route 27 at Great Missenden Station.

With the new double-deckers arriving in strength, further cascading of older types allowed the disposal of the last of the *Thames Valley* Guy utilities and the remaining Bristol K5G's from public service. The latter were Cars 392/4 and 400/2 (BRX 908/10/6/8) and 415-7 (CJB 134-6), and all were ousted in May, along with TV Guys 421/3/5 (CJB 140, CMO 653/5) and N&D examples H4/5 (CRX 282/3). These were followed by TV Guy 422 (CJB 141) in June, plus N&D examples H2 (CRX 280), H6 (FAD 253) and H7 (CRX 595), the last three without their engines. Similar bus H1 (CRX 279) was sold in July, but no further PSV's were disposed off until December. Of the K5G's, Cars 392/4 and 400 had their chassis broken up by the Company and the bodies went for scrap. Car 402 had originally been earmarked for conversion into a Stores Lorry, but was sold instead. It had been usual for one of the N&D Guys of the H1-5 to be allocated to the Kingsclere outstation, so its place was now taken by Bristol KSW 727 (JRX 802).

New Service Vehicles delivered in June were Commer 'Cob' Vans 37 (MRX 113) and 39 (MRX 114), along with Bedford CA5 van 41 (MRX 115), which were for Newbury Depot, the Clerk of Works and Reading Depot respectively. The first and last were in TV red and lettered accordingly, but that used by Mr. Abberfield was in a rather anonymous livery of grey – which it has been suggested made it less obvious the amount of time it was at Tom Pruett's house when engaged on various odd jobs there!

The vans were followed in July by a Ford Staff Car MRX 116 and the GM's new Wolseley MMO 731.

When the timetable from Saturday 23rd June was put out Route 32 was noted as not running between Routs Green and Chinnor until further notice, though quite why has not been discovered. This was reinstated on Saturday 8th September and Bristol LWL6B Car 614 (GJB 252) is seen at Wycombe Station on that route.

Over to the mid-west of the *Thames Valley* empire, the East Ilsley outstation was dispensed with from 8th September, with the Route 102 duty being transferred to Reading instead. The full route of West Ilsley – East Ilsley – Compton – Ashampstead – Pangbourne – Tilehurst – Reading was covered, and there were more short-workings between Reading and Pangbourne.

Bristol LS6G-type Car 685 (HBL 87) waits time on Station Hill for Route 102 to West Ilsley. This route had its origins in a Carrier's service on Reading's Market Days, the Ilsleys having been important villages in the sheep-rearing era.

Further LD's took to the road in June, with Car 759 (MBL 840) on LD6G chassis and with LD33/27R body allocated to Wycombe Marsh, whilst CLD31/25RD-bodied LD6G's 760/2/4 (MBL 841/3/5) went initially to Reading for London route duties on the A and B. More 'Lodekkas' followed in July, these having 5-cylinder Gardner engines and bus

Car 765 (MBL846) is seen when new at Maidenhead Bus Station on Local Service 63. Note the Hickies Piano advert, many of the adverts on double-deckers still being sign-written at that time. Note also the distinctive curved cab-tline of the LD-type and the high number of opening windows on the ECW body.

bodies of LD33/27R layout. These were Cars 765-9 (MBL 846-50), the first of which went to Maidenhead, whilst 766/7 were for Ascot, and the last pair went to Reading.

Route 7 to Nettlebed was not a service generally associated with new buses, so the old couple check with the driver of Car 769 (MBL 850) that they have the correct bus! The bus has yet to receive adverts.

Changes to services operated by Ascot came into force from June 1956, when new Route 52 was introduced. This rang mostly as Wokingham – Binfield (Royal Standard) - Bracknell – Bullbrook – Broad Lane (Kent's Factory), or from Binfield Road (Jocks Lane) or Easthampstead (Union), reflecting where new housing was being built along both sides of the Binfield Road on the Priestwood estates, plus the new employment opportunities in the factory estates being developed off Broad Lane and the brand

new Western Road. These were the embryonic Local Services for Bracknell, something that would require regular re-casting as the New Town expanded and the road systems were re-developed. Unfortunately, the fuel shortages caused by the Suez Crisis in the Autumn did lead to some reduction in the new route, though it was fully reinstated from Sunday 14th April 1957. The new operation raised the Ascot allocation to 16, though the pair of LD's soon became the usual performers on the Windsor Local Services.

As a result of the recent influx of Service Vehicles, August saw the sale of former Reading Depot Bedford 10/12cwt Van 27 (FJB 99), whilst the following month saw a clearout of redundant Staff Cars with the sale of Vauxhall 10hp DRX 476, ERX 580 and FRX 607, along with Ford 'Anglia' 8hp EDP 247.

The older Bristol double-deckers were now to be found on lesser duties, including K6A Car 450 (DBL 158) on Route 23 short-working to Furze Platt.

The Duple-bodied Guy 'Arabs' remained very active and would have many more years to run. Car H14 (HOT 392) was caught by the camera working Route 108 to Lambourn Woodlands, once the independent operation of Ernie Nobes before he joined the ranks of Newbury & District in July 1938.

A rare shot of the old 'Titan' TD1 No.29 (RX 1758) on tree-lopping duties in Broad Street, Wokingham. It is of course rather fitting that it was finally replaced in the same year that Engineer Basil Sutton retired, given the 28-year association by him with that type.

The decision had also been taken to replace the Leyland Titan TD1 Route Servicing Vehicle 29 (RX 1758) with another bus conversion, and during September Bristol K5G Car 405 (BRX 921) took the

place of it as No.43. Also on the non-PSV front, the 32-year old tradition of running petrol tankers on a commercial basis finally came to a close. The Board resolved at its meeting on 16th September to surrender the contract, and the quartet of Leyland 'Beaver' Petrol Tank Wagons 5,7,9 and 11 (ABL 769-72) were sold to the Regent Oil Company in October.

In the Staff Bulletin of 18th September applications were invited for o-m-o working from Reading-based crews, though only 5 Drivers actually volunteered, whilst a similar appeal at Newbury on 29th December brought even less of a response, which caused the Company to point out that the alternatives were likely to be route reductions and redundancies.

The large number of Bristol KSW6B's were putting in solid work all over the Thames Valley operating area, Car 699 (HMO 845) is seen at Mackenzie Street in Slough about to depart for Maidenhead via the A4.

Over at Reading KSW6B-type Car 735 (JRX 810) is covering Route 12 to Aldershot Bus station, though it was common to find those from the coach-seated batch on there once the 'Lodekkas' had displaced them from frontline London duties.

The poor response to the proposed o-m-o working at Reading meant that initially only Route 75 (Reading – Bracknell – Bagshot – Guildford) could be converted. Bristol LS's 712 and 724 (HMO 858/70) were fitted out with electronically-operated ticket machines and reduced to 41 seats plus a luggage pen at the front nearside of the saloon, taking up those duties from 15th October. It had been hoped to convert some saloons to cover the London Route A (Reading – Bracknell – Ascot – Staines – London), as it shared duty rosters with the 75, but the Suez Crisis from 11th October meant that the route had to be suspended in order to conserve fuel. O-m-o buses bore no external signage at this point, though a card sign was slotted into a holder on the driver's door stating 'Please Pay As You Enter'.

As a result of the temporary suspension of Route A plans to re-equip Route 112 (Newbury – Oxford) with coach-seated LD's was brought forward, with Cars 763/4 (MBL 844/5) were sent to Newbury, where the rear doors were much appreciated on days when the wind blew across the Berkshire Downs! The overall fuel situation led to the introduction of an emergency timetable from 17th December, which remained in force until March 1957. The subsequent increase in fuel duty resulted in a general fares rise of half a pence for a single journey and 1d for a return.

Also in December the lightweight Bristol SC4LK's started to arrive, with Cars 774-6 (NBL 731-3) having B35F bodies by Eastern Coach Works. These were to be used on Route 18 (Maidenhead – Marlow) over the weight-restricted bridge, though 774 spent some time initially allocated to Reading for evaluation, even

venturing out to Guildford on Route 75! It is also likely that their suitability for o-m-o working was considered as part of this, as it was also intended that the 18 would convert to one-man, whilst the number of SC's would make inter-working with the already converted Routes 16 and 17 (the back-roads Henley – Maidenhead routes) possible.

Partly as a result of this, December was not a good month to be a Bedford, as TV culled OWB-type Car 437 (CRX 546), which hadn't done much lately, plus OB-type coaches 164/5 (LJO 756/7) and 604-6 (FRX 313-5), there no longer being the need for lightweight coaches for Hayling Island excursions now that the weak bridge had been replaced. 437 did find a new role however, as it went to the Eileen Hurren Blind Fund, whilst all the others are believed to have gone to Cyprus for further service.

Highbridge buses were not the natural choice in the Thames Valley area, and once the East Ilsley route was taken over by Reading, their operations were restricted to the Newbury area. Car H10 (FMO 517) is seen at The Wharf awaiting duty on Route 113 to Hungerford 'the back way' via Inkpen and Kintbury.

It will be recalled that TV had only recently eliminated the pre-war Bristol K5G-type from public use, so it came as something of a surprise when the Company started to acquire some of the type over the Winter of 1956/7! However, these were no ordinary purchases, as they were from the *Brighton, Hove & District* fleet and were for a new venture in open-top riverside operation suggested by that operator's former General Manager Tom Pruett! As these was a seasonal operation the full account of this venture follows this chapter as a separate sub-chapter as that will afford a better overview of this rather unique idea, which also re-introduced the old tradition of 'going for a blow' on the top deck of the earlier generations of *Thames Valley* buses!

Top-less on the 'Valley
The Riverside Service 1957 - 1959

Car 771 (CAP 132) crosses Cookham Bridge back over into Berkshire on the route to Maidenhead.

The middle Thames valley has long been recognised as an important, perhaps even unique, inland 'resort', enjoyed by rich and poor alike. The combination of a varied and attractive river frontage below the foothills of the Chilterns, fringed by charming villages, lazy meadows, small towns with their distinctive bridges and the bustle of river life itself created the fine area in which the *Thames Valley Traction Co. Ltd.* had steadily developed its bus services.

From the outset the company brought the attractions of the area to the attention of locals and visitors alike. In timetables details were given of handy points for leaving the services to walk or visit the villages and country pubs. A day-long 'Anywhere' ticket had been introduced in April 1928, which at 3s 6d gave unlimited travel throughout the TV area. Guide books were produced suggesting tours and stopping off points and places of interest.

With the limited annual holiday of that era, such facilities were very popular, particularly with shop staff on their weekly half-day closing in local towns. Indeed, 'going for a blow' on a fine day on one of the open-top Thornycrofts of the 1922-1931 period had been a regular treat for many. However, the last of the open-top fleet had been disposed after the Summer of 1931, the experience was no longer available locally.

When in 1955 Tom Pruett was appointed as General Manager, he brought with him experience at Brighton, Hove & District of seasonal open-top operation, and his arrival was to turn the clock back some 25 years by re-introducing the facility once again on the *'Valley*! Mr. Pruett persuaded the TV Board to purchase 4 Bristol K5G's from his former employer to be used on a new 'riverside service' to be operated by open-toppers. The vehicles were all 1940 deliveries with the high-type radiator, and somewhat ironically

TV had only cleared that model out from the fleet just prior to their purchase. They were formerly BH&D fleet nos. 6353-6, becoming TV Cars 770-3 (CAP 206, 132, 176 and 211 respectively).

All carried Eastern Coach Works bodies, with those on 770/1/3 being converted to POT30/26R by BH&D on behalf of TV. Car 772 was converted by TV and all were finished in a livery of 'pale primrose' with maroon wings and bonnets. The vehicles were received in late 1956 and stored pending the start of the service.

Operation commenced in May 1957, and it was intended to run the service on Easter Sunday, Easter Monday, and then Sunday-only until Whit Sunday, after which a daily operation would come into force. The exception to that was Wednesday/Thursday 19th/20th June, when the buses were booked to act as grandstands at Ascot Races. It was envisaged that the buses would run until 30th September.

The upper deck of one of the open-top Bristol K5G's awaiting departure from Maidenhead Coach Station.

The initial departures were fixed at 10.00am from Reading Stations and 10.30am from Maidenhead Coach Station, then running on an hourly headway until the 6.00pm departure from Reading and the 6.30pm out of Maidenhead. The local press sampled the new service, fortunately on a fine day, and gave the facility a full-page write up. The overall journey time for the 20-mile route was 82 minutes, and the adult day return fare was 5 shillings.

Experience soon showed that the first journeys in the morning were poorly used, whilst a demand existed for a later evening timing. Therefore the times were amended from Saturday 6th June to omit the initial journeys, but to add one additional run at 7.00pm and 7.30pm from Reading and Maidenhead respectively. At the same time it was decided to amend the period of operation to run 'until further notice'. As is evident from the above, the two service buses were split between the Reading and Maidenhead garages, and it was intended that the others would be required to act as 'reliefs'. In fact Car 772 only joined the others from

Car 771 (CAP 132) passes the famous Boulters Lock.

8th June, as the conversion in the Company's workshops had taken longer than originally anticipated.

However, the weather for the Summer of 1957 was not particularly good, and loadings were therefore down as a result. As it was unlikely that all 4 buses would be required, one was sent to the Oxford-based subsidary *South Midland* fleet on 31st August. Car 770's new role was the operation of a tour of the Oxford Colleges and nearby Blenheim Palace. The livery was duly modified, with SM fleetnames placed in the ovals of beading as they were fitted to that coach fleet. It therefore became the only double-decker to be operated by the *South Midland* fleet under *Thames Valley* control. Returning to the riverside route, it should be noted that very good leaflets were produced, together with window stickers carried throughout the TV fleet. The open-toppers duly received full-size side adverts depicting the route taken. At the end of the Summer all four buses were placed in store at the Stokenchurch garage.

The experiences of 1957 led to a more cautious approach for the operations of 1958, with the service not commencing until Whit Sunday, followed by Whit Monday, thence Saturdays and Sundays only until 29th June, then daily until 31st August. In another effort to further improve the loadings the service was extended at the eastern end onto Windsor, to turn at the Windsor & Eton Riverside Station of the *Southern Region*. As an echo of the very popular pre-war combined rail/road/river excursions, it was hoped that train passengers would take a trip on the bus service to reach other places along the River Thames.

The extended service had a journey time of 1hr 51mins and the adult return fare was 6 shillings. Workings were still covered by Reading and Maidenhead-based vehicles, as TV never had a garage at Windsor, with the Maidenhead bus working 'shorts'

as positioning runs. Operations did not commence until 11.52am from Maidenhead (to form the 12.30pm from Windsor) and 12.30pm from Reading. The headway was also reduced to just 2-hourly. The weather again proved a problem, leading to some serious doubts about the wisdom of the operation! After Winter in store at Stokenchurch, the open-toppers were brought out for the 1959 season, with the service operating on Saturdays and Sundays only from 4th to 12th July, before taking up daily duties from 18th July until 31st August. Timings were retained from the previous year, and despite some fine spells, the weather was generally poor again!

The buses were once again stored over the Winter of 1959/60, and whilst at Stokenchurch they were used in the making of a minor film entitled 'Snowball'. The intention had been to resume operations again from 2nd July 1960, and indeed leaflets had been printed in readiness during March. However, the venture was reviewed as the Summer approached, and it was decided not to continue the battle with the elements! 773 (CAP 211) was sold to Red & White in June 1960 for use as a tree-lopper, TV already having its own converted K5G No.43 (BRX 921). 770-2 (CAP 206, 132, 176) were also sold to a dealer in July, bringing the end to an interesting experiment!

Car 770 (CAP 206) after transfer to South Midland.

1957

The outstanding pair of Bristol SC4LK-types was received for Route 18 (Maidenhead – Marlow) to go over to operation by the batch from 1st January. These were Cars 777/8 (NBL 734/5), but despite their layout there were no initial thoughts about one-man-operation. As it was, the unladen weight of these buses had crept up to 4tons 2quarters since the order had been placed, which meant that passengers over a limit of 15 had to leave the bus and walk over Marlow bridge instead, so perhaps the conductor had to decide who stayed on – even though the passengers were effectively on the bridge at the same time as the very bus they had left! Notices regarding the passenger limit were displayed on the front bulkhead of the bus.

Above – SC-type Car 777 (NBL 734) in 'as delivered' condition, with black fleet numbers and still crewed with a conductor. It is laid over at Quoiting Square, Marlow, a terminus since Marlow & District days.
Below – Car 778 (NBL 735) at Maidenhead after the white fleet numbers were introduced and Route 18 had gone one-man, note the 'Pay As You Enter' sign by the entrance.

More Newbury Drivers had finally come forward for o-m-o working and, from 26th January, a number of the lighter used routes were converted, some of those actually only running on set days. These were Routes 103 (Newbury – Ecchinswell); 108 (N'b – Hungerford

Newtown or Lambourn via Lambourn Woodlands), a former double-deck working; 114 (Newbury – East Woodhay); 116 (Newbury – Kintbury – Hungerford); 120 (Newbury – Hermitage – Frilsham); 126 (Newbury – Crookham Common); and Sundays-only Route 129 (Newbury – Didcot). For this work Newbury received Bristol LS-type Cars 706-9 (HMO 852-5), all of which were converted to B41F and fitted with electronically-operated ticket machines. It seems that quite early on in the saga of o-m-o discussions with the Union, it was agreed that the driver would no longer set the rear destination blinds, formerly a task undertaken by the conductor, so initially they were painted out in black, and sometime later panelled in.

February saw the death of one of Ascot's long-serving drivers, just a year prior to his retirement. He was Frederick Lovegrove, who lived at Brookside in New Road, North Ascot, and later by the Gold Cup pub in Fernbank Road, who in common with many others cycled daily over to the garage off the High Street. His grandson recalled to me how his wife would meet him at the stop on the Windsor-bound bus to hand him his lunchbox, collecting the empty one on his return. When he finished late, dinner would be cooked at the appropriate time, such was the regularity of the working arrangements in those days. After his death, his driver's cap remained on the mantelpiece for many years as a keepsake.

During February a start was made on disposing of the utility-bodied Bristol K6A's, once pride of the Ascot operations, but latterly employed on the Aldermaston works contracts. Cars 430/1/4 (CRX 541/2/5) all went that month, but the remainder would manage to see a further summer of use.

Also in February the Board learnt that the land for the new garage at Bracknell had now been identified, being situated in the new Market Street to link the re-located Cattle Market and Skimped Hill Lane, which was also convenient for the cattle pens still used at the station goods yard.

By March some problems had been experienced on late-night buses taking off-duty United States Air Force personnel back to their Greenham Common Base, so it was agreed that 3 passes would be issued in order that their Military Police could travel with them.

From 23rd March Route A (Reading – Bracknell – Ascot – Staines – London) became o-m-o using LS-type Cars 723/5 (HMO 869/71), which had been fitted with 41 coach seats taken from Bristol LD's 761/2 (MBL 842/3). Those 'Lodekkas' were re-seated with bus seats from the pair of LS's, plus those taken from others of the type converted to o-m-o use. LS Car 722 (HMO 868) was also converted to B41F for o-m-o as a spare for the A Route. However, at peak times there were reliefs using crew-operated double-deckers

Car 725 (HMO 871) is seen at Victoria Coach Station after conversion for the A Route. Note the coach seats, the PAYE sign on the driver's door and the flashing orange direction indicators fitted for London use, the latter feature not becoming universal for some years.

In fact, the single-decking of the A would only prove to a fairly short phase, as once Bracknell New Town got under way use of the route would increase, with weekend peak services seeing up to 4 double-deckers in use as Londoners visited their re-located relatives, and of course the *Green Line* route still terminated at Ascot despite calls for its extension.

LD6G-type Car 762 (MBL 843), now with bus seats but retaining the rear door, on Route 1A to Woodley.

In order to further extend the scope for o-m-o working Route 75 (Reading – Bracknell – Guildford) duties were combined with Route A, though standard LS saloons were used.

However, from 1st June o-m-o working did at last come to the Bristol SC's on Route 18 to Marlow, along with Route 18A (Maidenhead – Pinkneys Green – Halifax Road), as well as Routes 16 and 17 between Maidenhead and Henley which had been converted earlier. The opportunity was also taken to transfer the High Wycombe – Danesfield RAF Camp 'shorts' to the SC's instead of a Wycombe Marsh-based car. The batch could almost invariably be found on the above group of routes, but there were exceptions, such as the time one replaced a failed *Bristol Greyhound* coach all the way to Bristol, and another pressed into service on Route B to Victoria due to exceptional loadings!

The remaining Bedford OWB bus, Car 438 (CRX 547) was disposed of in June for use by the Hendon Old People's Welfare Committee, freshly repainted in TV livery and named 'Polly', the conversion work also including provision of a toilet and stretcher place. Beadle-bodied Bedford OB Cars 510-2 (EJB 232-4) were also withdrawn in June, though identical Car 520 (EJB 242) was retained as a spare for the Marlow route – even though there were far too many SC's to meet that exacting requirement.

Also withdrawn that month were former *Newbury & District* Guy 'Arabs' H8 (CRX 596) and H9 (EWO 484), both of which were sold without engines. Utility bodied Bristol K6A Car 432 (CRX 543) also departed by July. The purpose of removing the Gardner engines from certain sold vehicles was that they were to be re-conditioned for use in some of the new 'Lodekkas'!

A summer 1957 view of the Colonnade yard, with Windover-bodied Bristol L6B coach 491 (EJB 213), Guy 'Arab' H9 (EWO 484), the Route Servicing No.43 (BRX 921), Beadle-bodied Bedford OB Car 512 (EJB 234) and Duple-bodied Bedford OWB Car 438 (CRX 547). Seats from one of the N&D Guys were used to re-seat L6B Car 72 (EBD 235) during May, though similar Car 71 (EBD 234) retained coach seating.

New buses received during June were a pair of Bristol LD-types/ECW LD33/27R bodies, becoming Cars 780/1 (NBL 737/8), and both were sent to work from Newbury. The latter was rather fitting, as the chassis had been fitted with the reconditioned Gardner 5LW engines taken from withdrawn former *N&D* Guys!

Car 781 (NBL 738) working from Newbury Wharf on the busy Route 110 to Tadley, which terminated by the Company's Dormy Shed adjacent to Allen's Garage.

In recognition of the increasing duties now covered by the Ascot Garage, Conductor Sawkins was promoted to Inspector from 26th June, as 'Nobby' Clarke was fully engaged supervising at Windsor Central Station.

The day before that a farewell dinner had been held at the White Hart in Sonning in order to mark the retirement of John Dally as Traffic Manager on June 30th. Mr. Dally had been with the Company since its *British* days, commencing as Secretary in April 1917. That post was re-assigned to John Pearmain following implementation of the 1930 Road Traffic Act in order that the Traffic Manager could concentrate on matters relating to operations and service license applications. Although in his latter days he was perhaps regarded by younger members of the Traffic Office as over-cautious, he could rightly feel the credit for having taken the development of the *'Valley'* network through times good and bad, including two world wars. His strength lay in careful research and the thorough planning of timetables, and many a passenger would have been surprised to know just how much thought went into their services! He was a master of the black art of time-tabling, mixing steady headways with specific requirements, particularly as the latter met demand without the often wasteful mileage associated with contract journeys.

John Dally was, of course, the last of the original trio of Senior Managers, with T. Graham Homer and Basil Sutton having already departed, so an era had truly ended. He was succeeded by Mr. J. A. Stephenson, who was assisted by Mr. F. L. Beetham, effective from 1st July.

From 4th July certain journeys on Route 28 from Reading to Henley and Hambleden were put over to double-deckers then, after a lot of tree-cutting, from 16th of that month the whole route to High Wycombe became 'decker operated. Unfortunately, there was a total strike of crews between 20th to 28th July, so the implementation took place on the 29th instead.

Over at Newbury, Route 113 (Newbury – Kintbury – Inkpen – Hungerford) was double-decked from 15th July, which eliminated the need for relief workings and helped reduce operating costs over that road.

The classic lines of the Windover-bodied Bristol L6B coaches were becoming rather outdated, and 1957 would be the final season for the 1947/8 examples, of which Car 491 (EJB 213) is seen at the Colonnade.

The Summer of 1957 saw young Ian White starting his career at Wycombe Marsh garage. He was the son of Driver Frank ('Chalkey') White of Stokenchurch Dormy Shed, and as a lifetime bus enthusiast he has been able to provide an interesting insight into Marsh staffing at the time: R. Mouat-Biggs was Garage Foreman and went back to *British* days; with Frank Stacey (Assistant Garage Foreman); George Bishop and Norman Cook (Charge-hands); Archie Tubb, Ted Cooper, Vic Allen, Alf Miller, Keith Bishop, Claude Theobalds, Keith Loveday and Pete Gibson (Shift Fitters); E. McCormack 'Mac' and Albert West (Day Fitters); Evan Dalton (Night Fitter, Wycombe Marsh); Mr. Johnson (Night Fitter, Desborough Road); Jack Wingrove and Nigel Denton (Electricians); Bill Foster (Painter); Roy Puttick (Coachbuilder); Ted Ellander (Storekeeper); and lastly, but not least, Ian White as Trainee, doing the rounds of Storekeeping, Vehicle Electrics, Coachbuilding and Fitting.

Bristol KSW6B Car 696 (HMO 842) working on Route 28 following conversion to double-deckers. The advert was Hickies Pianos was often seen, and the shop still continues to supply musical instruments.

Further one-man-operation had been planned for the start of July, but had to be postponed due to the strike. This time the conversion affected the Ascot Garage, which had not had a scheduled saloon working for some time. Route 52 (Wokingham – Binfield Village – Easthampstead or Bullbrook) was converted, as was the Windsor – Winkfield – Bracknell – Easthampstead – Crowthorne route, now re-numbered as Route 53 (formerly the 2B), both going to o-m-o from 3rd August. The Bristol LS's converted for use at Ascot were Cars 712/3/21 (HMO 858/9/67), which were also Ascot's first brush with underfloor-engined buses.

The use of saloons on the 53 certainly made sense, as there were few regular passengers over the full route, though there remained a steady stream of visitors to the Easthampstead Union (later Church Hill House Hospital) and the TB Sanatorium at Pinewood. The latter was one of a number of establishments set up in countryside around London to take patients for 'fresh air' treatment (in those days before a smog-free city), and for some years *Brimblecombe Bros.* operated a link from Wokingham Station, whilst some London operators, including *Banfield's Coaches*, ran regular journeys for the benefit of visitors.

Bristol LS Car 720 (HMO 866) working Route 3 from Reading to Camberley. With LS's at both Crowthorne and Ascot, it is perhaps surprising that the 53 route did not become a joint operation.

On 5th/6th August a large World Girl Guide Camp was held in Windsor Great Park, so *London Transport* and the *'Valley* provided a joint service between the camp site at Spital and both the Windsor railway stations.

The only new bus delivered during August was Car 782 (NBL 739), a standard ECW LD33/27R-bodied LD which was fitted with one of the reconditioned Gardner 5LW engines. Once again the bus was sent to Newbury garage.

During September Strachan utility-bodied Bristol K6A Car 427 (CRX 197) was sold, leaving only Cars 426/8/9/33 (CRX 196/8, 540/4) of that type still active. It was also decided that month that Bristol L6B coaches 460-5 (DMO 664-9), which had Windover or Vincent half-cab bodies, would be re-built as service saloons. The bodies were becoming outdated, but they

Former United Counties Bristol L6B Car 71 (EBD 234) had been transferred from South Midland and is seen outside Maidenhead Garage. Note the Service Van by the office entrance of the building that had served as the Head Office from 1920-1922.

had also been constructed using unseasoned timber, and were not in good order. They were to be re-built to 30ft long and receive reconditioned Gardner 5LW engines, something of a metamorphous-in-reverse as the attractive coaches became ugly-duckling buses.

Route 113 to Inkpen had recently been converted to double-deck operation, and new LD5G-type Car 782 (NBL 739) awaits that duty at Newbury Wharf. Next to it is a visiting Southdown touring coach.

improve parking facilities. 6 more electronic ticket machines were approved for purchase in connection with the next phase of o-m-o conversions. Also once again discussed was the idea of a Camberley bus station. In hindsight, it is difficult to see why TV and *Aldershot & District* did not act in unison to make it happen, particularly as the town had been a border between the two concerns going back to the original territorial agreement, even the railway interest in each operator not achieving a solution.

Also seen at the Wharf is Bristol LS5G Car 687 (HBL 89) working o-m-o on Route 106. The Fire Station seen behind had been the Denham Bros. garage the time that Newbury & District was formed.

At the Board Meeting of 15th September it was agreed to earmark further properties in the Frogmoor area in order to consolidate the Company's holding there and

Just one further Bristol LD5G, again with a re-con engine and standard ECW LD33/27R body, arrived in October and became Car 783 (NBL 740), being allocated to Maidenhead.

Quite a few vehicles were sold that month, with K6A utility-bodied Cars 428/9 (CRX 198 and 540) departing, along with highbridge ex-*Red & White/Newbury & District* Guy 'Arab' Car H9 (EWO 484). The whole quartet of Windover-bodied Bristol L6B coaches originally used to re-equip the London Route A, Cars 487-91 (EJB 209-13), were sold after having been parked for some time in the Colonnade yard. A start was also made on disposal of the earlier Duple-bodied AEC 'Regal' coaches, with SM's 45/8 (LJO 758/61), 52 (MWL 744) and 62 (NWL 879) being selected, along with similar coach 142 (DMO 331) from the Newbury fleet. On the Service Vehicle front, the only change in 1957 took place in October, with the departure of Lorry No.25 (JGF 406), a former WD Commer purchased in 1948 which had served as the Wycombe Marsh stores lorry.

As one-man-operation spread, the Bristol LS saloons were to be found in wider locations. Car 714 (HMO 860) is seen in the Weldale Street yard of Reading Garage ready for service on Route 9A to Tadley.

Double-deck repaints from the Autumn of 1957 were supposed to be without the black lining to the upper-deck cream band, but that practice was ignored at Newbury, as Reg Hibbert and his 'lads' liked to do a 'proper' job! Reg also arranged for an off-peak duty of touching up the black paint on front mudguards, so it was rare to see a Newbury-based bus looking bad in that respect despite the many narrow roads traversed.

From 1st October two of the contracts to Milton Depot from Newbury were switched to being covered by SM coaches, and this continued for many years, and also accounted for why some of the older coaches were rarely seen in Oxford!

With the Winter timetable from Saturday 26th October a new Route 2B was formed as part of a recasting of

Local Services in the Ascot/Sunninghill/Sunningdale area, which now became:

Route 2A Ascot (Horse & Groom) – Cheapside (Post Office) – Sunninghill (Schools) – Sunningdale Park – Sunningdale (Schools) – Sunningdale (Station);
Route 2B Ascot (Horse & Groom) – Ascot (Station) – Sunninghill (Schools) – Sunningdale (The Rise) – Sunningdale (Station);
Route 2C Ascot (Horse & Groom) – Ascot (Station) – South Ascot (Marie Louise Club) – Sunninghill (Schools) – Sunningdale Park – Sunningdale (Schools) – Sunningdale (Station).

Still to be found working hard were the Bristol KS6B deliveries of 1950/1. Above – Car 591 (FMO 973) is in Reading Garage. Below – Car 594 (FMO 976) stands in the Southern yard at Reading awaiting relief duties on Route 2 to Windsor. Both have now lost the upper-deck cream band, the next stage in the simplification of the livery occurring during this period. Also note that on this and the previous page we see the transition from black fleet numbers to white ones.

A rare bird indeed was Car 779 (NBL 736), one of only 6 Bristol LDL6G's to be built. Note the offside emergency door behind the driver's cab.

In connection with the changes in the Ascot area, an agreement was made with Reading brewers H. & G. Simonds for buses to use the forecourt of the Sunningdale Hotel for turning of buses at the railway station.

Also from 26th October Route 60 (Maidenhead – Cookham – Bourne End – Little Marlow – Marlow) was reduced to run between Marlow and Little Marlow only, with extra journeys on Routes 18/18a compensating between Maidenhead and Marlow. Route 61 (Summerleaze Road – Maidenhead Bus Station – Marlow Road corner – All Saints Avenue – Pinkneys Green) was also deleted, again with all areas sufficiently covered by other services.

At the November Board Meeting it was decided to demolish the chequer-bricked row of cottages at Nos.73-9 Lower Thorn Street, along with those at Nos.37/9, in order to maximise parking space in the front yard.

From 1st November the operational arrangements for No.2 Area were revised, with High Wycombe continuing to cover the activities at Wycombe Marsh, Desborough Road and the Dormy Sheds at Fingest, Princes Risborough and Stokenchurch still under the control of Ernest Jeffries. However, a separate Maidenhead Area was formed, with Mr. C. E. Lewis now acting as Traffic Superintendent in his own right.

On 15th November the Traffic Manager and General Manager met and agreed that the open-top Bristol K5G's would be made available for use as grandstands at Royal Ascot Race Week in June 1958.

A further pair of Bristol LD's with reconditioned 5LW engines and standard ECW LD33/27R bodies arrived in November as Cars 784/5 (NBL 741/2), and these were allocated to Maidenhead and Reading. The sharp-eyed amongst you may have already noted that fleet number 779 had so far remained unclaimed, and at the time some might have wondered if another open topper was in the course of preparation.

Standard 'Lodekka' Car 785 (NBL 742) was amongst the last to be delivered with black fleet numbers, and is seen at Reading Stations on Woodley Route 1A.

However, it was actually one of the few 30ft long Bristol LDL6G chassis which carried an ECW LD37/33R body. The type was an interim model, and this example had originally been intended for *Southern Vectis*. It was received in November and allocated to Reading, where it soon earned the nickname 'Big Bertha'. The extra length might not seem much, but as the vehicle was a one-off, drivers often thought they had a standard LD and the rear end got quite a few scrapes. The author recalls that drivers

147

would regularly clip parked cars on the Local Services in Bracknell for this very reason! The vehicle weighed in at 8tons 4cwt 2qtrs against the standard LD at 7tons 10cwt 2qtrs. When new it was mostly found on Route 1A to Woodley, as new housing development in that area saw a sharp rise in passenger numbers, TV being responsible for all Woodley area services in those days.

The late '50's saw a number of routes warranting the use of double-deckers, and Bristol KSW6B Car 641 (GJB 279) awaits duty in the Southern yard on the 5B for Pangbourne and Yattendon.

On 1st December Mr. Bessell retired as Oxford Foreman and Mr. M. D. Munday took his place there. On the last day of that month Chief Inspector Harry Guley also retired and was replaced at Reading by Mr. C. W. Ankerson, who was Local Traffic Supervisor and retained that title, whilst Inspector Reg Pembroke became responsible for the preparation of the weekly working arrangements.

Also during December the last pair of Strachan utility-bodied Bristol K6A's were disposed of, with the sale of Cars 426/33 (CRX 196 and 544), ending the use of buses obtained under wartime conditions.

In the meantime a number of changes occurred on the services front. Route 62 was surveyed on 3rd December for its suitability for double-deck operation, though it was agreed that only 7ft 6ins buses would be scheduled on that road. A new joint venture with *London Transport* started on 11th December, with TV's double-decked Route 64 (Slough Station – Britwell) being shown in timetables alongside LT's Route 484 which, whilst not exactly the same route, covered much the same ground and offered increased opportunities between those points.

The Bristol saloons of the 1950-2 deliveries also continued to put in solid work on a wide variety of duties. LWL6B-type Car 631 (GJB 269) lays over in Lower Thorn Street yard with blinds set for a short-working on Route 9A, whilst alongside it is LL6B-type Car 544 (FMO 19) awaits the afternoon turn on Route 5A through to Chilton.

On 14th December a new o-m-o saloon working began over Route 1C (Reading Stations – Calcot Estate, with some projections to Theale), though this was perhaps regarded as only a temporary solution, as it duly disappeared when Routes 1 (Maidenhead – Reading) and 10 (Reading – Newbury) were joined end-to-end from 29th March 1958.

The only new bus delivered in December was Bristol LD6G/ECW LD33/27R Car 786 (NBL 743), which went to work from Wycombe Marsh Garage.

That month also saw the licensing application for a Southern Ireland tour to be operated by *South Midland,* and that was duly granted. However Mr. Pruett warned that the Company faced difficult times, with rising fuel costs and increased car ownership, but it was hoped that the development of Bracknell New Town would counter-balance that.

Bristol KSW6B Car 656 (HBL 58) had just been repainted when seen at Reading Stations on Route 9.

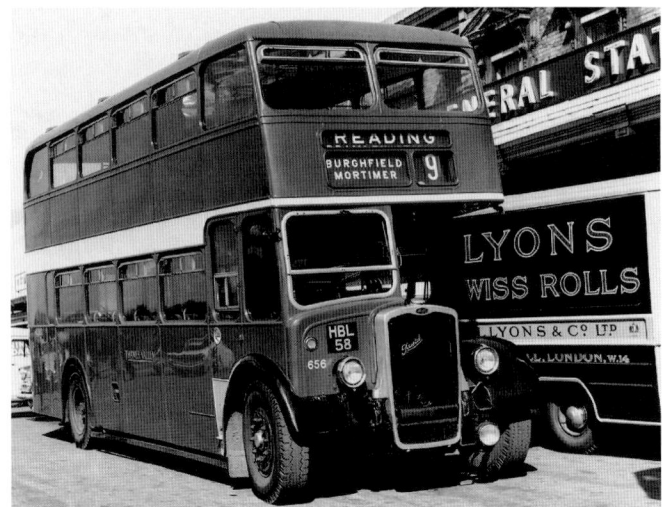

1958

Over the Winter of 1957/8 Duple-bodied AEC 'Regal' coaches 141/3/4 (DMO 330/2/3) and 145 (EBL 736) were officially re-classified as 'dual-purpose' vehicles, and they could be found on contract duties from various locations in the Newbury area. By January Duple bus-bodied 'Regal' Car 132 (DMO 321) was being rebuilt for o-m-o use, with the rear of the cab removed, plus an angled window over the bonnet to allow the driver to swivel around. It was also fitted with a reversing light, a rare sight in those days, and this was in lieu of the assistance that had previously been provided by the conductor. The seating capacity was reduced by one to 34 in order to make room for a luggage pen towards the front of the saloon, this conversion paving the way for other such conversions, which provided some useful buses of 7ft 6ins width for use on sparser rural services.

Duple-bodied AEC 'Regal' saloon Car 137 (DMO 326) clearly shows the angled window with the ticket machine mounted on the shelf behind, as fitted to this type on conversion to o-m-o. It is seen at The Wharf with a highbridge Duple-bodied Guy 'Arab' behind.

However, one surprise conversion to o-m-o was the surviving Beadle-bodied Bedford OB Car 520 (EJB 242), complete with a reversing light, despite being decidedly 'spare' to requirements by then! It was also, of course, the only petrol-engined vehicle remaining in the passenger fleet.

1950 Windover bodied Bristol L6B coaches 550/1 (FMO 25/6) had been working for *South Midland*, but in January 1958 they were transferred to serve from Maidenhead instead. Unlike the deliveries of 1947/8, these bodies were still in sound condition, but with the advent of underfloor-engined types their graceful lines were becoming rather dated in appearance.

Each Winter the open-top Bristol K5G's were put in store at Stokenchurch Dormy Shed, and Car 772 (CAP 176) is seen with old destination blinds being draped over the upper deck seating in order to keep dust and bird-droppings off!

The face of the Newbury-based fleet had steadily changed over the years since it came into *Thames Valley* control, but even at January 1958 it could still offer some interesting variety, as seen below:

Double-deckers -
Guy 'Arab' III 6LW/Duple H57R- Cars H10 (FMO 517), H13-6 (HOT 391-4)
Guy 'Arab' III 5LW/Duple L53RD- Cars 170/1 (FMO 515/6)
Bristol K6A/ECW L55R – Cars 439/40 (CRX 548/9), 443-5/51/2 (DBL 151-3/9/60)
Bristol K6B/ECW L55R – Cars 453 (DBL 161), 466/7 (DMO 670/1), 497 (EJB 219), 524 (FBL 26)
Bristol KSW6B/ECW L55R – Cars 648/50 (GJB 286/8), 668/9 (HBL 70/1), 702/4 (HMO 848/50), 726-8 (JRX 801-3)
Bristol LD6G/ECW CLD56RD – Cars 763/4 (MBL 844/5)
Bristol LD5G/ECW LD60R – Cars 780-2 (NBL 737-9)

A link with the past was the only Leyland 'Tiger' still active in the fleet, PS1-type Car 169 (LWL 995), which had received a new ECW body in 1951. It is seen in the low-height section of Newbury Garage, and note the warning stripes painted on the uprights!

Single-deckers –

AEC 'Regal' 0662/Duple B35F (132 as B34F) – Cars 131-40 (DMO 320-9)

AEC 'Regal' 0662/Duple DP35F – Cars 141/3/4 (DMO 330/2/3), 145 (EBL 736)

AEC 'Regal' 6821A/Lydney B35F – Cars 161-3 (FBL 919-21)

Bristol L6A/ECW B35R – Cars 455/8 (DBL 163/6), 478-80 (DMO 682-4)

Bristol L6B/ECW B35R – Car 538 (FMO 13)

Bristol LL6B/ECW B39R - Cars 556/64/5 (FMO 938/46/7)

Bristol LS6G/ECW B41F – Cars 685/6 (HBL 87/8)

Bristol LS5G/ECW B41F – Cars 706/7 (HMO 852/3)

Bristol LS6B/ECW B41F - Car 721 (HMO 867)

Coaches –

AEC 'Regal' III/Duple C35F – Cars 146-8 (EJB 146-8)

Leyland 'Tiger' PS1/ECW FC37F8 – Car 169 (LWL 995)

Bristol LS6G/ECW C39F – Car 673 (HBL 75)

Bristol LS6B/ECW C39F – Car 688 (HMO 834)

Notes –

161 was under repair at Reading after an accident

131/5/6/8/9 were de-licensed pending conversion to o-m-o or disposal

141/3/5 and 161-3 were de-licensed

133/40 were allocated to Hungerford

137/7 were allocated to Lambourn

727 was allocated to Kingsclere

One of the Crowthorne-based Bristol LS-types passes south along Finchampstead Road, just as a train on the Reading to Tonbridge line steams over the bridge. The headroom of this bridge is given as 13ft 3ins, but only in the centre, and over the years it claimed the roofs of 3 of the 'Valley's double-deckers, plus a number of lorries too!

Despite the evident need for economies in operation due to fuel costs and the difficulties of recruitment, the Company was still accommodating to requests by large local employers and in response to Local Councils. On the work front, further developments at AERE Harwell, AWRE Aldermaston and ROF Burghfield continued to keep many vehicles occupied, both on service routes and associated contract runs. However, TV did not have it all its own way, and from 31st January it lost contracts NE/7 and NE/8 (both from Newbury to RAF Milton Depot) to *Reliance Motor Services*, those contracts having been covered by *South Midland* coaches.

Route 9 (Reading – Burghfield – Mortimer) was used by many to travel out to work at the Royal Ordnance Factory, as well as the families living in the housing developments in that area. Bristol KSW6B Car 697 (HMO 843) is seen in the Lower Thorn Street yard.

Only 2 new buses entered service during January, as Cars 787/8 (NBL 744/5). Both were Bristol 'Lodekka' LD6G-types with Eastern Coach Works LD33/27R bodies, and the pair were allocated to Wycombe Marsh. However in contrast to the previous year, no passenger vehicles were disposed of during the first half of 1958.

Car 787 (NBL 744) was caught at Frogmoor Bus Station on a short-working to Marlow on Route 28.

Half-cab Bristols could still be found on Route 3a (Reading – Wokingham – Barkham – Finchampstead), and LWL6B-type Car 582 (FMO 964) is seen turning in Wokingham from Broad Street into the Market Place. The little café and bakers on the corner of Rose Street was later lost to road widening.

On the staff front Mr. M.D. Munday became Garage Foreman at Oxford, whilst Mr. J. F. Dickenson became Garage Foreman at Reading, both promotions being effective from 1st January. During that month the Newbury Garage 1943 Bedford OW-type Lorry (CMO 963) was disposed of without a replacement.

Another stronghold of rear-entrance saloons was the High Wycombe Local Services, and LWL6B Car 621 (GJB 259) is seen at the Desborough Road Garage.

In an interesting development on the Extended Tours, the Company applied to the Department of Industry & Commerce in Dublin for permission to operate a 9-day tour of Southern Ireland. Originally this proposal had also included a pick up point at the Cheltenham Coach Station, the intention being to take advantage of the numerous connections afforded there, but that element was not proceeded with.

In preparation for this new tour, TV's sole remaining Leyland, the ECW-bodied 'Tiger' PS1 Car 169 (LWL 995) was de-licensed, repainted and re-seated to 34 in order to provide additional comfort. The choice of such a relatively old coach had much to do with the arrangements made for its servicing whilst in the Irish Republic, where the make was well represented and, at that time, Bristols were a rarity. In this new role 169 once again reverted to the *South Midland* fleet-name, having originated in that fleet before passing to *Newbury & District* and then later to *Thames Valley!*

The extended tours programme of *South Midland* was indeed still going well, with tours centred on Pitlochry (Scotland), Newquay (Cornwall), Ilfracombe (North Devon), Torquay (South Devon), Porthcawl (South Wales), Llandrindod Wells (Central Wales), Grange-over-Sands (English Lakes) and several Wye Valley holidays based at Tintern. In addition to these activities, the express coach network was maintained, with the Oxford to London routes (via Henley or High Wycombe), London to Worcester, and Southsea from Oxford and Worcester. Joint services had also been developed with *Southdown* from Oxford to Brighton Southsea and Eastbourne, with *East Kent* to Margate, and with *Maidstone & District* to Hastings and Bexhill. *Full details are contained in David Flitton's '50 Years of South Midland 1921-1970' (see page 4).*

Another regular duty for TV's buses was for rail replacement when engineering requirements dictated closure of part of the line. Bristol K6B Car 453 (DBL 161) is seen outside the old Wokingham Station, with the taxi office to the right. The station buildings were typical, but not a thing from this view now remains!

It should be noted that the TV/SM booking offices were also agents for *Salters Steamers, London Coastal Coaches*, the continental tours of *Thos. Cook & Son*, and the coach-air link operated by *Skyways* from London Victoria for flights to Paris, along with the Butlin's Holiday Camps.

Although the importance of the Parcels Service may have declined compared to the days when the buses were some of the very few motors on the local roads, the Company still maintained over 180 agents throughout its area. Parcel rates were 1 shilling up to 4lbs weight, 1 shilling and 6 pence up to 14lbs and just 2 shillings for the maximum weight of 28lbs, and the joint arrangements for transferring parcels between the *'Valley* and *Reading Corporation* were still in place.

At the close of January AEC 'Regal' Car 132 (DMO 321) returned to service as a one-man-operated bus, and returned to Newbury Garage. Work commenced on 2 others from the same batch, and over the period to the end of July Cars 131/3/4/7/9 (DMO 320/2/3/6/8) were dealt with, though the others from that batch would be disposed of instead. The conversions were all down-seated to 34 in order to provide space for a luggage pen.

Vehicle deliveries from ECW in that period tended to be in ones or twos, this being in accordance with a system of 'sanctions', as chassis orders from Bristol Commercial Vehicles were known, the intention being to try to satisfy demand from all eligible operators.

Received in February was a further pair of Bristol 'Lodekkas' with standard ECW LD33/27R bodies as Cars 789/90 (NBL 746/7). 789 had a Gardner 5LW engine re-conditioned by the Company, and this was sent to Maidenhead, whereas 790 had a brand new Gardner 6LW unit and was allocated to Newbury.

Car 790 (NBL 747) is seen at The Wharf, on the side where a Thames Valley shelter had stood since the 1930's. By now the original wooden 'chalet-style' shelter had given way to a concrete and corrugated iron affair, other passengers at the bus station relying on the overhanging upper story of the Old Granary for shelter in wet weather.

The final go ahead for the Eire tour came when the east Midlands Traffic Commissioner granted the Road Service License on 5th February, and work on Car 169 (LWL 995) was duly completed. However, from 7th February, the Colonnade ceased to be an operational base, though it remained a busy place, with buses coming and going for overhauls and repaints, as well as still being the Coach Station for express services through Reading, as it had served in such a manner since Robert Thackray had constructed it in 1930.

During the first week of February, a sharp-eyed TV driver had averted a terrible tragedy whilst he steered his bus along Route 3 between Crowthorne and Sandhurst. Driver Norman Hitchman of Twyford saw what at first he took to be a bundle of newspaper in the road, the visibility being poor due to the weather being foggy. However, as he drew nearer, he realised it was in fact a baby , a 2-year old who had managed to crawl from his garden into the road, whereupon his luck was in as Norman brought his bus to a safe halt. He jumped from his cab and rescued the infant, who wore only his nappy, and the crew wrapped him in their greatcoats! Although they knocked on nearby doors for some 10 minutes, no parents could be found, so the child was left with one lady and the bus went on its way to Camberley, where the Police were told. Later the mother was successfully located, and she duly wrote to the Company expressing her gratitude for the crew's prompt action. In response, the TV spokesman told the local press *'our chaps are always very good with children and go out of their way to help them'*. What the Police said to mum isn't known!

As noted previously, the Bristol SC4LK saloons also covered duties on the 2 routes between Maidenhead and Henley, and Car 775 (NBL 732) is seen in the Market Place, Henley working Route 16 in snowy weather, alongside a Ford 'Anglia' car.

On 18th February the Traffic Manager visited Windsor to consider a suitable terminal point in connection with the proposal to extend the open-top Riverside Service to that town. Following on from that a meeting took place with British Railways (Southern Region) in order to secure use of the Eton & Riverside Station, which was a convenient point for both rail connections and the nearby Salters Steamers, whose mooring was just yards away on the Berkshire bank of the River Thames. The extension would bring the route mileage up to 30, and it was hoped that the weather would at last shine on the venture. It was agreed to provide a marked bay for the bus to wait in.

Bristol LL6B saloons were the mainstay of Wycombe Local Service 33. Desborough Road-based Car 559 (FMO 941) is seen at the Newlands Road terminus.

Some severe snow was experienced during the week ending 28th February, with the High Wycombe and Newbury areas bearing the brunt as usual. Services in the Wycombe area suffered some cancellations before roads were once again made passable. To the west 2 buses had to be abandoned at Applepie Hill on the road between Aldworth and Compton whilst working Route 102. One of these was Bristol LWL6B Car 581 (FMO 963), but the other was not recorded. Due to that the run from Compton School could not be completed, resulting in a dozen pupils having to stay over at the headmaster's house, both of the buses being recovered safely during the following day.

'Just as well it had a red roof, or we would never have found it' is what the weary gang who had just cleared the road in front of Car 581 after its night out on the Berkshire Downs must have been thinking!

153

March saw the arrival of another Bristol 'Lodekka', fitted with a reconditioned Gardner 5LW engine and standard ECW LD33/27R body. It became Car 791 (NBL 748) and entered service at Maidenhead. Here it is seen on Wokingham Station forecourt with the 'Molly Millar' pub behind, having worked to there on Route 21 via The Walthams. Unlike the photo showing Wokingham Station shown on page 152, the pub and other buildings have survived.

From 29th March the long established routes between Maidenhead and Reading (Route 1) and Reading and Newbury (Route 10) were joined together end-on-end, to be known as Route 1 throughout. One of the reasons behind this was the chronic shortage of drivers at Maidenhead, due mainly to the employment opportunities at the Slough Trading Estate.

KS6B-type Car 597 (FMO 979), now demoted from London Route B duties, offered coach seating, heaters and a platform door on the revised Route 1.

The 30-minute headway of the old Route 1 was retained, though the Reading to Newbury section now followed suit, whereas it had been on a 20-minute basis from the pattern inherited after the takeover of the *Ledbury Transport Company*. There were also numerous short-workings between Newbury and Colthrop Mills and between Reading and Wargrave.

An interesting comparison of the relative dimensions of Bristol LS-type Car 720 (HMO 866) and SC-type 777 (NBL 734), both seen parked outside Maidenhead Garage.

With other conversions to one-man-operation planned, a further order for 40 Setright Ticket Machines was placed in March.

Also received that month was the first examples of a new Bristol chassis for the Company, this being the successor to the LS. These MW6G coaches weighed in at 7tons 6cwts 3qtrs in comparison to the equivalent LS at 7tons 1cwt, primarily due to the fact that the new model had a separate chassis frame, whereas the LS design had the body built on a sub-frame. This quartet of coaches was for *South Midland* and they introduced a new style of livery evenly split between maroon and cream, with a distinct affinity to the style

154

adopted by *Royal Blue.* The livery very much suited their ECW C34F coachwork, though it had been a close call, as when Tom Pruett had asked his wife what livery she felt might appeal to potential female passengers, she had suggested pink!

This photo shows an example of both the lowbridge and highbridge Duple-bodied Guy 'Arab' MkIII's that came with the Newbury & District operations. On the left is Car 171 (FMO 516) laid over from duties on Route 106 to Lambourn, whilst H10 (FMO 517) rests between contract runs on a sunny day in 1958.

Repaints of coaches from the Spring of 1958 used the new scheme of lower panels in maroon and cream from the waistrail up, though the natural curves on the ECW streamlined bodies were followed, as with LWL coach 609 (GBL 873) helping out at Newbury.

Other notable repaints into the new scheme were Car 169 (LWL 995), the rebodied Leyland 'Tiger' PS1 and the better examples of the remaining AEC 'Regal' coaches of the *South Midland* fleet. This remained the standard scheme for both that fleet and the coaches of *Thames Valley,* though the proportions were variable.

MW6G coaches 800/1 (ORX 631/2) arrived during March, and they were followed in April by Cars 802/3 (ORX 633/4), and these were the first *South Midland* coaches registered in Berkshire, as indeed were all subsequent deliveries. All had glazed quarter lights for

touring work, but Car 803 had been selected for some special treatment, and it was put under wraps at Oxford.

In fact 803 had been entered for the British Coach Rally in Brighton on 20th April, which was somewhat unusual in view of the Bristol-ECW products only being available to State-owned companies. However, the fact that Mr. Pruett had previously served with the local *Brighton, Hove & District* no doubt had a lot to do with this. A party of officials, including the Newbury engineer Reg Hibbert (who still undertook all major dockings for the SM fleet) were treated to a hotel for the weekend in connection with this event.

Car 803 had received some additional attention at the coachbuilders, with the front grille and ECW 'wings' being chrome-plated. It had also been fitted with roof-mounted continental-style air-horns. To Oxford's considerable pride, the coach actually won the Concours d'Elegance, and the overall judging was based on the appearance of the coach and the skills of the driver. The former had been polished to a dazzling shine, whilst Driver Langridge certainly proved his worth on that day.

After the event the coach initially returned to Botley Road, where it was placed on display on the forecourt. On 30th April it was displayed at Maidenhead Bus Station, at Newbury Wharf on 1st May, and then to Reading Stations Square the following day, thereby reviving the old TV practice of placing new coaches on public show.

Driver Langridge and General Manager Tom Pruett receive trophies from the Mayor of Brighton as Car 803 (ORX 634) gleams in the seafront sunshine.

On a rather more mundane note, duty plate holders had started to appear throughout the service bus fleet from February onwards. This was in line with *London Transport* practice, though it was never fully adopted. Indeed, the author recalls the use of waterproof yellow crayons at some locations, whilst others used plates, the numbers referring to lists of scheduled buses introduced by Charlie Chun, who came from LT.

155

Bristol KSW6B Car 634 (GJB 272) reverses into Fairlawn Road, Tadley on route 9 from Reading, with guidance from the conductor. The Dormy Shed is to the left, and note the angled roofline, which owed its origins to when the shed was modified to take a double-decker. Also seen behind the bus is another of that type bound for Newbury on Route 110.

Thoughts were also being given to the reintroduction of the open-top Riverside Service, which had been extended to Windsor as discussed earlier. Although this actually appears in some official TV documents as Route C, this never appeared in timetables as such. It was decided to commence operation on 24th May on weekends only, then with a full service throughout the school holidays, though the frequency was reduced.

Bristol K5G Car 772 (CAP 176) is seen in the layover bay at the Eton & Riverside Station with side adverts now amended to reflect the longer route of 30 miles.

The staff Bulletin for 22nd May included an appeal for further volunteers to transfer to o-m-o duties at High Wycombe, as the Company wished to convert Routes 32 (High Wycombe – Bledlow Ridge – Chinnor), 34 (High Wycombe – North Dean – Speen) and 80 (High Wycombe – Lacey Green – Princes Risborough – Aylesbury). The initial response was not bad, but the Union did raise a number of objections, most issues relating to how the former duties carried out by the conductor would be covered or reduced. These had included supervising reversing manoeuvres, the setting of destination blinds and assisting passengers with pushchairs or bulky luggage. The latter had been accommodated in the rear boot fitted to most saloon buses, but as that would necessitate the driver leaving his ticket machine and cash-bag unattended, it was agreed to provide a luggage pen behind the front door. Rear destination boxes were initially over-painted, but were panelled over during subsequent body overhauls. Rear reversing lights were fitted to converted vehicles or specified on new deliveries intended for that role.

Bristol LS Car 687 (HBL 89) is seen at Ascot after conversion to o-m-o, with the rear destination boxes painted over and a reversing light had been fitted.

Further housing development on the Baughurst Estate led to diversions of Route 110 (Newbury – Thatcham – Tadley) in order to serve residents there, and this came into effect from 31st May. The route also contained a number of short-workings to serve the busy military stores at Thatcham (GSS) Depot, as well as Messrs. Croppers and the Colthrop Mills.

The Wycombe garages used the duty plates, which can be seen below the first nearside window on Bristol KS Car 591 (FMO 973) as it awaits departure to Booker on Route 38 from High Wycombe Station.

May saw no new additions to the fleet, though work was well underway on the Bristol chassis sent away for rebodying. TV had stripped the Windover/Vincent bodies from coaches 460-5 (DMO 664-9) and over the Winter the chassis had been lengthened at Reading Works to take 30ft long bodies similar to those being built on Bristol SC-types. TV was not unique in this and a number of other companies had programmes to turn redundant coaches into useful o-m-o saloons. The engines were Gardner 5LW's taken from wartime buses inherited from *Newbury & District*.

South Midland AEC 'Regal' coach 56 (MJO 667) was one of those to bear the maroon and cream scheme. It is seen at Oxford on the Worcester to London service.

LS coach 689 (HMO 835) is seen at Gloucester Green Bus Station in Oxford after transfer to South Midland.

As noted previously, a number of older coaches of the *South Midland* fleet were employed on contract runs, so Car 67 (OFC 206) found itself transferred to the TV fleet for the same purpose from June 1958, though it did not receive TV fleetnames. That same month saw TV's Bristol LS coaches 689/90/2/3 (HMO 835/6/8/9) being transferred to *South Midland* instead.

More of a case of 'swans turning into ugly ducklings', the rebuilt and rebodied former Bristol half-cab coaches became one-man saloons. Former Car 461 (DMO 665) became 795 as a result of the rebuild, but retained the original registration mark. It is seen turning into Reading Garage from Weldale Street.

During June the first of the Bristol LL5G rebuilds returned as Cars 795/6 (DMO 665/6), carrying fully-fronted, front-entrance 39-seater bodies by ECW, both buses initially being allocated to Maidenhead, mainly seeing use on Routes 16 and 17 between Maidenhead and Henley. In order to provide a suitable seat for the driver, ECW had devised a sliding version for access to the saloon, as the swivel version did not suit the position of the controls. Due to the lightweight build of the bodies they weighed in at exactly 6 tons, which was much lighter than the conventional LL-type and made them economical buses to operate. Though they were by no means attractive, they were nonetheless useful vehicles and were destined to see another 8-9 years service.

June also saw the end of an era, with the disposal of the final Inspector's motorcycle - that type of mobility

Half-cab rear-entrance Bristol L-series buses had been ordered in large numbers and were still to be found throughout the operating area. 1951 LWL6B Car 584 (FMO 966) is seen at Newbury Wharf between duties. Note the National Fire Service signs on the barn, a leftover from the war years.

having been provided since the formative years of TV, the honour going to Crowthorne Inspector Hester's BSA 250cc (DRD 659).

Another long-serving employee retired in June, when R. Mouat-Biggs ended his long career with *Thames Valley*. He had joined in the Summer of 1924 with the opening of the new Wycombe Marsh Garage, and he had for many years been Garage Foreman there. That garage had quadrupled in size over the years, along with having responsibility for the Dormy Sheds at Fingest, Princes Risborough and Stokenchurch, plus later still the 'running shed' at Desborough Road. He was well respected for having kept the wheels turning through some trying times, and the guest list at his farewell luncheon read like a roll call of the long-service staff, some of whom had originally served as local independents, along with his old boss, former Chief Engineer Basil Sutton. His place was taken by Mr. L.F. Stacey, whilst from 1st July the post of Assistant Engineer at Reading was taken by Mr. B. T. Hancock.

In the meantime the inaugural Eire tour commenced on 18th June, and Leyland 'Tiger' PS1 Car 169 (LWL 995) travelled to Fishgaurd on the western coast of Wales, in order to catch the overnight ferry across the Irish Sea.

TV's coastal express service from High Wycombe to Southsea remained a very popular facility, particularly as the rail journey was not very convenient. It also did

well for passengers from Marlow and Maidenhead, so much so that a coach would often start from the latter town. It ran every Sunday from June to September, plus also on Saturdays during July and August, and it was popular with Period Return bookings for those wishing to make a week of it or to travel on by ferry to the Isle of Wight.

The Bristol KSW6B's were also still putting in solid work on trunk routes, though Car 738 (JRX 813) was coach-seated with a platform door, having originally been ordered for London Route B.

No outgoing changes to the fleet had so far occurred in 1958, but in July a clearout of older saloons and coaches took place. As already noted, a number of routes had been double-decked, thus reducing the need for so many scheduled reliefs. A reduction in contract work also rendered some coaches redundant. These were Duple-bodied 1947 *South Midland* AEC 'Regal' coaches, all with classic half-cab bodywork, Cars 39/40/2 (LWL 996/7/9) and 69 (EJB 650 former N&D vehicle). On the bus front those ousted were Duple-bodied 'Regal' saloons, Cars 135/6/8/40 (DMO 324/5/7/9), new in 1947 to *Newbury & District*. These were joined by similar vintage ECW-bodied Bristol L6A Cars 455/7/8 (DBL 163/5/6) and other 1948 examples 472/4/6/7/81-5 (DMO 676/8/80/1/5-9).

Another interesting comparison shot shows rebuilt Bristol LL5G Car 796 (DMO 666) alongside LWL6B-type 617 (GJB 255). The circular yellow 'Pay As You Enter Sign' and the narrowing to a single line of the destination indicator indicates this view was taken a few years later, the location being Thorn Street yard.

July saw some minor amendments to Route 22 (Burnham – Everitts Corner section) in order that all journeys could be operated by double-deckers, and to address the growth of housing in that area. However, just as one situation was resolved, so another beset the Traffic Office, with the reduction of the weight limit on Marlow Bridge to just 2 tons from 14th July! Buses from the Maidenhead end of Route 18 worked as far as Quarry Wood Road, on the Berkshire bank of the River Thames at Bisham, whilst another bus provided a shuttle service on the Buckinghamshire side. That vehicle reached that point via Bourne End each morning, spending its day travelling back and forth between Marlow, Little Marlow and Marlow Common. As this duty did not fully utilise the bus, a number of variations were tried out, including some journeys through to Danesfield RAF Camp near Medmenham.

The closure of Marlow Bridge to buses meant that it was no longer necessary to use only lighter buses, so o-m-o LS-types could be found working to Bisham on route 18, leading to a new destination of 'Marlow Bridge Only' as seen on Car 715 (HMO 861). Also note the damaged front nearside corner!

The new restriction also removed any justification in retaining the last of the Beadle-bodied Bedford OB's, so Car 520 (EJB 242) was sold off in August. That same month also saw another *South Midland* Duple-bodied AEC 'Regal' coach, 51 (MWL 743) departing.

Whilst on the subject of Marlow, it should also be noted that a school journey ran for many years from the Maidenhead area for boys at Borlaise School, and that also terminated at Quarry Wood Road. In those days the walk through town to the school was not considered unreasonable, plus it saved the expense of running the bus via Bourne End.

LL5G rebuild Car 798 (DMO 668) at the Kingsbury Square terminus of Route 80 in Aylesbury.

The conversion of Routes 32, 34 and 80 to one-man-operation did go through from 26th July, although the Union had insisted on further changes to the working arrangements, which the Company had agreed to. The former *Gem Bus Service* Route 80 (High Wycombe – Aylesbury 'the pretty way', as one driver once described it to me) then became the frequent haunt of rebodied Bristol LL5G's, as some sections were rather narrow for the LS-type, the front overhangs of which suffered from numerous minor knocks.

In due course a number of the rebodied LL5G's were to be found at Newbury as o-m-o spread onto more routes in that area.

The conversion of 8-year old Bristol LL6B-types was rather unexpected, particularly as a number of them had already been disposed of to United Welsh. Car 566 (FMO 948) clearly shows the jacknife doors and the angled window over the bonnet in order to locate a ticket-machine shelf.

Indeed, as other o-m-o vehicles became available during 1958, Bristol LS Cars 685-7 (HBL 87-9) were converted back to B45F for crew operation. It should also be noted that quite a few of the LS saloons moved around at this time, which left the regular four at Crowthorne Dormy Shed as Cars 710/4/5/8 (HMO 856/60/1/4), with the usual cover for engineering being Car 720 (HMO 866). Despite this allocation, Route 3 (Reading – Wokingham – Crowthorne – Camberley) remained crew-operated.

Changes in working arrangements in the Newbury area also reduced the requirement there by 4 saloons, though the place of one of those on a contract was in fact taken by a *South Midland* coach.

The next route scheduled for the one-man treatment was the 1b (Reading – Winnersh – Hurst – Shurlock Row), which went over from 9th August. During that month there were representatives from *Wilts & Dorset* and *East Kent* visiting to see the various types of one-man conversions that TV had put in service.

Indeed, another phase was just commencing, with the selection of Bristol LL6B Cars 564-8 (FMO 946-50), though as it turned out no other half-cab buses would be so treated, so it would seem that this was merely seen as a way of providing some suitable buses at low cost in order to improve operating costs.

The conversions involved removing the original rear doorway and provided a driver-operated jacknife door at the front, along with a ticket-machine shelf set in an angled window, plus a modified driver's seat to allow easy access to the passengers and an alternative exit in the event of emergencies (the former opening window over the bonnet no longer being available). The work was carried out at Lowestoft by ECW, on one bus at a time, with Car 564 being the last to return in January 1959. All five were initially allocated to Newbury and used widely on the surrounding narrow roads to good effect, and all remained in service for yet another 10 years!

During August the remaining quartet of Bristol LL5G buses with new ECW FB39F bodies were delivered as Cars 794/7-9 (DMO 664/7-9), and all went to work from Wycombe Marsh Garage. Over the years these did move about, and there were even some exchanges of these with Newbury-based half-cab front-entrance LL6B's a few years later.

Newbury also received another Bristol L-series bus in September, in the shape of L6B-type Car 72 (EBD 235), which had originated with *United Counties* and later passed to *South Midland*. It had been built as dual-purpose, but later received bus seats, and is seen at the Wharf when laid over between contract duties.

160

In the meantime, and commencing on 9th August, the journeys previously operated as Route 1c between Reading and Calcot, were instead covered by diversion of Route 11 (Reading – Bucklebury), which took in the new housing off the Bath Road at Calcot.

Car 793 is seen on Route 63 at Maidenhead very soon after delivery and before any adverts were applied.

A further pair of Bristol LD6G's with ECW LD33/27R bodies was placed in service at Maidenhead during September as Cars 792/3 (NBL 749/50). These were the last new double-deck buses to be delivered without heaters or doors.

September was also the traditional month for clearing out old vehicles, and further Bristol L6A's that had recently been held in reserve were ousted. These were Cars 456/9 (DBL 164/7) and 478-80 (DMO 682-4), which had been stored at Stokenchurch. In October a cull of older *South Midland* coaches took place, with Duple-bodied AEC 'Regals' 41 (LWL 998), 46/7 (LJO 759/60) and 49/50 (MWL 741/2) all departing.

O-m-o Bristol LL6B Car 564 (FMO 946) was usually to be found on Route 106 to Upper Lambourn.

September also saw the sale of Morris 'Oxford' car, which had for some years been used by Basil Sutton, but latterly had been for general use at Reading. One new Service Vehicle acquired was an AEC 'Matador', which had been purchased from the Military Disposal Sales at Ruddington in Nottinghamshire. This was to form a new Recovery Vehicle, and the chassis was thoroughly overhauled over the Winter of 1958/9, and between April and November 1959 a modern cab body was constructed at Reading Works, incorporating some standard ECW items. As with some previous projects handled by the Works, this seems to have been a bit of a 'spare time' occupation mainly undertaken on quieter days, hence the length of preparation!

AEC 'Matador' Recovery Vehicle No.1 usually ran on trade plate 323 RD, and it is seen in Reading Works on completion, which included a contemporary style of AEC radiator grille and fleetname panels.

With so many detailed timetable changes during the year, September was notably in that the Winter edition contained no significant amendments. However, the former *Denham Bros.* terminus on what had become Route 115 (Newbury – Highclere) was moved from the Red House public house to nearby Crowshott Lane in response to Police concerns that the waiting bus represented a potential traffic hazard, this alteration taking effect from 27th September. Also of relevance on the services side, Peter Agg was promoted to Chief Schedules Officer that same month.

On the incoming vehicles front, the first 'Lodekkas' for service work with the improved features were received during October as LD6G-type Cars 808/9 (PRX 926/7). These had under-seat heaters on both decks and conductor-operated rear platform doors, both buses being sent to Wycombe Marsh for use on Route 20 (High Wycombe – Maidenhead – Windsor) and Route 30 (High Wycombe – Aylesbury).

From October Route 62 (Slough – Cippenham) was covered by a pair of Maidenhead-based double-decks, though only 7-and-a-half footers were scheduled.

Typifying the nature of many of the rural routes operated in the Newbury area, this scene shows LL6B Car 565 (FMO 947) pausing at Boxford on Route 106. Note the lack of markings at this Y-roads junction, and the old type of warning sign indicating approach to a school.

Over at Marlow, it proved possible to slightly re-arranged timings in order to reduce the number of buses required to cover the disjointed Route 18 duties on both sides of the Thames by one vehicle from 4th October.

Bristol LD6G Car 809 (PRX 927) awaits departure to Windsor on Route 20 at Frogmoor Bus Station. The fibreglass front cowl of the 'Lodekka' was neat in appearance but prone to accident damage.

The subject of the accessibility to public transport is by no means a new one, particularly in a population affected by the ravages of two world wars, something highlighted in a report noted by the General Manager.

The Minister of Transport had stated that there were over 1 million disabled persons out of the working population of 23 million, though that ignored all those whose mobility was impaired by old age or disabled children. Despite this, there were no specific proposals put forward, nor would vehicles be designed with such concessions for many years to come.

The Company did, however, continue to provide extensive information for prospective passengers who wished to explore its area by utilising the bus services. As had been the case for many years, a guidebook was issued and, by the late 1950's the cover had been updated to feature a Bristol LS saloon alongside the River Thames and heading to Oxford on Route 5. Within the pages were details of historical interest and other attractions where buses ran, and the free guide was subsidised by adverts within its 128 octavo pages.

Still hard at work on the Wycombe Local Services 26/26a were 1948/9 Bristol K's such as Car 507 (EJB 229) seen heading east to Wycombe Marsh. Note that the intermediate blind is faded from constant use on this route.

The Thames Valley network took its buses to many varied places, and here we see Bristol KS6B Car 597 (FMO 979), once the pride of the London B Service, in the more tranquil setting of the feudal estate village of Yattendon. Here the 'Royal Oak' had been the starting point for passengers since the days of the horse-drawn carrier's wagon, but now it was part of Route 5b between Reading and Newbury.

Another topical subject in 1958 was proposals to close branch line railways, though this was actually in advance of the infamous 'Beeching Report' of 1960. The West Wycombe Station closed to passenger traffic from 3rd November, but the location was well served by buses on TV routes emanating from High Wycombe, with Routes 30 (to Aylesbury), 32 (to Bledlow Ridge or Chinnor), 37 (to Fingest or Henley), 39 (to Stokenchurch or Watlington), 40 (to Radnage), 41 (to Ibstone) and 42 (between Loudwater and West Wycombe), as well as the Oxford – London coaches of *South Midland* and certain bus journeys of *City of Oxford* services.

On 5th November Company officers met with those of *British Railways (Western Region)* to discuss possible closure of the lines between Newbury and Lambourn and from Cholsey to Wallingford. Lambourn was, of course, an established outstation, whist the Cholsey to Wallingford road was already served by Route 5 from Reading to Oxford.

It should be noted that Ascot had continued to have a coach allocated throughout the Summer, Windover-bodied Bristol L6B Car 545 (FMO 20) covering 1958. However, from 4th November this was laid up at the back of the garage, awaiting a decision on its future. Not that Ascot had much space, with some buses parked out at night, and from December a further double-decker was allocated to cover school journeys, as there were few secondary schools in the area then.

L6B coach 545 (FMO 20) did in fact get a reprieve, returning to service after a repaint into the maroon and cream scheme and transfer to South Midland for Summer 1959 relief duties. It is seen at Victoria Coach Station in immaculate condition.

Three Bristol K-type double-deckers were transferred from Wycombe Marsh to Desborough Road Garage on 8th November in order to operate some of the journeys on the intensive Local Service Route 26/26a (Micklefield Estate – Wycombe Marsh – Desborough Road – Sands), and this also reduced dead mileage.

Visiting coaches were to be found at TV garages from time to time, and this ECW-bodied Bristol MW from Tillings Transport (3 BXB) was on hire to Thos. Cook & Son for a tour of Devon and Cornwall.

*Repaints of coaches into the new maroon and cream scheme continued throughout 1958/9. In the case of the Lydney/BBW-bodied Guy 'Arab' UF coaches, of which Car 87 (SFC 502) is seen **above**, this livery had the effect of enhancing their rather solid look. **Below**, the solitary AEC 'Regal' MkIV coach 85 (SFC 571), however, very much suited the scheme, and is seen freshly re-painted at Victoria Coach Station.*

Newbury got coach-seated KSW6B Car 741 (JRX 816) during November to operate on the 17-mile Route 122 which was jointly operated with *Wilts & Dorset* through to Basingstoke via Kingsclere.

The ranks of the Duple-bodied AEC 'Regal' coaches were further thinned during December, with disposals of *South Midland* 53 (MJO 278), 54/5 (MJO 664/5) and 60 (NWL 877), along with former *Newbury & District* examples 141/4 (DMO 330/3), both of which had latterly carried TV fleetnames.

Further Newbury area services went over to one-man-operation from 20th December, though some only ran on certain days. These were Route 101a (Newbury – Peasemore, Thursdays and Saturdays only), Route 105 (Newbury – Wantage – Childrey Ridgeway, which ran on Wednesdays and Saturdays), Route 114a (N'bury – West Woodhay, Thursdays and Saturdays) and 120a (Newbury – Aldworth, on Thursdays and Saturdays).

Also converted was the 'Boxford short' on Route 106, provided for school children. Route 103 (Newbury – Ecchinswell, which ran on Tuesdays, Thursdays and Saturdays) now became fully o-m-o, whilst a number of journeys on Route 116 (Newbury – Hungerford via the Bath Road) were also scheduled for such working, but not at peak times when double-deckers were still required. Similarly, except on Saturdays (when double-deckers took over), Route 115 (Newbury – Highclere) was one-man-operated. Arrangements for such working were quite complex, drivers requiring a very sound knowledge of the area!

Through the above arrangements, together with the elimination of relief buses by the double-decking of a number of routes, some economies had been achieved during 1958, though a number of rural routes were still regarded as marginal. Fortunately in those days operators were happy to take a wider view, allowing some uneconomical (but nonetheless essential) routes to be cross-subsidised by the profitable operations.

Such issues were indeed at the heart of the General Manager's Christmas Message from Tom Pruett. There was also some optimism, with the expansion of Bracknell New Town and the new opportunities that would bring. Existing services through that town were already showing an increase, as Route 2 passed the new factories at Broad Lane and Western Road.

At the end of December Local Traffic Superintendent T.H. Read retired at Maidenhead. His place was taken by W.E. Hobbs, transferred from High Wycombe, but that vacancy was not re-filled at that time.

1950 Bristol KSW6B Cars 601-3 (FMO 983-5) could be distinguished from a distance by having their registration plates across the base of the radiator. Car 602 is seen at Frogmoor for Great Missenden.

1959

Recent changes on route 18 (Maidenhead – Marlow Bridge) had reduced vehicle requirements by one bus, so one of the Bristol SC4LK's took over from one of the older L-series buses allocated for Routes 16 and 17 (both between Maidenhead and Henley).

January also saw a further clearout of AEC 'Regal's, with 1949/50 Duple-bodied *South Midland* examples 61 (NWL 878), 63/4 (NJO 217/8), 65-7 (OFC 204-6), along with similar 1947/8 coaches 143 (DMO 332), 145 (EBL 736) and 146/7 (EJB 146/7), all which had originated with *Newbury & District*.

In order to replace those coaches for contract duties, a batch of Bristol LL6B coaches was purchased from *United Counties*. These became Cars 821-9 (FRP 835/7-44), all which had been fitted with 8ft-wide axles, along with being built with ECW FC37F bodies of that width. They had originated from the same batch as those which had become SM Cars 75-8 (FRP 832-4/6) in May 1952 when the latter had acquired the *UCOC* Oxford – High Wycombe – London service, though those coaches still retained 7ft. 6ins axles. Cars 821-7 were allocated to *South Midland* and 828/9 to the *Thames Valley* fleet. The fleet numbers before these had already been allocated to new LD-types and LL5G-type rebuilds awaiting new bodies.

Car 829 (FRP 844) turns from Weldale Street into the Thames Valley Reading Garage from a contract run. Note the lamp-post to the left, painted in black and white as a aid to driving in the WW2 black-out.

Also received in January were a further pair of Bristol 'Lodekkas', these being fitted with the Bristol AVW engines taken from coaches rebuilt as LL5G buses. The bodies were of an improved specification, and of LD33/27RD layout. These became Cars 810/1 (PRX 928/9), and both were initially based at Reading and used on Route 1 (Maidenhead – Newbury). Quite soon after both were re-allocated to Wycombe Marsh, then moved again to Stokenchurch Dormy Shed for use on Routes 39/40/41 in place of a pair from the Bristol KSW6B's 729-31 (JRX 804-6).

Above – LD6B Car 811 (PRX 929) is seen when new at Newbury Wharf in Route 1. Note the sign-written advert for Langstons the Outfitters. Below – The same bus is seen working on Route 20 at Maidenhead Bus station, following transfer to Wycombe Marsh but prior to being sent to Stokenchurch.

Once a hive of wartime activity, the Shaw Factory of Vickers Armstrong finally closed its gates in January, which resulted in some bus journeys no longer being required. A number of routes had been developed by extending journeys on Routes 106 (from Lambourn), 113 (from Hungerford via Kintbury), 116 (also from Hungerford but via the Bath Road), 121 (Penwood) and 127 (from Wash Common), whilst double-deck reliefs ran in from various points around town.

However, it was the un-planned events in Maidenhead that dominated the traffic situation in late January, as from 4pm on 23rd it became impossible to operate Route 20 from Maidenhead due to extensive flooding of the River Thames. By 6pm the Yorkstream had backed up and flooded the Coach Station, whilst the Bus Station followed suit overnight. Buses on Route 18 between Summerleaze Road and the Bus Station had to cease, and *British Railways* agreed to accept holders of TV season tickets on services to High Wycombe, Bourne End, Cookham and Maidenhead. The Bath Road soon descended into to chaos, as all traffic passed through Maidenhead town centre then.

Ascot Garage was busier than ever, and this icy scene shows the original Course Road garage to the right, plus the adjacent building converted as an extension later on. One of its numerous Bristol KSW6B's stands inside, whilst another is parked at the yard end to the left but out of view in this shot.

In order to provide refreshments for crews during the floods at Maidenhead, a bus was kitted out as a mobile canteen and parked on the elevated land just to the west in St. Ives Road. Over the night of 26th -27th January the floods receded, so Route 20 resumed the full route from 7a.m. From 11a.m. the Bus Station returned to full use again, though some routes needed to avoid the remaining pockets of water in York Road and Bridge Avenue. Although the Summerleaze Road journeys resumed on 28th, the Coach Station remained under water, a situation made worse when freezing temperatures turned it all into 3-4 inches of ice, and it stayed like that until 2pm on 2nd February!

Maidenhead Coach Station at the height of the floods! The Paddington to Bristol Railway had fortunately been constructed on an embankment and forms the rear of the site. To the right is the bus stand allocated to Blue Bus Service of Bray which, being the last of the independent bus operators in the town, had been re-located here from the railway station forecourt. When it closed coaches stopped at the Bear Hotel.

During February The Board approved another batch of 40 Setright Ticket Machines, whilst further one-man conversions were being reviewed in order to counter rising costs. Indeed, the second batch of the home-made buses arrived in February as Cars 817-20 (FMO 21-4). These former Windover-bodied coaches on Bristol L6B chassis had been lengthened and re-engined to LL5G format by the Company, and then re-bodied by ECW as FB39F.

Re-bodied LL5G-type Car 818 (FMO 22) in original condition. Route 6b to Bramley was one of the routes converted to o-m-o once these buses were available.

These were equipped similar to the previous batch for one-man use, but for some reason they weighed in at 6tons 3cwts 3qtrs instead of the 6ton dead of the early examples. All were initially set to work from Reading, though Car 818 was very soon afterwards transferred to High Wycombe. Their arrival displaced the last of the Bristol L6A saloons, Cars 473/5 (DMO 677/9) and L6B saloon Cars 521-3 (FBL 23-5), though all were placed in store. These LL5G's worked on a variety of routes, particularly those calling for narrower vehicles and remained in service until 1968. In later years they became regular buses to cover servicing absences.

Bristol LL5G Car 817 (FMO 21) loads with market day shoppers in Market Place, Wokingham, bound for Finchampstead after Route 3a was duly converted to one-man working. In those days before universal use of fridges shopping for food was a more frequent task.

On 19th February Bristol LWL6B Car 620 (GJB 258) suffered severe damage after a lorry had careered down the notorious steep Amersham Hill and hit it in the rear. The bus was working the 1.05pm journey to Cadmore End on Route 36 at the time, having itself just travelled down the hill from the Railway Station terminus. Conductress Margaret Wiltshire, who went onto complete 40 years service on the 'Valley at High Wycombe, recalled the terrific bang and the screams of the passengers as the lorry rammed in the rear end as it halted at the Crendon Street junction. Damage to the rear was extensive, though due to the solid nature of the Bristol-ECW product, none of the passengers required hospital treatment. The pantechnican lorry had been full of new television sets, and some of the unbroken ones soon disappeared from the accident scene and before the Police arrived! The lorry came off worse from the encounter, as its body was totally wrecked, whilst the bus also sustained some front-end damage as it was shunted into a passing drop-side truck of the Post Office Telephones.

Due to more seats now being required on Route 37, one of the services now serving the former station at West Wycombe, this route received one of the Bristol LS saloons still crew-operated with 45 seats from 1st March. However, the general trend towards converting such buses to one-man use continued, with a further trio being made available for use at Reading that month. These were for conversion from 14th April of Routes 5a (Reading – Wantage), 6a (Reading – Odiham), 6b (Reading – Bramley) and 102 (Reading – West Ilsley). Thereafter, a mix of LS's and re-bodied LL's were to be found covering these mixed duties which took buses to a wide variety of places. From the same date Route 9 (Reading – Mortimer – Tadley) was extended through to the New Inn at Baughurst in reflection of housing development in that area, though it remained a double-deck operation .

In the meantime, on 28th March, the Campaign for Nuclear Disarmament, led by the Cannon Collins and Bertram Russell, staged a protest march from London to the AWRE plant at Aldermaston. A fair bit of distruption occurred to the TV services sharing the route taken by the marchers, though there was some compensation, as the buses carried around 500 people who had travelled to Reading to join the march there.

Further Bristol MW6G coaches were received in March as Cars 804/7 (PRX 930/3), followed in April by Cars 805/6 (PRX 931/2). These all had ECW C34F bodies fitted with glazed quarter lights for tours in the *South Midland* fleet.

MW coach 806 (PRX 932) is seen passing through the ancient town of Winchester on a private hire job.

As previously noted, the service bus fleet had been fitted with holders for duty plates, and these were in use officially from 20th April, though their use was by no means universal.

Bristol LS5G Car 706 (HMO 852) is seen laid over on Route 5a to Wantage. Buses for the Reading saloon routes could generally be found parked alongside the entrance to the Southern yard off Stations Square.

A truly exceptional private hire job called for these 19 'Lodekkas', seen awaiting loading at Wendover Way.

On 6th June the *Valley* was called on to provide cover for more than 1100 employees and families of the High Wycombe-based furniture makers Ercol. From Wycombe they were taken to London's Tower Bridge, where they boarded the famous 'Royal Sovereign' for a cruise down river to Southend-on-Sea. Once there a lunch for 1000 took place at The Kursal, where the Chairman Mr. L.R. Ercolani presented long-service medals and watches to staff, the remainder eating in other nearby restaurants. The firm's band provided the music throughout the day, and everyone much enjoyed themselves.

Further Bristol saloons, L6B-types 539/43 (FMO 14/8), were withdrawn and placed in store at Stokenchurch in April. At the same time similar buses 537/42 (FMO 12/7) were put in store at Desborough Road Garage, though none were sold until next year.

With so many routes being converted to o-m-o, the days of the older Bristol L-series saloons were ending. Car 539 (FMO 14) is seen here nearing the end of its service covering a short-working to Noakes Hill on Route 102.

As previously noted, the balance of the fleet had now turned toward double-deckers, though in order to achieve this switch the Company would need acquire more without too much expense, as we shall shortly see with some interest!

From 17th May Sunday services were added to Route 64 (Slough Station – Britwell), which was also covered by *London Transport* Route 441a (or Route 400 on Mondays to Saturdays) as was already the established joint arrangement.

'Lodekka' Car 813 (SMO 79) is seen as new at Frogmoor on Route 20 to Windsor. Note the change of style of upper-deck side opening windows to hopper-type, with only two being provided on each side.

Three Bristol LD6B's with ECW LD33/27RD bodies were received as Cars 812-4 (SMO 78-80) in June, all being sent to Wycombe Marsh Garage for use on trunk Routes 20 (to Windsor), 28 (to Reading) and 30 (to Aylesbury), where their rear doors and heaters were no doubt appreciated once colder weather came.

LD6B-type Car 814 (SMO 80) is also seen on Route 20 approaching the Windsor terminus at the Central Station. Note the duty plate in the holder, and also that the conductor-operated rear door has been left open due to the warm weather.

From 15th June some short-workings were added to the timetable for Route 5, this being to cover erstwhile trains between Cholsey and Wallingford, which had ceased operation on Saturday 13th. One single-decker was allocated to this duty and the journeys operated between the Railway Hotel in Cholsey and Wallingford Market Place.

As had become the regular tradition, the quartet of open-top Bristol K5G's, Cars 770-3 (CAP 206, 132, 176, 211) were turned out for The Derby at Epsom Race Course in June prior to commencement of the Riverside Service. A renewed sense of optimism on the route accompanied this, hoping for a good season!

Over at Bracknell, planning of the New Town came under the auspices of the Bracknell Development Corporation, who leased the site of the new garage to the Company. The contract for building the garage was signed during June and, at the same time land held in St. Ives Road, Maidenhead, adjacent to the bus station, was disposed of.

During June the final pair of Bristol L6A saloons were disposed of, these being Cars 473/5 (DMO 677/9). It should be noted that many of these vehicles built in the early post-war years had started to show severe body defects due to the use of unseasoned timber, and would have required a thorough rebuild.

However, as already noted, the double-decker was then in the ascendancy, and during June an interesting trio arrived at Lower Thorn Street from the *Bristol Omnibus* fleet! Cars 436/7 (KHU 624 and KHU 601) had been new in 1947 direct to the Bristol operator, and these were both K6B's. Car 438 (HTT 980) had originated with *Western National* in 1946, passing to *Bristol Omnibus* with its Stroud Area routes in 1950.

The latter had originally also been a K5G, but it was re-engined with a Bristol AVW unit by TV before use. These all carried the standard ECW 7ft 6ins wide 55-seater body, though they differed in some details from the indigenous examples. As they had the *BOC* single aperture blind layout, TV initially used them all with a 'Relief' stencil, which allowed the route number to be changed by the conductor whilst, as all had been new to a green-liveried fleet, they had red interiors (ECW practice being to give the opposite colour to the external finish as a general rule). This trio was usually to be found working for Reading, though they could sometimes be loaned to cover engineering absences at other garages. Car 436 would outlast the other pair by several years, and it was even selected for a thorough body rebuild in 1961, at which point it received the standard 3-piece front destination display.

Above *– Car 436 (KHU 624) in original condition with one-piece destination screen and seen in the Southern yard at Reading.* ***Below*** *– Car 438 (HTT 980) enters Stations Square in Reading on a Summer relief run on Route 2 in from Ascot Races.*

Former Bristol Omnibus Car 437 (KHU 601) awaits departure from Wokingham Market Place on Route 3. Note the range of shops then surrounding the market.

Double-deck operation was scheduled from June for Routes 18a (Maidenhead Bus Station – Halifax Road), 23 (Maidenhead – Pinkneys Green) and 64 (Slough Station – Britwell), and Maidenhead Garage was sent a further pair of such vehicles to cover these, whilst the Reading allocation was increased by one bus for relief duties.

LD6G-type Car 815 (SMO 81) at Maidenhead Bus Station working on Route 18a to Halifax Road.

July saw the arrival of the last pair of rear-entrance LD's ordered by TV, as Bristol Commercial Vehicles was now offering a front-entrance 30-footer capable of carrying 70 passengers. These became Cars 815/6 (SMO 81/2) and were both LD6G chassis with ECW LD33/27RD bodies, allocated to Maidenhead.

A number of route changes took place from 18th July, most of these affecting the services in the Slough area. Route 63 (Maidenhead – Curls Lane Estate) became Route 15, in the 'Maidenhead series', but the route was not altered. Over at Marlow, the existing journeys between Marlow – Little Marlow – Bourne End got a separate identity as Route 18b. At Slough Route 22 became the 60 and continued to provide the service to Maidenhead via the Bath Road. Route 22a (Maidenhead – Taplow – Cliveden – Burnham – Slough) became Route 63 and, with a diversion via Sheepcote Lane, went over to 7ft 6ins double-decks.

Bristol K6B Car 530 (FBL 32) stands in Maidenhead Garage with blinds set for the new Route 63.

The former 22b became Route 61 (St. Andrews Way – Trading Estate – Salt Hill – Slough Station), but the previous workings to Maidenhead were transferred to Route 65 (Maidenhead – Taplow – Burnham – Trading Estate – Salt Hill – Slough Station). Similarly the 'Burnham shorts' on Route 22 also migrated to the 'new' 65 (Maidenhead – Burnham – Slough).

The 'Hitcham Park shorts' from the original Route 22 were transferred under 'new' Route 66 (Maidenhead – Hitcham Park – Burnham – Slough), whilst Priory Park was served from Slough by a Route 67, all of this making the main Route 22 a much simpler operation. In all cases journeys working through the Trading Estate, as opposed to only serving the main gates, were indicated by an 'a' suffix.

1948 Bristol K6B Car 499 (EJB 221) passes by the Slough Working Men's Social Club on Route 67 to the Priory Estate.

From the same date a new Route 68 (Lent Rise – Burnham – Everitts Corner – Trading Estate – Salt Hill – Slough Station) came into use, which also had some 'a' journeys at peak times. However, this only ran generally on an hourly basis, being covered by a crew-operated saloon based at Maidenhead.

Many of these changes reflected the housing developments in the Slough area as, although the town had not been designated a New Town, it nonetheless had continued to receive former Londoners since after the First World War. Numerous others came from Wales and other areas where the traditional industries were in decline, the factories of the Trading Estate and other local large employers offering new work prospects. The bus services to carry these, together with similar requirements in the High Wycombe area, were the most intently worked of the *Valley's* routes.

From 18th July Route 20 (Windsor – High Wycombe) and Route 30 (High Wycombe – Aylesbury) were combined as a through route under the guise of Route 20. This ran as 20a when deviating through Little Kimble, as the old 30 had done on alternate journeys – these runs also omitting the section via Fifield Memorial Hall, so that was served alternately as well. This gave a total route mileage of 36 on the 20, with a running time of 2hrs 15mins, whilst the 20a was 34.7 with a journey time of 4 minutes less. Princes Risborough Dormy Shed continued to provide 2 buses for this operation, now updated to a pair of LD-types.

Bristol LD6B Car 811 (PRX 929) at Maidenhead Bus Station after transfer from Reading to Wycombe Marsh and working the new Route 20a. Note that the whole of the driver's windscreen opens.

By August it was found that the buses covering the rail replacement Cholsey – Wallingford journeys were not coping at times! As nothing further is heard of this it must be assumed that demand was duly met, perhaps also confirming that the railway passengers had deliberately been underestimated in order to close the line? This also reminds of a later *Thames Valley* story, when several routes were omitted from the timetable booklet, then not long afterwards they were withdrawn due to lack of use!

Ascot continued to have use of a coach throughout the Summer of 1959, but the identity has not been recorded, though an LWL6B of the 607-12 (GBL 871-6) batch was noted at times, probably from Reading.

The re-cast of services in the Slough area saw more use of double-deckers, though those working Route 66 via Burnham were 7ft 6ins, such as KS6B Car 589 (FMO 971) seen laid over at Maidenhead.

Throughout the decades Thames Valley had provided a special service to Fair Mile Hospital on Thursdays and Sundays for relatives wishing to visit patients at the Mental Hospital. Re-bodied Bristol LL Car 819 (FMO 23) and another of the batch prepare for the run in Lower Thorn Street yard.

Another personnel change took place in August, with the promotion of Mr. G. E. Morris to Assistant Traffic Supervisor at High Wycombe. It is worth noting that positions such as these were paramount to the smooth daily operations, as these were the eyes-and-ears of the Company, having to deal with everything that the crews, the weather and the public could present them with! They, and the Inspectors, are easily overlooked, but they are definitely the unsung heroes without whom the Company could not have built the good reputation it enjoyed.

Still active was odd-man-out and former United Counties/South Midland dual-purpose bodied Bristol L6B Car 71 (EBD 234), generally to be found on relief duties at Maidenhead. Note the additional side beading of the ECW 'express' body and the limited destination display.

Further housing developments in the Priestwood and Easthampstead areas of Bracknell led to changes in the services providing localised journeys and those bringing workers in from further afield. Existing Route 52, worked from Ascot Garage, has already provided a number of journeys primarily aimed at taking workers to the new factories opened in Broad Lane and Eastern Road, both off the London Road. This had provided an effective supplement to Route 2 (Reading – Wokingham – Binfield – Bracknell – Ascot – Windsor), but these journeys were transferred as short-workings to Route 2 from 22nd August, there now being no requirement for the journeys previously run through to Woodley Airfield from Ascot.

A further Bristol LS was sent to Ascot Garage for the new Route 52, and Car 687 (HBL 89) is seen on the forecourt on arrival – the blind display should not be taken literally!

A new Route 52 was formed to operate across the developing town, which gave a two-way link to the new factories being developed in Western Road. The new route had a basic 40-minute headway and was designed to be covered by one Bristol LS saloon throughout the day, the bus being garaged at Ascot. It ran from Priestwood as Moordale Avenue (starting in Englemere Road) – Western Road – Bracknell High Street (Regal) – Railway Station – Crowthorne Road – Reeds Hill (Institution) – South Hill Road (Golden Farmer). However, as South Hill Road was the not the through route to Crowthorne as it is today, the bus had to reverse at that point. Journeys were operated from 7.44am through to 10.30pm, which also provided useful runs for cinema-goers. The running time was only 15 minutes, with a 5-minute break at each end, whilst the Sunday service ran only during the afternoon and evening. This route was the first of the true Bracknell Local Services, generations of which would develop as the New Town expanded. The situation was further complicated by the phase of road changes in the town, with old routes often being obliterated as new roads were laid down, leading to a very complex history indeed!

172

Also affecting the Ascot allocation was the need for school journeys to Priestwood School, there being an increased intake of primary school children for which the planned new schools were not quite ready for. So from 8th September a further double-decker was sent to Ascot. Even so, another saloon was required to help out on Route 2 reliefs from 23rd September, with further housing developments in the Priestwood and Bullbrook areas.

In the meantime at High Wycombe, the Frogmoor Bus Station had been undergoing some improvements for both passengers and crews alike. A new staff canteen and public toilets were constructed, whilst the flow of buses was much improved. Very little of this was noted in official records as the Company had bought up most of the adjacent properties over the years. However, Nos. 45-9 Frogmoor were demolished to form a new two-way access to the bus station, buses previously having entered from the north of the site. This new entrance allowed buses to enter south of a new traffic island, separated from the outgoing ones which passed north of the island. The tapered island was much wider at the western end and there stood the new canteen. The area to the rear of Nos. 51/53 Frogmoor was cleared and paved, whilst the Inspector's Office was relocated at No.53. Loading platforms were provided and marked with new signage, whilst parked buses were no longer in potential conflict with service movements at the old entrance area, though the latter was fitted with a gate and retained for emergencies. A vehicle wash was provided at the western boundary, but the day-garage servicing facility was demolished to increase space.

Meanwhile, over to the west, arrangements were being considered to purchase a plot of land at Rewley Road, nearby Oxford's main railway station. Indeed, the site being considered was probably part of the old Midland Railway Station, though nothing further is heard of the plan. It would seem, however, that plans for a re-development of Gloucester Green by the City Council had resulted in the need to consider alternative locations, whilst the proposed site was of course convenient for both the railway and not far from the Botley Road Garage.

This slightly earlier view shows a trio of South Midland coaches about to depart from Gloucester Green just as heavy snow begins to fall. It also serves to emphasise that the express services ran throughout the year and carried a huge number of passengers. A pair of Duple-bodied AEC 'Regals' are followed by one of the dual-purpose Bristol L6B's taken over from United Counties but duly transferred to the Thames Valley fleet.

The end of the Summer timetable saw a number of vehicles going into store during late September, with open-top Bristol K5G's 771-3 (CAP 132, 176 and 211) going to Stokenchurch. Similar bus 770 (CAP 206) initially went into store at Botley Road, but was taken over to Stokenchurch during October.

Also placed in store at Stockenchurch were two of the trio of Lydney-bodied AEC 'Regal' 6821A-type buses Cars 162/3 (FBL 920/1), whilst the other example Car 161 (FBL 919) went into store at Fingest Dormy Shed, where it was joined by ECW DP31R-bodied Bristol L6B Car 71 (EBD 234). It is also worth noting that ECW B35R-bodied Bristol L6B Cars 539/43 (FMO 14/8) were still laid up at Stokenchurch, having been there since April.

South Midland's only double-decker, Bristol K5G Car 770 (CAP 206) in store at Botley Road.

As it was some of these buses, including the open-tops, were brought out during October for the making of a minor film 'Snowball', which even though it featured TV buses running about was still a box office flop!

On the properties front, October 1959 saw the Enquiry Office at High Wycombe relocate to No.37 Frogmoor (though timetable booklets continued to quote No.35), whilst Nos.35 and the ground floor of 37a were rented out as shops. The Traffic Office continued to occupy the upper floor of Nos.37/37a. However, despite this, and the improvements at Frogmoor, the longer-term goal of a single bus station for the town continued to be discussed. Also under review was the use of Tadley Dormy Shed, now home to just one Bristol KSW6B to cover Route 9. To this end the Traffic Manager visited the *Wilts & Dorset* Baughurst Dormy Shed in October, the site being the former premises of *Edith Kent*, who had sold it to *Venture* in 1937, when she had sold out to *Newbury & District,* the Basingstoke company having recently acquired her son Bill Kent's bus services!

October saw the departure of the mini-batch of ECW B35R-bodied Bristol L6B Cars 521-3 (FBL 23-5), all of which had always served at High Wycombe. Also ousted that month was ECW DP31R-bodied L6B-type Car 71 (EBD 234), along with Duple-bodied AEC 'Regal' coach 68 (EJB 649) of SM but new to N&D.

November led to further inroads into the ranks of the *South Midland* 'Regal' coaches, with the sale of 56 (MJO 667) and 57-9 (NFC 128-30), all Duple-bodied. On the bus front, the other former *United Counties* and *South Midland* Bristol L6B Car 72 (EBD 235) went, though this had been re-seated as a 35-seater bus after transfer to TV. Also departing were the trio of Lydney-bodied AEC 'Regal' buses 161-3 (FBL 919-21), the latter despite already being front entrance. Also withdrawn in November was Bristol K6B Car 454 (DBL 162), which after being stored at Stokenchurch, was the first of a number of the older double-deckers selected for a thorough body rebuild.

No new PSV's were received in the latter months of 1959, though the incoming double-deckers were very interesting indeed!

*Further second-hand Bristol K-types came from the Bristol Omnibus fleet. **Above** – Car 457 (KHU 605) is seen turning out of Bridge Avenue, Maidenhead on Local Service Route 19. **Below** – Car 459 (KHU 622) is also seen in Maidenhead but in Bridge Street from the TV Garage. Note that both have had their front destination apertures rebuilt to T-shape.*

Car 455 (KHU 604) also had its front destination screen rebuilt to T-shape using gear taken from the rear of Bristol LS's converted for one-man-operation. However, the rear ends had no displays at all. It is seen in the 'relief pool' at the Southern Yard – an apt name in wet weather when huge pot-holes filled up!

A further Bristol K6B from *Bristol Omnibus* became Car 455 (KHU 604), along with a quartet of K6A's from that same operator as Cars 456-9 (KHW 633, KHU 605, KHU 606 and KHU 622), all with standard ECW L27/28R bodies. They had all been new in 1947 and, after re-paints, they entered service in January 1960 (455 at Reading and 456 at Newbury), followed by 458 (at Reading) in February, 459 (Maidenhead) in March, then finally 457 (also Maidenhead) in May.

The former ENOC/UCOC Bristol K5G's were mostly fitted with 8ft wide bodies on 7ft 6ins wide chassis, so the overhang was evident when viewed from the front. Car 460 (FPU 510) is seen parked in the front yard western extension at Maidenhead Garage, and surely no one would have suspected it had been built before TV's own original batches of that type.

However, the other K-types acquired in November were somewhat less than standard, emanating as they did from 1937! Originating with *Eastern National,* all had subsequently passed to the *United Counties* fleet when the operating areas were re-defined between those two concerns in 1952. As new they had the high pre-war radiator and standard ECW lowbridge bodies but, as part of post-war refurbishment programmes, they had all received the lower PV2-type radiator and been re-bodied in 1951/2 with new 8ft wide ECW L27/28R bodies. These bodies also featured the full 3-piece destination displays of the 1952 deliveries, but at the rear they only had T-type apertures, nonetheless all being suitable for the standard TV blinds.

These took the numbers vacated by coaches rebuilt as buses, carrying on from the re-use of former saloon numbers taken by the acquisitions so far. All were prepared for service and allocated from 1st January 1960 as Cars 460/1 (FPU 510/509) at Maidenhead, Car 462 (FPU 515) at Ascot and Car 463 (FPU 517) at Reading.

Ascot's example, Car 462 (FPU 515) in seen on the road between North Ascot and Cranbourne on Route 2. Note the white steering wheel fitted to these buses when they were re-bodied as a reminder to drivers of their 8-foot width. The tree-lined roads in this area also serve as a reminder that they were originally part of a greater Windsor Forest, and they also kept the Route Servicing Crew busy too.

Local enthusiasts had been quite surprised with these latest developments, though there would be more to come yet. There is little doubt that the selection of the second-hand buses added much interest to the local transport scene, particularly as the buses were spread far and wide and the fleet and registration numbers were not in sequence. The author recalls that shortly after this as he became to be aware of *Thames Valley,* these buses had a lot to do with his curiosity!

Car 456 (KHW 633) was the first of the acquired double-deckers allocated to Newbury, and is seen parked at The Wharf shortly after being sent there.

In the meantime, on the staff front, Mr. Jack Giles was promoted to Garage Foreman at Wycombe Marsh from 1st October, a position he had filled temporarily since Mr. Mouat-Biggs' retirement. November saw the departure of another long-serving employee, with the retirement of Mr. E. Stephens, Garage Foreman at Maidenhead, who is should also be noted spent some years responsible for maintaining the *Marlow & District* fleet of Karrier buses.

Further developments in the Bracknell area showed in two ways during November. The single-decker sent to assist on Route 2 (Reading – Wokingham – Bracknell – Ascot – Windsor) had to be replaced by a double-decker in response to increased loadings as housing was let to families coming in from London. Also, the Western Road-based Wayne Pumps were given the order for two fuel pumps for the new Bracknell Garage then under construction in Market Street.

The rear elevation of Car 458 (KHU 606) shows that no destination apertures were provided when these buses were out-shopped with T-shape front screens. Note also the number of adverts for cars, all three of these being sign-written for durability.

By far the finest of all the second-hand stock was Car 463 (FPU 517), which the Author often rode on when it was later allocated to Bracknell. Here it is seen at St. Mary's Butts/Gun Street coming in on Route 4a.

1960

Over the Winter of 1959/60 further discussions took place regarding the setting up of a Bus Station at Reading, the latest proposal centring on the large area of land leased by Messrs. Vincents off Station Hill. Originally leased from the *Great Western Railway*, it now came under the Nationalised *British Railways (Western Region)*. However, it would still be some years before such a feature was constructed.

This frontal shot of Car 464 (FPU 511) clearly shows the wider body on the 7ft 6 ins chassis. Note also how far over the steering wheel is within the driver's cab. This bus is recalled as the second best of all the K's acquired, and it is seen at Newbury Wharf.

January saw two more Bristol K5G's arriving from *United Counties*. Both had followed similar early histories to the previous examples received, being re-bodied post-war. One became Car 464 (FPU 511) and was identical to 460-3 in having an 8ft-wide body new in 1952, and this was sent to work from Newbury. The other, however, had been involved in a further body swap, during which it was paired with a 1947 7ft. 6ins ECW body! This vehicle evidently required more pre-service attention, but emerged in March as Car 465 (FPU 513). It was sent to Maidenhead, working alongside the native 1947-50 examples, though its stay was relatively short and ended in October 1962.

The only 'thin FPU' was Car 465 (FPU 513), which could be distinguished on the road by being the only 7ft 6ins K-type with a square number plate. It is seen at Maidenhead Bus Station acting as a relief on the busy short-workings on Route 21 to the factories on the White Waltham Airfield about a year later.

The last passenger train ran on the Lambourn Valley Branch on 4th January, so the service on Route 106 saw some enhancements in order to provide alternative links. One of these involved a bus leaving The Wharf at 7.01am in order to form a new 7.35am departure from Lambourn Square which ran through to Newbury Station. Further direct journeys reaching Newbury Station were also provided at 11.55am and 5.20pm, whereas all other runs continued to terminate at The Wharf. A Sunday service was also maintained, with two journeys extended through to the Station at 2.40pm and 7.30pm. A further double-decker was allocated to each of Routes 106 and 108 (Newbury Wharf – Stockcross –Wickham – Shefford Woodlands – Lambourn Woodlands – Lambourn Square, though both worked from the Newbury end.

Bristol K6A Car 439 (CRX 548) is seen helping out on Route 106 at Newbury.

The acquired buses were used widely, often as reliefs, and Car 461 (FPU 509) is seen nearing Windsor.

Another area then seeing considerable development in housing was Woodley, just a few miles to the east of Reading, so from January a double-deck relief was put on Route 1a in order to provide further capacity for the first of three major phases of estate building. As the factory traffic to that same area had now largely dried up, the increase in population provided a good alternative. Indeed, from February, the service was increased in frequency, with journeys serving various terminal points to match the spread of housing, with buses running to Colemans Moor Road, Tippings Lane or Raversbourne Drive, though all served Western Avenue and Woodley Roundabout, whilst at the appropriate times there were projections to the Airfield Industrial Estate.

Bristol K6A Car 444 (DBL 152) enters Reading Depot from Weldale Street between turns on Route 1a.

On 12th January there were extensive snowfalls over the Company's area, resulting in the loss of 3,650 route miles before roads became passable once again. Fortunately, the snow passed quickly and did not give rise to any significant flooding this time.

Although both *Thames Valley* and *London Transport* buses used Mackenzie Street, just across from the forecourt of Slough Station, the situation was not ideal and discussions took place during February regarding the construction of a proper joint bus station, though it was accepted that such a proposal would require a Public Enquiry.

One of the most intently-worked services was Route 60 via 'main road' between Maidenhead and Slough. 1958 Bristol LD5G Car 791 (NBL 748) loads at the Mackenzie Street stands near Slough Railway Station. As it was, Slough like Reading, would have to wait a number of years more before bus stations would be constructed.

Work was, however, progressing well with the new garage at Bracknell, and it was resolved that both the Ascot Garage and Crowthorne Dormy Shed would be disposed of once it was occupied.

During January a further pair of Bristol LS saloons was converted for one-man-working, these being Cars 686/7 (HBL 88/89), and both were Reading cars.

February saw the departure of another of the old guard, as Stanley Read retired from his post as Vehicle Records Clerk. It was he who had maintained the immaculate records of the 'Sutton era' and, those of us who have studied *Thames Valley* would know a lot less without his detailed records!

Takeovers of other operators was infrequent in post-war years, but on 3rd February a meeting took place at the request of Mr. West of *Bray Transport* and the Traffic Manager regarding the possible disposal of that business. Of particular interest might have been the worker's services to the ICI Research Plant at Jealotts Hill, situated as it was about halfway between Bracknell and Maidenhead, plus school runs contracted to Berkshire County Council. However, TV also recalled that it had previously attempted to provide services to the Jealotts Hill site, without much success, whilst the shortage of drivers made the prospect of part-time contracts unattractive at that point in time, so nothing came of the proposal.

178

Indeed, such was the shortage of drivers that the Company reviewed the allocation of coaches for Private Hire that year, reducing those allocations to:

Desborough Road	3	39-seat Bristol LS/ECW
	1	37-seat Bristol LWL/ECW
Maidenhead	3	39-seat Bristol LS/ECW
	1	37-seat Bristol LWL/ECW
Newbury	1	39-seat Bristol LS/ECW
Reading	2	37-seat Bristol LWL

As will be noted, Ascot had no coach allocated for the first time in years, though bookings would be covered by other locations. In respect of Newbury, this was the most drastic of reductions, though it was anticipated that *South Midland* coaches could cover any greater needs when they arose. By March the situation at the Maidenhead Garage was so bad that two of its coach allocation had to be transferred to Reading.

During recent times many of the larger destination displays had been simplified, as in the case of 1949 Bristol K6B Car 498 (EJB 220). Where there would have been three lines previously in the intermediate box, one line (but straight to the point) is now shown.

The only change to the passenger fleet in February was the demise of the last Duple-bodied AEC 'Regal' coach from the *South Midland* fleet, in the shape of Car 70 (ERX 937), one of those originally with N&D. Coaches of this type had indeed carried the fleetnames of all three concerns during their working lives, one being noted with *Thames Valley* fleetname, *Newbury*

& *District* displayed in one destination aperture and 'on hire to *South Midland*' in the other!

Bristol L6B coach 552 (FMO 934) is seen outside the Iffley Road Garage in the Summer of 1960. Unlike some of the newer coaches, these vehicles could enter the height-restricted garage, which would itself be sold not long afterwards.

The future of the remaining Windover-bodied Bristol L6B coaches was reviewed and, after re-painting into the new livery, Cars 545/51/2/4/5 (FMO 20/6, FMO 934 /6/7) were all sent to work for *South Midland*. All transferred in May, except 552 which went in March, and they were kept busy out of Oxford and Newbury until October. Car 551 continued through to November 1961, making it the last of that type in use.

On the Service Vehicle front, two new Bedford CAV vans were delivered as No.45 (UJB 298) in a grey livery for the Clerk of Works based at Reading, and No.47 (UJB 299), in red livery as Depot Van for High Wycombe. Outgoing Service Vehicles were Bedford 10/12cwt No.15 (DJB 914), the previous Wycombe van, and No.17 (DJB 943), one of the Reading-based ex-WD Ford (Canada) V8 4-wheel drive Breakdown Wagons, now ousted by the recently completed AEC 'Matador'. Former Clerk of Works Van No.39 (MRX 114) was retained for the Advert Fixer. Readers will note the continuing use of odd numbers for the SV fleet, which originated when the even-numbered *Ledbury Transport* fleet was still being maintained.

From 5th March a new route commenced in Slough as 69 (Priory Estate – Windsor Lane Cross Roads – Everitts Corner – Trading Estate (West Gate) – Trading Estate (Main Gate) – Salt Hill – Slough Station), which operated 'a' journeys through the Trading Estate and was covered by two double-decks.

179

One of the next batch of acquired buses turned out to be rather a surprise, as will be seen below! Car 475 (FLJ 978) stand on Station Hill in Reading awaiting a relief journey to Pangbourne on Route 5. Note that the intermediate box on 3-piece displays now often just showed the slanted 'Thames Valley'.

A similar theme continued for the fleet changes during March, with outgoing Bristol L6B/ECW B35R saloons 534-7 (FMO 8-12) and 543/4 (FMO 18/9) all going to join the others at *United Welsh!* The operator had its own agenda, which was to speed up disposal of types supplied when under *Red & White* control. As the TV fleet numbers did not clash with those of the new owner, all were retained for their new role.

Car 474 (JT 9360) in the Southern Yard for Route 9.

The incoming buses for March were all second-hand Bristol K-types, though there was variety amongst them. The four had been offered by *Hants & Dorset* and, in common with much of that fleet, they had been

through a re-bodying process. Those becoming Cars 472-4 (JT 9354/5/60) were new in 1938, but received PV2 radiators and new ECW L27/28R bodies in 1949. They were K5G's, as was the fourth example, but its history was rather more complex. It was new in 1942 and was later fitted with a Brush body taken from another 1938 K5G. That body had been much rebuilt by *H&D*, but the 6-bay layout was retained, the great number of windows earning it the nickname 'Boeing' at TV (due to the resemblance to that type of airliner), whilst at Windsor County Boy's school we dubbed it the 'Stone Age Flier'. It became Car 475 (FLJ 978), and apparently TV's Engineer Mr. Campbell knew nothing about its odd origins until it turned up in the yard (much to the amusement of his staff!). These were also the first buses I had seen with 2-letter marks and I initially imagined them to be even older.

About to leave as relief bus on Route 6 to Spencers Wood is Car 473 (JT 9355). Fortunately 473/4 took the standard TV destination blinds.

Car 475 was also unusual in that it only seated 54, there being a double-seat at the rear of the top deck where a 3-seater would normally be found, and I recall this was due to the layout of the rear emergency door. Nonetheless, it put in over 4 year's service, based mainly at Reading, but with occasional loans to Bracknell, and at least it had heaters! Car 472 went to Newbury and 473/4 to Reading, though all lost the distinctive sun-visors over the cab windscreen as favoured by their previous owner. As 472 had an odd front destination box layout, that was replaced by a T-type layout using gear taken from LS's converted for o-m-o before out-shopping.

Car 472 (JT 9354) arrived at Newbury with no rear destination aperture, as can be seen in this view taken shortly afterwards. It also provides an interesting comparison with the rear of Duple-bodied Guy 'Arab' Car H14 (HOT 392), one of the highbridge examples.

The other new vehicles received in March were touring coaches for *South Midland*, all being ECW C34F-bodied Bristol MW6G's, and these became Cars 830-2 (UJB 196-8), and they were followed in April by 833 (UJB 199). These were well-appointed bodies and the MW's gave good service for many years, some even being rebuilt as service buses in due course!

Coach 833 (UJB 199) in original condition. A number of these coaches had front ends fitted with the standard MW grille in due course after accidents.

An unusual sight at Victoria Coach Station was Car 621 (GJB 259), a Bristol LWL6B-type on hire to South Midland. As this was a Wycombe car, it seems likely that it had taken over from a coach with problems in that area.

On the double-deck coach front, the Company had ordered 5 of the new Bristol FLF chassis to receive special bodies as the next generation of London route rolling stock, and these were in course of preparation.

A number of special services were operated on Sundays to provide suitably timed connections for churchgoers, and could be found within the public timetables. An example was the link from Cippenham to the Roman Catholic Church in Lower Britwell Road, Burnham and, from 6th March, the route was slightly diverted in order that double-deckers could be used. Another regular special, which did not appear in the public timetables, ran on Sundays for many years from Slough and Maidenhead to Pinewood Hospital. This was situated near Crowthorne and had built as a TB isolation hospital in the relative fresh air and trees.

There was some major disruption again at Maidenhead Bridge on 18th March, though this time it was a bad road smash rather then the customary floods. All the same, some 600 miles were lost before the carriageway was cleared, and this affected all TV services between Maidenhead and Slough.

On a brighter note, *Thames Valley* gave its practical support to an event held in aid of World Refugees, when it provided 4 buses free of charge to take people home from a special charity film show at The Rialto in Maidenhead on 25th March. Although no details of the operation were recorded, it is presumed that the buses ran outwards in each direction from the town and turned once everyone had alighted.

A further pair of ex-*United Counties* Bristol K-types was acquired in April and these became Cars 476/7 (GNO 688/98), and were the last purchases of that particular scheme.

Their Essex registrations confirm that they too had originated with *Eastern National*, and these were 1938 buses that had also transferred to *United Counties* and were given the post-war PV2 radiator and new 8ft wide ECW bodies in 1952. However, by the time they were sold, both had received 7ft 6ins ECW L27/28R bodies new in 1948 from other vehicles in that fleet! However, as they had the standard 3-piece destination screens no alterations were required before they took to the road in June. Car 476 went to Reading and 477 to Maidenhead. It would seem that the latter was not a great success, with the vehicle being out of use from July 1960 to January 1961 for some reason, this bus seeing the least use of all those purchased.

Above- Car 476 (GNO 688) is seen on Station Hill on Route 1. Below – Car 477 (GNO 698) finally returned to service and saw some use at Reading. It enters St. Mary's Butts from the south, having run a relief on Route 4a in from Arborfield Camp.

Although many of the second-hand K's stayed based at a single garage, whereas others did move around a bit, particularly those at Reading, which were loaned out to cover engineering absences. Their presence made the fleet a little more varied, looking out for the 'foreign' registrations out on the road. They were all interesting in some way or another, with a variety of interior finishes and window arrangements. However, I must admit to 3 particular favourites: Car 436 (KHU 624), which went the best of them all; Car 463 (FPU 517), which had the best bodywork; and Car 475 (FLJ 978) for just being so weird – though in the Winter of 62/63, when it covered my school journey, its heaters were much appreciated!

Royal Ascot Week was another time when buses not usually seen on Route 2 would help out, and Car 590 (FMO 972) a 1950 Bristol KS6B returns to Stations Square in Reading. Note the double-front adverts.

Indeed, the Company operated a number of facilities for schoolchildren, though mostly these were suitably timed journeys on established routes, short-workings where appropriate or projections onto the schools. The use of contract services was much less then, as public bus services were more widespread, and usually the Education Authority tended to regard contracts as a last resort. One such journey was the 8.52am on Route 53, which started at Chavey Down (after a short dead run from Ascot Garage), then ran past Winkfield Church and Mushroom Castle (a local nursery that featured on the local destination blind!) to reach the Cranbourne School on the edge of Windsor Great Park.

With the growth of Bracknell New Town, it soon became apparent that there would not be sufficient secondary school places, so Berkshire County Council asked TV to supply a 'special' to run between Bracknell to Windsor County Grammar School for Boy's – which in turn was the establishment I found myself assigned to after passing my 11-plus in 1962! The years I was there provided my grounding on the TV fleet which, aided by my Ian Allan 'British Bus Fleets No.3' which helped me to identify all the types.

A regular performer for some years on Route 75 (Reading – Bracknell – Bagshot – Guildford) was LS-type Car 724 (HMO 870), seen here in Farnham Road Bus Station at the Surrey terminus. Cars 723-5 always stood slightly higher off the ground at the front from the others of the type, and also they had vents each side of the Bristol/ECW badge. Also distinguishing in earlier years was the fact that only 723/4 had maker's badges with a cream background.

The 6th of May saw another royal event which drew large crowds into London, and additional journeys were laid on to mark the wedding of Princess Margaret to Anthony Armstrong-Jones. The Oxford route via Henley and Maidenhead was provided with extra departures and relief coaches were drafted into help, though residents of High Wycombe were placed in the care of the *Green Line* services, and Route B from Reading was also enhanced.

May was a relatively quiet month for fleet changes, with just a trio of 1950 Bristol L6B Cars 538/40/2 (FMO 13/5/7) leaving to join others at *United Welsh.*

Over at the far western tip of the Thames Valley area, coach-seated Bristol KSW6B Car 743 (JRX 818) was doing the honours on Route 106 at Swindon. This was a 29.5 mile run, taking 1hr 33mins, though it only ran 3 or 4 times per day. The origins of this route traces back to a market-day carrier's service of Ernie Nobes.

The open-top Bristol K5G's came out of store and were licensed on 1st June for The Derby. Indeed the timetables for the 1960 season had been printed, these being a separate sheet from the main timetable booklet, as had been the practice so far, but when the situation was reviewed, it was decided not to operate them again. To be fair, the Company had persevered for three Summers, all of which had been poor weather. It was resolved that they would all be sold, and also that time was up for the quartet of Guy UF coaches Cars 86-9 (SFC 501-4).

The Ascot coach duty was re-filled from 1st June with the transfer of ECW 'Queen Mary'-bodied Bristol LL-type Car 829 (FRP 844), out of store at Desborough Road. At the same time identical coach 828 (FRP 843) emerged from hibernation for allocation to Reading, though it was mainly used on relief duties, seeing the least use of all the ex-*United Counties* examples.

The only known photo of Car 828 (FRP 843) in use is this one at the re-fuelling point in Reading Garage.

Over at Newbury, the lack of a vehicle capable of towing duties was of growing concern to Reg Hibbert, so he was allowed (assuming he asked, of course!) to fit a tow-bar under the rear panel of Bristol LL6B Car 565 (FMO 947), after which it could be seen from time to time towing in a failed bus from wherever it had expired. Whenever such a situation occurred, 565 would be exchanged off service when it next entered The Wharf and the recovery team would set off. This also explains why, whilst identical Cars 564/6 (FMO 946/8) were regularly to be found out-stationed at Lambourn, 565 was always kept 'at home' instead.

40 more Setright Ticket Machines were authorised in June, whilst the Service Vehicle fleet saw the disposal of Ford 'Anglia' car HDP 401, as used by the High Wycombe Inspectors.

However, the major event of June was the opening of the new Bracknell Garage in Market Street. This was a purpose-built garage which could house 30 buses under cover, plus a further 15 parked outside in a yard. It was constructed at the junction of Skimped Hill Lane and the newly-opened Market Street.

Seen after transfer to Bracknell Garage, former Crowthorne Dormy Shed Car 718 (HMO 864) is covering an old Ascot Garage short-working on Route 2 between Wokingham and Ascot. Note that the bus is travelling east from the Bush Hotel stop in Wokingham, also the sign for the erstwhile open-air Martin's Pool and the Heelas store, all now gone.

Indeed, the famous Bracknell Cattle Market had also been re-located from its long-established site behind the Hinds Head pub at the top of the old High Street. Buses entered the garage at the northern end, where re-fuelling took place, and there was a bus-washing machine positioned centrally within the building. Two inspection pits were provided opposite the main entrance in a workshop area, whilst the offices and canteen were situated to the right of the entrance.

Twenty four vehicles were transferred to the garage, with Crowthorne Dormy Shed contributing 1953/4 Bristol LS6B saloons 710/4/5/8 (HMO 856/60/1/4), all of which were still crew-operated 45-seaters, 3 of which covered Route 3 (Camberley - Crowthorne – Wokingham – Reading) and 3a (Finchampstead – Barkham – Wokingham – Emmbrook – Reading). Similar 1954 examples 712/3/21 (HMO 858/9/67) were transferred from Ascot Garage, and they covered Routes 52 (Priestwood – Easthampstead) and 53 (Windsor – Winkfield – Bracknell – Crowthorne), as well as the coach allocation 1951 Bristol LL6B/ECW FC37F8 Car 829 (FRP 844).

KSW Car 643 had been as Ascot since new in 1951.

This shot of Bracknell Garage from the southern yard was taken a few years later, when Bristol LS Car 706 (HMO 852) had been transferred to cover additional services as the Local Services were developed. All Bracknell LS workings soon became one-man, and it is perhaps strange that the garage never provided any journeys on Route 75 to Guildford?

184

On the double-deck front, Ascot contributed a number of Bristol KSW6B/ECW L27/28R buses, with Cars 640-5 (GJB 278-83) of 1951, 701/3/5 (HMO 847/9/51) of 1953/4 and 744-7 (JRX 819-22) new in 1954, and these covered Route 2 (Windsor – Ascot – Bracknell – Wokingham – Reading) and the 2a/2b/2c group of Ascot – Sunninghill – Sunningdale Local Services.

Also transferred were a pair of Bristol LD5G's with ECW LD33/27R bodies, Cars 766/7 (MBL 847/8), and these generally covered the Windsor Local Service Routes 51/51a/51b since new in 1956. Also drafted to the new garage was former *United Counties* Bristol K5G Car 462 (FPU 515), which then became the regular performer on the Windsor Boy's Special in addition to relief duties on Route 2.

Above – Bristol LD5G Car 767 (MBL 848) at Ascot Garage. Note the painted advert, which had a duck egg green background and was a feature of this bus for many years. Below – K5G Car 462 (FPU 515) was at Bracknell for some time.

The honour of being the first bus into the new garage went to LS-type 712 (HMO 858), which broke the ribbon, though the LWL6B coach bringing the party

of officials from Reading embarrassed itself by failing en route!

The garage assumed operation of all the routes inherited from Ascot Garage and Crowthorne Dormy Shed, and all existing crews were transferred to the new location. On Route 2 (Reading – Wokingham – Bracknell – Ascot – Windsor) those journeys in the Windsor direction which had started from Ascot High Street now started from Station Road in Bracknell instead. Incoming journeys from Windsor now finished at the Regal Cinema in Bracknell, leaving the bus to just coast down the hill into the garage. Early starts for Reading still started from Ascot (Horse & Groom), but ran out there dead. Late buses from Reading were not, however, curtailed at Bracknell, running through to Ascot (Horse & Groom) before returning dead to Bracknell. This caused quite a few bad feelings with the crews who lived in the Ascot area, knowing they had just passed home and then having to make their own way back! Dave Howard, who was the Schedules Clerk from the opening of the garage recalled how he would let the conductor drop off in such circumstances when he was travelling, paying in on his behalf!

The Ascot KSW's put in long years of high mileages on Route 2, and Car 705 (HMO 851) is seen opposite the White Hart Hotel in Windsor with a full load on a sunny day, when the river would have been very busy.

The first Route 53 (Windsor – Winkfield – Bracknell – Crowthorne) journey of the day now started at Chavey Down rather than Plaistow Green, which was useful for those living in the nearby new housing in Bullbrook, whereas the final journey of the day ran through to the Regal Cinema in Bracknell. Buses on the Windsor Local services had always run dead to take up duties from the Prince Albert in Clewer Road, on the edge of Windsor and this practice continued.

Bristol KSW6B Car 644 (GJB 282) working Route 2c from Sunningdale Station to Ascot. Note the Thames Valley timetable cases on the railings of Giddy & Giddy the estate agents.

Similarly, the Ascot – Sunninghill – Sunningdale Local Services, Routes 2a/2b/2c were covered by buses sent dead to Ascot (Horse & Groom). The buses worked over Route 3 (Camberley – Crowthorne – Wokingham – Reading) by Bracknell continued to take up duties from Crowthorne (Prince Alfred) after a dead run from the garage, as did the last journey from the Camberley direction at night – though in due course this ran on service through to Bracknell. The 3 journeys to Little Sandhurst were now extended onto Little Sandhurst Stores, though they were still under that route. The bus for Route 3a (Finchampstead – Barkham – Wokingham – Emmbrook - Reading) also still started from the Greyhound pub in Longwater Road, in Finchampstead village, though later some changes were made to reduce the wasted mileage.

On 14th June the new *South Midland* tour of Western Counties of Ireland commenced, the honour of cover for this going to Bristol MW6G coach 803 (ORX 634) which had won the award at the Brighton Rally. These extended tours were, in the days before the advent of package holidays abroad, quite upmarket and popular.

Coach 803 (ORX 634) is seen working on the Irish Tour at the end of July 1960, rather too dusty to be a concours d'elegance winner on this occasion!

Indeed, these tours were meticulously planned and operated by hand-picked drivers. Some involved daily outings from a base, whilst others were continuous tours. These resulted in *South Midland* coaches being seen at bus depots many miles from home, re-fuelling and washing facilities also being arranged, whilst the drivers carried emergency contact details for operators who could assist in the event of a breakdown. The tours for the 1960 season were as follows:

Tour	Days	Cost
Southern Counties of Ireland	9	£32.18s
Western Counties of Ireland	9	£32.18s
Scotland	10	£36.15s
English Lakes	8	£25.10s
Cornwall	8	£25.00s
Welsh Coast	8	£22.10s
Mid Wales	8	£19.19s
North Devon	8	£21.00s
South Devon	8	£18.00s
Wye Valley (based at Tintern)	8	£16.16s
Wye Valley (based at Symonds Yat)	8	£16.16s

The Wye Valley tours were in the hands of ex-UCOC Bristol L6B's, and Car 73 (EBD 236) is at Victoria Coach Station for the Symonds Yat tour. Scotland, the Irish tours, English Lakes, Cornwall and Welsh Coast were covered by Bristol MW's, whilst Bristol LS-types operated Mid Wales, North Devon and South Devon.

It is worth noting that all publicity for the tours also included prices direct from London, as the coaches started there if required, plus pick-up points in Slough, Maidenhead, High Wycombe and Henley in addition to Oxford. The American market was catered for by the inclusion of costs in dollars. For the latter in particular, an additional list of itineraries was drawn up which combined two tours at a time, making the full list of options up to 29!

Indeed, the coaches of both *Thames Valley* and *South Midland* could also be found regularly far away from home when called upon to provide relief workings for *Associated Motorways* express routes at peak times. Newbury Garage was particularly well placed, lying alongside the A4 and A34 trunk routes, whilst Oxford was ideally placed to also serve the A34 and roads to the Cotswolds and Wales. Sometimes the call would come to replace a broken down coach, though mostly the work was planned but at short notice. A number of drivers kept an overnight bag packed in case they were called upon, as a journey did not always mean they would return that day, as often this would result in a somewhat triangular route. To give an example, a driver and coach sent from Oxford or Newbury might initially cover a trip to Portsmouth or Bournemouth but, as loading charts were kept open to the last moment, an Inspector there might request that it then formed a relief to (say) Cheltenham for the following morning, later picking up the opportunity to work back to Oxford! Copies of the Driver's Guide issued by *Associated Motorways* detailed all the routes, stops and terminal arrangements, along with emergency phone numbers and bus garages which could give aid. All the drivers I have interviewed agreed, however, that such workings made a welcome change to daily routines and a chance to put your foot down!

Very few saloons had been purchased since the LS-types of 1952-5, so they still handled front-line duties such as Route 5 (Reading – Wallingford – Oxford). Car 717 (HMO 863) is seen at Gloucester Green Bus Station in Oxford. In fact the LS's would remain on this crew-operated duty right through until 1964.

From 18th June operation of former *Blue Star* Route 9a (Reading – Grazeley – Aldermaston – Tadley) was switched from the Tadley Dormy Shed to Reading and converted to o-m-o working. This saloon operation had been a feature of Tadley Shed since the route had been acquired from *John Spratley* in November 1937, but now only the double-decker for Route 9 (Reading – Mortimer – Tadley – Baughurst) was still kept there. Jack Lambden ('Tadley Jack' as he was known by all the locals) remained the driver, having started at the outstation way back in the Summer of 1925.

Inevitably, use of the shed was duly reviewed, and arrangements were made to transfer the Bristol KSW bus and its crew to the *Wilts & Dorset* garage at Heath End in Baughurst with effect from 6th August, which was about a mile and a half to the east. The Tadley Shed was then sold to the adjacent Allen's Garage on whose land it already stood and, apart from the addition of windows, remained is use for some years.

Time was allowed in the schedules for the Baughurst-based bus to call into Reading Garage for re-fuelling and for the conductor to pay in the previous day's takings. Bristol KSW Car 729 (JRX 804) is seen in the exit onto Lower Thorn Street after such a visit.

Another Bristol KSW stronghold was the busy Route 4 (Reading – Arborfield – Yateley – Camberley), which had earlier on been a Dormy Shed working for a pair of Leyland 'Titans' kept in a corrugated iron shed by Yateley church. Car 668 (HBL 70) lays over in the Southern Yard between duties.

As noted above, the open-top K5G's and the Guy UF coaches were up for disposal and, as was the usual practice at that time, their availability was initially circulated to other State-owned operators.

Bristol MW6G dual-purpose Car 852 (VJB 943) is seen when new at Victoria Coach Station on Route A.

This practice of inter-company disposals had led to the L-series saloons passing to *United Welsh*, and had also been the 'shopping list' for TV's acquisition of K-type double-deckers. However, this latest round of disposals had something of a twist, as the Guy coaches went to *Red & White*, as did open-top K5G Car 773 (CAP 211). The latter left in June and went for use as a tree-lopper, whereas the coaches left in July for a new career as dual-purpose saloons, looking very much at home in the fleet of the operator that had originally ordered them from the associated Lydney Coach Works! The other open-toppers left during July, but none was destined for public service, whilst the one that went to Chepstow has survived in preservation.

Car 852 (VJB 943) arrived in July, followed by 853 (VJB 944) in August, both being specified with ECW DP41F bodies in order to replace Bristol LS Cars 723/5 (HMO 869/71) in their role as the buses used for Route A (Reading – Bracknell – Ascot – Staines – London). They took up these duties from September 1st, when the dual-purpose bodied LS's were moved to Newbury, though retaining their coach seating.

The other arrival for July was also coach-seated, being the first of 5 new double-deckers for London Route B, as Car 834 (UJB 200). This 30ft long Bristol FLF-type had a 6-cylinder Bristol engine and CH37/38F body by Eastern Coach Works.

Car 834 leaves Victoria when new. Note the sliding door, which was controlled by the driver, and made these unique amongst FLF production deliveries.

As compensation for the loss of the Guys, Bristol LWL coaches 608/9 (GBL 872/3) were transferred to South Midland in July, along with Windover-bodied Bristol L6B Car 550 (FMO 25). Car 608 is seen at Gloucester Green on a relief journey to London.

Also during July it was decided that the 6 AEC 'Regal' saloons still in use at Newbury would be sold as soon as the new Bristol MW6G saloons on order were received. Indeed, the first pair of these did arrive in July/August, they were assigned elsewhere.

Above - the lower saloon of Car 834 (UJB 200) shows the style of green and buff moquette used and the headrests fitted. Below - additional luggage space was provided under the stairs and to the right in a full-height case rack. Also note the sliding door, fitted only to this batch (though it was tried on the FLF prototype and later replaced with a jack-knife door).

The re-bodied Leyland 'Tiger' PS1 coach had recently enjoyed something of a renaissance with allocation to the Irish Tour, but as that role was now taken by an MW6G coach, Car 169 (LWL 995) had spent 1960 on more mundane contract duties to AERE Harwell.

It had, of course, run under the fleetnames *South Midland, Newbury & District, Thames Valley,* then *South Midland* once again, but its other significance was in being the last Leyland PSV in the TV fleet, the make having featured continuously since 1928! It was withdrawn at the end of July, but even then its working days were not over, as it passed to *Frostways* of Kennington, Oxford, who continued to use it on contract work. Indeed, this and other sales of *South Midland* coaches to local firms resulted in a complaint from the Oxford Manager, who said that such coaches were dirty and poorly kept, and was concerned the public might take them as still being his charges!

In August six of the older saloons out-stationed in the Newbury area for contracts were replaced by 5 coaches transferred from Oxford and a saloon from Reading. Bristol LL6B Car 822 (FRP 837) was one of the coaches involved and is seen in the Botley Road Garage at Oxford.

In those days public bodies such as the British Transport Commission regularly produced films as promotion for their activities, these being shown between feature films at the cinema. In connection with one on touring coaches, *South Midland* loaned one of the 34-seater Bristol MW6G coaches to the BTC Film Unit for 29th-30th August, which was a nice 'jolly' for the driver, along with his 15 minutes of fame!

Although the Irish Tours were a success, the Company was aware that the Irish Sea was often rough, and that ferry sailings were disrupted or even cancelled. With that in mind, the General Manager met in August with representatives from *Aer Lingus*, regarding the possibility of a coach/air/coach link. Also aligned to that thinking was an application to the Traffic Commissioner for an Oxford to Bristol Airport transfer link which was lodged on 1st September, but this was not put in place after all due to high costs.

September was otherwise a quiet month on the traffic side, and this was no doubt due to the considerable effort expended on the switch over from Ascot and Crowthorne to the new Bracknell Garage.

A picture that sums up Marlow & District, with the famous (but rather weak) suspension bridge that was to be a constant trial for bus operators. Ramsden-bodied Karrier CL4-type KX 3638 is crossing the bridge from Marlow, despite the blind display.

A particularly significant retirement took place on the last day of September, with the departure of Ernest Jeffries. Also sometimes referred to as 'Mr. Marlow & District', he had indeed started his bus career in 1925, when he commenced such operations under the guidance of his employer Reginald Clayton, who was also Director of Karrier Motors of Huddersfield. As Clayton lived at The Heights, above Marlow on the Henley Road, the first pair of buses was kept there, and in fact Jeffries was actually his chauffeur!

Ernest was soon singled out as a man with the talents to succeed in the business and so made the rapid transformation to Manager of the growing enterprise. *Marlow & District Motor Services* soon moved to a new head office (and residence for Ernest) at 8 Glade Road, near Marlow Station. A substantial garage was built over the rear garden for the growing fleet, and it was accessed via the un-made Victoria Road which ran parallel to Glade Road.

Services were expanded, mainly it should be noted, to form a practical test-bed for the Karrier products, a feat all the more remarkable that this occurred right in the heart of *Thames Valley* country! However, a territorial agreement was reached in May 1926, but following shares held in TV by the *Great Western Railway* in 1931 the hold by the *'Valley* increased until outright acquisition took place in May 1933.

Throughout all these changes Ernest Jeffries remained as Manager, and his natural talents for organisation earned him much respect with staff and public alike.

These skills were also acknowledged by *Thames Valley*, and following the closure of the Marlow premises in favour of operation by Maidenhead Garage, and the transfer of administration to Reading, Ernest was appointed as Traffic Superintendent for the High Wycombe area. In that role he steered operations there through the busy period of acquisitions of the 1930's, and the difficult days of the Second World War, all with his usual efficiency. He was also very active with the social side, particularly at bowls, and he even represented England from 1948-50. His place was taken by Mr. G.E. Morris with effect from 1st October.

On the vehicle front, outgoing stock in September consisted of 1950 ECW B35R-bodied Bristol L6B's 539/41 (FMO 14/6) and 1950 ECW B39R-bodied Bristol LL6B Cars 556-8/61 (FMO 938-40/3), all of which went to *United Welsh!* Also departing was AEC 'Regal' 0662-type Car 133 (DMO 322), which had been recently taken off contract work in the Newbury area.

The days of the 1947 Duple-bodied AEC 'Regals' were numbered. Car 132 (DMO 321) is seen at The Wharf after conversion to o-m-o, despite retaining the sliding door, although now power-assisted.

On the Service Vehicle fleet, September saw the sale of the Maidenhead Depot Van No.23 (EBL 533), a Bedford 10/12cwt new in 1947. However, this was not replaced, as such an allocation there ceased in favour of direct deliveries from the Central Stores in Reading.

One particularly interesting transfer, at least from the point of view of a budding *Thames Valley* enthusiast, was Bristol K5G Car 475 (FLJ 978), which was sent to Bracknell as an additional vehicle in September.

Car 475 (FLJ 978) in the Southern Yard at Reading. Note the 6-bay construction of the lower deck.

Flooding in the region occurred again on 4th and 5th November, and Maidenhead operations were affected in respect of Routes 20/20a, the section between that town and Cookham not running. The same situation returned in December for 4 days, and both times any TV season tickets could be used on the rail services. It is of course worth recording that in former times, when Thornycrofts and Tilling-Stevens buses had roamed the River Thames valley, they could generally cope with moderate floods on these services, the drivers relying on the Thames-side railings and other roadside posts as guides!

A further step forward on one-man working affected former Crowthorne Shed Route 3a (Reading – Wokingham – Barkham – Finchampstead), covered by one bus also provided by Reading Garage, which went over to such operation using Bristol LS saloons from 5th November. The schedules remained the same as before, including short-workings timed for school children between Emmbrook (Rifle Volunteer and Dog & Duck) and Wokingham, plus some others from Emmbrook and Reading and between Finchampstead and Wokingham. This saved 96hrs 25mins of staff pay per week. It is also worth recalling that the total number of buses between Wokingham and Reading per day was 85, with only minutes between some!

Car 717 (HMO 863) is seen following the conversion of Route 3a to one-man-operation, about to leave from Stations Square in Reading.

Within Wokingham all services still focussed on the Market Place area for stopping points. Buses on the A (Reading – London), 2 (Reading – Windsor) and 75 (Reading to Guildford) had their main westerly stop by the northern flank of the triangular site housing the Old Town Hall, where the 21 (from Maidenhead) also called before pressing onto the Railway Station. On the opposite side of the road was the Bush Hotel, where the eastbound buses of those services stopped. Routes 3 (Reading – Camberley), 3a (Reading – Finchampstead) and 4a (Reading – Arborfield – Wokingham) also called or terminated in the Market Place on the eastern and western flanks of the site. The 4a also ran onto the Railway Station, which was useful for Army personnel from Arborfield Garrison who needed to travel further afield on leave.

Bristol L6B coach 555 was the last of the Windover-bodied examples to remain in service.

In the meantime the surviving Windover-bodied L6B Bristol coaches had spent the Summer working for *South Midland*, and they were often seen at Victoria Coach Station mingling amongst much newer types. However, time eventually caught up with them when in November Cars 545 (FMO 20) and 550-4 (FMO 25/6 and FMO 934-6) were disposed of. That left only Car 555 (FMO 937), which was stored and returned to service the following year. Also ousted in November was exposed-radiator fully-fronted L6B coach 74 (EBD 237), which had come from *United Counties*.

Coahc-seated Bristol FLF Car 836 (UJB 202) enters Victoria Coach Station from Buckingham Palace Road, overlooked by the large winged statue over the portico of the rail-air bus terminal of British Overseas Airways Corporation. All of this batch had painted adverts for Huntley & Palmers Biscuits and, in due course another for South Midland Coach Tours on the offside panel behind the staircase (seen blank here).

In November the remainder of the 5 coach-seated Bristol FLF's were received, but these had Gardner 6-cylinder engines in place of the Bristol unit fitted to Car 834, which was for evaluation purposes on a route with high mileage and generally faster road speeds. These became Cars 835-8 (UJB 201-4), and all had ECW CH37/28F bodies, the loss of seats on the lower deck being to accommodate the luggage racks. All were nominally allocated to Reading, though two spent the night in Samuelson's Garage at Victoria in rotation. Unlike the original 'Lodekka' concept, these were a new generation of flat-floor buses, hence the chassis designation <u>F</u>lat-floor <u>L</u>ong-wheelbase <u>F</u>ront-entrance.

The interior view, looking forward, of one of the MW saloons, Cars 854-7 (VJB 945-8). These buses were in use at Newbury throughout most of their long working lives, though later some transfers to High Wycombe did occur.

Also received in November were the first new saloons for Newbury Garage for some time, the staff by then being firmly of the opinion that the *Valley* only sent them old buses! These were Bristol MW6G chassis with ECW B41F bodies built as one-manners, and they became Cars 854/5 (VJB 945/6). In December identical Cars 856/7 (VJB 947/8) followed along, and these were used on a wide variety of duties, some of which were inter-worked during the days or over the weekly cycle still associated with that market town.

Bristol MW6G Car 856 (VJB 947) prepares to work Route 120 to Frilsham, a pleasant half-hour journey through Hermitage, with Thursday and Saturday only links to Curridge. Most of the Newbury area routes followed the pattern set under Newbury & District, and those could be traced back to the network of the Country Carrier's.

With these MW buses now to hand, the Company was able to dispose of the remaining Duple-bodied AEC 'Regal' saloons recently taken off contract duties as part of the cascading of older stock in the Newbury area. Cars 131/2/4/7 (DMO 320/1/3/6) all departed in December, this being another significant stage in the elimination of types from the *Red & White* era. The last of the once extensive fleet of AEC 'Regal' half-cab coach had gone back in February, leaving only the ECW-bodied underfloor-engined 'Regal' MkIV coach 85 (SFC 571) to represent that make. However, this coach would actually outlast the contemporary Bristol LS's by 2 years right on through to 1967!

On the double-deck front, the erstwhile *Newbury & District* fleet was now represented by lowbridge Duple-bodied Guy 'Arab' MkIII 5LW Cars 170/1 (FMO 515/6) and Duple highbridge Guy 'Arab' MkIII 6LW Cars H10 (FMO 517) and H13-6 (HOT 391-4), all of which would remain active in the Newbury area through to 1968. These actually remained the property of N&D, the legal lettering reading as 'Newbury & District Motor Services Ltd., on hire to the Thames Valley Traction Co. Ltd., 83 Lower Thorn Street, Reading'. Although none has survived to preservation, an identical bus from the *Red & White* fleet fortunately has, as these were indeed one of the classic combinations of chassis and body types of that era.

Car 170 (FMO 515) leaves the stop in Euclid Street, Swindon on its regular Route 106, an almost 30-mile run up through Liddngton, over the Lambourn Downs and along the Lambourn valley into Newbury.

December also witnessed yet another pair of Bristol LL6B's travelling west and over the border to *United Welsh* in Swansea, though Cars 562/3 (FMO 944/5) would not be the last to make that journey. Some years later the trade would be the other way round when the TV fleet, and especially Newbury, looked like an outpost of the Welsh operator, the full story of which will appear in the next (and final) volume of the story of *Thames Valley*.

The first of a batch of 13 Bristol FLF6G's for trunk services were received during December, fitted with ECW H38/32F bodies, their higher capacity reducing the need for relief buses at times. The batch would not be completed for nearly a year, with only Cars 839/40 (WJB 223/4) arriving that month and being allocated to Reading.

The Staff at Reading were sad to hear of the death of long-service Traffic Superintendent Jack Dear on 4th December. He was one of the nucleus of employees who had steered the Traffic Office through the decades from the 1920's.

From 5th December arrangements were made for the contracts between Abingdon and Harwell and Oxford and Harwell to be covered by *South Midland* coaches, having previously been handled by Newbury-based vehicles. Also, in the interests of economy, a study took place of the routes used within Reading town by the various scheduled services, after which modifications were made to the effect that 21,000 miles were saved per annum.

From17th December Route 21 (Maidenhead – White Waltham – Waltham St. Lawrence – Shurlock Row – Binfield – Wokingham) was fully double-decked,

with 6 double-deckers scheduled in place of the 7 service saloons and relief cars previously in use. Prior to this one of the 'Lodekka' LD-types was taken down to the Crauford Arch, under the London - Bristol rail line and was tested for clearance. Only 4 of the daily journeys ran beyond Shurlock Row to Wokingham, the rest of the service being most intently used between Maidenhead and the factories on the White Waltham airfield and the airfield itself, along with housing developments in the Woodlands Park and Cox Green areas, whilst also offering a further local service to those in the Boyn Hill area to the west of the town centre.

The Chief Engineer, Ian Campbell, had been offered that position with *United Automobile Services* up at Darlington, so he had the customary farewell lunch on 19th December before taking up the new post from January 1961.

No stage carriage journeys were operated by *Thames Valley* on Christmas Day, though *South Midland* ran a couple of trips on both the London routes, as was its custom. The Union, however, wanted a further day in lieu granted for working on Boxing Day, which resulted in an all-out strike (Oxford excluded) on 27th.

70-seater Bristol FLF6G Car 839 (WJB 223) awaits departure at Reading Stations Square for Woodley on Route 1a. Note the painted Wolfe & Hollander furniture store adverts.

The period from 1946 to 1960 had seen remarkable changes in the *Thames Valley* fleet and a further consolidation of operations through the acquisition of *Newbury & District* and *South Midland*. It had been an interesting period of hard work and had seen bus services at their zenith. There had been a number of issues as well, with steady increases in operating costs since the end of World War Two but, as 1960 closed, *Thames Valley* was still found to be in good shape.

*Throughout my rendition of the Thames Valley saga I have been fortunate to have had the opportunity of interviewing or corresponding with many people with some connection to the Company, along with others who were there to make first-hand observations. Without them, this story could never have been told in the detail that it has. Over a pie-and-a-pint Reg Hibbert assisted me in seeking out old N&D colleagues, whilst researches throughout the TV area provided numerous contacts. Whenever appropriate such items have included within the main text, but two contributions that have come from erstwhile members of the Head Office Staff I believe warrant coverage in their own right. In both cases, these are the personal observations of young men embarking on their first proper employment, aided by the fact that both already had an interest in buses – so welcome to **The Guest Pages**.*

Life in the Traffic Office in 1960 by Peter Wilks

When Peter started working at *Thames Valley* in January 1960, he joined a Company that had 40 years of history behind it and many of the Traffic Department staff had long service. Peter's insight into the daily workings and the characters with whom he shared the office give something of the flavour of how such operators functioned in those days.

Peter worked for Frank Robinson ('Mr. Rob'), who had joined the Company in 1924, and managed the Traffic Office, especially the publicity and printing of the roadside 'case bills' (as the timetables displayed at bus stops were known). His No.2 was Stanley Renouf ('Mr. Ren'), who also maintained immaculate records of TV's dealings with the Traffic Commissioners, which Peter found fascinating lunchtime reading.

Peter worked on various tasks for John Stevenson (the Traffic Manager), Frank Beetham (Assistant Traffic Manager), as well as Mr. Rob, and he also looked after the Private Hire Diary. At that time *Thames Valley* still had a lot of bookings in the Reading and Newbury areas, mainly through the tireless efforts of Ted White at The Wharf and Stan Brooker at Reading, whilst Ken Rogerson generated some at Maidenhead. However, it seems much of this was priced rather more to retain custom than strictly on costs. *South Midland* very much went its own way as usual and administered all its own private hire work.

It seemed that Mr. Rob felt that he had been overlooked in terms of promotion when the Assistant Traffic Manager post was established in 1950, though he kept up his spirits by bursting into song no matter where he was in the building and by playing piano in a band led by Reading music shop proprietor Norman Hackett! Generally the atmosphere in the office was quite relaxed and no one seemed to mind if Peter took a photo out of the window if he saw an interesting bus, or by detouring from trips to the printers via Stations Square to see what was about. The hours were quite long though, as he travelled in from Marlow daily on the 7.35am service 28, returning on the 5.40pm, plus every other Saturday morning, as many workers did in those days.

Morning tea breaks were taken in the canteen at the rear of the garage, where the wooden slatted seats from wartime utilities had been re-used – ideal for people from the Central Works with dirty overalls, but not so good for office staff! Next to the canteen was the Recreation Room (a Nissen hut type building, popularly known as 'Rat Hall' for reasons which could be guessed at), behind which in a storeroom Peter discovered lots of interesting old files and photos to aid his study of the TV fleet and its workings. There was a fixed lunch break from 1.00 p.m. to 2.15 p.m. A staff bus (known as the "Liberty Boat") was provided from the office to Stations Square and onwards to Wokingham (in reality it was the 12.55 p.m. Service 2), which catered for the many staff who lived on the Wokingham Road. The return working conveniently brought back the staff for 2.15 p.m.!

Peter rarely came across the General Manager, Tom Pruett, and to a junior clerk he seemed a bit gruff and forbidding. His office seemed rather grand, and Mr. Ren didn't approve of such expense saying 'it's all come out of the conductor's bag'.

The Traffic Manager, John Stevenson, is recalled as a very precise man, even to the point of annoying Mr Rob at times, but high standards were his byword. His deputy, Frank Beetham, had come from *West Yorkshire*. The Reading Area Traffic Superintendent was Jack Dear, whilst Arthur Waldron is recalled as the very well thought of Assistant Traffic Superintendent based at Newbury. The High Wycombe Traffic Superintendent was Ernest Jeffries, and if he had been to Reading for a meeting, he gave Peter a lift back to Marlow, when interesting chats on his old *Marlow & District* days took place.

Peter had already met the Chief Engineer, Ian Campbell, as he had originally been considering going into engineering, and he found him willing to chat to him in the corridor on the vehicle front. Indeed, Peter recalls that when the quartet of buses were purchased from *Hants & Dorset*, Mr. Campbell admitted that he did not know Car 475 had a 'funny body' until it was delivered to Reading!

Peter was of course already interested in the *Thames Valley* fleet, and he was not alone. He soon met Peter Pribik, who spent most of his working life in the Schedules Office, whilst Mike Waring was in

Engineering Records (later to *Hants & Dorset, West Yorkshire* and *Wallace Arnold*), David Howard was in Schedules (later to *Northampton Corporation, Tyne & Wear Metro, Eastbourne Corporation* and then as head of *Isle of Man Transport*). Together with Howard Thomas (who went on to independent operators), they would explore the system on Saturday afternoons, ranging as far as Swindon or to the wilds of Childrey Ridgeway!

Left to right: David Howard, Ian Jones and Mike Waring standing in the doorway of a Bristol FLF.

Life in the Engineers Records Office, as seen through the eyes of Michael Waring

At age 16 I was interviewed by Company Secretary John Pearmain, a man I recall as well-spoken and courteous. This led to the offer of a job as Junior Clerk in the Engineers Record Office in November 1959 at the weekly rate of £3 19s 6d, plus a free-travel bus pass.

The Engineers Record Office was on the upper floor of the offices situated at the south end of the Reading Garage, next to the Schedules Office and the Cashiers Office. The décor was of painted brick walls in green gloss and upper areas and window frames in Tilling cream, and it looked like it had been like that since the major reconstruction of 1938-9, whilst the floors were covered in the same kind of lino found in the ECW bodies of the early 1950's.

On the same floor was the office of Chief Inspector Reg Pembroke and the Setright Ticket Machine

Repair Shop manned by two mechanics headed by Ken Deacon had been a Fitter back in Tilling-Stevens days, so he knew a thing or two about mechanical contrivances!

A large wall-mounted board in the office adjoining the Assistant Chief Engineer was used to determine vehicle allocations. It had been divided up into Depots, sub-divided into separate sections for double-deckers, single-deckers and coaches, then with with squares of about 1 inch Only parent garages were indicated, as any allocations to Dormy Sheds, or in the case of Desborough Road at High Wycombe or Iffley Road at Oxford, were left as determined locally.

Cup hooks were screwed into the board, upon which formica discs, engraved with Car Numbers, could be hung to indicate allocations. Discs with white numbers on red were for double-deckers, red letters on white for single-deckers and white numbers on green for coaches. There were also some discs with white numbers on black, but I cannot now recall what they represented.

Each month required changes to the allocations due to new vehicles arriving, others being sold, de-licensing for major dockings and serious accident victims, so I got very familiar with where all the vehicles were when this task fell to me. Over the Winter a lot of the coaches were laid up, so the de-licensed section of the board got very full then.

Fleets Lists were produced based on these allocations and duplicated off using a Roneo Machine on large sheets of paper. The associated licensing of vehicles was also a significant task, particularly as buses not likely to see use for a time were routinely de-licensed to save money. At the end of each month someone would need to go off to the local Licensing Office by The Forbury with the paperwork and a cheque, always a chance to get out of the office for a while!

The head of the Engineering Department was Chief Engineer Ian Campbell, a tall slim, quietly-spoken Scot, who was kindly and well respected. I was also impressed that he found time to chat to me and answer my queries on the fleet. One day I recall asking him why, shortly beforehand, the Company had taken back some of the pre-war Bristol K5G's they had sold to *Eastern National,* only to break them up. He told me this was because it had been discovered that they had not paid the nominal £1 transfer fee (usual then for inter-company transfers of vehicles with only limited written-down value), so TV didn't want them to have the profit from the scrap!

Whenever I went into the Chief Engineer's office I admired the large model of a Leyland 'Titan' TD1 which the chassis manufacturer had apparently given out to larger customers, each painted in the livery of that operator, and I wonder what ever happened to it? The Assistant Engineer was Brian Hancock, not quite as approachable as Mr. Campbell, but a good engineer with previous experience with Bristol Commercial Vehicles and REME, later becoming Engineer with the Isle of Wight operator *Southern Vectis* and others.

The newest vehicle in the fleet at the close of 1960 was Bristol FLF6G Car 840 (WJB 224), which is on Station Hill on a very damp day awaiting the nod from the Duty Inspector to form a relief on the London B.

Mr. Hancock shared his office with the Engineers Secretary Vashti, who had worked for Basil Sutton since leaving school just after the Second World War.

The Engineers Record Office was supervised by Stanley Read, who when I joined was soon to retire and was training his successor. Record-keeping was done with the aid of Cardex Cabinets, in which trays of flip-over cards could be accessed by removing the tray onto a desk. Des Stagg was the new man, and he was re-trained from his previous post in the Stores Department. The records were very thorough and gave a complete history of all that happened with that Car, included all dockings, mileages run and re-paints. Files for each Car were also kept for any paperwork.

The Works was supervised by Tom Sheppard, a life-long employee in his 50's, who seemed amiable enough. His office was in the centre of the Works and had good all-round vision like a control tower, so he could virtually see everything that was going on. Jimmy Lewington looked after the Stores, and was again easy going.

The Reading Garage staff were under the control of Garage Foreman Jimmy Dickenson, another life-long employee, who had started out maintaining the buses and liked to recall how difficult t was to start the old Tilling-Stevens 'on the handle'. He referred to them

as 'Tillys' and was a tall man with white hair, who always wore a long white coat and had the air of someone at the helm. He was ably assisted by other Chargehands who had worked their way up the ladder from Fitters, and I recall Len Jones, Jack Dodds and Bob Elder.

We always had regular contact with the other Garage Foremen in the course of our duties. Jack Giles was at Maidenhead, Frank Stacey at High Wycombe, Stan Tucker at Ascot, Reg Hibbert at Newbury and Mr. Munday at Oxford. Stan Tucker seemed to overlap on Traffic and Engineering somewhat, probably due to it being a small depot, and all the staff there had a soft spot for him. Mr. Munday was the youngest of them all and was always late with his paperwork and, when chased, would say he was just finishing it, which always raised a smile! Reg Hibbert had the usual Scouse wit and had come to us from N&D. I remember riding out to Newbury one evening on my new Privilege Pass (around 1961) and met him in the garage. I asked him why his 'Lodekkas' 763/4 had been repainted with black lining out – Newbury did its own re-paints then, so he said they were so good they only needed a touch-up and varnish, then I thought he winked, or was it a twitch?

A regular sight for Mike was a bus freshly turned out from the Reading Works. Bristol LD-type Car 791 (NBL 748) is seen in the Lower Thorn Street yard as it awaits return to its allocated depot. A thorough overhaul and re-paint has returned it to 'as new'.

There was the inevitable clash between Engineering and Traffic at times, when buses were called in for re-paints and the operating garage didn't want to release them, but otherwise the programme would see each bus re-painted every 2 years, whilst coaches would be generally dealt with over the Winter under a separate programme.

Bus adverts were an important source of income for bus operators, as well as a means of publicising tours and excursions. When I started adverts were either on paper or sign-written directly on. I have a feeling that some exterior adverts may have been transfers, e.g. the roof ads on saloon buses. The letting was arranged through British Transport Advertising and was a mixture of local firms and national brand-names and newspapers, whilst the interior adverts also included local events and were changed more frequently. TV was one of the few nationalised operators to specify the double-front ads, and Car 596 (FMO 978) below shows it with painted ones for Cooks of Reading, who were local house-builders.

In one instance the advertiser, Archer's Stationery of Slough, took all the available external positions for a set of painted ads, so Car 699 (HMO 845) was dubbed 'the Archer's bus'.

We had our own Advert Fixer, Derek Parsons, a one-time driver, who now covered the whole fleet in his van, fixing all the printed ads himself. The painted ads were undertaken by in two stages, with Derek preparing the background colour for the sign-writer Mr. Shunn and his assistant Alf to complete the advert as well as those for *Reading Corporation*. The fixing of adverts and even painting was undertaken during the working day, Monday to Friday, so opportunities had to be found to do this. Arrangements were usually made with the Garage Foreman to keep buses for painted ads back for peak-time working only. Occasionally, painted backgrounds might be prepared, only for the bus to be sent unexpectedly, leaving the surface like sandpaper, so you can imagine Derek's comments when that occurred!

Mike soon found he could tell many of the buses by their adverts alone, a method used by the author, who like Michael Plunkett and Bob Crawley in earlier years, had made up charts of such details!

Operators acquired by Thames Valley 1946 – 1960

H. D. Farmer (Gem Bus Service)   **26.03.1949**
The Harrow Inn, Hughenden Valley, High Wycombe.
Bus service High Wycombe – Lacey Green – Princes Risborough – Monks Risborough.

Newbury & District M. S. Ltd.   **01.01.1950**
The Wharf, Newbury - Transferred from Red & White United Transport when Nationalised.
All bus services and licenses for excursions and tours, Enquiry Office at The Wharf, Garage in Mill Lane.
The Newbury & District company remained in existence, though to the public the name disappeared around 1952.

South Midland M. S. Ltd.   **01.01.1950**
118 High Street, Oxford – Transferred from Red & White United Transport when Nationalised.
All coach operations, Head Office, Enquiry Office and Café at Gloucester Green and Garage in Iffley Road.
The South Midland name was retained for the Oxford based operation through to the end of 1970, when they were transferred to City of Oxford Motor Services Ltd.

R. E. Jackson (Crescent Coaches)   **01.06.1951**
St Andrews Crescent, Windsor – Jointly acquired with London Transport.
Bus Service Slough – Cippenham.

United Counties Omnibus Co. Ltd.   **01.05.1952**
Northampton – Transferred to South Midland.
Express coach service Oxford – High Wycombe – London and Garage in Botley Road.

Frowen & Hill (Borough Bus Service)   **01.12.1954**
St. Leonards Road, Windsor.
Bus service Windsor – Clewer Green – Windsor.

United Counties Car 807 (EBD 234) is seen as new in Nottingham. This vehicle passed to South Midland as Car 71, then transferred to the Thames Valley fleet in due course. It has the ECW 'express' type body on Bristol L6B chassis and is in green and cream livery.

THE THAMES VALLEY FLEET 1946 - 1960

Where two fleet numbers are shown pre-1951, e.g. 294/18, the vehicle was transferred to the Ledbury or N&D fleet

Details of re-numbering in later years are shown in the appropriate places, e.g 774/S301

Vehicles passing to Alder Valley are noted in the disposals column as To AV plus new fleet number

Standard body codes:		B - single-deck saloon bus		DP - dual-purpose bus with coach seating		C - coach		
L - Lowbridge double-decker		H - highbridge double-decker		LD - Lodekka low height double-decker				
F - fully-fronted on half-cab chassis		CH - double-decker with coach seating		CLD - Lodekka with coach seating				
Entrance position:		F - front entrance	R - rear entrance	C - centre entrance	D - dual entrance	RD - rear door fitted		
		ROS - rear open staircase						
Other codes:		8 (as suffix) - 8ft wide body on 7ft 6ins chassis			52 (in brackets) year body built			
Example:		CLD31/25RD = Coach-seated Lodekka with 31 seats on upper deck, 25 seats on lower deck and rear doors						

Fleet No.	Reg. No.	Chassis Make	Chassis Type	Bodybuilder	Body Type	Date New	Date Acq.	Date Out
144	MO 9316	Tilling-Stevens	B9A	Brush	B35R	May-27	New	Jan-46
150	MO 9322	Tilling-Stevens	B9A	Brush	B35R	Jun-27	New	Jan-46
152	MO 9324	Tilling-Stevens	B9A	Brush	B35R	Jun-27	New	Feb-46
153	MO 9325	Tilling-Stevens	B9A	Brush	B35R	May-27	New	Jan-46
156	MO 9328	Tilling-Stevens	B9A	Brush	B35R	May-27	New	Jan-46
164	RX 1753	Leyland	Titan TD1	Leyland	L24/24ROS	May-28	New	Oct-49
165	RX 1754	Leyland	Titan TD1	Leyland	L24/24ROS	May-28	New	Oct-49
166	RX 1755	Leyland	Titan TD1	Leyland	L24/24ROS	May-28	New	Oct-49
167	RX 1756	Leyland	Titan TD1	Leyland	L24/24ROS	May-28	New	Oct-49
168	RX 1757	Leyland	Titan TD1	Leyland	L24/24ROS	Jun-28	New	Oct-49
169	RX 1758	Leyland	Titan TD1	Leyland	L24/24ROS	Jun-28	New	Sep-56
Car 169 was converted to TV Route Servicing Vehicle No.29 in October 1949								
170	RX 1759	Leyland	Titan TD1	Leyland	L24/24ROS	Jun-28	New	Oct-49
171	RX 1760	Leyland	Titan TD1	Leyland	L27/24R	Jun-28	New	Jul-50
172	RX 1761	Leyland	Titan TD1	Leyland	L24/24ROS	Jul-28	New	Oct-49
173	RX 1762	Leyland	Titan TD1	Short	L24/24ROS	Jul-28	New	Oct-49
174	RX 1763	Leyland	Titan TD1	Short	L24/24ROS	Jul-28	New	Oct-49
175	RX 1764	Leyland	Titan TD1	Short	L24/24ROS	Jul-28	New	Oct-49
179	RX 4341	Leyland	Titan TD1	Leyland	L27/24R	Jun-29	New	Oct-52
180	RX 4342	Leyland	Titan TD1	Leyland	L27/24R	Jun-29	New	Oct-52
181	RX 4343	Leyland	Titan TD1	Leyland	L27/24R	Jun-29	New	Jan-53
182	RX 4344	Leyland	Titan TD1	Leyland	L27/24R	Jun-29	New	Aug-52
183	RX 4345	Leyland	Titan TD1	Leyland	L27/24R	Jun-29	New	Aug-52
184	RX 4346	Leyland	Titan TD1	Leyland	L27/24R	Jun-29	New	Jul-52
185	RX 4347	Leyland	Titan TD1	Leyland	L27/24R	Jun-29	New	May-52
186	RX 4348	Leyland	Titan TD1	Leyland	L27/24R	Jun-29	New	Jul-52
187	RX 4349	Leyland	Titan TD1	Leyland	L27/24R	Jun-29	New	Oct-52
190	RX 4352	Leyland	Titan TD1	Leyland	L27/24R	Jun-29	New	Oct-52
199	RX 5561	Leyland	Titan TD1	Leyland	L27/24R	Oct-29	New	Oct-51
200	RX 5562	Leyland	Titan TD1	Leyland	L27/24R	Oct-29	New	by Feb-51
201	RX 5563	Leyland	Titan TD1	Leyland	L27/24R	Feb-30	New	by Sep-51
202	RX 5564	Leyland	Titan TD1	Leyland	L27/24R	Feb-30	New	Feb-51
203	RX 5565	Leyland	Titan TD1	Leyland	L27/24R	Feb-30	New	by Apr-51
204	RX 5566	Leyland	Titan TD1	Leyland	L27/24R	Feb-30	New	by Apr-51
205	RX 5567	Leyland	Titan TD1	Leyland	L27/24R	Feb-30	New	Mar-52
206	RX 5568	Leyland	Titan TD1	Leyland	L27/24R	Mar-30	New	by Sep-51
207	RX 5569	Leyland	Titan TD1	Leyland	L27/24R	Mar-30	New	by Apr-51
208	RX 5570	Leyland	Titan TD1	Leyland	L27/24R	Mar-30	New	by Apr-51
209/2	RX 5571	Leyland	Lion LT1	Brush	B32R	Feb-30	New	Feb-50
210/4	RX 5572	Leyland	Lion LT1	Brush	B32R	Feb-30	New	Feb-50
211/6	RX 5573	Leyland	Lion LT1	Brush	B32R	Feb-30	New	Feb-50
212/8	RX 5574	Leyland	Lion LT1	Brush	B32R	Feb-30	New	Feb-50
213/10	RX 5575	Leyland	Lion LT1	Brush	B32R	Feb-30	New	Aug-50
214/12	RX 5576	Leyland	Lion LT1	Brush	B32R	Feb-30	New	Feb-50
215/20	RX 5577	Leyland	Lion LT1	Brush	B32R	Feb-30	New	Mar-50
216/22	RX 5578	Leyland	Lion LT1	Brush	B32R	Feb-30	New	Feb-50
217/38	RX 5579	Leyland	Lion LT1	Brush	B32R	Jan-30	New	Mar-50
218/42	RX 5580	Leyland	Lion LT1	Brush	B32R	Jan-30	New	Feb-50
219	RX 6110	Leyland	Titan TD1	Leyland	L27/24R	Mar-30	New	by Apr-51
220	RX 6111	Leyland	Titan TD1	Leyland	L27/24R	Mar-30	New	Aug-50
221	RX 6112	Leyland	Titan TD1	Leyland	L27/24R	Mar-30	New	by Sep-51
222	RX 6242	Leyland	Titan TD1	Leyland	L27/24R	May-30	New	by Apr-51
223	RX 6243	Leyland	Titan TD1	Leyland	L27/24R	May-30	New	by Apr-51
224	RX 6244	Leyland	Titan TD1	Leyland	L27/24R	May-30	New	Jul-50
225/46	RX 6245	Leyland	Lion LT2	Brush	B29R	Jul-30	New	by Sep-51
226/50	RX 6246	Leyland	Lion LT2	Brush	B29R	Jul-30	New	by Sep-51
227/52	RX 6247	Leyland	Lion LT2	Brush	B29R	Jul-30	New	Jul-50
228/54	RX 6248	Leyland	Lion LT2	Brush	B29R	Jul-30	New	Mar-51

Fleet No.	Reg. No.	Chassis Make	Chassis Type	Bodybuilder	Body Type	Date New	Date Acq.	Date Out
229/14	RX 6249	Leyland	Lion LT2	Brush	B29R	Jul-30	New	Jan-50
230/62	RX 6250	Leyland	Tiger TS3	Brush	B29R	Jul-30	New	Jul-50
232	RX 8165	Leyland	Titan TD1	Leyland	L27/24R	Mar-31	New	Oct-51
233	RX 8166	Leyland	Titan TD1	Leyland	L27/24R	Mar-31	New	Jul-50
234	RX 8167	Leyland	Titan TD1	Leyland	L27/24R	Mar-31	New	by Sep-51
235	RX 8168	Leyland	Titan TD1	Leyland	L27/24R	Mar-31	New	Oct-52
236	RX 8169	Leyland	Titan TD1	Leyland	L27/24R	Mar-31	New	Aug-50
237	RX 8170	Leyland	Titan TD1	Leyland	L27/24R	Mar-31	New	Apr-51
244	RX 9541	Leyland	Tiger TS4	Brush	B31R	Feb-32	New	Jul-53
245	RX 9699	Leyland	Tiger TS4	Brush	B32R	Mar-32	New	Mar-51
246	RX 9700	Leyland	Tiger TS4	Brush	B32R	Mar-32	New	Apr-51
247	RX 9701	Leyland	Tiger TS4	Brush	B32R	Mar-32	New	Nov-51
248	RX 9702	Leyland	Tiger TS4	Brush	B32R	Mar-32	New	Aug-52
249	RX 9703	Leyland	Tiger TS4	Brush	B32R	Mar-32	New	Aug-53
250	RX 9704	Leyland	Tiger TS4	Brush	B29R	May-32	New	Oct-51
252	RX 9706	Leyland	Tiger TS4	Brush	B29R	Apr-32	New	Jan-52
253	RX 9707	Leyland	Tiger TS4	Brush	B29R	May-32	New	Sep-52
255	RX 9709	Leyland	Tiger TS4	Brush	B29R	May-32	New	Jul-51
256	RX 9710	Leyland	Tiger TS4	Brush	B31R	May-32	New	Nov-51
258	GN 5145	Leyland	Tiger TS3	Leyland	B31R	May-31	Sep-33	Oct-49
			Car 258 was originally Premier Line, acquired by Eastern National O C on takeover of Aylesbury O C, then to TV					
259	GN 5139	Leyland	Tiger TS3	Leyland	C26R	May-31	May-34	Oct-49
			Car 259 was originally Premier Line, then to LPTB before being passed onto to TV					
262	JB 5841	Leyland	Tiger TS7	Duple	C32F	Apr-35	New	Apr-54
264	JB 5843	Leyland	Tiger TS7	Duple	C32F	Apr-35	New	Sep-54
265	JB 5844	Leyland	Tiger TS7	Brush	B32R	Jun-35	New	Mar-51
266	JB 5845	Leyland	Tiger TS7	Brush	B32R	Jul-35	New	Aug-52
267	JB 5846	Leyland	Tiger TS7	Brush	B32R	Jul-35	New	Oct-52
268	JB 5847	Leyland	Tiger TS7	Brush	B32R	Jun-35	New	Mar-51
269	JB 5848	Leyland	Tiger TS7	Brush	B32R	Jul-35	New	Mar-51
270	JB 5849	Leyland	Tiger TS7	Brush	B32R	Jun-35	New	Mar-51
271	JB 5850	Leyland	Tiger TS7	Brush	B32R	Jun-35	New	Jun-52
272	JB 5851	Leyland	Titan TD4	ECW	L24/24R (40)	Sep-35	New	Sep-50
273	JB 5852	Leyland	Titan TD4	Brush	L24/24R	Sep-35	New	Aug-53
274	JB 5853	Leyland	Titan TD4	Brush	L24/24R	Sep-35	New	Aug-53
275	JB 5854	Leyland	Titan TD4	Brush	L24/24R	Sep-35	New	Mar-53
276	JB 5855	Leyland	Titan TD4	Brush	L24/24R	Sep-35	New	Aug-52
277	JB 5856	Leyland	Titan TD4	Brush	L24/24R	Sep-35	New	Aug-53
294/18	JB 7494	Leyland	Tiger TS7	Brush	B32R	Dec-35	New	Oct-51
295	JB 7495	Leyland	Tiger TS7	Brush	B32R	Dec-35	New	Aug-52
296	JB 7496	Leyland	Tiger TS7	Brush	B32R	Dec-35	New	Mar-51
297	JB 7497	Leyland	Tiger TS7	Brush	B32R	Dec-35	New	Jul-50
298	JB 7498	Leyland	Tiger TS7	Brush	B32R	Dec-35	New	Mar-51
299	JB 7499	Leyland	Tiger TS7	Brush	B32R	Dec-35	New	Feb-51
302	JB 8341	Leyland	Tiger TS7	Brush	DP32R	Feb-36	New	Mar-51
303	JB 8342	Leyland	Tiger TS7	Brush	DP32R	Feb-36	New	Oct-52
304	JB 8343	Leyland	Tiger TS7	Brush	DP32R	Feb-36	New	Oct-52
305	JB 8344	Leyland	Tiger TS7	Brush	DP32R	Feb-36	New	Aug-52
306	JB 8345	Leyland	Tiger TS7	Brush	DP32R	Feb-36	New	May-52
307	JB 8346	Leyland	Tiger TS7	Brush	DP32R	Feb-36	New	Nov-50
308	JB 8347	Leyland	Tiger TS7	Brush	DP32R	Mar-36	New	Sep-50
309/24	JB 8348	Leyland	Tiger TS7	Brush	B32R	Feb-36	New	Sep-52
310/26	JB 8349	Leyland	Tiger TS7	Brush	B32R	Feb-36	New	Jul-50
311/28	JB 8350	Leyland	Tiger TS7	Brush	B32R	Feb-36	New	Aug-51
321/30	ABL 751	Leyland	Tiger TS7	Eastern Coach Works	B32R	Mar-37	New	Oct-52
322/32	ABL 752	Leyland	Tiger TS7	Eastern Coach Works	B32R	Mar-37	New	Aug-53
323/34	ABL 753	Leyland	Tiger TS7	Eastern Coach Works	B32R	Mar-37	New	Aug-53
324/36	ABL 754	Leyland	Tiger TS7	Eastern Coach Works	B32R	Mar-37	New	Sep-52
325/40	ABL 755	Leyland	Tiger TS7	Eastern Coach Works	B32R	Mar-37	New	Aug-53
326/44	ABL 756	Leyland	Tiger TS7	Eastern Coach Works	B32R	Mar-37	New	Sep-52
327	ABL 757	Leyland	Tiger TS7	Eastern Coach Works	B32R	Mar-37	New	Mar-51
328	ABL 758	Leyland	Tiger TS7	Eastern Coach Works	B32R	Mar-37	New	Aug-53
329	ABL 759	Leyland	Tiger TS7	Eastern Coach Works	B32R	Mar-37	New	Sep-52
330	ABL 760	Leyland	Tiger TS7	Eastern Coach Works	B32R	Mar-37	New	Jul-50
331/48	ABL 761	Leyland	Tiger TS7	Eastern Coach Works	B32R	Mar-37	New	Oct-52
332	ABL 762	Leyland	Tiger TS7	Eastern Coach Works	B32R	Mar-37	New	Oct-53
333/184	ABL 763	Leyland	Tiger TS7	Eastern Coach Works	B32R	Mar-37	New	Oct-52
334	ABL 764	Leyland	Tiger TS7	Eastern Coach Works	B32R	Mar-37	New	Aug-53
335	ABL 765	Leyland	Titan TD4	Brush	L26/26R	Feb-37	New	Aug-53

Fleet No.	Reg. No.	Chassis Make	Chassis Type	Bodybuilder	Body Type	Date New	Date Acq.	Date Out
336	ABL 766	Leyland	Titan TD4	Brush	L26/26R	Feb-37	New	Aug-53
337	ABL 767	Leyland	Cub KPZ2	Brush	B24F	May-37	New	Sep-52
338	ABL 768	Leyland	Cub KPZ2	Brush	B24F	May-37	New	Sep-52
339	AJB 811	Leyland	Titan TD5	Brush	L26/26R	May-37	New	Aug-53
340	AJB 812	Leyland	Titan TD5	Brush	L26/26R	May-37	New	Aug-53
341	AJB 813	Leyland	Titan TD5	Brush	L26/26R	May-37	New	Jul-53
342/179	AJB 814	Leyland	Tiger TS8	Brush	B32R	May-37	New	Apr-53
343/185	AJB 815	Leyland	Tiger TS8	Brush	B32R	May-37	New	Jul-53
344/180	AJB 816	Leyland	Tiger TS8	Brush	B32R	May-37	New	Nov-53
345	AJB 817	Leyland	Tiger TS8	Brush	B32R	May-37	New	Sep-54
346/182	AJB 818	Leyland	Tiger TS8	Brush	B32R	May-37	New	Apr-53
347	AJB 819	Leyland	Tiger TS8	Brush	B32R	May-37	New	May-51
348	AJB 820	Leyland	Tiger TS8	Brush	B32R	May-37	New	Oct-53
359	ARX 981	Leyland	Tiger TS8	Eastern Coach Works	B32R	Feb-38	New	Jul-50
360	ARX 982	Leyland	Tiger TS8	Eastern Coach Works	B32R	Feb-38	New	Jul-50
361	ARX 983	Leyland	Tiger TS8	Eastern Coach Works	B32R	Mar-38	New	Dec-53
362	ARX 984	Leyland	Tiger TS8	Eastern Coach Works	B32R	Mar-38	New	Sep-52
363	ARX 985	Leyland	Tiger TS8	Eastern Coach Works	B32R	Feb-38	New	Sep-54
364	ARX 986	Leyland	Tiger TS8	Eastern Coach Works	B32R	Feb-38	New	Jul-50
365	ARX 987	Leyland	Tiger TS8	Eastern Coach Works	B32R	Mar-38	New	Sep-50
366	ARX 988	Leyland	Tiger TS8	Eastern Coach Works	B32R	Mar-38	New	Sep-54
367	ARX 989	Leyland	Tiger TS8	Eastern Coach Works	B32R	Mar-38	New	Sep-50
368/186	ARX 990	Leyland	Tiger TS8	Eastern Coach Works	B32R	Mar-38	New	Dec-53
369	ARX 991	Leyland	Titan TD5	Eastern Coach Works	L24/24R	May-38	New	May-53
370	ARX 992	Leyland	Titan TD5	Eastern Coach Works	L24/24R	May-38	New	May-54
371	BBL 557	Leyland	Tiger TS8	Eastern Coach Works	B32R	Jun-38	New	May-54
372/181	BBL 558	Leyland	Tiger TS8	Eastern Coach Works	B32R	Jun-38	New	Mar-54
373	BBL 559	Leyland	Tiger TS8	Eastern Coach Works	B32R	Jun-38	New	Mar-54
374	BBL 560	Leyland	Tiger TS8	Eastern Coach Works	B32R	Jun-38	New	Mar-54
375	BBL 561	Leyland	Tiger TS8	Eastern Coach Works	B32R	Jun-38	New	Oct-53
376	BBL 562	Leyland	Tiger TS8	Eastern Coach Works	B32R	Jun-38	New	Jul-50
377	BBL 563	Leyland	Tiger TS8	Eastern Coach Works	B32R	Jun-38	New	Mar-51
378	BBL 564	Leyland	Tiger TS8	Eastern Coach Works	B32R	Jun-38	New	Jun-53
379/183	BBL 565	Leyland	Tiger TS8	Eastern Coach Works	B32R	Jun-38	New	Dec-53
380	BBL 566	Leyland	Tiger TS8	Eastern Coach Works	B32R	Jun-38	New	Mar-54
381	BMO 980	Leyland	Tiger TS8	Harrington	C32F	Jun-39	New	Oct-54
382	BMO 981	Leyland	Tiger TS8	Harrington	C32F	Jun-39	New	Apr-54
383	BMO 982	Leyland	Tiger TS8	Harrington	C32F	Jun-39	New	Oct-54
384	BMO 983	Leyland	Tiger TS8	Harrington	C32F	Jun-39	New	Oct-54
385	BMO 984	Leyland	Tiger TS8	Harrington	C32F	Jun-39	New	Apr-54
386	BMO 985	Leyland	Tiger TS8	Harrington	C32F	Jun-39	New	Oct-54
387	BMO 986	Leyland	Tiger TS8	Harrington	C32F	Jun-39	New	Oct-54
388	BMO 987	Leyland	Tiger TS8	Harrington	C32F	Jul-39	New	Oct-54
389	BMO 988	Leyland	Tiger TS8	Harrington	C32F	Jul-39	New	Oct-54
390	BMO 989	Leyland	Tiger TS8	Harrington	C32F	Jul-39	New	Oct-54
391	BRX 656	Bristol	K5G	Eastern Coach Works	L24/24R	Jun-39	New	Sep-55
392	BRX 908	Bristol	K5G	Eastern Coach Works	L24/24R	Sep-39	New	May-56
393	BRX 909	Bristol	K5G	Eastern Coach Works	L24/24R	Sep-39	New	Oct-54
394	BRX 910	Bristol	K5G	Eastern Coach Works	L24/24R	Sep-39	New	May-56
395	BRX 911	Bristol	K5G	Eastern Coach Works	L24/24R	Sep-39	New	Apr-54
396	BRX 912	Bristol	K5G	Eastern Coach Works	L24/24R	Sep-39	New	Apr-54
397	BRX 913	Bristol	K5G	Eastern Coach Works	L24/24R	Sep-39	New	Oct-54
398	BRX 914	Bristol	K5G	Eastern Coach Works	L24/24R	Oct-39	New	Apr-54
399	BRX 915	Bristol	K5G	Eastern Coach Works	L24/24R	Oct-39	New	Apr-54
400	BRX 916	Bristol	K5G	Eastern Coach Works	L24/24R	Oct-39	New	May-56
401	BRX 917	Bristol	K5G	Eastern Coach Works	L24/24R	Oct-39	New	Nov-54
402	BRX 918	Bristol	K5G	Eastern Coach Works	L24/24R	Oct-39	New	May-56
403	BRX 919	Bristol	K5G	Eastern Coach Works	L24/24R	Oct-39	New	Apr-54
404	BRX 920	Bristol	K5G	Eastern Coach Works	L24/24R	Oct-39	New	Oct-54
405	BRX 921	Bristol	K5G	Eastern Coach Works	L24/24R	Oct-39	New	To SV
				Car 405 was converted to TV Route Servicing Vehicle No.43 in October 1956				
406	BRX 922	Bristol	K5G	Eastern Coach Works	L24/24R	Oct-39	New	Oct-54
407	BRX 923	Bristol	K5G	Eastern Coach Works	L24/24R	Oct-39	New	Oct-54
408	BRX 924	Bristol	K5G	Eastern Coach Works	L24/24R	Oct-39	New	Apr-54
409	BRX 925	Bristol	K5G	Eastern Coach Works	L24/24R	Oct-39	New	Oct-54
410	CJB 131	Bristol	K5G	Eastern Coach Works	L24/24R	Dec-40	New	Oct-54
411	FM 7455	Leyland	Cub KP3	Brush	B26F	Dec-32	Dec-40	Sep-52
				Car 411 was exchanged for 'Tiger' TS3 Car 260 with Crosville M.S. For use on the Marlow Bridge route				
412	HF 6041	Leyland	Titan TD1	Leyland	L27/24R	May-29	Jun-41	May-52

Car 412 was originally Wallesey C. T., later with W. Alexander, to TV via dealers

Fleet No.	Reg. No.	Chassis Make	Chassis Type	Bodybuilder	Body Type	Date New	Date Acq.	Date Out
413	CJB 132	Bristol	K5G	Eastern Coach Works	L27/28R	May-42	New	Sep-55
414	CJB 133	Bristol	K5G	Eastern Coach Works	L27/28R	Apr-42	New	Sep-55
415	CJB 134	Bristol	K5G	Eastern Coach Works	L27/28R	Apr-42	New	May-56
416	CJB 135	Bristol	K5G	Eastern Coach Works	L27/28R	May-42	New	May-56
417	CJB 136	Bristol	K5G	Duple	UL27/28R	Nov-42	New	May-56
418	CJB 137	Guy	Arab 1 5LW	Duple	UL27/28R	Dec-42	New	Aug-55
419	CJB 138	Guy	Arab 1 5LW	Duple	UL27/28R	Dec-42	New	Aug-55
420/187	CJB 139	Guy	Arab 1 5LW	Strachan	UL27/28R	Jan-43	New	Aug-55
421	CJB 140	Guy	Arab 1 5LW	Strachan	UL27/28R	Feb-43	New	May-56
422	CJB 141	Guy	Arab 1 5LW	Brush	UL27/28R	Feb-43	New	Jun-56
423	CMO 653	Guy	Arab 1 5LW	Brush	UL27/28R	May-43	New	May-56
424	CMO 654	Guy	Arab 1 5LW	Brush	UL27/28R	May-43	New	Oct-55
425	CMO 655	Guy	Arab 1 5LW	Brush	UL27/28R	May-43	New	May-56
426	CRX 196	Bristol	K6A	Strachan	UL27/28R	Jan-45	New	Dec-57
427	CRX 197	Bristol	K6A	Strachan	UL27/28R	Mar-45	New	Sep-57
428	CRX 198	Bristol	K6A	Strachan	UL27/28R	Jun-45	New	Nov-57
429	CRX 540	Bristol	K6A	Strachan	UL27/28R	Jul-45	New	Nov-57
430	CRX 541	Bristol	K6A	Strachan	UL27/28R	Aug-45	New	Feb-57
431	CRX 542	Bristol	K6A	Strachan	UL27/28R	Aug-45	New	Feb-57
432	CRX 543	Bristol	K6A	Strachan	UL27/28R	Sep-45	New	by Jul-57
433	CRX 544	Bristol	K6A	Strachan	UL27/28R	Oct-45	New	Dec-57
434	CRX 545	Bristol	K6A	Strachan	UL27/28R	Nov-45	New	Feb-57
435	DR 9636	Leyland	Titan TD2	Mumford	L24/24R	Mar-32	Mar-45	Mar-53
436	DR 9846	Leyland	Titan TD2	Mumford	L24/24R	Jun-32	Mar-45	Oct-52

Cars 435/6 were ex-Plymouth C.T., purchased through Western National O. C. on behalf of the Tilling Group

Fleet No.	Reg. No.	Chassis Make	Chassis Type	Bodybuilder	Body Type	Date New	Date Acq.	Date Out
437	CRX 546	Bedford	OWB	Duple	B26F	Dec-45	New	Dec-56
438	CRX 547	Bedford	OWB	Duple	B26F	Dec-45	New	Jun-57
3885	JVW 430	Bristol	K5G	Eastern Coach Works	L27/28R	Jan-44	On Loan	Mar-46

This K5G was the postwar Bristol/ECW prototype and was on loan for Route 2 from Ascot garage 16th-23rd March

Fleet No.	Reg. No.	Chassis Make	Chassis Type	Bodybuilder	Body Type	Date New	Date Acq.	Date Out
439	CRX 548	Bristol	K6A	Eastern Coach Works	L27/28R	May-46	New	Mar-64
440	CRX 549	Bristol	K6A	Eastern Coach Works	L27/28R	May-46	New	Dec-63
441	CRX 550	Bristol	K6A	Eastern Coach Works	L27/28R	Jun-46	New	Jan-66
442	CRX 551	Bristol	K6A	Eastern Coach Works	L27/28R	Jun-46	New	Apr-62
443	DBL 151	Bristol	K6A	Eastern Coach Works	L27/28R	Sep-46	New	Apr-63
444	DBL 152	Bristol	K6A	Eastern Coach Works	L27/28R	Sep-46	New	Oct-62
445	DBL 153	Bristol	K6A	Eastern Coach Works	L27/28R	Sep-46	New	Apr-63
446	DBL 154	Bristol	K6A	Eastern Coach Works	L27/28R	Oct-46	New	Feb-65
447	DBL 155	Bristol	K6A	Eastern Coach Works	L27/28R	Oct-46	New	Jul-65
448	DBL 156	Bristol	K6A	Eastern Coach Works	L27/28R	Nov-46	New	May-65
449	DBL 157	Bristol	K6A	Eastern Coach Works	L27/28R	Dec-46	New	Oct-62
450	DBL 158	Bristol	K6A	Eastern Coach Works	L27/28R	Dec-46	New	Oct-65
451	DBL 159	Bristol	K6A	Eastern Coach Works	L27/28R	Dec-46	New	Oct-62
452	DBL 160	Bristol	K6A	Eastern Coach Works	L27/28R	Dec-46	New	Feb-66
453	DBL 161	Bristol	K6B	Eastern Coach Works	L27/28R	Jan-47	New	Feb-63
454	DBL 162	Bristol	K6B	Eastern Coach Works	L27/28R	Apr-47	New	Oct-65
455	DBL 163	Bristol	L6A	Eastern Coach Works	B35R	Jan-47	New	Jul-58
456	DBL 164	Bristol	L6A	Eastern Coach Works	B35R	Jan-47	New	Sep-58
457	DBL 165	Bristol	L6A	Eastern Coach Works	B35R	Jan-47	New	Jul-58
458	DBL 166	Bristol	L6A	Eastern Coach Works	B35R	Jan-47	New	Jul-58
459	DBL 167	Bristol	L6A	Eastern Coach Works	B35R	May-47	New	Sep-58
460	DMO 664	Bristol	L6B	Windover	C32F	Sep-47	New	see 794
461	DMO 665	Bristol	L6B	Vincent	C32F	Feb-48	New	see 795
462	DMO 666	Bristol	L6B	Windover	C32F	Sep-47	New	see 796
463	DMO 667	Bristol	L6B	Windover	C32F	Oct-47	New	see 797
464	DMO 668	Bristol	L6B	Vincent	C32F	Feb-48	New	see 798
465	DMO 669	Bristol	L6B	Windover	C32F	Oct-47	New	see 799
466	DMO 670	Bristol	K6A	Eastern Coach Works	L27/28R	Nov-47	New	Dec-63
467	DMO 671	Bristol	K6A	Eastern Coach Works	L27/28R	Dec-47	New	Nov-62
468	DMO 672	Bristol	K6B	Eastern Coach Works	L27/28R	Mar-48	New	Mar-65
469	DMO 673	Bristol	K6B	Eastern Coach Works	L27/28R	Mar-48	New	Oct-66
470	DMO 674	Bristol	K6B	Eastern Coach Works	L27/28R	Apr-48	New	Apr-63
471	DMO 675	Bristol	K6B	Eastern Coach Works	L27/28R	Apr-48	New	May-66
472	DMO 676	Bristol	L6A	Eastern Coach Works	DP31R	Jan-48	New	Jul-58
473	DMO 677	Bristol	L6A	Eastern Coach Works	DP31R	Jan-48	New	Jun-59
474	DMO 678	Bristol	L6A	Eastern Coach Works	DP31R	Jan-48	New	Jul-58
475	DMO 679	Bristol	L6A	Eastern Coach Works	DP31R	Jan-48	New	Jun-59
476	DMO 680	Bristol	L6A	Eastern Coach Works	DP31R	Jan-48	New	Jul-58
477	DMO 681	Bristol	L6A	Eastern Coach Works	DP31R	Jan-48	New	Jul-58

Fleet No.	Reg. No.	Chassis Make	Chassis Type	Bodybuilder	Body Type	Date New	Date Acq.	Date Out
478	DMO 682	Bristol	L6A	Eastern Coach Works	DP31R	Mar-48	New	Sep-58
479	DMO 683	Bristol	L6A	Eastern Coach Works	DP31R	Mar-48	New	Sep-58
480	DMO 684	Bristol	L6A	Eastern Coach Works	DP31R	Mar-48	New	Sep-58
481	DMO 685	Bristol	L6A	Eastern Coach Works	DP31R	Mar-48	New	Jul-58
482	DMO 686	Bristol	L6A	Eastern Coach Works	DP31R	Mar-48	New	Jul-58
483	DMO 687	Bristol	L6A	Eastern Coach Works	DP31R	Mar-48	New	Jul-58
484	DMO 688	Bristol	L6A	Eastern Coach Works	DP31R	Mar-48	New	Jul-58
485	DMO 689	Bristol	L6A	Eastern Coach Works	DP31R	Apr-48	New	Jul-58
486	DMO 690	Bristol	L6A	Eastern Coach Works	DP31R	May-48	New	Jul-58
487	EJB 209	Bristol	L6B	Windover	C33F	Sep-48	New	Oct-57
488	EJB 210	Bristol	L6B	Windover	C33F	Sep-48	New	Oct-57
489	EJB 211	Bristol	L6B	Windover	C33F	Sep-48	New	Oct-57
490	EJB 212	Bristol	L6B	Windover	C33F	Sep-48	New	Oct-57
491	EJB 213	Bristol	L6B	Windover	C33F	Sep-48	New	Oct-57
492	EJB 214	Bristol	K6B	Eastern Coach Works	L27/28R	Nov-48	New	Dec-63
493	EJB 215	Bristol	K6B	Eastern Coach Works	L27/28R	Dec-48	New	Aug-65
494	EJB 216	Bristol	K6B	Eastern Coach Works	L27/28R	Dec-48	New	Aug-65
495	EJB 217	Bristol	K6B	Eastern Coach Works	L27/28R	Dec-48	New	Aug-65
496	EJB 218	Bristol	K6B	Eastern Coach Works	L27/28R	Dec-48	New	Jul-65
497	EJB 219	Bristol	K6B	Eastern Coach Works	L27/28R	Jan-49	New	Jul-66
498	EJB 220	Bristol	K6B	Eastern Coach Works	L27/28R	Jan-49	New	Jul-65
499	EJB 221	Bristol	K6B	Eastern Coach Works	L27/28R	Dec-48	New	Dec-65
500	EJB 222	Bristol	K6B	Eastern Coach Works	L27/28R	Jan-49	New	Dec-65
501	EJB 223	Bristol	K6B	Eastern Coach Works	L27/28R	Jan-49	New	Dec-63
502	EJB 224	Bristol	K6B	Eastern Coach Works	L27/28R	Jan-49	New	Dec-65
503	EJB 225	Bristol	K6B	Eastern Coach Works	L27/28R	Jan-49	New	Aug-65
504	EJB 226	Bristol	K6B	Eastern Coach Works	L27/28R	Jan-49	New	Jul-66
505	EJB 227	Bristol	K6B	Eastern Coach Works	L27/28R	Jan-49	New	Dec-65
506	EJB 228	Bristol	K6B	Eastern Coach Works	L27/28R	Jan-49	New	Aug-66
507	EJB 229	Bristol	K6B	Eastern Coach Works	L27/28R	Jul-49	New	Nov-66
508	EJB 230	Bristol	K6B	Eastern Coach Works	L27/28R	Jul-49	New	Aug-66
509	EJB 231	Bristol	K6B	Eastern Coach Works	L27/28R	Jul-49	New	Mar-66
510	EJB 232	Bedford	OB	Beadle	DP27F	Jun-49	New	Jun-57
511	EJB 233	Bedford	OB	Beadle	DP27F	Jun-49	New	Jun-57
512	EJB 234	Bedford	OB	Beadle	DP27F	May-49	New	Jun-57
513	EJB 235	Bristol	K6B	Eastern Coach Works	L27/28R	Jul-49	New	Jan-67
514	EJB 236	Bristol	K6B	Eastern Coach Works	L27/28R	Aug-49	New	Jan-67
515	EJB 237	Bristol	K6B	Eastern Coach Works	L27/28R	Aug-49	New	Feb-66
516	EJB 238	Bristol	K6B	Eastern Coach Works	L27/28R	Aug-49	New	Aug-66
517	EJB 239	Bristol	K6B	Eastern Coach Works	L27/28R	Aug-49	New	Jul-66
518	EJB 240	Bristol	K6B	Eastern Coach Works	L27/28R	Aug-49	New	Jul-66
519	EJB 241	Bristol	K6B	Eastern Coach Works	L27/28R	Aug-49	New	Jul-66
520	EJB 242	Bedford	OB	Beadle	DP27F	May-49	New	Aug-58
521	FBL 23	Bristol	L6B	Eastern Coach Works	B35R	Oct-49	New	Oct-59
522	FBL 24	Bristol	L6B	Eastern Coach Works	B35R	Nov-49	New	Oct-59
523	FBL 25	Bristol	L6B	Eastern Coach Works	B35R	Nov-49	New	Oct-59
524	FBL 26	Bristol	K6B	Eastern Coach Works	L27/28R	Nov-49	New	Oct-66
525	FBL 27	Bristol	K6B	Eastern Coach Works	L27/28R	Dec-49	New	Jul-66
526	FBL 28	Bristol	K6B	Eastern Coach Works	L27/28R	Jan-50	New	Jan-67
527	FBL 29	Bristol	K6B	Eastern Coach Works	L27/28R	Feb-50	New	Jan-67
528	FBL 30	Bristol	K6B	Eastern Coach Works	L27/28R	Feb-50	New	Jan-67
529	FBL 31	Bristol	K6B	Eastern Coach Works	L27/28R	Mar-50	New	Mar-67
530	FBL 32	Bristol	K6B	Eastern Coach Works	L27/28R	Apr-50	New	Nov-66
531	FBL 33	Bristol	K6B	Eastern Coach Works	L27/28R	Apr-50	New	Mar-67
532	FMO 7	Bristol	K6B	Eastern Coach Works	L27/28R	Apr-50	New	May-67
533	FMO 8	Bristol	K6B	Eastern Coach Works	L27/28R	Apr-50	New	May-67
534	FMO 9	Bristol	L6B	Eastern Coach Works	B35R	Dec-49	New	Mar-60
535	FMO 10	Bristol	L6B	Eastern Coach Works	B35R	Jan-50	New	Mar-60
536	FMO 11	Bristol	L6B	Eastern Coach Works	B35R	Feb-50	New	Mar-60
537	FMO 12	Bristol	L6B	Eastern Coach Works	B35R	Mar-50	New	Mar-60
538	FMO 13	Bristol	L6B	Eastern Coach Works	B35R	Mar-50	New	Mar-60
539	FMO 14	Bristol	L6B	Eastern Coach Works	B35R	Mar-50	New	Sep-60
540	FMO 15	Bristol	L6B	Eastern Coach Works	B35R	May-50	New	May-60
541	FMO 16	Bristol	L6B	Eastern Coach Works	B35R	May-50	New	Sep-60
542	FMO 17	Bristol	L6B	Eastern Coach Works	B35R	May-50	New	May-60
543	FMO 18	Bristol	L6B	Eastern Coach Works	B35R	May-50	New	Mar-60
544	FMO 19	Bristol	L6B	Eastern Coach Works	B35R	Jun-50	New	Mar-60
545	FMO 20	Bristol	L6B	Windover	C33F	Mar-50	New	Nov-60
546	FMO 21	Bristol	L6B	Windover	C33F	Mar-50	New	See 817

Fleet No.	Reg. No.	Chassis Make	Chassis Type	Bodybuilder	Body Type	Date New	Date Acq.	Date Out
547	FMO 22	Bristol	L6B	Windover	C33F	Mar-50	New	See 818
548	FMO 23	Bristol	L6B	Windover	C33F	Mar-50	New	See 819
549	FMO 24	Bristol	L6B	Windover	C33F	Mar-50	New	See 820
550	FMO 25	Bristol	L6B	Windover	C33F	Jun-50	New	Nov-60
551	FMO 26	Bristol	L6B	Windover	C33F	Jun-50	New	Nov-60
552	FMO 934	Bristol	L6B	Windover	C33F	Jun-50	New	Nov-60
553	FMO 935	Bristol	L6B	Windover	C33F	Jul-50	New	Nov-60
554	FMO 936	Bristol	L6B	Windover	C33F	Jul-50	New	Nov-60
555	FMO 937	Bristol	L6B	Windover	C33F	Jul-50	New	Oct-61
39	LWL 996	AEC	Regal 0662	Duple	C35F	May-47	Jan-50	Jul-58
40	LWL 997	AEC	Regal 0662	Duple	C35F	May-47	Jan-50	Jul-58
41	LWL 998	AEC	Regal 0662	Duple	C35F	May-47	Jan-50	Oct-58
42	LWL 999	AEC	Regal 0662	Duple	C35F	May-47	Jan-50	Jul-58
45	LJO 758	AEC	Regal 0662	Duple	C35F	Aug-47	Jan-50	Oct-57
46	LJO 759	AEC	Regal 0662	Duple	C35F	Aug-47	Jan-50	Oct-58
47	LJO 760	AEC	Regal 0662	Duple	C35F	Aug-47	Jan-50	Oct-58
48	LJO 761	AEC	Regal 0662	Duple	C35F	Jan-48	Jan-50	Oct-57
49	MWL 741	AEC	Regal 0662	Duple	C35F	Jan-48	Jan-50	Oct-58
50	MWL 742	AEC	Regal 0662	Duple	C35F	Jan-48	Jan-50	Oct-58
51	MWL 743	AEC	Regal 0662	Duple	C35F	Jan-48	Jan-50	Aug-58
52	MWL 744	AEC	Regal 0662	Duple	C35F	Jan-48	Jan-50	Oct-57
53	MJO 278	AEC	Regal 0662	Duple	C35F	Jan-48	Jan-50	Dec-58
54	MJO 664	AEC	Regal III	Duple	C35F	Mar-48	Jan-50	Dec-58
55	MJO 665	AEC	Regal III	Duple	C35F	Apr-48	Jan-50	Dec-58
56	MJO 667	AEC	Regal III	Duple	C35F	Apr-48	Jan-50	Nov-59
57	NFC 128	AEC	Regal III	Duple	C35F	Sep-48	Jan-50	Nov-59
58	NFC 129	AEC	Regal III	Duple	C35F	May-49	Jan-50	Nov-59
59	NFC 130	AEC	Regal III	Duple	C35F	May-49	Jan-50	Nov-59
60	NWL 877	AEC	Regal III	Duple	C30F	Jun-49	Jan-50	Dec-58
61	NWL 878	AEC	Regal III	Duple	C33F	Jun-49	Jan-50	Jan-59
62	NWL 879	AEC	Regal III	Duple	C30F	Jun-49	Jan-50	Oct-57
63	NJO 217	AEC	Regal III	Duple	C33F	Jul-49	Jan-50	Jan-59
64	NJO 218	AEC	Regal III	Duple	C33F	Jul-49	Jan-50	Jan-59
65	OFC 204	AEC	Regal III	Duple	C30F	Mar-50	Jan-50	Jan-59
66	OFC 205	AEC	Regal III	Duple	C32F	Mar-50	Jan-50	Jan-59
67	OFC 206	AEC	Regal III	Duple	C32F	Mar-50	Jan-50	Jan-59
68	EJB 649	AEC	Regal III	Duple	C35F	Sep-48	Jan-50	Oct-59
69	EJB 650	AEC	Regal III	Duple	C35F	Sep-48	Jan-50	Jul-58
70	ERX 937	AEC	Regal III	Duple	C35F	Jul-49	Jan-50	Feb-60

These AEC coaches were acquired with South Midland Motor Services Ltd. of Oxford, 68-70 formerly Newbury & District MS

Fleet No.	Reg. No.	Chassis Make	Chassis Type	Bodybuilder	Body Type	Date New	Date Acq.	Date Out
94	CMO 523	Bedford	OWB	Duple	UB30F	Nov-42	Jan-50	Oct-51
95	CMO 624	Bedford	OWB	Duple	UB30F	Jan-43	Jan-50	Oct-51
96	CMO 657	Bedford	OWB	Duple	UB30F	Feb-43	Jan-50	Oct-51
99/H1	CRX 279	Guy	Arab II 5LW	Park Royal	UH30/26R	Nov-44	Jan-50	Jul-56
100/H2	CRX 280	Guy	Arab II 5LW	Park Royal	UH30/26R	Nov-44	Jan-50	Jun-56
101/H3	CRX 281	Guy	Arab II 5LW	Park Royal	UH30/26R	Oct-44	Jan-50	Jun-55
102/H4	CRX 282	Guy	Arab II 5LW	Park Royal	UH30/26R	Oct-44	Jan-50	May-56
103/H5	CRX 283	Guy	Arab II 5LW	Park Royal	UH30/26R	Nov-44	Jan-50	May-56
104/H6	FAD 253	Guy	Arab II 5LW	Park Royal	UH30/26R	Mar-44	Jan-50	Jun-56
105/H7	CRX 595	Guy	Arab II 5LW	Massey	UH30/26R	Sep-45	Jan-50	Jun-56
106/H8	CRX 596	Guy	Arab II 5LW	Massey	UH30/26R	Sep-45	Jan-50	Jun-57

94-6 and 100-106 were acquired with Newbury & District Motor Services Ltd. of Newbury, 104 formerly Cheltenham Distrct

Fleet No.	Reg. No.	Chassis Make	Chassis Type	Bodybuilder	Body Type	Date New	Date Acq.	Date Out
121	FS 8582	AEC Regal	0642 5LW	ECOC	B35R	Jul-34	Jan-50	Oct-51
122	FS 8560	AEC Regal	0642 5LW	ECOC	B35R	Jun-34	Jan-50	Mar-51
123	FS 8562	AEC Regal	0642 5LW	ECOC	B35R	Jul-34	Jan-50	Feb-51
124	FS 8567	AEC Regal	0642 5LW	ECOC	B35R	Jun-34	Jan-50	Mar-51
125	FS 8576	AEC Regal	0642 5LW	ECOC	B35R	Jul-34	Jan-50	Mar-51
126	FS 8572	AEC Regal	0642 5LW	ECOC	B35R	Jul-34	Jan-50	Mar-51
127	FS 8566	AEC Regal	0642 5LW	ECOC	B35R	Jun-34	Jan-50	Mar-51
128	FS 8574	AEC Regal	0642 5LW	ECOC	B35R	Jul-34	Jan-50	Mar-51
129	FS 8575	AEC Regal	0642 5LW	ECOC	B35R	Jul-34	Jan-50	Mar-51
130	FS 8565	AEC Regal	0642 5LW	ECOC	B35R	Jun-34	Jan-50	Mar-51

These AEC buses were acquired with N&D, but were originally Scottish MT, bodies originally from North Western RCC

Fleet No.	Reg. No.	Chassis Make	Chassis Type	Bodybuilder	Body Type	Date New	Date Acq.	Date Out
131	DMO 320	AEC	Regal 0662	Duple	B35R	Apr-47	Jan-50	Dec-60
132	DMO 321	AEC	Regal 0662	Duple	B35R	Apr-47	Jan-50	Dec-60
133	DMO 322	AEC	Regal 0662	Duple	B35R	Apr-47	Jan-50	Sep-60
134	DMO 323	AEC	Regal 0662	Duple	B35R	Apr-47	Jan-50	Dec-60
135	DMO 324	AEC	Regal 0662	Duple	B35R	Apr-47	Jan-50	Jul-58
136	DMO 325	AEC	Regal 0662	Duple	B35R	Apr-47	Jan-50	Jul-58

Fleet No.	Reg. No.	Chassis Make	Chassis Type	Bodybuilder	Body Type	Date New	Date Acq.	Date Out
137	DMO 326	AEC	Regal 0662	Duple	B35R	Apr-47	Jan-50	Dec-60
138	DMO 327	AEC	Regal 0662	Duple	B35R	Apr-47	Jan-50	Jul-58
139	DMO 328	AEC	Regal 0662	Duple	B35R	Apr-47	Jan-50	Aug-60
140	DMO 329	AEC	Regal 0662	Duple	B35R	Apr-47	Jan-50	Jul-58
141	DMO 330	AEC	Regal 0662	Duple	C35F	Aug-47	Jan-50	Dec-58
142	DMO 331	AEC	Regal 0662	Duple	C35F	Oct-47	Jan-50	Oct-57
143	DMO 332	AEC	Regal 0662	Duple	C35F	Oct-47	Jan-50	Jan-59
144	DMO 333	AEC	Regal 0662	Duple	C35F	Oct-47	Jan-50	Dec-58
145	EBL 736	AEC	Regal 0662	Duple	C35F	Nov-47	Jan-50	Jan-59
146	EJB 146	AEC	Regal III	Duple	C35F	Mar-48	Jan-50	Jan-59
147	EJB 147	AEC	Regal III	Duple	C35F	Mar-48	Jan-50	Jan-59
148	EJB 148	AEC	Regal III	Duple	C35F	Mar-48	Jan-50	Jan-59
151	EJB 521	AEC	Regent III	Lydney	H30/26R	Mar-48	Jan-50	Jan-51
These vehicles were acquired with Newbury & District M. S. Ltd., 151 was later transferred to Venture in exchange for Guys								
152	AGJ 929	AEC	Regal 0662	ECOC	B32R	Apr-33	Jan-50	Jan-52
153	AGX 455	AEC	Regal 0662	Burlingham	UB34F	Apr-33	Jan-50	Oct-51
154	TG 1819	AEC	Regal 0662	Burlingham	UB34F	Jun-31	Jan-50	Oct-51
155	AGP 841	AEC	Regal 0662	Burlingham	UB34F	Apr-33	Jan-50	Oct-51
157	FAX 349	AEC	Regal 0662	Burlingham	UB34F	circa-30	Jan-50	Oct-53
These AEC's were acquired with N&D, all being secondhand rebuilds through Red & White								
160/H9	EWO 484	Guy	Arab I 5LW	Lydney	H30/26R	Jun-43	Jan-50	Jun-57
This Guy was acquired with N&D, but was originally a Red & White vehicle which was rebodied before transfer								
161	FBL 919	AEC	Regal 6821A	Lydney	B35F	Feb-50	New	Nov-59
162	FBL 920	AEC	Regal 6821A	Lydney	B35F	Feb-50	New	Nov-59
163	FBL 921	AEC	Regal 6821A	Lydney	B35F	Mar-50	New	Nov-59
These AEC buses had been ordered for Newbury & District Motor Services Ltd. and delivered as shown								
164	LJO 756	Bedford	OB	Duple	C29F	Jul-47	Jan-50	Dec-56
165	LJO 757	Bedford	OB	Duple	C29F	Mar-48	Jan-50	Dec-56
166	CWL 953	Leyland	Tiger TS7	Harrington	C32F	Apr-36	Jan-50	c.Mar-51
167	BWL 349	Leyland	Tiger TS7	Harrington	C32F	May-35	Jan-50	c.Mar-51
168	CWL 951	Leyland	Tiger TS7	Harrington	C32F	Apr-38	Jan-50	c.Mar-51
169	LWL 995	Leyland	Tiger PS1	ECOC (new 1936)	DP31R	Feb-47	Jan-50	Jul-60
These vehicles were acquired with N&D, but were all originally South Midland Motor Services Ltd.								
170	FMO 515	Guy	Arab 111 5LW	Duple	L27/27RD	Feb-50	New	Apr-68
171	FMO 516	Guy	Arab 111 5LW	Duple	L27/27RD	Feb-50	New	Apr-68
These Guy buses were ordered for Newbury & District Motor Services Ltd. and delivered as shown								
172/H10	FMO 517	Guy	Arab 111 6LW	Duple	H31/26R	May-50	New	Mar-68
This Guy bus was ordered for Venture, Basingstoke, but diverted to Newbury, for the rest of the batch see 175-8 below								
173/H11	EWO 490	Guy	Arab II 5LW	Park Royal (new 1950)	H30/26R	Jul-43	Jan-51	Oct-55
174/H12	EWO 492	Guy	Arab II 5LW	Park Royal (new 1950)	H30/26R	Jul-43	Jan-51	Oct-55
These Guys were originally Red & White, rebodied before transfer to Venture, then to Newbury for standardisation								
175/H13	HOT 391	Guy	Arab 111 6LW	Duple	H31/26R	Apr-50	Jan-51	Mar-68
176/H14	HOT 392	Guy	Arab 111 6LW	Duple	H31/26R	Apr-50	Jan-51	Apr-68
177/H15	HOT 393	Guy	Arab 111 6LW	Duple	H31/26R	Apr-50	Jan-51	Mar-68
178/H16	HOT 394	Guy	Arab 111 6LW	Duple	H31/26R	Apr-50	Jan-51	Mar-68
These Guys were acquired with N&D, but were originally Venture of Basingstoke, transferred for standardistion								
556	FMO 938	Bristol	LL6B	Eastern Coach Works	B39R	Aug-50	New	Sep-60
557	FMO 939	Bristol	LL6B	Eastern Coach Works	B39R	Aug-50	New	Sep-60
558	FMO 940	Bristol	LL6B	Eastern Coach Works	B39R	Aug-50	New	Sep-60
559	FMO 941	Bristol	LL6B	Eastern Coach Works	B39R	Aug-50	New	Mar-67
560	FMO 942	Bristol	LL6B	Eastern Coach Works	B39R	Nov-50	New	Apr-68
561	FMO 943	Bristol	LL6B	Eastern Coach Works	B39R	Nov-50	New	Sep-60
562	FMO 944	Bristol	LL6B	Eastern Coach Works	B39R	Nov-50	New	Dec-60
563	FMO 945	Bristol	LL6B	Eastern Coach Works	B39R	Nov-50	New	Dec-60
564	FMO 946	Bristol	LL6B	Eastern Coach Works	B39R	Nov-50	New	May-67
565	FMO 947	Bristol	LL6B	Eastern Coach Works	B39R	Dec-50	New	Aug-68
566	FMO 948	Bristol	LL6B	Eastern Coach Works	B39R	Dec-50	New	Jun-68
567	FMO 949	Bristol	LL6B	Eastern Coach Works	B39R	Dec-50	New	Aug-68
568	FMO 950	Bristol	LL6B	Eastern Coach Works	B39R	Dec-50	New	Aug-68
569	FMO 951	Bristol	LL6B	Eastern Coach Works	B39R	Dec-50	New	May-68
570	FMO 952	Bristol	LL6B	Eastern Coach Works	B39R	Jan-51	New	Oct-61
571	FMO 953	Bristol	LL6B	Eastern Coach Works	B39R	Jan-51	New	Dec-67
572	FMO 954	Bristol	LL6B	Eastern Coach Works	B39R	Feb-51	New	Jan-61
573	FMO 955	Bristol	LL6B	Eastern Coach Works	B39R	Jan-51	New	Oct-61
574	FMO 956	Bristol	LL6B	Eastern Coach Works	B39R	Jan-51	New	Aug-68
575	FMO 957	Bristol	LL6B	Eastern Coach Works	B39R	Jan-51	New	Oct-61
576	FMO 958	Bristol	LL6B	Eastern Coach Works	B39R	Feb-51	New	Oct-61
C5000	LHY 949	Bristol	LDX6G	Eastern Coach Works	LD33/35R	Oct-49	Mar-51	Mar-51
This bus was on demonstration from BCV and was in the BT&CC fleet, being used from 3rd-9th March on Route 2								

Fleet No.	Reg. No.	Chassis Make	Chassis Type	Bodybuilder	Body Type	Date New	Date Acq.	Date Out
577	FMO 959	Bristol	LWL6B	Eastern Coach Works	B39R	Mar-51	New	Apr-62
578	FMO 960	Bristol	LWL6B	Eastern Coach Works	B39R	Mar-51	New	Apr-62
579	FMO 961	Bristol	LWL6B	Eastern Coach Works	B39R	Mar-51	New	Apr-62
580	FMO 962	Bristol	LWL6B	Eastern Coach Works	B39R	Mar-51	New	Apr-62
581	FMO 963	Bristol	LWL6B	Eastern Coach Works	B39R	Mar-51	New	Feb-62
582	FMO 964	Bristol	LWL6B	Eastern Coach Works	B39R	Mar-51	New	Mar-66
583	FMO 965	Bristol	LWL6B	Eastern Coach Works	B39R	Mar-51	New	Apr-62
584	FMO 966	Bristol	LWL6B	Eastern Coach Works	B39R	Mar-51	New	Sep-62
585	FMO 967	Bristol	LWL6B	Eastern Coach Works	B39R	Mar-51	New	Feb-62
586	FMO 968	Bristol	KS6B	Eastern Coach Works	L27/28R	Aug-50	New	Mar-68
587	FMO 969	Bristol	KS6B	Eastern Coach Works	L27/28R	Sep-50	New	Sep-68
588	FMO 970	Bristol	KS6B	Eastern Coach Works	L27/28R	Sep-50	New	Jul-68
589	FMO 971	Bristol	KS6B	Eastern Coach Works	L27/28R	Nov-50	New	May-68
590	FMO 972	Bristol	KS6B	Eastern Coach Works	L27/28R	Nov-50	New	Aug-68
591	FMO 973	Bristol	KS6B	Eastern Coach Works	L27/28R	Nov-50	New	Dec-67
592	FMO 974	Bristol	KS6B	Eastern Coach Works	L27/28R	Nov-50	New	Aug-68
593	FMO 975	Bristol	KS6B	Eastern Coach Works	L27/28R	Nov-50	New	Aug-68
594	FMO 976	Bristol	KS6B	Eastern Coach Works	L27/28R	Nov-50	New	Oct-68
595	FMO 977	Bristol	KS6B	Eastern Coach Works	CL27/26RD	Jan-51	New	Dec-68
596	FMO 978	Bristol	KS6B	Eastern Coach Works	CL27/26RD	Jan-51	New	Apr-69
597	FMO 979	Bristol	KS6B	Eastern Coach Works	CL27/26RD	Jan-51	New	Oct-68
598	FMO 980	Bristol	KS6B	Eastern Coach Works	CL27/26RD	Jan-51	New	Apr-69
599	FMO 981	Bristol	KS6B	Eastern Coach Works	CL27/26RD	Jan-51	New	Feb-69
600	FMO 982	Bristol	KS6B	Eastern Coach Works	CL27/26RD	Jan-51	New	Oct-68
601	FMO 983	Bristol	KSW6B	Eastern Coach Works	L27/28R	Dec-50	New	Apr-69
602	FMO 984	Bristol	KSW6B	Eastern Coach Works	L27/28R	Dec-50	New	Sep-69
603	FMO 985	Bristol	KSW6B	Eastern Coach Works	L27/28R	Dec-50	New	Oct-68
604	FRX 313	Bedford	OB petrol	Duple	C29F	Jun-50	New	Dec-56
605	FRX 314	Bedford	OB petrol	Duple	C29F	Jul-50	New	Dec-56
606	FRX 315	Bedford	OB petrol	Duple	C29F	Jul-50	New	Dec-56
None	JB 7289	Bedford	WLB	Duple	C20F	Oct-35	Jun-51	Jun-51
None	JB 9860	Bedford	WTB	Duple	B26F	Aug-36	Jun-51	Jun-51
None	BJB 580	Bedford	WTB	Duple	C20F	Oct-38	Jun-51	Jun-51
None	CRX 333	Bedford	OWB	Duple	UB26F	Jan-45	Jun-51	Jun-51
None	EBL 967	Bedford	OB	Mulliner	B26F	Dec-47	Jun-51	Jun-51

These Bedford vehicles were acquired with Crescent Coaches, Windsor, all were re-sold without being used

Fleet No.	Reg. No.	Chassis Make	Chassis Type	Bodybuilder	Body Type	Date New	Date Acq.	Date Out
607	GBL 871	Bristol	LWL6B	Eastern Coach Works	FC35F	Jul-51	New	Dec-63
608	GBL 872	Bristol	LWL6B	Eastern Coach Works	FC35F	Jul-51	New	Apr-64
609	GBL 873	Bristol	LWL6B	Eastern Coach Works	FC35F	Aug-51	New	May-64
610	GBL 874	Bristol	LWL6B	Eastern Coach Works	FC35F	Aug-51	New	Apr-64
611	GBL 875	Bristol	LWL6B	Eastern Coach Works	FC35F	Aug-51	New	Dec-63
612	GBL 876	Bristol	LWL6B	Eastern Coach Works	FC35F	Aug-51	New	May-62
613	GJB 251	Bristol	LWL6B	Eastern Coach Works	B39R	Oct-51	New	Mar-68
614	GJB 252	Bristol	LWL6B	Eastern Coach Works	B39R	Oct-51	New	Aug-64
615	GJB 253	Bristol	LWL6B	Eastern Coach Works	B39R	Jan-52	New	Aug-68
616	GJB 254	Bristol	LWL6B	Eastern Coach Works	B39R	Jan-52	New	Apr-69

Car 616 ceased PSV duties July 1965, serving as an Enquiry Office at Maidenhead, then as a driver training vehicle

Fleet No.	Reg. No.	Chassis Make	Chassis Type	Bodybuilder	Body Type	Date New	Date Acq.	Date Out
617	GJB 255	Bristol	LWL6B	Eastern Coach Works	B39R	Jan-52	New	Feb-65
618	GJB 256	Bristol	LWL6B	Eastern Coach Works	B39R	Jan-52	New	Feb-65
619	GJB 257	Bristol	LWL6B	Eastern Coach Works	B39R	Jan-52	New	Jul-66
620	GJB 258	Bristol	LWL6B	Eastern Coach Works	B39R	Jan-52	New	Dec-68
621/259	GJB 259	Bristol	LWL6B	Eastern Coach Works	B39R	Jan-52	New	May-70
622	GJB 260	Bristol	LWL6B	Eastern Coach Works	B39R	Feb-52	New	Mar-65
623	GJB 261	Bristol	LWL6B	Eastern Coach Works	B39R	Feb-52	New	May-64
624	GJB 262	Bristol	LWL6B	Eastern Coach Works	B39R	Feb-52	New	Apr-68
625/263	GJB 263	Bristol	LWL6B	Eastern Coach Works	B39R	Feb-52	New	Jun-70
626	GJB 264	Bristol	LWL6B	Eastern Coach Works	B39R	Feb-52	New	Mar-68
627/265	GJB 265	Bristol	LWL6B	Eastern Coach Works	B39R	Feb-52	New	Feb-71
628	GJB 266	Bristol	LWL6B	Eastern Coach Works	B39R	Mar-52	New	Nov-68
629/267	GJB 267	Bristol	LWL6B	Eastern Coach Works	B39R	Apr-52	New	Jun-70
630	GJB 268	Bristol	LWL6B	Eastern Coach Works	B39R	Mar-52	New	Dec-68
631/269	GJB 269	Bristol	LWL6B	Eastern Coach Works	B39R	Mar-52	New	May-70
632	GJB 270	Bristol	LWL6B	Eastern Coach Works	B39R	Apr-52	New	Oct-68
633	GJB 271	Bristol	LWL6B	Eastern Coach Works	B39R	Apr-52	New	Nov-68
634	GJB 272	Bristol	KSW6B	Eastern Coach Works	L27/28R	Jun-51	New	Dec-68
635	GJB 273	Bristol	KSW6B	Eastern Coach Works	L27/28R	Jul-51	New	Mar-69
636	GJB 274	Bristol	KSW6B	Eastern Coach Works	L27/28R	Jul-51	New	Mar-69
637	GJB 275	Bristol	KSW6B	Eastern Coach Works	CL27/26RD	Oct-51	New	Sep-69
638	GJB 276	Bristol	KSW6B	Eastern Coach Works	CL27/26RD	Oct-51	New	Apr-69

Fleet No.	Reg. No.	Chassis Make	Chassis Type	Bodybuilder	Body Type	Date New	Date Acq.	Date Out
639	GJB 277	Bristol	KSW6B	Eastern Coach Works	CL27/26RD	Oct-51	New	Apr-69
640	GJB 278	Bristol	KSW6B	Eastern Coach Works	L27/28R	Oct-51	New	Apr-69
641	GJB 279	Bristol	KSW6B	Eastern Coach Works	L27/28R	Oct-51	New	May-69
642	GJB 280	Bristol	KSW6B	Eastern Coach Works	L27/28R	Oct-51	New	May-69
643	GJB 281	Bristol	KSW6B	Eastern Coach Works	L27/28R	Nov-51	New	May-69
644	GJB 282	Bristol	KSW6B	Eastern Coach Works	L27/28R	Nov-51	New	May-69
645	GJB 283	Bristol	KSW6B	Eastern Coach Works	L27/28R	Nov-51	New	Apr-69
646	GJB 284	Bristol	KSW6B	Eastern Coach Works	L27/28R	Nov-51	New	Apr-69
647	GJB 285	Bristol	KSW6B	Eastern Coach Works	L27/28R	Nov-51	New	May-69
648	GJB 286	Bristol	KSW6B	Eastern Coach Works	L27/28R	Jan-52	New	Nov-69
649	GJB 287	Bristol	KSW6B	Eastern Coach Works	L27/28R	Jan-52	New	May-69
650	GJB 288	Bristol	KSW6B	Eastern Coach Works	L27/28R	Jan-52	New	Mar-70
79	SFC 565	Bristol	LS6G	Eastern Coach Works	C37F	Jun-52	New	Sep-65
80	SFC 566	Bristol	LS6G	Eastern Coach Works	C37F	Jun-52	New	Sep-65
81	SFC 567	Bristol	LS6G	Eastern Coach Works	C37F	Jun-52	New	Sep-65
82	SFC 568	Bristol	LS6G	Eastern Coach Works	C37F	Oct-52	New	Sep-65
83	SFC 569	Bristol	LS6G	Eastern Coach Works	C37F	Oct-52	New	Sep-65
84	SFC 570	Bristol	LS6G	Eastern Coach Works	C37F	Oct-52	New	Oct-61
85	SFC 571	AEC	Regal IV	Eastern Coach Works	C37F	Aug-52	New	Oct-67
71	EBD 234	Bristol	L6B	Eastern Coach Works	DP31R	Aug-48	May-52	Oct-59
72	EBD 235	Bristol	L6B	Eastern Coach Works	DP31R	Sep-48	May-52	Nov-59
73	EBD 236	Bristol	L6B	Eastern Coach Works	FC31F	May-50	May-52	Oct-61
74	EBD 237	Bristol	L6B	Eastern Coach Works	FC31F	May-50	May-52	Nov-60
75	FRP 832	Bristol	LL6B	Eastern Coach Works	FC37F8	Feb-51	May-52	Dec-62
76	FRP 833	Bristol	LL6B	Eastern Coach Works	FC37F8	Feb-51	May-52	May-63
77	FRP 834	Bristol	LL6B	Eastern Coach Works	FC37F8	Feb-51	May-52	Aug-63
78	FRP 836	Bristol	LL6B	Eastern Coach Works	FC37F8	Feb-51	May-52	Mar-63
These vehicles were acquired by South Midland from United Counties Omnibus Co. Ltd.								
UC.951	JWO 213	Leyland Royal	Tiger PSU1/13	Lydney	C41F	Apr-52	May-52	Nov-52
UC.2051	JWO 546	Leyland Royal	Tiger PSU1/13	Lydney	C41F	Apr-52	May-52	Nov-52
These coaches were loaned by Red & White to cover for the delayed Guy Arab UF coachesand were operated from Oxford								
651	HBL 53	Bristol	KSW6B	Eastern Coach Works	L27/28R	Jul-52	New	Mar-70
652	HBL 54	Bristol	KSW6B	Eastern Coach Works	L27/28R	Jul-52	New	Mar-70
653	HBL 55	Bristol	KSW6B	Eastern Coach Works	L27/28R	Aug-52	New	Nov-69
654	HBL 56	Bristol	KSW6B	Eastern Coach Works	L27/28R	Sep-52	New	Jul-70
655	HBL 57	Bristol	KSW6B	Eastern Coach Works	L27/28R	Sep-52	New	Jul-70
656	HBL 58	Bristol	KSW6B	Eastern Coach Works	L27/28R	Sep-52	New	Nov-69
657	HBL 59	Bristol	KSW6B	Eastern Coach Works	L27/28R	Sep-52	New	May-70
658	HBL 60	Bristol	KSW6B	Eastern Coach Works	L27/28R	Sep-52	New	Jun-70
659	HBL 61	Bristol	KSW6B	Eastern Coach Works	L27/28R	Nov-52	New	Sep-69
660	HBL 62	Bristol	KSW6B	Eastern Coach Works	L27/28R	Nov-52	New	Sep-69
661	HBL 63	Bristol	KSW6B	Eastern Coach Works	L27/28R	Nov-52	New	Sep-69
662	HBL 64	Bristol	KSW6B	Eastern Coach Works	L27/28R	Nov-52	New	Jun-70
663	HBL 65	Bristol	KSW6B	Eastern Coach Works	L27/28R	Jan-53	New	Nov-70
664	HBL 66	Bristol	KSW6B	Eastern Coach Works	L27/28R	May-53	New	Jul-70
665	HBL 67	Bristol	KSW6B	Eastern Coach Works	L27/28R	May-53	New	Feb-71
666	HBL 68	Bristol	KSW6B	Eastern Coach Works	L27/28R	May-53	New	Feb-71
667	HBL 69	Bristol	KSW6B	Eastern Coach Works	L27/28R	Jun-53	New	Apr-71
668	HBL 70	Bristol	KSW6B	Eastern Coach Works	L27/28R	Jun-53	New	Dec-70
669	HBL 71	Bristol	KSW6B	Eastern Coach Works	L27/28R	Jun-53	New	May-70
670	HBL 72	Bristol	KSW6B	Eastern Coach Works	L27/28R	Jun-53	New	Dec-70
671	HBL 73	Bristol	LS6G	Eastern Coach Works	C39F	Jun-52	New	Oct-67
672	HBL 74	Bristol	LS6G	Eastern Coach Works	C39F	Jul-52	New	Aug-66
673	HBL 75	Bristol	LS6G	Eastern Coach Works	C39F	Jul-52	New	Oct-65
674	HBL 76	Bristol	LS6G	Eastern Coach Works	C39F	Sep-52	New	Nov-66
675	HBL 77	Bristol	LS6G	Eastern Coach Works	C39F	Sep-52	New	Oct-67
676	HBL 78	Bristol	LS6G	Eastern Coach Works	C39F	Sep-52	New	Jul-68
677/100	HBL 79	Bristol	LS6G	Eastern Coach Works	B45F	Nov-52	New	Jul-71
678/101	HBL 80	Bristol	LS6G	Eastern Coach Works	B45F	Nov-52	New	Sep-71
679/102	HBL 81	Bristol	LS6G	Eastern Coach Works	B45F	Jan-53	New	Aug-71
680	HBL 82	Bristol	LS6G	Eastern Coach Works	B45F	Mar-53	New	Mar-69
681/103	HBL 83	Bristol	LS6G	Eastern Coach Works	B45F	Feb-53	New	To AV 201
682/104	HBL 84	Bristol	LS6G	Eastern Coach Works	B45F	Mar-53	New	To AV 202
683/105	HBL 85	Bristol	LS6G	Eastern Coach Works	B45F	Apr-53	New	To AV 203
684/106	HBL 86	Bristol	LS6G	Eastern Coach Works	B45F	May-53	New	Mar-71
685/107	HBL 87	Bristol	LS6G	Eastern Coach Works	B45F	May-53	New	To AV 204
686	HBL 88	Bristol	LS5G	Eastern Coach Works	B45F	Jun-53	New	Oct-68
687	HBL 89	Bristol	LS5G	Eastern Coach Works	B45F	Aug-53	New	Nov-68
86	SFC 501	Guy Arab	UF 6HLW	Lydney/BBW	C41C	Apr-53	New	Jul-60

Fleet No.	Reg. No.	Chassis Make	Chassis Type	Bodybuilder	Body Type	Date New	Date Acq.	Date Out
87	SFC 502	Guy Arab	UF 6HLW	Lydney/BBW	C41C	May-53	New	Jul-60
88	SFC 503	Guy Arab	UF 6HLW	Lydney/BBW	C41C	Mar-53	New	Jul-60
89	SFC 504	Guy Arab	UF 6HLW	Lydney/BBW	C41C	Apr-53	New	Jul-60
1863	OTT 2	Bristol	LD6B	Eastern Coach Works	LD33/25R	May-53	On loan	Jun-53
This 'Lodekka' was operated on trial from Ascot garage during June 1953 and came from Western National O. Co. Ltd.								
90	TWL 55	Bristol	LS6B	Eastern Coach Works	C37F	Jun-53	New	See S315
91	TWL 56	Bristol	LS6B	Eastern Coach Works	C37F	Jun-53	New	See S316
92	TWL 57	Bristol	LS6B	Eastern Coach Works	C37F	Jun-53	New	See S317
93	TWL 58	Bristol	LS6B	Eastern Coach Works	C37F	Jul-53	New	See S318
94	TWL 59	Bristol	LS6B	Eastern Coach Works	C37F	Aug-53	New	See S319
95	TWL 60	Bristol	LS6B	Eastern Coach Works	C37F	Oct-53	New	See S320
688	HMO 834	Bristol	LS6B	Eastern Coach Works	C39F	Oct-53	New	See S309
689	HMO 835	Bristol	LS6B	Eastern Coach Works	C39F	Oct-53	New	See S310
690	HMO 836	Bristol	LS6B	Eastern Coach Works	C39F	Oct-53	New	See S311
691	HMO 837	Bristol	LS6B	Eastern Coach Works	C39F	Feb-54	New	See S312
692	HMO 838	Bristol	LS6B	Eastern Coach Works	C39F	Feb-54	New	See S313
693	HMO 839	Bristol	LS6B	Eastern Coach Works	C39F	Feb-54	New	See S314
694	HMO 840	Bristol	KSW6B	Eastern Coach Works	L27/28R	Jul-53	New	Nov-70
695	HMO 841	Bristol	KSW6B	Eastern Coach Works	L27/28R	Jul-53	New	Jun-71
696	HMO 842	Bristol	KSW6B	Eastern Coach Works	L27/28R	Sep-53	New	May-71
697	HMO 843	Bristol	KSW6B	Eastern Coach Works	L27/28R	Sep-53	New	Aug-70
698	HMO 844	Bristol	KSW6B	Eastern Coach Works	L27/28R	Sep-53	New	Apr-71
699	HMO 845	Bristol	KSW6B	Eastern Coach Works	L27/28R	Oct-53	New	Dec-70
700	HMO 846	Bristol	KSW6B	Eastern Coach Works	L27/28R	Oct-53	New	Jun-70
701	HMO 847	Bristol	KSW6B	Eastern Coach Works	L27/28R	Oct-53	New	Apr-71
702	HMO 848	Bristol	KSW6B	Eastern Coach Works	L27/28R	Oct-53	New	Jan-71
703	HMO 849	Bristol	KSW6B	Eastern Coach Works	L27/28R	Dec-53	New	Dec-70
704	HMO 850	Bristol	KSW6B	Eastern Coach Works	L27/28R	Dec-53	New	Jan-71
705	HMO 851	Bristol	KSW6B	Eastern Coach Works	L27/28R	Jan-54	New	Mar-71
706/108	HMO 852	Bristol	LS5G	Eastern Coach Works	B45F	Oct-53	New	Mar-71
707/109	HMO 853	Bristol	LS5G	Eastern Coach Works	B45F	Oct-53	New	Nov-69
708/110	HMO 854	Bristol	LS5G	Eastern Coach Works	B45F	Nov-53	New	Feb-71
709/111	HMO 855	Bristol	LS5G	Eastern Coach Works	B45F	Dec-53	New	Feb-71
710	HMO 856	Bristol	LS6B	Eastern Coach Works	B45F	Nov-53	New	Nov-68
711/117	HMO 857	Bristol	LS6B	Eastern Coach Works	B45F	Jan-54	New	May-70
712/118	HMO 858	Bristol	LS6B	Eastern Coach Works	B45F	Jan-54	New	To AV 208
713/119	HMO 859	Bristol	LS6B	Eastern Coach Works	B45F	Jan-54	New	May-70
714/120	HMO 860	Bristol	LS6B	Eastern Coach Works	B45F	Jan-54	New	Jul-70
715	HMO 861	Bristol	LS6B	Eastern Coach Works	B45F	May-54	New	Dec-65
716	HMO 862	Bristol	LS6B	Eastern Coach Works	B45F	May-54	New	Mar-69
717/121	HMO 863	Bristol	LS6B	Eastern Coach Works	B45F	Jun-54	New	To AV 211
718/122	HMO 864	Bristol	LS6B	Eastern Coach Works	B45F	Jun-54	New	Sep-70
719/123	HMO 865	Bristol	LS6B	Eastern Coach Works	B45F	Nov-54	New	Jan-71
720/144	HMO 866	Bristol	LS6B	Eastern Coach Works	B45F	Nov-54	New	Nov-69
721/145	HMO 867	Bristol	LS6B	Eastern Coach Works	B45F	Nov-54	New	Nov-69
722/146	HMO 868	Bristol	LS6B	Eastern Coach Works	B45F	Dec-54	New	To AV 227
723	HMO 869	Bristol	LS6B	Eastern Coach Works	B45F	Jun-55	New	Nov-68
724/147	HMO 870	Bristol	LS6B	Eastern Coach Works	B45F	Jun-55	New	To AV 228
725	HMO 871	Bristol	LS6B	Eastern Coach Works	B45F	Jun-55	New	Nov-68
726	JRX 801	Bristol	KSW6B	Eastern Coach Works	L27/28R	Aug-54	New	Jun-71
727	JRX 802	Bristol	KSW6B	Eastern Coach Works	L27/28R	Aug-54	New	Feb-71
728	JRX 803	Bristol	KSW6B	Eastern Coach Works	L27/28R	Sep-54	New	Feb-71
729	JRX 804	Bristol	KSW6B	Eastern Coach Works	L27/28R	Aug-54	New	Apr-71
730	JRX 805	Bristol	KSW6B	Eastern Coach Works	L27/28R	Sep-54	New	Apr-71
731	JRX 806	Bristol	KSW6B	Eastern Coach Works	L27/28R	Sep-54	New	Feb-71
732	JRX 807	Bristol	KSW6B	Eastern Coach Works	L27/28R	Sep-54	New	Feb-71
733	JRX 808	Bristol	KSW6B	Eastern Coach Works	L27/28R	Sep-54	New	To AV 27
734	JRX 809	Bristol	KSW6B	Eastern Coach Works	L27/28R	Sep-54	New	Mar-71
735	JRX 810	Bristol	KSW6B	Eastern Coach Works	L27/28R	Sep-54	New	Feb-71
736	JRX 811	Bristol	KSW6B	Eastern Coach Works	L27/28R	Sep-54	New	Feb-71
737	JRX 812	Bristol	KSW6B	Eastern Coach Works	L27/28R	Sep-54	New	Feb-71
738	JRX 813	Bristol	KSW6B	Eastern Coach Works	CL27/26RD	Sep-54	New	Oct-70
739	JRX 814	Bristol	KSW6B	Eastern Coach Works	CL27/26RD	Sep-54	New	Jun-71
740	JRX 815	Bristol	KSW6B	Eastern Coach Works	CL27/26RD	Sep-54	New	Jun-71
741	JRX 816	Bristol	KSW6B	Eastern Coach Works	CL27/26RD	Sep-54	New	Jul-71
742	JRX 817	Bristol	KSW6B	Eastern Coach Works	CL27/26RD	Sep-54	New	Mar-71
743	JRX 818	Bristol	KSW6B	Eastern Coach Works	CL27/26RD	Sep-54	New	Jul-71
744	JRX 819	Bristol	KSW6B	Eastern Coach Works	L27/28R	Oct-54	New	Feb-71
395	724 APU	Bristol	SC4LK	Eastern Coach Works	B35F	Oct-54	Jan-55	Jan-55

Fleet No.	Reg. No.	Chassis Make	Chassis Type	Bodybuilder	Body Type	Date New	Date Acq.	Date Out
745	JRX 820	Bristol	KSW6B	Eastern Coach Works	L27/28R	Sep-55	New	To AV 28
746	JRX 821	Bristol	KSW6B	Eastern Coach Works	L27/28R	Sep-55	New	Jun-71
747	JRX 822	Bristol	KSW6B	Eastern Coach Works	L27/28R	Sep-55	New	Apr-71
748	JRX 823	Bristol	KSW6B	Eastern Coach Works	L27/28R	Sep-55	New	To AV 29
749	JRX 824	Bristol	KSW6B	Eastern Coach Works	L27/28R	Sep-55	New	Jun-71
750	MBL 831	Bristol	LD6G	Eastern Coach Works	CLD31/25RD	May-56	New	To AV 523
751	MBL 832	Bristol	LD6G	Eastern Coach Works	CLD31/25RD	Mar-56	New	To AV 524
752	MBL 833	Bristol	LD6G	Eastern Coach Works	CLD31/25RD	Mar-56	New	To AV 525
753	MBL 834	Bristol	LD6G	Eastern Coach Works	CLD31/25RD	Mar-56	New	To AV 526
754	MBL 835	Bristol	LD6G	Eastern Coach Works	CLD31/25RD	Mar-56	New	To AV 527
755	MBL 836	Bristol	LD6B	Eastern Coach Works	LD33/27R	Mar-56	New	To AV 528
756	MBL 837	Bristol	LD6B	Eastern Coach Works	LD33/27R	Mar-56	New	To AV 529
757	MBL 838	Bristol	LD6B	Eastern Coach Works	LD33/27R	Mar-56	New	To AV 530
758	MBL 839	Bristol	LD6G	Eastern Coach Works	LD33/27R	May-56	New	To AV 531
759	MBL 840	Bristol	LD6G	Eastern Coach Works	LD33/27R	Jun-56	New	To AV 532
760	MBL 841	Bristol	LD6G	Eastern Coach Works	CLD31/25RD	Jun-56	New	To AV 533
761	MBL 842	Bristol	LD6G	Eastern Coach Works	CLD31/25RD	May-56	New	To AV 534
762	MBL 843	Bristol	LD6G	Eastern Coach Works	CLD31/25RD	Jun-56	New	To AV 535
763	MBL 844	Bristol	LD6G	Eastern Coach Works	CLD31/25RD	May-56	New	To AV 536
764	MBL 845	Bristol	LD6G	Eastern Coach Works	CLD31/25RD	Jun-56	New	To AV 537
765	MBL 846	Bristol	LD5G	Eastern Coach Works	LD33/27R	Jul-56	New	To AV 538
766	MBL 847	Bristol	LD5G	Eastern Coach Works	LD33/27R	Jul-56	New	To AV 539
767	MBL 848	Bristol	LD5G	Eastern Coach Works	LD33/27R	Jul-56	New	To AV 540
768	MBL 849	Bristol	LD5G	Eastern Coach Works	LD33/27R	Jul-56	New	To AV 541
769	MBL 850	Bristol	LD5G	Eastern Coach Works	LD33/27R	Jul-56	New	To AV 542
770	CAP 206	Bristol	K5G	Eastern Coach Works	OT30/26R	Aug-40	Jul-57	Jul-60
771	CAP 132	Bristol	K5G	Eastern Coach Works	OT30/26R	Jul-40	Apr-57	Jul-60
772	CAP 176	Bristol	K5G	Eastern Coach Works	OT30/26R	Aug-40	Apr-57	Jul-60
773	CAP 211	Bristol	K5G	Eastern Coach Works	OT30/26R	Sep-40	Apr-57	Jun-60
These buses were purchased from Brighton, Hove & District Omnibus Co. Ltd. for the open-top riverside route								
774/S301	NBL 731	Bristol	SC4LK	Eastern Coach Works	B35F	Dec-56	New	Dec-69
775/S302	NBL 732	Bristol	SC4LK	Eastern Coach Works	B35F	Dec-56	New	Dec-69
776/S303	NBL 733	Bristol	SC4LK	Eastern Coach Works	B35F	Dec-56	New	Dec-69
777/S304	NBL 734	Bristol	SC4LK	Eastern Coach Works	B35F	Jan-57	New	Nov-69
778	NBL 735	Bristol	SC4LK	Eastern Coach Works	B35F	Jan-57	New	Apr-63
779	NBL 736	Bristol	LDL6G	Eastern Coach Works	LD37/33R	Nov-57	New	To AV 548
780	NBL 737	Bristol	LD5G	Eastern Coach Works	LD33/27R	Jun-57	New	To AV 549
781	NBL 738	Bristol	LD5G	Eastern Coach Works	LD33/27R	Jun-57	New	To AV 550
782	NBL 739	Bristol	LD5G	Eastern Coach Works	LD33/27R	Aug-57	New	To AV 551
783	NBL 740	Bristol	LD5G	Eastern Coach Works	LD33/27R	Oct-57	New	To AV 552
784	NBL 741	Bristol	LD5G	Eastern Coach Works	LD33/27R	Nov-57	New	To AV 553
785	NBL 742	Bristol	LD5G	Eastern Coach Works	LD33/27R	Nov-57	New	To AV 554
786	NBL 743	Bristol	LD6G	Eastern Coach Works	LD33/27R	Dec-57	New	To AV 555
787	NBL 744	Bristol	LD6G	Eastern Coach Works	LD33/27R	Jan-58	New	To AV 556
788	NBL 745	Bristol	LD6G	Eastern Coach Works	LD33/27R	Jan-58	New	To AV 557
789	NBL 746	Bristol	LD5G	Eastern Coach Works	LD33/27R	Feb-58	New	To AV 558
790	NBL 747	Bristol	LD6G	Eastern Coach Works	LD33/27R	Feb-58	New	To AV 559
791	NBL 748	Bristol	LD5G	Eastern Coach Works	LD33/27R	Mar-58	New	To AV 560
792	NBL 749	Bristol	LD6G	Eastern Coach Works	LD33/27R	Sep-58	New	To AV 561
793	NBL 750	Bristol	LD6G	Eastern Coach Works	LD33/27R	Sep-58	New	To AV 562
794	DMO 664	Bristol	LL5G	Eastern Coach Works	FB39F	see 460	Aug-58	Mar-67
795	DMO 665	Bristol	LL5G	Eastern Coach Works	FB39F	see 461	Jun-58	Jan-67
796	DMO 666	Bristol	LL5G	Eastern Coach Works	FB39F	see 462	Jun-58	Aug-67
797	DMO 667	Bristol	LL5G	Eastern Coach Works	FB39F	see 463	Aug-58	Mar-67
798	DMO 668	Bristol	LL5G	Eastern Coach Works	FB39F	see 464	Aug-58	Nov-66
799	DMO 669	Bristol	LL5G	Eastern Coach Works	FB39F	see 465	Aug-58	Nov-66
800	ORX 631	Bristol	MW6G	Eastern Coach Works	C34F	Mar-58	New	See 159
801	ORX 632	Bristol	MW6G	Eastern Coach Works	C34F	Mar-58	New	See 160
802	ORX 633	Bristol	MW6G	Eastern Coach Works	C34F	Apr-58	New	See 161
803	ORX 634	Bristol	MW6G	Eastern Coach Works	C32F	Apr-58	New	See 162
804	PRX 930	Bristol	MW6G	Eastern Coach Works	C34F	Mar-59	New	See 163
805	PRX 931	Bristol	MW6G	Eastern Coach Works	C34F	Apr-59	New	See 164
806	PRX 932	Bristol	MW6G	Eastern Coach Works	C34F	Apr-59	New	See 166
807	PRX 933	Bristol	MW6G	Eastern Coach Works	C34F	Mar-59	New	See 165
808	PRX 926	Bristol	LD6G	Eastern Coach Works	LD33/27RD	Oct-58	New	To AV 563
809	PRX 927	Bristol	LD6G	Eastern Coach Works	LD33/27RD	Oct-58	New	To AV 564
810	PRX 928	Bristol	LD6B	Eastern Coach Works	LD33/27RD	Jan-59	New	To AV 565
811	PRX 929	Bristol	LD6B	Eastern Coach Works	LD33/27RD	Jan-59	New	To AV 566

Fleet No.	Reg. No.	Chassis Make	Chassis Type	Bodybuilder	Body Type	Date New	Date Acq.	Date Out
812	SMO 78	Bristol	LD6G	Eastern Coach Works	LD33/27RD	Jun-59	New	To AV 567
813	SMO 79	Bristol	LD6G	Eastern Coach Works	LD33/27RD	Jun-59	New	To AV 568
814	SMO 80	Bristol	LD6G	Eastern Coach Works	LD33/27RD	Jun-59	New	To AV 569
815	SMO 81	Bristol	LD6G	Eastern Coach Works	LD33/27RD	Jul-59	New	To AV 570
816	SMO 82	Bristol	LD6G	Eastern Coach Works	LD33/27RD	Jul-59	New	To AV 571
817	FMO 21	Bristol	LL5G	Eastern Coach Works	FB39F	see 546	Feb-59	Jul-68
818	FMO 22	Bristol	LL5G	Eastern Coach Works	FB39F	see 547	Feb-59	Jun-68
819	FMO 23	Bristol	LL5G	Eastern Coach Works	FB39F	see 548	Feb-59	May-68
820	FMO 24	Bristol	LL5G	Eastern Coach Works	FB39F	see 549	Feb-59	Mar-68
821	FRP 835	Bristol	LL6B	Eastern Coach Works	FC37F8	Feb-51	Jan-59	Oct-61
822	FRP 837	Bristol	LL6B	Eastern Coach Works	FC37F8	Feb-51	Jan-59	Mar-62
823	FRP 838	Bristol	LL6B	Eastern Coach Works	FC37F8	Mar-51	Jan-59	Jul-63
824	FRP 839	Bristol	LL6B	Eastern Coach Works	FC37F8	Feb-51	Jan-59	Mar-62
825	FRP 840	Bristol	LL6B	Eastern Coach Works	FC37F8	Mar-51	Jan-59	Jan-62
826	FRP 841	Bristol	LL6B	Eastern Coach Works	FC37F8	Feb-51	Jan-59	Oct-61
827	FRP 842	Bristol	LL6B	Eastern Coach Works	FC37F8	Feb-51	Jan-59	Mar-62
828	FRP 843	Bristol	LL6B	Eastern Coach Works	FC37F8	Feb-51	Jan-59	Oct-61
829	FRP 844	Bristol	LL6B	Eastern Coach Works	FC37F8	Feb-51	Jan-59	Oct-61
				Bristol LL6B coaches 821-9 were purchased from the United Counties Omnibus Co. Ltd				
436	KHU 624	Bristol	K6B	Eastern Coach Works	L27/28R	Sep-47	Jun-59	Jul-66
437	KHU 601	Bristol	K6B	Eastern Coach Works	L27/28R	Sep-47	Jun-59	Dec-63
438	HTT 980	Bristol	K6B	Eastern Coach Works	L27/28R	Oct-46	Jun-59	May-62
455	KHU 604	Bristol	K6B	Eastern Coach Works	L27/28R	Sep-47	Nov-59	Dec-63
456	KHW 633	Bristol	K6A	Eastern Coach Works	L27/28R	Nov-47	Nov-59	Mar-63
457	KHU 605	Bristol	K6A	Eastern Coach Works	L27/28R	Sep-47	Nov-59	Feb-65
458	KHU 606	Bristol	K6A	Eastern Coach Works	L27/28R	Sep-47	Nov-59	Apr-63
459	KHU 622	Bristol	K6A	Eastern Coach Works	L27/28R	Sep-47	Nov-59	Feb-65
				These 8 Bristol K's were purchased from the Bristol Omnibus Co. Ltd, 438 being a K5G when bought				
460	FPU 510	Bristol	K5G	Eastern Coach Works	L27/28R8 (51)	Nov-37	Nov-59	Oct-64
				Car 460 was withdrawn from PSV use in October 1964 and became the Tree Lopper/Route Servicing Vehicle ED53				
461	FPU 509	Bristol	K5G	Eastern Coach Works	L27/28R8 (52)	Nov-37	Nov-59	Jul-65
462	FPU 515	Bristol	K5G	Eastern Coach Works	L27/28R8 (52)	Nov-37	Nov-59	Jan-65
463	FPU 517	Bristol	K5G	Eastern Coach Works	L27/28R8 (51)	Nov-37	Nov-59	Feb-66
464	FPU 511	Bristol	K5G	Eastern Coach Works	L27/28R8 (51)	Nov-37	Jan-60	May-65
465	FPU 513	Bristol	K5G	Eastern Coach Works	L27/28R (47)	Nov-37	Jan-60	Oct-62
				These buses were purchased from United Counties O.C.Ltd., rebodied in the years shown in brackets				
472	JT 9354	Bristol	K5G	Eastern Coach Works	L27/28R (49)	May-38	Mar-60	Mar-64
473	JT 9355	Bristol	K5G	Eastern Coach Works	L27/28R (49)	Jul-38	Mar-60	Mar-64
474	JT 9360	Bristol	K5G	Eastern Coach Works	L27/28R (49)	Jul-38	Mar-60	Sep-64
475	FLJ 978	Bristol	K5G	Brush (bebuilt H&D)	L28/26R	Apr-42	Mar-60	Nov-64
				These buses were purchased from Hants & Dorset M.S. Ltd., some rebodied as shown in brackets				
476	GNO 688	Bristol	K5G	Eastern Coach Works	L27/28R (48)	Jul-38	Apr-60	Apr-63
477	GNO 698	Bristol	K5G	Eastern Coach Works	L27/28R (48)	Jul-38	Apr-60	Oct-62
				These buses were purchased from United Counties O.C.Ltd., rebodied in the years shown in brackets				
830	UJB 196	Bristol	MW6G	Eastern Coach Works	C34F	Mar-60	New	See 167
831	UJB 197	Bristol	MW6G	Eastern Coach Works	C34F	Mar-60	New	Jan-71
832	UJB 198	Bristol	MW6G	Eastern Coach Works	C34F	Mar-60	New	Jan-71
833	UJB 199	Bristol	MW6G	Eastern Coach Works	C34F	Apr-60	New	Jan-71
834	UJB 200	Bristol	FLF6B	Eastern Coach Works	CH37/28F	Jul-60	New	To AV 601
835	UJB 201	Bristol	FLF6G	Eastern Coach Works	CH37/28F	Nov-60	New	To AV 602
836	UJB 202	Bristol	FLF6G	Eastern Coach Works	CH37/28F	Nov-60	New	To AV 603
837	UJB 203	Bristol	FLF6G	Eastern Coach Works	CH37/28F	Nov-60	New	To AV 604
838	UJB 204	Bristol	FLF6G	Eastern Coach Works	CH37/28F	Nov-60	New	To AV 605
839	WJB 223	Bristol	FLF6G	Eastern Coach Works	H38/32F	Dec-60	New	To AV 606
840	WJB 224	Bristol	FLF6G	Eastern Coach Works	H38/32F	Dec-60	New	To AV 607
852/179	VJB 943	Bristol	MW6G	Eastern Coach Works	DP41F	Jul-60	New	To AV 251
853/180	VJB 944	Bristol	MW6G	Eastern Coach Works	DP41F	Aug-60	New	To AV 252
854/181	VJB 945	Bristol	MW6G	Eastern Coach Works	B41F	Nov-60	New	To AV 253
855/182	VJB 946	Bristol	MW6G	Eastern Coach Works	B41F	Nov-60	New	To AV 254
856/183	VJB 947	Bristol	MW6G	Eastern Coach Works	B41F	Dec-60	New	To AV 255
857/184	VJB 948	Bristol	MW6G	Eastern Coach Works	B41F	Dec-60	New	To AV 256

Notes: Seating capacities are shown for vehicles as they were new, or their configuration at 1946 if older vehicles. A number of vehicles were re-seated during their working lives, particularly coaches demoted from touring duties to express coach work, or saloons converted for one-man operation. These conversions are noted within the main text.

This Fleet List is largely compiled Thames Valley official records, plus some additional information from the PSV Circle. Any variance with imformation contained in previous volumes should be regarded as corrected information.

F. No.	Reg. No.	ChassisMake/Model	Type	Date New	Date In	Date Sold	Purpose	Allocation
							Appendix 2	

SERVICE VEHICLE FLEET 1946 - 1960

F. No.	Reg. No.	ChassisMake/Model	Type	Date New	Date In	Date Sold	Purpose	Allocation
3	DP 7413	Morris Commercial	1-ton lorry	Mar-26	New	Oct-49	Route servicing	Reading
4	DP 7414	Morris Commercial	1-ton lorry	Mar-26	New	Oct-49	Depot lorry	Maidenhead
	DP 9140	BSA 7.7hp sidecar	Motorcycle	Nov-27	New	Jan-50	Engineering	Ascot
6	RX 3755	Austin 7hp	Van	Feb-29	New	Apr-51	Publicity Dept.	Reading
8	JB 4217	Austin 10hp	Van	May-34	New	Nov-51	Engineering	Reading
2	PP 5930	Morris Commercial	1-ton lorry	Apr-26	Mar-34	Oct-49	Depot lorry	Wycombe
	BBL 443	Austin 7hp	Car	Mar-38	New	Sep-50	Inspectors	
1	WO 9157	Leyland Cub (Perkins)	Lorry	Feb-35	Jun-40	Oct-54	Stores lorry	Reading
	UD 9244	Austin 10hp	Car	Jan-38	Apr-41	Mar-55	Staff car	
	ELT 722	Austin 10hp	Car	Jan-38	Apr-41	Sep-50	Staff car	
	EXY 823	Austin 10hp	Car	May-38	Apr-41	Mar-55	Staff car	
	FLY 286	Austin 10hp	Car	Mar-39	Apr-41	Sep-50	Staff car	
	FXD 202	Austin 10hp	Car	May-39	Apr-41	Jun-49	Inspectors	Reading
	PV 6530	Austin 10hp	Car	Feb-40	Apr-41	Oct-49	Engineer	Reading
	CJB 670	Austin 10hp	Car	May-41	New	Sep-50	Staff car	
	GJO 54	BSA 600cc	Motorcycle	Oct-38	Sep-43	Mar-49	Inspectors	Crowthorne
	FHA 257	Austin 10hp	Car	Nov-38	Feb-45	Mar-55	Staff car	
	ELX 440	Wolseley 8hp	Car	Feb-38	Sep-45	Jul-51	GM's car	Reading
	DJB 865	Vauxhall 10hp	Car	Oct-46	New	May-55	Inspectors	Wycombe
15	DJB 914	Bedford 10/12cwt	Van	Nov-46	New	Feb-60	Depot van	Wycombe
17	DJB 943	Ford (Canada) V8	4WD lorry	Ex-WD	Nov-46	Feb-60	Breakdown	Reading
19	*111 RD*	Ford (Canada) V8	4WD lorry	Ex-WD	Nov-46	Jan-72	Breakdown	Reading
21	*112 RD*	Dodge (America)	6-wheel lorry	Ex-WD	Nov-46	Feb-58	Breakdown	Reading
	DRX 476	Vauxhall 10hp	Car	May-47	New	Sep-56	Engineering	Reading
23	EBL 533	Bedford 10/12cwt	Van	Sep-47	New	Sep-60	Depot van	Maidenhead
25	JGF 406	Commer Q4 3-ton	Lorry (Ex-WD)	May-47	Sep-48	Oct-57	Depot lorry	Wycombe
	ERX 580	Vauxhall 10hp	Car	Jan-49	New	Sep-56	Clerk of Works	Reading
	ERX 607	Vauxhall 10hp	Car	Jan-49	New	Sep-56	Private Hire Man.	Reading
	DRD 659	BSA 250cc	Motorcycle	Mar-49	New	Jun-58	Inspectors	Crowthorne
27	FJB 99	Bedford 10/12cwt	Van	Jul-49	New	Aug-56	Depot van	Reading
	EDP 247	Ford Anglia 8hp	Car	Aug-49	New	Sep-56	Inspectors	Reading
29	RX 1758	Leyland Titan TD1	Tree-lopper	Ex-bus	Oct-49	Oct-56	Route servicing	Reading
	FMO 152	Morris Oxford	Car	Nov-49	New	Sep-58	Engineer's car	Reading
	CMO 963	Bedford OW 3-ton	Lorry	Sep-43	Jan-50	Jan-58	Depot lorry	Newbury
	EUW 584	Austin	Van	Feb-38	Jan-50	Jul-51	Depot van	Oxford
	EGK 623	Morris 8hp	Car	Jan-39	Jan-50	Jun-51	Staff car	Oxford
	LFC 562	Austin 16hp	Car	Sep-46	Jan-50	May-55	Traffic Supt. Car	Oxford
	ELJ 27	Morris 8hp	Car	Jul-38	Jan-50	May-54	Inspectors	Newbury
	AMO 960	Hillman Minx	Car	Jul-37	Jan-50	May-55	Depot engineer	Newbury
	FRX 9	Morris Oxford	Car	Mar-50	New	Feb-61	Traffic Supt. Car	Reading
	FRX 647	Morris Oxford	Car	Jun-50	New	Feb-61	Traffic Supt. Car	Wycombe
	FDP 101	Ford Pilot V8	Car	Nov-50	New	Jul-55	GM's car	Reading
31	GJB 552	Bedford 10/12cwt	Van	Mar-51	New	Oct-65	Depot van	Reading
	GJB 729	Austin A40	Car	Apr-51	New	Oct-58	Accountant's car	Reading
	GJB 786	Vauxhall Velox	Car	Apr-51	New	Sep-61	Traffic Manager	Reading
35/27	RWL 71	Bedford 10/12cwt	Van	Jun-51	New	Oct-65	Depot van	Oxford
	RWL 72	Vauxhall Wyvern	Car	Jun-51	New	Jun-61	Staff car	Oxford
33	GMO 943	Austin A40	Van	Oct-51	New	Nov-66	Publicity Dept.	Reading
	VV 8163	Morris 8hp	Car	Oct-39	May-52	May-55	Traffic dept.	Oxford
	HDP 401	Ford Anglia 8hp	Car	May-53	New	Jun-60	Inspectors	Wycombe
35	KBL 963	Fordson Thames 4D	Lorry	Sep-54	New	Nov-66	Stores lorry	Reading
	JRD 479	Ford Popular 10hp	Car	Dec-54	New	Jul-62	Inspectors	Newbury
	JRD 982	Ford Popular 10hp	Car	Oct-54	New	Jul-62	Asst. Traffic Man.	Reading
	LBL 331	Vauxhall Velox	Car	Apr-55	New	Jul-62	GM's car	Reading
	XFC 888	Morris Oxford II	Car	May-55	New	Jul-62	Traffic Supt. Car	Oxford
37	MRX 113	Commer Cob	Van	Jun-56	New	May-68	Depot van	Newbury
39	MRX 114	Commer Cob	Van	Jun-56	New	Apr-67	Clerk of Works	Reading
41	MRX 115	Bedford CA5	Van	Jun-56	New	Oct-65	Depot van	Reading

210

F. No.	Reg. No.	ChassisMake/Model	Type	Date New	Date In	Date Sold	Purpose	Allocation
	MRX 116	Ford	Car	Jul-56	New	Jul-62	Staff car	
	MMO 731	Wolseley	Car	Jul-56	New	Jun-62	GM's car	Reading
43	BRX 921	Bristol K5G	Tree-lopper	Ex-bus	Oct-56	Nov-64	Route servicing	Reading
RV.1	*323 RD*	AEC Matador	Crane Lorry	Ex-WD	Jan-60	To AV	Recovery Vehicle	Reading
45	UJB 298	Bedford CAV	Van (grey livery)	Feb-60	New	Nov-68	Clerk of Works	Reading
47	UJB 299	Bedford CAV	Van	Feb-60	New	Mar-69	Depot van	Wycombe

Notes: Motorcycle DP 9140 had originally been allocated to the Uxbridge garage.

3 (DP 7413) had a high platform for tree-cutting.

Vans 6 (RX 3755) and 8 (JB 4217) had originally been staff cars and were converted in June 1939 and January 1942.

8 (JB 4217) was transferred to Ascot in July 1949 to replace the BSA motorcycle with sidecar.

2 (PP 5930) was new as a 14-seater bus to Marlow & District Motor Services.

19 and 21 operated on the Trade Plates as shown in italics, 19 also ran on Trade Plate 533 MO.

Lorries 17, 19 and 21 were purchased from Government Surplus sales at Mount Farm, Dorchester, Oxfordshire.

29 (RX 1758) was former double-deck Car 169, and 43 (BRX 921) was formerly bus 405

31 (GJB 552) was allocated to Ascot garage by August 1957. Car DRX 476 went to Newbury in April 1955 for Engineering use.

Van EUW 584 and cars EGK 623 and LFC 562 were owned by South Midland M.S. Ltd., as were RWL 71 and RWL 72.

Car VV 8163 was acquired with the United Counties Omnibus Co. Ltd. operations at Oxford.

Cars AMO 960 and ELJ 27 and lorry CMO 963 were owned by Newbury & District M. S. Ltd.

Van RWL 71 was apparently also numbered 35 in error, being re-numbered as 27 c.1957.

RV.1 used Trade Plate 323 RD and had a new body constructed by Thames Valley.

Photos _Top left - No.35 (KBL 963) at Reading; top right - No.31 (GJB 552) at Ascot; centre left No.43 (BRX 921) at Reading; centre_
Below: _right No.33 (GMO 943) at Frogmoor; bottom left No.37 (MRX 113) at Newbury; bottom right No.25 (JGF 406) at Newbury._

From the late wartime period repaints had white paint in place of grey bands or roofs. New deliveries from Bedford OWB Cars 437/8 (CRX 546/7) had roofs in red, and from May 1946 older types were repainted in that style. Any pre-war lining out on panels disappeared during repaints, whilst the white gave way to cream. The black lining to cream bands was officially discontinued from 1957, though repaints at Newbury continued the practice for a while. Black was used for the mudguards of service cars.

ECW-bodied Bristol LL6B Car 567 (FMO 949) shows the standard livery for new post-war service saloons.

Saloon buses had a cream waistrail, but from Bristol L6A Car 455 (DBL 163) through to Bristol LWL Car 633 (GJB 271) the cream was applied to side window surrounds and advert panel of the ECW bodies, though there was no cream on the front or rear. Older cars were not, however, repainted into this scheme.

Harrington-bodied Leyland 'Tiger' TS8 384 (BMO 983) coach in red and cream phase - its fourth livery.

Coaches varied in their liveries, and some batches carried several schemes. The Duple-bodied Leyland 'Tiger' TS7 Cars 262/4 (JB 5841/3) were repainted after war service as red with a cream flash and red mudguards. The Harrington-bodied 'Tiger' TS8 Cars 381-90 (BMO 980-9) were repainted in 1946 as green

with cream side flash and roof. The Bristol L6B coaches of the 1947/8 deliveries were predominately cream, with the Windover-bodied 460/2/3/5 (DMO 664/6/7/9) having green wings, mudguards and radiator grille, whilst the Vincent-bodied examples 461/4 (DMO 664/8) had green side flash, mudguards and radiator grille. These were all repainted for 1950 in red with a cream waistrail (Windovers) or side flash (Vincents), due to problems with the original finish. The Harrington-bodied TS8's were also repainted to red with a cream side flash for 1949, all of these having red mudguards and radiator grilles.

The 1949 Windover-bodied L6B's for the London A route, Cars 487-91 (EJB 209-13), were painted all red except for a cream waistband and were the first postwar coaches to carry fleetnames on the sides. As they were regarded as 'service coaches' they had black radiator grilles. The 1950 examples, Cars 545-550 (FMO 20-6, FMO 934-7), were painted red with cream window surrounds and red mudguards and red radiator grille, though the latter was later black.

Windover-bodied Bristol L6B coach 546 (FMO 21) in red with cream window surrounds as new in 1950.

Bedford OB coaches 604-6 (FRX 313-5) of 1950 were red all over except for the customary Duple side flash. The Bristol LWL6B coaches 607-12 (GBL 871-6), and the rebodied Leyland 'Tiger' PS1 Car 169 (LWL 995) were delivered in cream with black mudguards, though the latter were repainted red after a couple of seasons, then again a couple of years later as maroon.

Bristol LS6G Car 671 (HBL 73) in cream and black. Note the return to glazed quarter lights for this batch.

The underfloor-engined Bristol LS coaches for both TV and *South Midland* were delivered in cream with window surrounds and mudguards in black, and one 1953 SM example had the ECW 'wings' painted black too. However, the black was considered heavy looking and was replaced by red from 1955, and again by maroon after another season or two. The Guy 'Arab' UF coaches followed the same pattern as the LS's, with black, red and maroon relief in succession.

The former *United Counties* Bristol coaches were acquired in cream with green mudguards, the latter feature initially repainted as black, then again as red, and later still in maroon. The pair of dual-purpose bodied Bristol L6B Cars 71/2 (EBD 234/5) were acquired in the green and cream 'express' style livery, and remained in that until transferred to TV in 1953, when they were repainted like the native L-types but without regard to their additional side trim.

Bristol LS6B Car 714 (HMO 860) seen after white fleet numbers had been introduced.

With the advent of underfloor-engined saloons on the LS chassis, the livery effectively returned to the early post-war style, with all-over red save for a cream waistrail and black mudguards.

Bristol 'Lodekka' Car 750 (MBL 831) as delivered. Note the painted 'Huntley & Palmers' advertisements.

The open-top Bristol K5G's were officially described as 'pale primrose' in their livery, though this may be due to *Brighton, Hove & District's* shade of cream always appearing more yellowy that that used by TV-rather more of an ice-cream shade? The mudguards and bonnet sides were painted maroon, and it must be acknowledged that these early uses of maroon as relief did lead to the unique livery (amongst BTC fleets that is) adopted for *South Midland* from 1958. Apparently Mrs. Pruett had been consulted on a new coach livery and had suggested pink, but fortunately not adopted!

Newbury & District

The vehicles inherited carried the standard *Red & White* livery of red, white and black. Repaints by TV of the Bedford OB's replaced their black mudguards with red, but the AEC 'Regal' coaches were repainted in TV's shade of red and the white areas replaced by cream, though the black mudguards remained. Re-bodied Leyland 'Tiger' PS1 coach 169 (LWL 995) was treated the same as TV's Bristol LWL's (see TV livery notes).

The saloon livery was simplified to red and cream, though black mudguards remained. The Duple-bodied 'Regals' were first red all-over with a cream flash, but some (at least) had cream window surrounds (but red flash) later on. Double-deckers had originally had white window surrounds, but TV repainted them into red with cream bands, though as some bodies lacked upper deck beading, the overall effect was quite plain.

N&D's highbridge Guy 'Arab' Car 172 (FMO 517) is shown in original condition in the darker red and white livery, leaving Gloucester Green, Oxford on the joint route with City of Oxford to Newbury.

AEC 'Regal' coach 50 (MWL 742) in R&W style.

South Midland

These were all in the red, white and black scheme of their former group, which very well suited the Duple style of coachwork. TV substituted its own shade of red, a little paler than that used by *Red & White*, but otherwise the scheme remained basically the same, with cream replacing white, but retaining black on the mudguards. From 1955 the 'Regals' were repainted into all-over cream, with red mudguards, which were later repainted maroon in line with changes to the TV fleet. At the time this changed it was considered to paint the side flash red, but was not taken up. Those coaches surviving beyond 1958 received the livery of maroon and cream in line with newer stock.

'Regal' coach 51 (MWL 743) in cream and red livery.

Fleet Numbers and Fleetnames

These were black until 1960 and were displayed on the bonnet side and rear panel. After 1960 they were white and displayed on the front, rear and bonnet. A few vehicles in the mid-1950's were delivered with fleet numbers prefixed 'TV' and ran as such, though this was a coachbuilder's error, as the list supplied by the Company had been marked TV or SM to distinguish which fleet the vehicles were intended for. Coaches carried their numbers less prominently, half-cabs continuing the pre-war practice of having them on the nearside dumb-iron of the chassis. Full-fronted types had them over the filler caps and on the rear panel generally, but batches varied.

Former *Newbury & District* and *South Midland* cars had gold fleet numbers when acquired, but these were replaced by black, then later white, as appropriate for *Thames Valley* stock. The open-top Bristols had black fleet numbers and were also notable in having blinds with white lettering on a maroon background.

Bristol K-type Car 453 (DBL 161) in original form with larger fleetname and painted 'Simonds' adverts.

The larger shaded *Thames Valley* fleetname, with its central dot, was replaced by a smaller, un-shaded serif style from January 1954. The *Newbury & District* fleetname was carried for a couple of years, until stocks were used up. *South Midland* coaches also got the thinner fleetname, altering their overall look.

Above, former N&D 'Regal' bus 140 (DMO 329,) and below, Guy 'Arab' 102 (CRX 282) in later liveries.

Appendix 4 Newbury & District

The full and interesting story of this independent was covered in my 1987 book 'A History of Newbury & District Motor Services Ltd., 1932-1952', which has been out of print for some years.

However, to give a short appreciation of the development of N&D we must first visit the bus scene in the Newbury area in the period leading up to the implementation of the 1930 Road Traffic Act. Whilst *Thames Valley* had tried hard periodically to establish services in the area, it had to resign itself to running just the route to Reading and its large shed in Mill Lane never lived up to its expectations. Also the *Great Western Railway* had operated quite a network of local routes, but the local operators had beaten them off as well. The local firms also benefited from loyal passengers, as they developed their services in response to local needs.

Leylands were an early choice for large capacity buses, including No.40 (VA 7943) a PLSC1 of 1928.

When the 1930 Act came into force, the burden on individual operators, in particular those who were one man outfits, put them at a definite disadvantage over the larger operators who could afford to add more employees to deal with licensing matters. It was that background that convinced Theo Denham that the best approach was to band together as a co-operative, so he called a meeting in the Spring of 1932, suggesting to the other local operators that they form a company. The initial reaction was lukewarm, though a number of others did join once the company had been set up.

The initial partners were *Denham Bros.*, who ran mainly bus services, plus a little private hire and lorry work, *Charles Durnford & Sons*, who were established as local coach operators and house removers, and *A. Andrews & Son (Favourite Coaches)*, who ran coaches and had some contract work. Durnfords also brought with them expertise in engineering, whilst the Andrews family were skilled coachbuilders and painters, Percy Andrews also being a skilled mechanic, and Theo Denham was a good organiser and became Secretary of N&D.

Typical purchases of the mid-1930's fleet were GMC No.31 (CC 9415) and Gilford VM 3669, one of a number for which fleet numbers are unknown.

N&D pursued a policy of getting local concerns to join with them, and this often involved the former independents becoming employees of the Company, as well as shareholders. In other cases the business was acquired outright, or the owner had other business ventures, so in the following list the term 'amalgamated' is as used by the Company at the time to indicate someone who came into the fold:

9/32 **John Prothero**, *Beedon, amalgamated*
9/32 **George Hedges**, *Brightwalton, amalgamated–*
(Later resumed independent operation as Reliance)
10/32 Tom Holman, *Ecchinswell, continued coal and carrier's business*
10/32 **Pocock Bros.**, *Cold Ash, amalgamated*
1/33 **Freddie Spanswick**, *Thatcham, amalgamated*
1/34 **Durnford Bros.**, *Newbury, re-amalgamated*
1/34 **Catherine Geary**, *Great Shefford, continued taxi and haulage business*
1/34 **John Burt**, *Inkpen, amalgamated*
1/34 **George Brown**, *Wash Common, sold out*
2/34 **George Howlett**, *Bucklebury, amalgamated*
3/34 **W. J. White & Son**, *Hermitage, amalgamated*
1/35 **Walter Cleeveley**, *Newbury, also a publican*
10/35 **Charlie Ballard**, *Bradfield, continued garage business*
4/37 **Edith Kent**, *Kingsclere, sold out and retired*
5/37 **Pass & Co.**, *Newbury, continued as Ford agents and garage proprietors.*
7/38 **Ernie Nobes**, *Lambourn Woodlands, amalgamated*

The standard 20-seater soon became the A-type Thornycroft, of which No.46 (PG 1099) was one of 18 purchased – note the empty spare-wheel carrier.

These acquisitions greatly added to the network of bus services, excursion and private hire, and also haulage work, all of which enhanced N&D's local reputation as passengers still felt connected to those who had previously served them on a daily basis.

As to the fleet, particularly one formed from so many different sources, it was a very mixed one indeed. In the first 2 years of operation, no fewer than 20 chassis makers were represented, whilst the list of known bodybuilders exceeds 16! During the mid-1930's some degree of standardisation was achieved, initially favouring Thornycrofts and GMC's for the smaller buses, with larger ones being Leyland, Tilling-Stevens, Gilford and Dennis types. The coach fleet also had Gilfords and GMC's, plus Stars, whilst the Dennis 'Ace' was much sought for bus and coach work from the late 1930's, such a vehicle being the first vehicle bought new by N&D in July 1935! Of course many of the inherited stock had been new to the constituent operators.

Coaching was always a very important facet of N&D business, the network of local contacts again being essential. Haulage and removals also remained important, and two phrases coined by Durnfords in their independent days summed it all up – 'we go to the seaside daily' and 'we move house every day'!

Tilling-Stevens were an early Denham's favourite so more were later added, including No.45 (TV 6036).

Wartime conditions put N&D under great pressure, the Newbury area being dotted with shadow factories and military establishments, as well as receiving a lot of evacuees and refugees. The strain of large increases in loadings, and the toll taken on the ageing fleet by the lack of skilled labour and materials, weakened the Company, making it seek an opportunity to sell out.

This came to the attention of *Red & White United Transport*, itself a very successful independent that had been expanding out of its native South Wales. Indeed, it had the intention to form a swathe through

The next phase of standardisation of 20-seaters was the Dennis 'Ace', of which N&D amassed 22 plus 1 'Mace'. No.65 (JY 4752)had a Mumford body.

from the eastern bank of the Severn and down to the South Coast, and had already acquired *Cheltenham & District* and had a base in the Stroud area. Indeed, had the plan to buy *Hants & Sussex* ever come off, that goal would have been achieved. So the acquisition of N&D fitted in well with that overall plan, and it was purchased in January 1944. *Red & White* consolidated its holdings in the region with the acquisition of the Basingstoke-based *Venture Ltd.* in March 1945 and *South Midland* of Oxford in October 1945, coaching being another priority.

Whilst it was sad to see the end of an independent N&D, the new owner retained the separate identity and invested heavily in both organisation and vehicles at a time when the latter were by no means easy to obtain. With their customary skills of refurbishing old vehicles for further service, the Chepstow works produced some useful additions to the fleet by giving new engines and bodies (some secondhand) to old chassis. There were also new additions, though to utility standards, plus other buses transferred from other companies within the group, whilst existing N&D vehicles worthy of retention were thoroughly overhauled and repainted, the livery changing from the green and cream of the old company to red, white and black.

More Leylands followed, including No.56 (HD 4371), a 1931 'Lion' LT2 ex-Yorkshire Woollen.

A new garage was provided by extending the Mill Lane premises, whilst the network of outstations still functioned as before, in fact even more buses were kept at outlying locations by drivers on contracts who took them home, and some of these part-timers also worked at the contract places, so the buses stayed out too, rarely being seen in Newbury.

The R&W era brought a number of AEC vehicles from various sources, with 'Regal 4' No.125 (FS 8576), with ex-SMT chassis and a body from North Western, and ex-Burnley, Colne & Nelson centre-door 'Regent' No.117 (HG 1221) amongst their variety.

Red & White United Transport was a successful group with interests abroad and in the Guernsey, but with the coming of the nationalisation of road transport, it had decided to sell out voluntarily, and so its companies came under State control in 1949. This led to both *N&D* and *South Midland* being placed under the control of *Thames Valley* from 1st January 1950, any public identity of the Newbury company fading after about 2 years. However, as the Company name appeared on the blinds of coaches, it was often displayed by nostalgic drivers!

Appendix 5   South Midland

The full and well researched story of this operator has been written by David Flitton and remains available – please see page 4 for full details. For that reason only the most basic outline is included here.

This Company, like so many others of its kind, sprang from the aftermath of the Great War, but from the outset it always adopted its own style and showed new directions. Registered as the *South Midland Transport & Touring Company* in April 1921, it was one of the first in the land to run a daily express coach service, linking its Oxford base with London from June 1921.

30-seater Dennis charabanc FC 4010 new in 1921.

The network was further expanded to Worcester from April 1930, plus a regular Summer link to Southsea had been added in 1929. Other attempts at expansion to Leicester and Nottingham did not survive, but the Company managed to triumph over fierce competition from *City of Oxford* and other competitors on the express front, changing its name to *South Midland Motor Services Ltd.* in October 1930. The vehicle policy seems sound from the outset, an important factor in the continued success of the operation, with the original Dennis charabancs giving way to newer types of that make, plus Gilfords, then a succession of Leyland 'Tiger' models, some of which even got re-bodied later on.

Gilford No.19 (WL 9058) new in 1930 with Arnold & Comben bodywork seen on the Worcester route.

The outbreak of War meant an initial increase in trade with lots of contract work, but the compulsory end to express services in October 1942 for reasons of fuel economy was a severe blow. That and a building deficit of routine maintenance, caused the Company to seek a buyer, which *Red & White* was happy to take on board. As with *Newbury & District* the fleet was maintained by refurbishments, overhauls and even some loaned vehicles, but once the War was over, orders for new vehicles were put in hand, with the Oxford-based fleet receiving good numbers of new Duple-bodied AEC 'Regal' coaches. A number of transfers between N&D and SM tidied matters up in due course, with SM's pair of Bedford OB's and surviving 4 Leylands going to Newbury in exchange for further 'Regals'.

Leyland 'Tiger' TS3 No.29 (JO 1599) was re-bodied by Harrington and is seen at the Berkshire inland 'resort' of California-in-England, Finchampstead.

A sound programme of extended tours was brought in after the War, and this became a very important facet of the *South Midland* operations. However, with the sale of *Red & White* to the State in 1949, control of SM passed to *Thames Valley*. The latter retained the separate identity right through to 1970, the value of the good reputation being well appreciated, whilst the intensive express routes and the extended tours programme all benefited from the tremendous demand for travel in the 1950's. Under TV's guidance further tours were added, including the first ventures to Ireland, something that became a speciality of the SM fleet.

A one-off in the fleet was Leyland 'Tiger' TS6 No.33 (AFC 531) with typical Harrington bodywork.

The old red, white and black livery was replaced by a new cream and black scheme from 1952 onwards, red replacing black after a year, then again by maroon, until the unique scheme of maroon and cream came in from 1958, some of the AEC 'Regal' coaches surviving to wear all these liveries!

The Oxford operation was kept fairly separate from the main *Thames Valley* scene, but it was common to find both TV and Newbury-based vehicles on loan to Oxford, whilst transfers between the fleets occurred regularly. At first the maintenance was largely handled at Newbury, which had been part of the R&W plan for the new garage there, but in 1952 the operation of the express service to London via

High Wycombe was acquired from *United Counties*. With that came a garage in Botley Road, and that was developed as the new base for the Oxford operations, which then became more self-sufficient on maintenance.

No. 39 (LWL 996) a Duple-bodied AEC 'Regal' coach supplied under the R&W vehicle policy.

Following the formation of the *National Bus Company,* it was decided to transfer the operation to the other Oxford-based company, *City of Oxford*, a strange twist in the long-running competition back to the pioneering days of both concerns. The *South Midland* name was still used for a time, but that was not the same animal, and is for others to dwell upon.

Bristol L6B's No.73 (EBD 236) ex-UCOC and No.545 (FMO 20) transferred from Thames Valley.

Appendix 6 - Scheduled Vehicle Allocations to Garages, Dormy Sheds etc. 1946-1960

Town/Village	Location		H	1946	1947	1948	1949	1950	1951	1952	1953	1954	1955	1956	1957	1958	1959	1960
Ascot	Course Road	G	R	10	12	12	12	12	12	12	13	13	15	16	17	17	17	19
Baughurst	The Street (W&D)	DS	R															1
Bracknell	Market Street	G																24
Chilton Foliat	*Parked by driver*	OS	N					2	2	2	1	??						
Crowthorne	Cambridge Road	DS	R	4	4	4	4	4	4	4	4	4	4	4	4	4	4	4
East Ilsley	Swan, High Street	OS	N					1	1	1	1	1	1	1				
Fingest	Turville Road	DS	W	2	2	2	2	2	2	2	2	2	2	2	2	2	2	2
High Wycombe	Desborough Rd.	G	W	16	16	16	??	??	??	18	18	18	18	18	??	) 58	) 60	) 60
High Wycombe	London Road	G			??	??	39	??	??	??	35	37	37	37	37	??	)	) 60
Hungerford	*Parked by driver*	OS	N					2	2	2	2	2	3	??	2	2	2	2
Kingsclere	Crown, N'bury Rd.	OS	N					1	1	1	1	1	1	1	1	1	1	1
Lambourn	Newbury Street	OS	N					4	4	4	5	5	4	3	2	2	2	2
Lambourn W'ds	*Parked by driver*	OS	N								1							
London	Samuelson's Garage	OS	R		2	2	2	2	2	2	2	2	2	2	2	2	2	2
London	Samuelson's (SM)	OS	O					2	2	3	3	3						
London	LT Stockwell (SM)	OS	O										3	3	3	3	3	3
Maidenhead	Bridge Street	G		??	??	60	??	??	59	66	68	68	68	68	74	78	75	80
Newbury	Mill Lane	DS	R			2	2											
Newbury	Mill Lane (N&D)	G			2	2		??	41	47	47	??	48	50	45	58	50	50
Oxford	Iffley Road (SM)	G	O					*	*	*	*	*	*	*	*	) 48	) 48	) 41
Oxford	Botley Road (SM)	G								*	*	*	*	*	*	)	)	)
Princes Risboro'	Longwick Road	DS	W	2	2	2	2	2	2	2	2	2	2	2	2	2	2	2
Reading	Lower Thorn St.	G		??	??	80	??	??	80	81	80	80	80	79	??	80	84	84
Reading	The Colonnade	W	R		#	#	#	#	#	#	#	#	#	#	#			
Stokenchurch	London Road	DS	W	2	2	2	2	2	2	2	2	2	2	2	2	2	2	2
Tadley	Fairlawn Road	DS	R	2	2	2	2	2	2	2	2	2	2	2	2	2	2	2
West Ilsley	*Parked by driver*	OS	N					1	1	1								
Worcester	Newport St. (SM)	OS	O					3	3	3	3	3	3	3	3	3	3	3

Key: OS = Out-station of non-TV premises. DS = Dormy Shed. G = Garage with maintenance facilities. W = Works.

Notes: The home garages of Reading, Maidenhead, Wycombe (London Road, Wycombe Marsh), Newbury or Oxford are shown in the 'H' column. Baughurst was a Wilts & Dorset Dormy Shed and was used in place of Tadley from August 1960. However, the single-deck allocation had ceased at Tadley from June 1960 and was transferred to Reading Garage. Scheduled allocations for the main garages do not include spare buses or coaches, though those for smaller locations are exact numbers, some being for contract operations. Where ?? is shown, exact figures are not available.
The Colonnade was essentially a works, but during the period indicated it was used as an operational base for coaches and relief vehicles due to lack of accommodation at Lower Thorn Street, that role ceasing in February 1958.
* Operational figures are not available for the Oxford garages, but the licensed off-peak fleet was typically 28, whilst the peak season fleet was 41, inclusive of any outstationed at London or Worcester. Iffley Road could accommodate 15 under cover and Botley Road 41, each location also having some outside parking. Once Botley Road had been acquired, Iffley Road became its subsidary running shed.
The TV shed in Newbury had been occupied by the Ministry of Supply, so the 2 buses were parked at the N&D garage during the period shown. After N&D was acquired, the TV shed became the Newbury body and paint shop.
Crowthorne Dormy Shed was incorrectly described as Wellington Road in previous volumes, please note correct address.
Ascot Garage and Crowthorne Dormy Shed were replaced by Bracknell Garage in June 1960.

Garage codes were used from about 1951 on Scheduled Working Arrangements and were as follows:

A - Ascot	H - Hungerford	P - Princes Risborough
B - Bracknell	K - Kingsclere	R - Reading
C - Crowthorne	L - Lambourn	S - Stokenchurch
CF - Chilton Foliat	LW- Lambourn Woodlands	T - Tadley
D - Desborough Road	M - Maidenhead	V - Victoria (Samuelson's Garage)
E - East Ilsley	N - Newbury	W - Wycombe Marsh (London Road)
F - Fingest	O - Oxford	WY - West Ilsley

Other operators using Thames Valley premises:
Wilts & Dorset kept one bus at the Newbury Garage following the acquisition of Venture Ltd. in 1950.
Royal Blue outstationed a coach in a lock-up garage provided by TV at Frogmoor, by 1957 this was kept at the Desborough Road Garage.

Appendix 7 - Summary of Schedule Workings from 1st January 1955

Monday to Friday Schedules - the types shown are those usually employed on the route

Garage Codes:
A – Ascot, C – Crowthorne, D – Desborough Road, E – East Ilsley, F – Fingest, K – Kingsclere, L – Lambourn, M – Maidenhead, N – Newbury, P – Princes Risborough, R – Reading, S – Stokenchurch, T – Tadley, V – Victoria, W –Wycombe Marsh

Route A Reading – London
R – Bristol KSW coach seats
Route B Reading – London
R, V – Bristol KSW coach seats
Route 1 Reading – Maidenhead
M, R – Bristol KS and KSW
Route 1a Reading – Woodley
R – Bristol K
Route 1b Reading – Shurlock Row
R – Bristol LL
Route 2 Reading – Windsor
A, R – Bristol KSW
Route 2a Ascot – Sunningdale
A – Bristol K
Route 2b Windsor – Winkfield – Easthampstead A – Bristol K
Route 2c Ascot – Sunningdale
A – Bristol K
Route 3 Reading – Camberley
C, R – Bristol LS
Route 3a Reading – Wokingham – Finchampstead C - Bristol L
Route 3a Reading – Emmbrook
R – Bristol LS
Route 4 Reading – Camberley
R – Bristol KSW
Route 5 Reading – Oxford
Joint with City of Oxford route 34
R- Bristol LS
Route 5a Reading – Wantage
R – Bristol LL
Route 5a Reading - Chilton
R – Bristol L
Route 5b Reading – Yattendon – Newbury N, R – Bristol LS
Route 5b Reading – Pangbourne
R – Bristol K
Route 5b Newbury – Hampstead Norris N – Guy Arab Highbridge
Route 6 Reading – Basingstoke
R – Bristol KS coach seats
Route 6a Reading – Odiham
R – Bristol K or KS
Route 6b Reading – Bramley
R - Bristol LS
Route 7 Reading – Nettlebed
R – Bristol K
Route 8 Reading – Henley
R – Bristol K or KS
Route 9 Reading – Tadley
R, T – Bristol K and KS
Route 9a Reading – Tadley
R, T – Bristol L and LL
Route 10 Reading – Newbury
N, R – Bristol KSW

Route 11 Reading – Bucklebury
R – Bristol LS
Route 12 Reading – Aldershot
Joint with Aldershot & District
R – Bristol KS/KSW coach seats
Route 16 Maidenhead – Henley
M – Bristol LL
Route 17 Maidenhead – Henley
M – Bristol LL
Route 18 Maidenhead – Marlow
M – Bedford OB
Route 18a Maidenhead – Pinkneys Green M – Bristol K
Route 19 Maidenhead – Sealeys Stores M – Bristol K
Route 20 Windsor – High Wycombe
M, W - Bristol KSW
Route 21 Maidenhead – The Walthams – Wokingham
M – Bristol LWL and LS
Route 22 Maidenhead – Slough
M – Bristol K, KS and KSW
Route 22a Maidenhead – Dropmore – Slough
M – Bristol LL
Route 23 Maidenhead – Cookham Dean M – Bristol K
Route 24 Maidenhead – Cookham Dean M – Bristol LS
Route 25 High Wycombe – Flackwell Heath W – Bristol LS
Route 26/26a HW Local Service
Joint with LTE route 326/326a
W – Bristol K
Route 27 High Wycombe – Great Missenden D – Bristol K
Short-workings W – Bristol L
Route 28 High Wycombe – Reading
R, W – Bristol LWL and LS
Marlow shorts W – Bristol LL
Route 30 High Wycombe – Aylesbury
P, W – Bristol KSW
Route 31 H. Wycombe – Lacey Green
D, W – Bristol LS and LL
Route 32 High Wycombe – Bledlow Ridge W – Bristol LL
Route 33 HW Local Service
D – Bristol LWL
Route 34 High Wycombe – Speen
W – Bristol LL
Route 35 High Wycombe – Downley Common W – Bristol LS
Route 36 H.Wycombe – Lane End
F, W – Bristol L
Route 37 H.W. – Henley, Turville, Frieth or Lane End
F, W – Bristol L
Route 38 High Wycombe – Booker
D – Bristol K
Route 39 H. Wycombe – Watlington
S, W – Bristol KSW
Route 40 – H. Wycombe – Radnage
S, W - Bristol KSW
Route 41 High Wycombe – Ibstone
S, W – Bristol KSW
Route 42 Loudwater – W. Wycombe
D – Bristol KSW or LWL (shorts)
Route 50 Reading – Abingdon
Joint with City of Oxford route 40
R – Bristol LS
Route 51 Windsor Local Service
A – Bristol KSW
Route 60 Maidenhead – Bourne End – Marlow M – Bristol L

Route 61 Summerleaze Road – Pinkneys Green M - Bristol L
Route 62 Slough – Cippenham
M – Bristol L
Route 63 M'head – Curls Lane
M – Bristol K
Route 75 Reading – Guildford
Joint with Aldershot & District
R – Bristol LWL
Route 80 High Wycombe – Lacey Green – Aylesbury D – Bristol L
Route 81 High Wycombe – Booker
D – Bristol K
Route 101 – Newbury – East Ilsley
N – Guy Arab Highbridge
Route 101a Newbury – Peasemore
N – Bristol LL
Route 102 West Ilsley – East Ilsley – Reading E, N Guy Arab Highbridge
Route 103 Newbury – Ecchinswell
N – Bristol LL
Route 104 Newbury – Ashford Hill – Kingsclere N – Bristol LL
Route 105 Newbury – Wantage or Childrey Ridgeway N – Bristol LL
Route 106 Newbury – Lambourn – Swindon L, N Guy Arab Lowbridge plus Bristol L on shorts (L)
Route 106a Lambourn – Hungerford
L – Bristol L
Route 108 Newbury – Wickham or Lambourn Woodlands or Hungerford Newtown N - Guy Arab Highbridge
Route 109 Newbury – Cold Ash
N – Bristol K
Route 110 Newbury – Thatcham – Tadley N – Bristol KS
Route 111 Newbury – Bucklebury Common N - Bristol K or KS
Route 112 Newbury – Oxford
Joint with City of Oxford MS
N – Guy Arab Highbridge
Route 113 Newbury – Kintbury – Hungerford N – Bristol LL
Route 114 N'bury – East Woodhay
N – Bristol K or KS
Route 114a N'bury – West Woodhay
N – AEC Regal coach
Route 115 Newbury – Highclere
N – Bristol K
Route 116 N'b – Hungerford via A4
N – Bristol K
Route 120 N'b – Frilsham/Curridge
N - Bristol L
Route 120a Newbury – Aldworth
N – Bristol L
Route 121 Shaw Factory – Camp Close N – Bristol K
Route 122 Newbury – Kingsclere – Basingstoke *Joint with Wilts & Dorset*
K – Guy Arab Highbridge
Route 126 N'b – Crookham Cmn.
N – Guy Arab Highbridge
Route 127 Wash Common – Shaw Factory N – Bristol K
Route 128 Valley Rd. – Shaw Estate
N – Bristol K
Route 128a Bartlemy Cl. – Broadway
N – Bristol K
Route 129 Newbury Station – Didcot Station
N – Bristol LL
Please note: 129 was Sundays only

ASCOT-
Double-deckers: Bristol K6A 433, 434, 439, 440, 441, 442, Bristol KSW6B 640, 641, 642, 643, 644, 645, 646
Coaches: Bristol L6B 488

HIGH WYCOMBE - including Wycombe Marsh, Desborough Road, Fingest, Princes Risborough and Stokenchurch -
Double-deckers: Bristol K5G 413, 414, 417, Guy 'Arab' 1 5LW 422, 423, Bristol K6A 446, 447,451, Bristol K6B 469, 505, 506, 507, 508, 509, 513, 517, 518, 519, 528, 529, Bristol KS6B 589, 591, Bristol KSW6B 601, 602, 636, 647
Single-deckers: Leyland 'Tiger' TS7 303, 309, 326, 329, 332, 334, Leyland 'Tiger' TS8 348, 363, 366, Bristol L6A 472, 473, 474, 478, 479, 480, Bristol L6B 522, 523, 536, 537, 542, 543, Bristol LL6B 570, 571, 572, Bristol LWL6B 577, 578, 579, 618, 619, 620, 621, 625, 626, 627, 628
Coaches: Leyland 'Tiger' TS8 381, Bristol L6B 460, 462, 463, 465, 487, 552, 553, 555, Bristol LWL6B 607, 608, Bristol LS6G 671

MAIDENHEAD -
Double-deckers: Leyland 'Titan' TD1 182, Leyland 'Titan' TD4 274, 275, 277, Leyland 'Titan' TD5 339, Bristol K5G 403, 404, 408, 409, 410, Bristol K6A 427, 432, 443, 450, Bristol K6B 470, 498, 499, 500, 501, 502, 503, 504, 514, 515, 516, 527, 530, Bristol KS6B 592, 593, Bristol KSW6B 635, 649
Single-deckers: Leyland 'Tiger' TS4 244 (in use as office), Leyland 'Tiger' TS7 305, 325, 328, Leyland 'Tiger' TS8 345, 374, 375, 380, Bristol L6A 455, 456, 457, 458, 459, 475, 481, 482, 483, 538, 541, Bristol LL6B 561, 562, 563, 567, 568, 569, 573, 574, 575, 576, Bristol LWL6B 622, 623, 624
Coaches: Leyland 'Tiger' TS8 384, 387, Bristol L6B 461, 464, 550, 551, Bristol LWL6B 609

NEWBURY – incl. Chilton Foliat, East Ilsley, Hungerford, Kingsclere, Lambourn and West Ilsley –
Double-deckers: Leyland 'Titan' TD1 179, 180, 181, 187, 190, Guy 'Arab' 1 5LW 160, 418, 420, 421, 424, 425, Guy 'Arab' 11 5LW 99, 100, 101, 102, 103, 173, 174, Guy 'Arab' 111 5LW 170, 171, Guy 'Arab' 111 6LW 172, 175, 176, 177, 178, Bristol K6A 467, Bristol KSW6B 648, 650
Single-deckers: Leyland 'Tiger' TS7 333, Leyland 'Tiger' TS8 342, 343, 344, 346, 361, 362, 368, 372, 379, AEC 'Regal' 0662 131, 132, 133, 134, 135, 136, 137, 138, 139, 140, 157, AEC 'Regal' 6821A 161, 162, 163, Bristol L6B 521, Bristol LL6B 557, 558, 559, 560
Coaches: Leyland 'Tiger' TS7 262, 264, Leyland 'Tiger' PS1/1 169, AEC 'Regal' 0662 48, 53, 141, 142, 143, 144, 145, AEC 'Regal' 111 146, 147, 148, Bristol LS6G 673

OXFORD - including Worcester and Victoria –
Coaches: AEC 'Regal' 0662 39, 40, 41, 42, 45, 46, 47, AEC 'Regal' 111 54, 55, 56, 57, 58, 59, 60, 61, 62, 63, 64, 65, 66, 68, 69, Bristol L6B (dual-purpose) 71, 72, Bristol L6B 73, 74, Bristol LL6B (8ft. bodies) 75, 76, 77, 78, Bristol LS6G 79, 80, 81

Opposite – The oldest and newest, Leyland 'Titan' TD1 Car 179 (RX 4341) and Bristol LS6G coach 673 (HBL 75).

READING - incl. Crowthorne, Tadley and Victoria –
Double-deckers: Leyland 'Titan' TD1 183, 235, Leyland 'Titan' TD2 435, 436, Leyland 'Titan' TD4 273, 335, 336, Leyland 'Titan' TD5 340, 341, 369, 370, Bristol K5G 391, 392, 393, 394, 395, 396, 397, 398, 399, 400, 401, 402, 405, 406, 407, 415, 416, Bristol K6A 426, 428, 429, 430, 431, 444, 445, 448, 449, 452, 466, Bristol K6B 453, 454, 468, 471, 492, 493, 494, 495, 496, 497, 524, 525, 526, 531, 532, 533, Bristol KS6B 586, 587, 588, 590, 594, 595, 596, 597, 598, 599, 600, Bristol KSW6B 634, 637, 638, 639,
Single-deckers: Leyland 'Tiger' TS7 321, 322, 323, 324, Leyland 'Tiger' TS8 371, 373, 378, Bristol L6A 476, 477, 484, 485, 486, Bristol LL6B 556, 564, 565, 566, Bristol LWL6B 580, 581, 582, 583, 584, 585, 613, 614, 615, 616, 617
Coaches: Bristol L6B 491, 546, 547, 549, Bedford OB 604, Bristol LWL6B 610, 611, 612, Bristol LS6G 672

DELICENSED -
Double-deckers: Leyland 'Titan' TD1 184, 185, Leyland 'Titan' TD4 276, Guy 'Arab' 1 5LW 419, Guy 'Arab' 11 5LW 104, 105, 106 (*new, awaiting licensing)
Single-deckers: Leyland 'Tiger' TS4 248, Leyland 'Tiger' TS7 267, 331, Bedford OWB 437, 438, Bedford OB 510, 511, 512, 520, * Bristol LWL6B 629, 630, 631, 632, 633
Coaches: AEC 'Regal' 111 70, Bedford OB 164, 165, 605, 606, Leyland 'Tiger' TS8 382, 383, 385, 386, 388, 389, 390, Bristol L6B 489, 490, 545, 548, 554

221

ASCOT –
Double-deckers: Bristol K6A 441, Bristol KSW6B 640, 641, 642, 643, 644, 645, 646, 701, 703, 705, 744, 745, 746, 747, Bristol LD5G 766, 767
Coaches: Bristol L6B 545

HIGH WYCOMBE – including Wycombe Marsh, Desborough Road, Fingest, Princes Risborough and Stokenchurch – (2 LWL6B at Fingest, 2 KSW6B Princes Risborough and 2 KSW6B at Stokenchurch) -
Double-deckers: Bristol K6B 471, 505, 506, 507, 508, 509, 517, 518, 519, 528, 529, Bristol KS6B 589, 591, Bristol KSW6B 601, 602, 636, 647, 652, 662, 694, 695, 700, 729, 730, 731, Bristol LD6G 758, 759, 787, 788
Single-deckers: Bristol L6B 72, 522, 523, 537, Bristol LL6B 559, 570, 571, 572, Bristol LWL6B 577, 578, 579, 618, 619, 620, 621, 625, 626, 627, 628, 629, 630, Bristol LS6G 679, 680, 681, Bristol LS6B 710, 711, 712, 718
Coaches: Bristol LWL6B 607, Bristol LS6G 671, 676

MAIDENHEAD –
Double-deckers: Bristol K5G (open-top) 771, 772, 773, Bristol K6A 442, 450 Bristol K6B 470, 498, 499, 500, 501, 502, 503, 504, 513, 514, 516, 527, 530, Bristol KS6B 592, 593, Bristol KSW 603, 635, 649, 651, 657, 661, 666, 667, 698, 699, 732, 733, 734, Bristol LD5G 765, 783, 784, 789, 791 Bristol LD6B 755, 757
Single-deckers: Bedford OB 520, Bristol L6A 456, 459, 473, 475, 477, 486, Bristol L6B 71, 541, Bristol LL6B 560, 561, 562, 563, 566, 573, 574, 575, 576, Bristol LL5G 795, 796, Bristol LWL6B 582, 622, 623, 624, 631, Bristol LS6G 677, 683, Bristol LS6B 713, 714, 715, Bristol SC4LK 774, 775, 776, 777, 778
Coaches: Bristol L6B 550, 551, Bristol LWL6B 608, 609, Bristol LS6B 691

NEWBURY – including Hungerford, Kingsclere and Lambourn – (133/40 at Hungerford, 134/7 at Lambourn and 727 at Kingsclere) -
Double-deckers: Bristol K6A 439, 440, 443, 444, 445, 451, 452, 466, 467, Bristol K6B 453, 454, 468, 469, 497, 524, Bristol KSW6B 648, 650, 668, 669, 702, 704, 726, 727, 728, Bristol LD5G 780, 781, 782, 790, Bristol LD6G 763, 764, Guy 'Arab' III 5LW 170, 171, Guy 'Arab' III 6LW H10, H13, H14, H15, H16
Single-deckers: AEC 'Regal' 0662 131, 132, 133, 134, 135, 136, 137, 138, 139, 140, AEC 'Regal' 6821A 161, 162, 163, Bristol L6A 455, 458, 478, 479, 480, Bristol L6B 535, 536, 538, 543, Bristol LL6B 556, 557, 558, 564, 565, Bristol LS6G 685, 686, Bristol LS5G 706, 707, Bristol LS6B 716, 721
Coaches: AEC 'Regal' 0662 141, 143, 144, 145, 146, 147, 148, Leyland 'Tiger' PS1 169, Bristol LS6B 688, Bristol LS6G 673

OXFORD – includes Worcester and London
Double-deckers: Bristol K5G (open-top) 770
Coaches: AEC 'Regal' 0662 39, 40, 41, 42, 26, 47, 49, 50, 51, 53, AEC 'Regal' III 54, 55, 56, 57, 58, 59, 60, 61, 62, 63, 64, 65, 66, 67, 68, 69, 70, AEC 'Regal' IV 85, Bristol L6B 73, 74, Bristol LL6B 75, 76, 77, 78, Bristol LS6G 79, 80, 81, 82, 83, 84, Bristol LS6B 90, 91, 92, 93, 94, 95, 689, 690, 692, 693, Guy UF 6HLW 86, 87, 88, 89, Bristol MW6G 800, 801, 802, 803

Bristol L6B Car 540 (FMO 15) was the single-deck Tadley allocation for Route 9a.

READING – incl. Crowthorne, Tadley and Victoria – (1 KSW6B and 1 L6B at Tadley, 4 LS-type at Crowthorne and 2 LD-types at Samuelson's Garage, Victoria)
Double-deckers: Bristol K6A 446, 447, 448, 449, Bristol K6B 492, 493, 494, 495, 496, 525, 526, 531, 532, 533, Bristol KS6B 586, 587, 588, 590, 594, 595, 596, 597, 598, 599, 600, Bristol KSW6B 634, 637, 638, 639, 653, 654, 655, 656, 659, 660, 663, 664, 665, 670, 696, 697, 735, 736, 737, 738, 739, 740, 741, 742, 743, 748, 749, Bristol LD6G 750, 753, 754, 760, 761, 762, 786, Bristol LD5G 768, 769, 785, Bristol LDL6G 779
Single-deckers: Bristol L6B 521, 534, 539, 540, 542, 544, Bristol LWL6B 580, 581, 583, 584, 585, 613, 614, 615, 616, 617, 632, 633, Bristol LS5G 708, 709, Bristol LS6G 678, 682, 684, 687, Bristol LS6B 717, 719, 720, 723, 724, 725
Coaches: Bristol L6B 549, Bristol LWL6B 610, 611, 612, Bristol LS6G 672, 674

DELICENSED -
Double-deckers: Bristol KSW6B 658, 660, Bristol LD6B 756, Bristol LD6G 751, 752
Single-deckers: Bristol L6A 457, 472, 474, 476, 481, 482, 483, 484, 485 (all for disposal), Bristol LL6B 567, 568, 569, Bristol LS6B 722
Coaches: Bristol L6B 546, 547, 548, 552, 553, 554, 555

'Big Bertha' Bristol LDL6G Car 779 (NBL 736) on the 1a.

ASCOT –
Double-deckers: Bristol K5G 462, Bristol KSW6B 640, 641, 642, 643, 644, 645, 701, 703, 705, 744, 745, 746, 747, Bristol LD5G 766, 767
Single-deckers: Bristol LS6B 712, 713, 721

HIGH WYCOMBE - **including Wycombe Marsh, Desborough Road, Fingest, Princes Risborough and Stokenchurch –** (2 LWL6B at Fingest, 2 LD-types at Princes Risborough and 2 LD-types at Stokenchurch) -
Double-deckers: Bristol K6B 468, 469, 494, 495, 496, 505, 506, 507, 508, 509, 513, 517, 518, 519, 528, 533, Bristol KS6B 586, 591, Bristol KSW6B 601, 602, 636, 647, 652, 658, 662, 694, 695, 729, 730, 731, Bristol LD6G 758, 759, 786, 787, 788, 808, 809, 812, 813, 814
Single-deckers: Bristol LL5G 794, 797, 798, 799, 818, Bristol LL6B 558, 559, 570, 571, 572, 573, 574, Bristol LWL6B 579, 614, 618, 619, 620, 621, 625, 626, 627, 628, Bristol LS6G 678, 679, 680, 681, 682, 684, 685
Coaches: Bristol LWL6B 607, Bristol LS6G 671, 675

The Bristol SC's were a permanent Maidenhead allocation, and Car 777 (NBL 734) is seen outside Maidenhead Depot awaiting service on Route 17 to Henley via Burchetts Green and Hurley.

MAIDENHEAD –
Double-deckers: Bristol K5G 460, 461, Bristol K6B 454, 470, 471, 492, 493, 497, 498, 499, 500, 501, 502, 503, 504, 514, 515, 516, 527, 530, 531, Bristol KS6B 587, 598, 592, 593, 598, 599, 600, Bristol KSW6B 603, 635, 649, 651, 655, 657, 661, 666, 667, 698, 699, 732, 733, 734, Bristol LD5G 765, 783, 784, 789, 791, Bristol LD6B 755, 756, 757, 815, 816, Bristol LD6G 792, 793
Single-deckers: Bristol LL5G 795, 796, Bristol LL6B 560, 561, 562, 563, 569, 575, 576, Bristol LWL6B 577, 578, 613, 615, 622, 623, 624, Bristol LS6G 677, 683, Bristol LS6B 715, Bristol SC4LK 774, 775, 776, 777, 778
Coaches: Bristol LWL6B 609, Bristol LS6B 691

NEWBURY – including Hungerford, Kingsclere and Lambourn –
Double-deckers: Bristol K5G 464, Bristol K6A 439, 440, 443, 444, 452, 456, 466, 467, Bristol K6B 453, 524, 525, 532, Bristol KS6B 595, 596, 597, Bristol KWS6B 669, 702, 704, 726, 727, 728, 741, Bristol LD5G 780, 781, 782,

Bristol LD6G 763, 764, 790, Guy 'Arab' III 5LW 170, 171, Guy 'Arab' III 6LW H10, H14, H15, H16
Single-deckers: AEC 'Regal' 0662 131, 132, 133, 134, 137, 139, Bristol L6B 541, Bristol LL6B 556, 561, 564, 565, 566, 567, Bristol LWL6B 583, 584
Coaches: Bristol LS6B 688, Bristol LS6G 673, Leyland 'Tiger' PS1 169

OXFORD - including Worcester and London
Coaches: Bristol LL6B 75, 76, 77, 821, 822, 825, 826, 827, Bristol LS6B 690, 692, Bristol LS6G 79, 80, 81, 82, 84, Bristol MW6G 800, 801, Guy UF 6HLW 86, 88, 98

READING – incl. Crowthorne, Tadley and Victoria –
(1 KSW6B and 1 L6B at Tadley, 4 LS-type at Crowthorne and 2 LD-types at Samuelson's Garage, Victoria)
Double-deckers: Bristol K5G 438, 463, Bristol K6A 441, 442, 446, 448, 449, 450, Bristol K6B 436, 437, 455, 526, 529, Bristol KS6B 588, 590, 594, Bristol KSW6B 634, 637, 638, 639, 646, 648, 650, 653, 654, 656, 659, 660, 663, 664, 665, 668, 670, 696, 697, 700, 735, 736, 737, 738, 739, 749, 742, 743, 748, 749, Bristol LD5G 768, 769, 785, Bristol LD6G 750, 751, 752, 753, 754, 760, 761, 762, Bristol LDL6G 779, Bristol LD6B 810, 811
Single-deckers: Bristol L6B 538, 539, 540, 542, 543, Bristol LL5G 817, 819, 820, Bristol LL6B 557, Bristol LWL6B 580, 581, 582, 585, 616, 617, 629, 630, 631, 632, 633 Bristol LS5G 686, 687, 706, 707, 708, 709, Bristol LS6B 710, 711, 714, 716, 717, 718, 719, 720, 722, 723, 724, 725
Coaches: Bristol LS6B 693, Bristol LS6G 672, 674

DELICENSED –
Double-deckers: Bristol K5G (open-top) 770, 771, 772, 773 (in store at Stokenchurch), Bristol K6A 447, 451, 457, 458, 459, Guy 'Arab' III 6LW H13
Single-deckers: Bristol L6B 535, 536, 537, 544 (for sale)
Coaches: AEC 'Regal' IV 85, Bristol L6B 73, 74, 545, 550, 551, 552, 553, 554, 555, Bristol LL6B 78, 823, 824, 828, 829, Bristol LWL6B 608, 610, 611, 612, Bristol LS6B 90, 91, 92, 93, 94, 95, Bristol LS6G 83, 676, 689, Bristol MW6G 802, 803, 804, 805, 806, 807, Guy UF 6HLW 87 – all these were delicensed for the Winter and would return to service in due course.

Bristol KSW6B Car 669 (HBL 71) is seen laid over in the High Street at Hungerford, there being bays marked out for buses on the wide street also used for the market. It is on Route 113 to Newbury by way of Inkpen and Kintbury.

Index to Other Operators In the Main Text

A

Aer Lingus *189*

Aldershot & District Traction Co. Ltd. *13 18 67 111 112 113 127 145*

Alpha Coaches (Carter) *17 19*

Associated Motorways Ltd. *44 78 84 187*

B

B&M Bus Service (Keep) *119*

Banfield's Coaches *144*

Barnsley & District Electric Traction Co. Ltd. *110*

Beta Bus Service (Fuller & Pomroy) *12*

Birch Bros. Ltd. *29*

Blue Belle Coaches *45*

Blue Bus Service (West Bros.) *33 166*

Blue Star Service (Spratley) *9 187*

Borough Bus Service (Frowen & Hill) *118 132 197*

Bray Transport Ltd. *33 178*

Brighton, Hove & District Omnibus Co. Ltd. *25 26 120 124 129 133 138 155*

Brimblecombe's Coaches *55 106 144*

Bristol Greyhound *1 84 142*

Bristol Omnibus Co. Ltd. *16 65 95 128 169 170 174 175*

British Overseas Airways Corporation *192*

Bristol Tramways & Carriage Co. Ltd. *124*

British Automobile Traction Co. Ltd. *55 60 110 143 144*

British Road Services *110 134*

British Railways *165*

C

Central Scottish Motor Traction Co. Ltd. *34*

Cheltenham District Traction Co. Ltd. *49 63*

Chiltern Bus Co. Ltd. *8*

City of Oxford Motor Services Ltd. *13 30 38 41 44 46 55 60 61 66 83 95 163*

Cook, Thos. & Son Ltd. *152 163*

Crescent Coaches (Jackson) *68 73 197*

Crosville Motor Services Ltd. *5 13 82 87 121*

D-E

Denham Bros. *145*

Eastbourne C.T. *195*

Eastern Counties Omnibus Co. Ltd. *42 76 95 97 108 120 123*

Eastern National Omnibus Co. Ltd. *7 13 65 80 97 111 122 123 175 182 196*

East Kent Road Car Co. Ltd. *70 151 160*

Enterprise Coaches (Taylor) *59*

F-G-H

Ford, A. & Son *123*

Frostways, Kennington *189*

Gem Bus Service (Farmer) *32 159 197*

Gough's Bus Service *33 34 72 131*

Great Western Railway/British Railways (Western Region) *11 13 16 33 118 163 177 190*

Green Line Coaches Ltd. *23 61 142 183*

Hants & Dorset Motor Services Ltd. *13 20 28 76 80 83 97 105 180 194 195*

Hants & Sussex Motor Services Ltd. *43*

Huntley, S. & Son *100*

I-J-K

Isle of Man Transport *195*

Imperial (A. Moore & Son) *14*

Kemps Bus Service *23 78*

Kent's Coaches (E.G. Kent) *123 174*

Kent, W.E. *100 174*

King Alfred Motor Services Ltd. *46*

Kingsclere Coaches (E.G. Kent) *100*

L-M

Ledbury Transport Co. Ltd. *6 17 29 54 56 57 77 134 152 154 179*

Lincolnshire Road Car Co. Ltd. *97 123*

London Coastal Coaches *66 152*

London Transport *43 61 68 69 84 95 101 114 144 148 155 168 178*

Maidstone & District Motor Services Ltd. *151*

Marlow & District Motor Services Ltd. *12 66 69 95 121 141 176 190 194*

N

Newbury & District Motor Services Ltd. *8 17 20 43 44 45 46 49 50 52 54 56 63 66 67 68 72 73 77 78 83 92 100 101 103 110 114 116 125 128 129 131 135 137 142 143 145 146 149 151 155 157 158 164 165 174 179 189 192 193 197*

Nobes, Ernest *137*

Northern General Transport Co. Ltd. *42*

Northampton C.T. *195*

North Western Road Car Co. Ltd. *46*

O-P

Penn Bus Co. Ltd. *24*

Pixey Bus Service (Harris) *14 69 132*

Plymouth Corporation Transport *5 6 7 92 97*

Premier Line Ltd. *5 36 39*

R

Reading Corporation Transport *6 18 23 26 34 35 37 38 55 81 125 126 152 197*

Red & White United Transport Ltd. *8 20 43 44 45 46 49 50 51 52 55 56 63 65 70 73 81 83 87 91 92 100 108 114 125 129 146 180 188 192*

Regent Petroleum *28 31 94 137*

Reliance Motor Services Ltd. (Hedges) *57 65 150*

Ribble Motor Services Ltd. *83*

Royal Blue Coaches *84 108 155*

S

Salter's Steamers *66 152 173*

Scottish Motor Traction Co. Ltd. *46 51 114*

Skyways Air-link *152*

Smith's Luxury Coaches (Reading) Ltd. *10 54*

Southdown Motor Services Ltd. *70 125 145 151*

Southern National Omnibus Co. Ltd. *97*

Southern Railway/British Railways (Southern Region) *8 10 14 18 23 28 36 48 51 105*

Southern Vectis Omnibus Co. Ltd. *147 196*

South Midland Motor Services Ltd. *43 44 45 46 50 51 54 55 56 57 58 64 65 67 70 71 72 77 79 80 81 82 84 86 87 89 90 92 93 95 101 102 103 104 105 106 107 108 111 114 115 116 120 123 124 131 133 146 148 149 150 151 154 155 157 158 159 160 161 163 164 165 167 172 173 179 181 186 187 188 189 193 194 197*

T

T&B Haulage *10*

Thackray's Way – *see Ledbury Transport Co. Ltd.*

Thomas Tilling Ltd. /Tilling's Transport Ltd. *30 98 163*

Tyne & Wear Metro *195*

U-V

United Automobile Services Ltd. *13 193*

United Counties Omnibus Co. Ltd. *13 79 82 83 95 122 125 145 160 165 172 174 175 177 181 182 183 185 191 197*

United Welsh Services Ltd. *53 180 188 190 193*

Varsity Express *82*

Venture Ltd. *20 43 36 49 52 55 63 100 129 174*

W-X-Y-Z

Wallace Arnold *195*

Wallasey Corporation Transport *5 59 82 83*

Westcliff-on-Sea Motor Services Ltd. *36 39 48 65 111*

Western National Omnibus Co. Ltd. *97 102 169*

West Yorkshire Road Car Co. Ltd. *13 107 122 128 194 195*

White, W.J. & Son *44*

Wilts & Dorset Motor Services Ltd. *43 46 55 63 83 87 99 100 122 131 160 164 174 187*